HITLER'S FOREIGN FIGHTERS

HITLER'S FOREIGN FIGHTERS

Foreign Recruitment in the
Heer and *Waffen-SS* 1939–1945

DR ANTONIO J. MUÑOZ

FRONTLINE
BOOKS

HITLER'S FOREIGN FIGHTERS
Foreign Recruitment in the Heer and Waffen-SS 1939-1945

First published in Great Britain in 2026
by Frontline Books
An imprint of
Pen & Sword Books Ltd
Yorkshire - Philadelphia

ISBN 9781036199258

A CIP catalogue record for this book is available from the British Library

Typeset by Lapiz Digital
Printed and bound in the UK by CPI Group (UK) Ltd,
Croydon, CR0 4YY.

Printed on paper from a sustainable source by
CPI Group (UK) Ltd, Croydon, CR0 4YY

The Publisher's authorised representative in the EU for product safety is
Authorised Rep Compliance Ltd., Ground Floor, 71 Lower Baggot Street,
Dublin D02 P593, Ireland.
www.arccompliance.com

For a complete list of Pen & Sword titles please contact
PEN & SWORD BOOKS LTD
47 Church Street, Barnsley, South Yorkshire, S70 2AS, England
E-mail: enquiries@pen-and-sword.co.uk
Website: www.pen-and-sword.co.uk
or
PEN & SWORD BOOKS
1950 Lawrence Rd, Havertown, PA 19083, USA
E-mail: uspen-and-sword@casematepublishers.com

CONTENTS

DEDICATION

In memory of David Littlejohn, British author and historical trailblazer.

LIST OF FIGURES, MAPS AND TABLES

Figures

Tables

AUTHOR'S NOTE

The idea for this book has been with me for many decades, during which I have gathered extensive data on the subject. I now believe that this body of knowledge is ready to be presented. In studying the history of the Second World War, particularly the Axis forces, one often encounters broad narratives: the rise of Nazi Germany, the devastation of the Eastern Front, and the eventual collapse of the Third Reich. Within these sweeping accounts, however, exist countless smaller stories – stories that complicate the picture and challenge our assumptions. One of the most neglected concerns the men who fought in German uniform but were not themselves German. Whether ethnic Germans living outside the Reich, volunteers from Western Europe, or conscripts from Eastern Europe and beyond, their presence in the *Wehrmacht* and *Waffen-SS* was far more substantial than often acknowledged.

This work explores a central paradox: how could a regime committed to uncompromising racial ideology, celebrating the ideal of the 'pure' Aryan soldier, come to rely so heavily on foreigners, many of whom it had previously deemed inferior? The answer lies in the tension between ideology and necessity. At the outbreak of war, Nazi recruitment policies were rooted firmly in racial theory: the *Wehrmacht* and *Waffen-SS* sought *Volksdeutsche* from annexed territories and Germanic 'kindred' peoples from Scandinavia, the Low Countries and elsewhere. Yet catastrophic losses on the Eastern Front in 1941 and 1942 revealed the limits of ideology, compelling the Germans to draw on manpower sources they had once rejected. By the final stages of the war, men from virtually every corner of Europe – many who did not speak German, identify with German culture, or sympathise with Nazi goals – wore German uniforms.

Writing about this subject presents particular challenges. The topic is not neutral. Accounts of foreigners in German service can easily be distorted: post-war apologetics may romanticise a so-called 'crusade against Bolshevism', while other narratives oversimplify or impose ideological judgments, ignoring the diversity of motives and experiences among these men. My approach has been to resist both temptations. This is not a story about heroes or villains, but about how ideology, coercion, opportunism and survival intersected in one of history's most destructive wars.

In preparing this work, I have relied on a wide range of sources: archival collections in Germany and Eastern Europe, captured German records preserved by the Allies, wartime propaganda materials, and scholarly studies of national volunteer movements. Memoirs and testimonies have been used with caution, revealing personal detail while reflecting the biases of memory and post-war political agendas. Sorting through these voices has been essential – acknowledging their value while recognising their limitations.

Terminology presents additional challenges. Nazi categories were often shifting and contradictory. The *Volksdeutsche,* for example, were divided into groups ranging from those fully assimilated into German culture to those who spoke little or no German and had lived for generations in Slavic or Balkan lands. Encoded in bureaucratic systems such as the *Volksliste,* these distinctions reflected both racial obsession and pragmatic manpower needs. My aim is to clarify these distinctions without becoming trapped by the logic – or the illogic – of the Nazi system itself. What emerges is a portrait of a military system in crisis – a regime clinging to racial exclusivity at the outset of war, only to draft men who bore little resemblance to the Aryan ideal by war's end. Some men willingly embraced Nazi ideology and participated in atrocities; others were drawn into German service through coercion, manipulation or circumstance. Many joined for reasons that defy easy categorisation: the hope of fighting communism, the promise of better rations, fear of reprisals, or the lure of adventure. Presenting this range of motives is not to justify or excuse, but to understand. War rarely conforms to neat ideological categories, and the story of foreign volunteers in German service is a reminder of the complexity of human behaviour under extreme circumstances.

I hope readers approach this book with inquiry rather than judgment. Second World War history is often flattened into simple binaries – good and evil, victim and perpetrator, collaboration and resistance. While these categories have their place, they can obscure the human realities in between. This book reveals how a regime founded on racial purity ultimately undermined its own principles in the pursuit of survival, and how men from dozens of nations found themselves, voluntarily or involuntarily, wearing the uniform of Hitler's armies. Finally, this book does not seek to glorify or romanticise these formations. Their service occurred within a criminal regime responsible for unprecedented destruction and genocide. A sober and critical approach is essential. Yet dismissing the subject as unworthy of study does a disservice to history.

To understand the Nazi war machine fully, one must examine not only its ideological core but also the margins, where ideology was bent, compromised or abandoned. What emerges is a portrait of a military system in crisis. Its transformation reflects the desperation of the Third Reich, as a nation of eighty million sought to fight the entire world. It also underscores a broader truth about war: it compels states to make choices they would otherwise consider unthinkable. My hope is that this book contributes to a fuller understanding of that process and illuminates a neglected aspect of the Second World War.

INTRODUCTION

Evolution of Recruitment Policies: *Volksdeutsche*, and Foreign Volunteers

At the outbreak of the Second World War, the recruitment policies of the *Wehrmacht* and *Waffen-SS* were largely shaped by Nazi racial ideology – an ideology that prioritised ethnic Germans, or *Volksdeutsche*, and 'racially pure' Aryans as the core of the Third Reich's military forces. Early recruitment efforts focused primarily on soldiers from Germany, and more specifically, those who were seen as ideologically aligned with Nazi principles. Scandinavians, Danes, Dutch and other Germanic peoples were the primary targets for volunteer recruitment, and their inclusion was seen as a natural extension of the racial unity espoused by the regime. However, by 1941, military necessity began to alter this vision, especially after the catastrophic losses suffered by the *Wehrmacht* on the Eastern Front. Despite their fervent belief in the superiority of the 'Aryan' race, the Nazis were forced to confront the reality of an overstretched army and a desperate need for manpower.

This led to a gradual relaxation of earlier racial purity policies and the reluctant inclusion of foreign recruits, many of whom were seen as racially inferior according to Nazi doctrine. This shortage even extended to the *Waffen-SS*, who had to compete with the *Luftwaffe* (Air Force), *Kriegsmarine* (Navy) and *Heer* (Army) for German recruits. *SS-Obergruppenführer und General der Waffen-SS* Gottlob Berger, who was head of the *SS-Hauptamt* (SS Main Office), very quickly turned to ethnic Germans from outside of the Reich, as a viable recruiting source which the other branches were not yet tapping into. At the time (1940), the three branches of the *Wehrmacht* (Armed Forces) were only concentrating on the *Volksdeutsche* who were inside the new Reich territories annexed from Czechoslovakia, Luxembourg, Poland and France. Thus, ethnic Germans from Romania, and particularly Hungary, were a source of untapped manpower that the *Waffen-SS* very quickly exploited.[1]

Volksdeutsche: The Initial Focus on Ethnic Germans

As described above, one of the first groups to be targeted for military service were the *Volksdeutsche* – ethnic Germans living within the newly-established borders of the Reich, particularly in occupied territories or former German lands. The incorporation of regions like western Poland, Alsace-Lorraine, and the Sudetenland into Nazi Germany by 1940 gave the Nazis a large pool of men who were seen as racially compatible and aligned with the German cause. Many of these men, although they were ethnically German, were culturally distinct, often speaking dialects of German or even no German at all. In addition, these *Volksdeutsche* were divided into several principal groups based on the level of German ancestry which they possessed as well as their command of the German language. In regions like western Poland and the Sudetenland, these men were recruited into the *Wehrmacht* as early as 1940, and by 1941, this practice was formalised.

The Nazis saw these populations as an extension of the German *Volk* (people); ethnic Germans who had been separated from the Reich after the First World War due to the shifting borders of Europe. Men from the Sudetenland and Alsace-Lorraine, for example, were quickly conscripted into the ranks of the *Wehrmacht,* as in the eyes of the Nazi regime these areas were seen as rightfully belonging to the German nation. While this early recruitment emphasised ethnic and cultural affinity, it also revealed a tension between Nazi racial ideology and military reality. Some recruits, especially those from regions where German was not spoken, faced discrimination and mistrust, despite their supposed racial alignment. The military bureaucracy, however, was pragmatic and determined to tap into this expanding pool of manpower, which had been forcibly integrated into the Reich.

The Expansion to Other Ethnic Groups: A Reluctant Shift in Policy

By the start of 1942, the war on the Eastern Front began to drain the German military of its core soldiers. The devastating losses during the winter of 1941/42, during the battle for Stalingrad and the subsequent Soviet offensives, further exposed the fragility of the Nazi military system, which had relied primarily on Germanic and ethnic-German soldiers. The Red Army's relentless push forced Hitler to reevaluate his military's ability to maintain its fighting strength without resorting to a broader, more diverse recruitment pool. It was clear that if the Germans were to avoid collapse, they would need to expand the military beyond its traditional racial parameters. Initially, this shift in recruitment was cautious and highly controlled. In 1942, Hitler forbade foreign units from growing larger than battalions to maintain the illusion of racial purity.

But as the German army faced increasing defeat and attrition, commanders began to circumvent these orders. They found ways to organise foreign troops into new formations by recruiting enough men for a regiment, but dividing them into battalions, which were technically within the permissible limits of Adolf Hitler's current policy. For example, an entire regiment of men might be split into multiple battalions, such as the *I. (Bataillon)* of the '448th Eastern Battalion' [*I. /448*] and the *II. (Bataillon)* of the '448th Eastern Battalion' [*II. /448*], each appearing on paper as a legitimate 'battalion', but effectively comprising two battalions.

By 1943, as losses mounted, even regiments of foreign soldiers were authorised. By 1944, the Germans had established several divisions of foreign troops, like the 1st Cossack Cavalry Division, and the 162nd (Turkestani) Infantry Division. These numerous formations were ethnically diverse, and often from groups once considered racially inferior by Nazi standards. The *Waffen-SS* began to recruit not only from the occupied Eastern territories but also from regions as diverse as the Caucasus, Central Asia, and even the Banat and Bosnia in Yugoslavia. The recruitment of non-Germanic people in the *Waffen-SS* began in 1943. It marked a stark departure from the original vision of a racially pure and culturally homogeneous military and highlighted the pragmatic nature of Nazi decision-making under duress. With regard to the *Volksdeutsche*, the Germans divided them into several categories in order to better employ this manpower resource. To do this, the Third Reich established several categories named the *Volksliste* (*Deutsche Volksliste*, DVL) – introduced primarily in annexed Polish territories (especially the Warthegau region) in 1939–40. It divided Polish citizens of German ancestry into four main groups:

> Category I: *Volksdeutsche* ('Ethnically German') – Persons of German descent who had engaged themselves in favour of the Reich before 1939.
> Category II: *Deutschstämmige* ('Of German Descent') – Persons of German descent who had remained passive to their Germanic heritage.
> Category III: *Eingedeutschte* ('Voluntarily Germanised') – Indigenous persons considered by the Nazis as partly Polonised (mainly Silesians and Kashub).
> Category IV: *Deutsche nur auf dem Papier* ('German in name only') – Persons who possessed a German surname, but were wholly assimilated to Polish society in body and mind.

Category I were, as explained, ethnic Germans who had identified themselves as German before 1939. These *Volksdeutsch* were commonly members of German organisations, often pro-Nazi in nature. Category II *Volksdeutsche* were basically passive ethnic Germans who kept some Polish identity but had clear Germanic ancestry. The Nazis believed that this category of *Volksdeutsch* could be 're-Germanised'. Category III *Volksdeutsch* were partially Germanised Poles of mixed Polish-German ancestry. They were believed to be considered assimilable over time. Finally, Category IV, referred to as the '*Rückgedeutschte*' – Poles with distant German roots, least reliable, under 'probation' from Reich authority to be considered 'German'. However, this was not the only system found in the Reich.

For example, the SS had its own racial selection criteria for *Waffen-SS* recruitment of *Volksdeutsche* outside the Reich. In the Balkans, ethnic-German communities (*Donauschwaben, Gottscheers,* etc.) were often grouped simply as '*Volksdeutsche*' without a four-tier *Volksliste*. This is how the *Waffen-SS* recruited, for example, ethnic Germans from the Banat region of Yugoslavia (*7. SS-Freiwilligen-Gebirgs-Division 'Prinz Eugen'*). In occupied Soviet territories, Heinrich Himmler's *Reichskommissar für die Festigung deutschen Volkstums* (RKFDV, Reich Commissioner for the Strengthening of German Nationhood) applied 'A', 'B' and 'C' racial groups for resettlement and military purposes. As an example, in 1942 the *Waffen-SS* recruits comprising the SS Recruit Training Regiment located in Bobruisk, Belarus were composed of 70 per cent Romanian ethnic Germans and 30 per cent Russian ethnic Germans.

Ethnic Germans of Category IV: A Final Reluctance

By 1944, as the war reached its direst phase, the Nazis faced an existential crisis. Manpower shortages were so severe that the regime began to draft even those who had been deemed ineligible for service earlier in the war. These included ethnic Germans from Category IV, men who could not even speak German and had little connection to German culture. Initially, Category IV men were excluded from military service due to their lack of linguistic ability and cultural integration, but the increasingly dire situation on the Eastern and Western Fronts forced the Nazis to lower their standards. Despite their complete lack of connection to Nazi ideology and the German language, these men were conscripted and assigned to various units, sometimes in an effort to bolster divisions that were rapidly losing their strength.

This move represented the ultimate pragmatism of the Nazi military machine: a willingness to overlook the strictures of racial purity when survival and victory were at stake. By now, the ideal of the 'racially pure' German soldier had been completely eroded by the necessities of war, as soldiers from all walks of life – including those with little connection to the Nazi cause – were pressed into service. For example, when the Allies landed in Normandy in June 1944, they took a good number of men prisoner, wearing the uniform of the *Feldheer* (Field Army), who claimed they were Polish citizens forcibly conscripted into the *Wehrmacht*.

The *Waffen-SS*: From Ideological Purity to Pragmatic Diversity

The *Waffen-SS*, initially the most ideologically driven and racially exclusive part of the Nazi military apparatus, was perhaps the most impacted by this shift. Originally composed of Germans and 'racially acceptable' foreigners such as Scandinavians and Dutch volunteers, by the mid-1940s the SS was forced to incorporate foreign nationals from an ever-broadening array of ethnic backgrounds. By 1943 even Bosnian Muslims were being conscripted into the ranks of the *Waffen-SS*. Many of these non-Germanic volunteers that were recruited by the *Waffen-SS* had little or no ideological alignment with Nazi principles. For the *Waffen-SS*, the pragmatic need for soldiers outweighed the strict racial policies that had once defined the organisation. The division of non-German recruits into different categories revealed the sheer diversity of the units, which were now composed of soldiers from across Europe, the Baltic States, and even the USSR. The expansion of the *Waffen-SS*, despite the growing inclusion of non-Germanic recruits, also highlighted the contradictions at the heart of Nazi military policy. The SS's racial purity had been compromised by the practical realities of war, as men from ethnically diverse backgrounds, often motivated by anti-Soviet sentiment or the promise of autonomy, were drawn into service.

A Military of Necessity

The Nazi military machine's recruitment policies underwent a profound transformation from 1940 to 1944, shifting from a rigid adherence to racial purity and ideological conformity to a more pragmatic, necessity-driven approach. As the war spiralled into crisis, the Nazis found themselves relying on men from increasingly diverse backgrounds, many of whom had previously been considered racially inferior. This evolution in policy – from the early focus on ethnic Germans and racially acceptable groups to the expansion of foreign troops from all corners of Europe and beyond – underscores the tension between Nazi ideology and the imperatives of war. By the final stages of the conflict, the *Wehrmacht* and *Waffen-SS* had incorporated men from the farthest reaches of the Nazi empire, including those with little desire to fight for Nazi goals. The extent of recruitment was so large, that by the start of 1944, one out of five soldiers on the Russian Front wearing the uniform of the *Feldheer* was a non-German volunteer.

Chapter 1

THE ARYAN ARMY

In 1939, the German *Wehrmacht,* particularly its *Heer* (Army), was largely composed of conscripts and volunteers from within Germany's pre-1937 borders. However, following the *Anschluss* of Austria (1938) and the annexation of the Sudetenland after the Munich Agreement (also in 1938), the pool of potential recruits expanded to include large numbers of German-speaking Austrians and ethnic Germans (*Volksdeutsche*) from these newly incorporated territories. The Austrian military was incorporated into the *Heer* by simply employing entire divisions composed of Austrians. In line with Nazi racial ideology, the Reich leadership considered these populations to be part of the broader German racial community, and thus young men of military age from the Sudetenland were rapidly inducted into the army – many even before the outbreak of war. This was part of the regime's effort to consolidate national unity and reinforce the notion of a Greater German Reich.

The *Waffen-SS,* originally established as a small paramilitary praetorian bodyguard unit for Adolf Hitler and the Nazi leadership, was at the time of Poland's invasion still evolving into a full-fledged combat arm of the military. While the regular *Heer* focused more on traditional military training and operations, the *Waffen-SS* was ideologically driven and subject to stricter racial vetting. Entry into the *Waffen-SS* during the late 1930s and early war period required proof of 'Aryan' ancestry, often to as far back as 1750 in some cases. Applicants underwent rigorous racial examinations, including physical evaluations, ancestry checks, and political screening. There was even a height requirement if a young German wanted to join the *Leibstandarte SS Adolf Hitler* formation. The idea was not simply to create an effective military force, but an elite corps that embodied Nazi racial ideals both physically and ideologically.

This racial exclusivity set the *Waffen-SS* apart from the broader *Wehrmacht*. Although the *Wehrmacht* also prioritised ethnic Germans and excluded Jews and other 'non-Aryans' under the Nuremberg Laws, it was generally less ideologically rigid than the SS. The *Heer* made some pragmatic exceptions over time (especially as manpower shortages intensified), but in 1939, both the army and the SS were still seen as racially homogeneous institutions – composed primarily of men deemed to be of pure Germanic or Nordic stock. This initial racial composition contributed to a sense of elitism and ideological commitment, particularly within the *Waffen-SS*, whose members often saw themselves as the racial and martial vanguard of the Nazi movement.

The Exemptions

At the start of the war, however, there were instances where *Mischlinge* – persons of partial Jewish descent as described in the Nazi 1935 Nuremberg racial laws – were exempted from being classified as Jews and permitted to serve in the *Wehrmacht* (including the *Heer*, *Kriegsmarine*, and *Luftwaffe*). This occurred through a combination of legal loopholes, individual exemptions (so-called 'German Blood' declarations), and personal intervention by high-ranking Nazi officials, including Hitler himself in some cases. Under the Nuremberg Laws, a *Mischling* of the first degree had two Jewish grandparents and did not practice Judaism or was not married to a Jew. A *Mischling* of the second degree had one Jewish grandparent. Neither were considered 'full Jews', but they were racially suspect and could face discrimination, especially from 1940 onward. At the start of the war, many *Mischlinge* were already serving in the *Wehrmacht*, having joined before strict enforcement of racial policies in the military began.

Over time, they were increasingly dismissed or transferred to non-combat roles. However, many exemptions were made. Hitler personally signed approximately 1,200 individual exemptions for the (*Ausnahmegenehmigungen*) – *Mischlinge* to continue serving in the *Wehrmacht*, especially in the, *Luftwaffe* and in the *Kriegsmarine*. Wilhelm Keitel, head of the *Oberkommando der Wehrmacht* (OKW – Armed Forces High Command), and Hermann Göring (head of the *Luftwaffe*) were known to have supported some of these exemptions, especially for skilled officers or decorated veterans. Some *Mischlinge* received the status of what was termed as the '*Deutschblütigkeitserklärung*' ('Declaration of German Blood'), which effectively 'Aryanised' them legally. Exact figures are difficult to determine because many files were destroyed and records were not always consistent.

However, historian Bryan Rigg (in *Hitler's Jewish Soldiers*) provides estimates based on extensive archival research and interviews. For the *Heer,* he estimates that approximately 55,000–60,000 men of partial Jewish ancestry (mostly *Mischlinge*) served at various times during the war. Some were officers, including field-grade ranks (Majors, Colonels). For the *Luftwaffe*, it is believed that around 2,000–3,000 served. Göring was known for granting exemptions, especially for pilots or technical specialists. As for the German Navy (*Kriegsmarine*), Professor Rigg believes that 1,000–2,000 *Mischlinge* may have served. There were some notable cases. For example, *Kriegsmarine* captain Bernhard Rogge (who later became a rear admiral), commanded the raider *Atlantis* and had a *Mischling* officer under his command. Another was *Generalfeldmarschall* Erhard Milch, one of the highest-ranking *Luftwaffe* officers, who was widely believed to be a *Mischling,* but Hitler signed a declaration of Aryan status for him, effectively erasing the issue. Despite Nazi racial doctrine, pragmatism often overrode ideology. The service of *Mischlinge* in the *Wehrmacht* is a stark example of the contradictions within the Third Reich, where racial laws were applied unevenly, and personal connections or military necessity could determine one's fate.

Hitler's New Order

By September 1939, a number of Sudeten Germans had already been integrated into both the *Wehrmacht* and the *Waffen-SS.* However, even though some Sudeten Germans were serving in the *Waffen-SS* as early as 1939, it was in limited numbers and mostly in supporting or administrative roles, or in pre-war volunteer formations that were absorbed into the *Waffen-SS* after the annexation of the Sudetenland in late 1938. Full-scale recruitment and integration into combat units took off more significantly from 1940 onward, especially with the formation of divisions like the *SS-Division 'Totenkopf'* and later in foreign units. The annexation of the Sudetenland had not only brought strategic industrial and defensive assets into the Reich's fold but also thousands of military-age ethnic Germans. These men, considered by the regime as natural Germans despite their previous Czechoslovak citizenship, were absorbed into the German military apparatus. Many joined *Wehrmacht* units, while a select few were able to meet the stricter criteria of the *Waffen-SS.*

Their inclusion helped bolster early manpower and was also a symbolic affirmation of the Nazi claim to unite all Germans under one Reich. It is also important to note that the *Waffen-SS* was still relatively small in 1939. It consisted of units such as the *Leibstandarte SS 'Adolf Hitler'* Regiment (LSSAH) which formed part of the *SS-Verfügungstruppe*

(SS-VT), which would later form the core of the expanded *Waffen-SS* divisions. These early SS combat formations were manned almost exclusively by racially 'pure' Germans, often fanatically loyal to the regime, and were used in tandem with the regular army in the Polish campaign. This collaboration, however, sometimes led to friction with the *Wehrmacht*'s traditional officer corps, which viewed the SS as politically driven and unprofessional, despite their zeal.

The start of the Second World War saw both the German *Heer* and the emerging *Waffen-SS* composed almost entirely of men considered racially Aryan under Nazi ideology. The annexation of territories like the Sudetenland had already contributed thousands of racially acceptable recruits to the Reich's expanding war machine. While the *Wehrmacht* remained largely pragmatic in its outlook, the *Waffen-SS* was carefully constructed as an ideological elite, reflecting Himmler's vision of a racially pure military vanguard. This foundation would begin to erode by mid-war as the need for manpower overcame racial purism, but in 1939, the Nazi regime still clung firmly to its racial ideals in military recruitment.

Racial Vetting and Recruitment Standards in the *Waffen-SS*

Following the ideology of racial purity promoted by Heinrich Himmler, the *Waffen-SS* had one of the most rigorous selection processes in the Third Reich. In its early years – especially prior to and during the invasion of Poland – candidates were expected to provide genealogical proof of Aryan ancestry, sometimes tracing back to the mid-eighteenth century. Racial examiners from the *Rasse- und Siedlungshauptamt-SS* (RuSHA, SS Race and Settlement Main Office), evaluated not only bloodlines but physical features such as skull shape, eye and hair colour, and even posture and dental condition. Recruits had to embody the so-called 'Nordic ideal', which was arbitrarily defined by pseudoscientific criteria.

The RuSHA was a key institution of the SS in Nazi Germany. It was established to implement racial policy within the SS and oversee the settlement of ethnic Germans in occupied territories. This department had numerous functions. The high racial standards of the RuSHA made the early *Waffen-SS* small but elite in the eyes of the Nazi regime. Units such as the *Leibstandarte SS Adolf Hitler* or other SS combat units which formed part of the *SS-Verfügungstruppe,* were not just military formations – they were also ideological symbols. The regime promoted them as the future racial aristocracy of the Germanic world. This obsession with racial purity was more than propaganda; it directly impacted who could serve, who could rise in rank, and who would be denied entry despite military aptitude.

Absorption of the Austrian Army

After the *Anschluss* in March 1938, when Nazi Germany annexed Austria, the Austrian military and population were rapidly integrated into the structures of the Third Reich – particularly the *Wehrmacht* and, to a lesser extent, the *SS-Verfügungstruppe*. Absorption of Austrians into the *Wehrmacht* occurred in steps. First the Austrian *Bundesheer* was dissolved. This occurred shortly after the *Anschluss* of 12 March 1938. Six days later (18 March 1938) the Austrian *Bundesheer* was formally merged into the German *Wehrmacht*. Officers and men were either absorbed directly into German units or used to form new ones. In many cases, entire Austrian units were reflagged under *Wehrmacht* command, especially the mountain troops.

Conscription of Austrian men was now enforced. Austrian men of military age were conscripted into the *Wehrmacht* as German citizens. This is because Austria was treated as just another region of the Reich and was no longer a separate nation. From 1938 onward, Austrian conscripts made up a substantial part of the *Wehrmacht*, particularly in the mountain infantry. There was also a concerted effort for cultural assimilation within the *Wehrmacht* of Austrian troops, as well as rank adjustments. The *Wehrmacht* command evaluated Austrian officers for ideological and military reliability. Some higher-ranking Austrian officers were demoted or dismissed, while others were retained and absorbed into German command structures. These demotions or forced retirements often were decided upon the apparent loyalty (or lack thereof) of the officer in question. Some Austrians were allowed to join the *SS-Verfügungstruppe* as early as 1938–9, though under selective conditions.

These were the same racial and ideological requirements like all men wishing to join SS units. The *SS-Verfügungstruppe* required 'Aryan' purity and a record of political reliability. Since Austrians were now considered 'Reich Germans', they became eligible to apply, especially if they were members of the NSDAP, Hitler Youth, or the Austrian SS, which had been operating illegally before 1938. For former Austrian SS members – those who had been members while it was illegal to do so, they were absorbed into the *Allgemeine-SS* and the *SS-Verfügungstruppe* after 1938. Austrians who joined the *SS-Verfügungstruppe* were trained alongside their German counterparts and saw early action in the invasion of Poland (1939) and later in France (1940). By 1941,

Austrians are estimated to have made up 8–13 per cent of the *Waffen-SS*, depending on the period and source. That percentage was smaller in 1939 but already noticeable. After the *Anschluss*, Austrians were quickly incorporated into the *Wehrmacht*. This integration marked the beginning of Austria's significant and often overlooked contribution to Germany's military forces, particularly in elite units like the *Waffen-SS*.

Sudeten Germans and the Integration of the *Volksdeutsche*

The Sudeten Germans, incorporated into the Reich following the 1938 Munich Agreement, represented one of the first major populations of ethnic Germans from outside Germany's pre-1937 borders to be militarily mobilised. Many among them harboured strong nationalist and anti-Czech sentiments, with some already organised in paramilitary groups such as the *Sudetendeutsches Freikorps*. As a result, the Nazi regime considered them racially suitable and ideologically aligned, making their incorporation into the German war effort both politically symbolic and practically valuable. By late 1938 and early 1939, Sudeten men of military age were drafted into the *Wehrmacht* and, where they met racial criteria, into the *Waffen-SS*. Their integration not only bolstered manpower but also reinforced the Nazi vision of *Volksgemeinschaft* – a racially unified German national community extending beyond the Reich's pre-war borders. The recruitment of Sudeten Germans thus served a dual purpose: meeting the Reich's growing military needs and legitimising Hitler's pan-German ideology of uniting all ethnic Germans under one state.

This process of integrating *Volksdeutsche* expanded further following the invasion of Poland in September 1939, when the Reich annexed regions such as the Warthegau, Danzig-West Prussia, and parts of Upper Silesia. These territories contained substantial ethnic German populations who had preserved their German identity despite long-standing Polish rule. After annexation, the Nazi regime moved swiftly to incorporate them, often through the controversial *Deutsche Volksliste*, which classified individuals based on perceived racial desirability and loyalty. Military-age *Volksdeutsche* from these Polish territories were rapidly conscripted into the *Wehrmacht* and, if deemed racially acceptable, the *Waffen-SS*. While not all were volunteers – many were pressured or coerced – their participation served the dual purpose of reinforcing the regime's ideological claim to the annexed lands and expanding its military ranks. By 1940, thousands of ethnic Germans from beyond the Reich's 1937 frontiers were serving in German uniforms, often indistinguishable from their Reich-born counterparts. In the eyes of the Nazi leadership, these men – whether from the

Sudetenland or annexed Polish territories – embodied the racial unity and martial vigour that the Third Reich aspired to project.

Ethnic Germans in Alsace-Lorraine and in Luxembourg

Following the rapid defeat of France in June 1940, the Nazi regime implemented a de facto annexation of Alsace and Lorraine (specifically the *Moselle département*), regions with contested historical ties to Germany. Though never formally annexed under international law, both of these territories were administratively absorbed into the German Reich – Alsace into *Gau Baden* and Lorraine into *Gau Westmark* – and subjected to policies of forced assimilation. German became the mandatory language of administration and instruction, French institutions were dismantled, and German nationality was imposed upon the local population. By August 1942, the Nazi regime had extended universal conscription to young men from these regions, treating them as Reich citizens for military purposes.

Tens of thousands of Alsatians and Lorrainers – many of whom identified as French or retained dual cultural identities – were forcibly drafted into the *Wehrmacht*, with a smaller number conscripted into the *Waffen-SS*, where selection was based more rigidly on ideological and racial criteria. These conscripts became known as the '*Malgré-nous*' ('Against our will'), a term that entered historical and legal discourse in post-war France to denote the involuntary nature of their service. Many were deployed to the Eastern Front, where combat conditions were particularly severe, and where disproportionate casualty rates were recorded among conscripts from Alsace-Lorraine. In Luxembourg, a parallel process unfolded. The Grand Duchy, occupied by German forces in May 1940, was gradually integrated into *Gau Moselland* and subjected to policies of enforced Germanisation.

The Nazis declared Luxembourgers to be Reich citizens in August 1942, explicitly to facilitate their conscription into the German military. Approximately 10,000 men from Luxembourg were conscripted, the vast majority into the *Wehrmacht*, with a limited number assigned to the *Waffen-SS*. The population reacted with broad opposition culminating in the general strike of August 1942, which was brutally suppressed by the Nazi authorities. Many young men resisted conscription by fleeing, going into hiding, or joining underground resistance groups. The forced conscription of men from Alsace-Lorraine and Luxembourg was not only a violation of international law, but also an act of political violence that fractured families and communities. In the post-war period, many *Malgré-nous* survivors faced suspicion and stigma, as well as bureaucratic hurdles in being recognised as victims of the occupation rather than collaborators. Over time, the French and Luxembourg governments officially recognised the coerced nature of these enlistments, and reparative measures were undertaken, albeit unevenly. The incorporation of these western borderland populations into the German war machine underscores the racial and political opportunism of the Nazi regime. Even as it maintained rigid racial standards for voluntary service in the *Waffen-SS*, the state pragmatically conscripted men from annexed territories when manpower shortages became acute – illustrating the contradictions between ideological purity and military necessity.

The fact that the Germans had to resort to forceful conscription of people who up until 1939 had not been German citizens, only showed the fact that the *Wehrmacht* was being stretched to the limit because of all of its military commitments. Even expanded recruitment within the Reich was not enough to cover the heavy losses that the *Wehrmacht* was suffering in the air, on land and at sea. A nation of eighty million people was fighting the world. It was madness. The period from 1942 to 1943 was a time when the *Wehrmacht* was experiencing heavy losses. Therefore, the recruitment of Reich Germans was expanded to the 17 to 45 age group for most branches. Prior to this, the average age group in the *Wehrmacht* ranged from 18–35 years of age. The period from 1944 to 1945 was a chaotic one where further heavy losses were taken by the German military, forcing the recruitment of men for military service from 16 to 60-year-olds, including teenagers and older reservists. In reality, however children as young as 12 and men as old as 70 fought in the *Volkssturm*.

Tensions Between the *Waffen-SS* and the *Heer*

Though both the *Wehrmacht* and the SS adhered to Nazi racial doctrines to varying degrees, tensions existed between them from the beginning. The *Wehrmacht* officer corps, many of whom came from the *Junker* class – the old Prussian military aristocracy – often regarded the SS as an amateurish political force, lacking proper military professionalism. Meanwhile, the SS viewed the army as insufficiently ideological and too conservative. Himmler's long-term goal was to create the *Waffen-SS* as a parallel army that would one day eclipse the traditional military. This political rivalry began to emerge in earnest even during the Polish campaign. Still, in 1939, cooperation was the norm. *Waffen-SS* units were assigned to front-line operations and supported the *Heer* logistically and militarily. However, atrocities committed by SS troops during the invasion – such as the execution of Polish civilians and POWs – began to set the SS apart not just ideologically but behaviourally. However, this abhorrent behaviour would eventually come to infect the *Heer*, especially the *Ostheer* – the Eastern Army that would launch the invasion of the Soviet Union and fight along the Eastern Front until the end of the war. This distinction would deepen as the war progressed, with the *Waffen-SS* becoming increasingly autonomous and expanding its recruitment base beyond racially 'pure' Germans.

The Role of Ideology in Combat Doctrine

Unlike the *Wehrmacht*, which was steeped in traditional German military doctrine, the early *Waffen-SS* emphasised ideological indoctrination as central to its training. SS recruits were taught that they were not just soldiers but racial warriors (*Rassekrieger*) fighting for the future of the Germanic race. Political instruction took up a significant portion of their training, reinforcing ideas of anti-Bolshevism, anti-Semitism, and loyalty to Hitler. This ideological component helped foster fanaticism, which contributed to both battlefield aggression and participation in war crimes. This emphasis on racial ideology initially made the *Waffen-SS* distinct from the regular army, shaping how it would evolve as the war progressed. However, as stated earlier, the war in the East would be fought by the *Ostheer* with particular cruelty – to the point where army units quite often behaved just as abominably as SS formations. Between 1941 and 1945, the war in the East would truly become a *vernichtungskrieg* (war of annihilation). Initially small and racially exclusive, the *Waffen-SS* would eventually grow into a vast multinational force – but in 1939, its core identity was as a racial elite, tightly controlled by Himmler and shaped by Nazi racial ideology.

Barbarossa and the Erosion of Racial Exclusivity

By the time *Unternehmen Barbarossa* commenced on 22 June 1941, the *Waffen-SS* and *Heer* had already drawn significantly on *Volksdeutsche* from annexed Polish territories. The early classification of these men as racially valuable Germans, combined with their proximity to the Eastern Front, made them a convenient and ideologically acceptable pool of manpower. In particular, many were recruited into SS and police rear-area security units, performing police duties and anti-partisan operations – especially in the occupied Soviet territories. Others were absorbed into auxiliary police units, the *SS-Totenkopfverbände*, or even ethnic German militias like the ethnic-German *Sonderdienst* and *Wehrdienst* which served in Poland. The *SS-Totenkopfverbände* was the manpower source to man the Nazi concentration and extermination camps. Many of these SS and police forces that operated in the rear areas or in occupation duties all across Europe, sometimes took part in atrocities.

As the war dragged on and the racial standards of the *Heer* and *Waffen-SS* eroded further, *Volksdeutsche* from occupied Poland – especially those from *Deutsche Volksliste* categories I and II – were increasingly treated as equivalent to Reich Germans. However, those in categories III or IV, or those with perceived 'Polish' traits, often faced discrimination within the military hierarchy. Still, by 1943–4, the lines between *Reichsdeutsche* and certain *Volksdeutsche* had become blurred, and the *Waffen-SS* had shifted from being an exclusively Aryan elite to a multinational and multiethnic combat force driven by pragmatic military necessity rather than ideological purity. The year 1943 was the year where non-Aryan formations began to be recruited into the *Waffen-SS*. This ideological change had occurred in the *Heer* even earlier – in 1941 with the Russian campaign. Then, the German command quickly realised the lack of sufficient forces available in the rear areas, to properly patrol and govern the vast swaths of occupied territory.

Non-German Recruitment: From Ideological Purity to Military Utility

As the war dragged on, the *Waffen-SS* underwent a dramatic transformation. By 1943–4, it had evolved from a racial elite to a multinational fighting force, including volunteers, conscripts, and collaborators from countries such as Latvia, Estonia, Lithuania, Ukraine, Turkestan, Georgia, Armenia, Azerbaijan, Bosnia-Hercegovina, Albania, France, Belgium, and even India – e.g., the Indian Legion. The Indian Legion was a *Heer* formation: *(verstärktes) Infanterie-Regiment 950 (indisch)*. While earlier recruitment had been restricted to Germanic peoples (e.g., Norwegians, Danes, Swedes, Dutch, and Belgian Flemings), later formations included non-Germanic units, like the *13. Waffen-Gebirgs-Division der-SS 'Handschar'* or the *15. Waffen-Grenadier-Division der-SS (Lettische Nr. 1)*, clearly reflected an abandonment of earlier racial standards. Although these foreign units were typically assigned to second-line or anti-partisan duties, many saw extensive combat and suffered heavy casualties, especially on the Russian Front. To maintain internal cohesion, the *Waffen-SS* began to develop a dual-structure system – retaining elite 'Germanic' divisions at the core, while peripheral and foreign divisions were administered with more flexibility and less ideological scrutiny. The original notion of the SS as a racial vanguard was quietly diluted in favour of military utility.

Sudeten Germans in Later *Waffen-SS* and *Wehrmacht* Units

Sudeten Germans continued to serve in large numbers throughout the war, especially in units operating in Bohemia-Moravia, on the Eastern Front, and later in defensive operations against the advancing Red Army. By the war's later stages, many of these men had become integrated into mixed formations, serving alongside *Reichsdeutsche, Volksdeutsche,* and even non-German recruits. The initial ideological scrutiny that had governed recruitment in 1939 had given way to a pragmatic emphasis on manpower and survival. In addition to their front-line service, some Sudeten Germans were also recruited into SS, police battalions, the *Sicherheitsdienst* (SD, SS Security Service), and rear-area units involved in anti-partisan operations or atrocities in occupied territories. Their status as loyal ethnic Germans gave them a privileged position under Nazi racial laws, but their roles varied widely depending on skillset, political loyalty and location. As the Reich collapsed, many Sudeten Germans would find themselves branded as traitors or collaborators by the post-war Czechoslovak government, leading to mass expulsions and loss of property after 1945.

Racial Ideology vs. Wartime Realities

What began in 1939 as an ideologically rigid system rooted in Nazi racial theory had by 1944 become a sprawling, heterogeneous military machine. The *Waffen-SS,* once limited to a racial elite from the Reich and select Germanic countries, had transformed into a polyglot force of around 900,000 men, many of whom would not have met the racial or ideological standards of the early years, and many who had been drafted against their will. This shift was not merely a logistical adaptation, but a reflection of the growing contradiction between Nazi ideology and wartime necessity. Still, the myth of the *Waffen-SS* as a racial elite persisted in propaganda and internal SS rhetoric, even as it became less tenable in practice. The early focus on racial purity – embodied by the first SS volunteers and their careful vetting – served a symbolic purpose for the Nazi regime. But the harsh realities of total war, particularly on the Eastern Front, ultimately forced the regime to compromise its core principles in Favour of survival. The Sudeten Germans, as early symbols of Hitler's 'national unification', were both beneficiaries and eventual victims of this ideological contradiction.

Chapter 2

RECRUITMENT OF ETHNIC GERMANS IN THE NEWLY-ANNEXED TERRITORIES

The SS department responsible for recruiting and assigning *Volksdeutsche* (ethnic Germans outside the Reich) to *Waffen-SS* units was the *SS-Hauptamt* (SS Main Office), the central administrative office for the SS during much of the Second World War. This office oversaw personnel, administration, training and recruitment. Within the *SS-Hauptamt* was *Amt II* (Recruitment) which managed recruitment of all categories of SS personnel, including *Volksdeutsche* volunteers and conscripts. It coordinated the screening, selection and assignment of recruits to *Waffen-SS* divisions. It also worked closely with local ethnic-German organisations and *Volksliste* authorities to identify potential recruits. In addition, the RuSHA played a supporting role by handling ethnic classification, *Volksliste* administration and ensuring racial suitability for SS service. Recruitment and assignment were also influenced by the *SS-Verfügungstruppe* (SS-VT) command structure, which later became the *Waffen-SS*.

The Sudetenland

The break-up of the Czechoslovak state began with the Nazi absorption of Czech regions bordering the Reich in which approximately 3.2 to 3.5 million ethnic Germans were living. These were the so-called Sudeten Germans led by Konrad Henlein. The total number of men who were of ethnic-German ancestry who could possibly serve in the *Wehrmacht* was around 350,000–400,000. Of these, around 250,000 were in the preferred age group (18 to 25) and eligible for immediate conscription. Some Sudeten Germans had already formed paramilitary units like the *Sudetendeutsches Freikorps*, which worked with the German *Abwehr* and SS.[1] On 18 March 1939 the Czechoslovak state was finally dissolved and Slovakia became an independent state under Father Jozef Tiso, a former Catholic priest. The Czech region became a 'protectorate' of the Reich and was split up into two principal provinces named '*Böhmen und Mähren*' ('Bohemia and Moravia').[2] Reich Minister Constantine *Freiherr* von Neurath was now appointed Reich Protector of Bohemia and Moravia. František Chvalkovsky was given the title of Minister of the Protectorate government to Berlin, which he held from 27 April 1939 until he was killed during an air raid in Berlin in 1944. He had been Minister without portfolio during the interim government of the Protectorate of Bohemia and Moravia from mid-March 1939 until his appointment on 27 April. Earlier, he had been Czechoslovak Foreign Minister from 4 October 1938 until 14 March 1939. Dr. Ottokar Fischer was initially assigned as Minister of the Interior for the Protectorate from March to April 1939.

Fischer was replaced in late April 1939 by General Joseph Jezak who became Interior Minister in the Protectorate government from July 1939 until September 1941. Jezak had been a senior Czech Gendarmerie officer and had served extensively in the Austro-Hungarian Army prior to 1918. Immediately the new 'Protectorate' required a police force which consisted of 17,000 Czech *Gendarmerie* under the new Minister of the Interior.[3] In addition, a small Czech 'Army' of some 5,000 men, according to one source, or 6,500 NCOs and men and 280 officers according to another,[4] was allowed to remain armed as a 'show' force and to act as palace guards and for various ceremonial duties. This small Czech contingent was lightly armed and equipped. By 1944 5,000 out of the 7,000-man Czech force had become too unreliable to continue even with their ceremonial or palace guard duties. As a result, 2,000 of the more 'reliable' Czech Army men were retained in the Protectorate while the other 5,000 were transferred to northern Italy in May 1944. These 5,000 men were reformed as a construction unit and were employed there building defences for the German Army in the Ossola Valley.[5] Colonel Emanuel Moravic, who had been assigned as Propaganda Minister in the collaborationist Czech government, was given the post of commander of this construction brigade.

Service in the Heer *and* Waffen-SS

Sudeten Germans were distributed to many German formations, but there were certain German infantry divisions that were staffed with a significant proportion of *Volksdeutsche* from the Sudetenland.

Certain German divisions were also the recipients of large numbers of Czechoslovak weapons. After the occupation of Czechoslovakia in March 1939, the Germans captured an enormous stockpile of Czech arms (from factories like ČKD, Zbrojovka Brno, and Škoda), including Vz. 24 rifles, ZB-26 and ZB-30 light machine guns (ancestors of the British Bren gun), Vz. 37 heavy machine guns, Vz. 36 and vz. 38 field artillery pieces, as well as the LT vz. 35 and LT vz. 38 (later renamed Pz.Kpfw. 35(t) and Pz.Kpfw. 38(t)) tanks. The divisions that were primarily equipped with Czech weapons were formations raised as the 2.-5. *Welle* (2nd to the 5th Wave) divisions. The Czech equipment and arms were distributed particularly to 'second-rate' divisions and early mobilisation formations, especially in the 2nd through 5th Waves. The 2nd- and 3rd-Wave divisions, raised in August 1939 and September–October 1939 respectively, were fully or heavily equipped with Czech weapons. The following divisions, in particular, were outfitted almost entirely with such matériel:

- *62. Infanterie-Division*
- *63. Infanterie-Division*
- *64. Infanterie-Division*
- *65. Infanterie-Division*
- *66. Infanterie-Division*
- *67. Infanterie-Division*
- *68. Infanterie-Division*[6]
- *69. Infanterie-Division*
- *70. Infanterie-Division*
- *71. Infanterie-Division*
- *72. Infanterie-Division*
- *73. Infanterie-Division*

As far as the LT vz. 35 and LT vz. 38 tanks produced in the Skoda factories were concerned, the German *6. Panzer-Division* (converted from *1. Leichte-Division* in October 1939) was heavily equipped with Pz.35(t) tanks. Two other panzer divisions, *7. Panzer-Division* and *8. Panzer-Division*, contained the LT vz. 38, a.k.a. Pz.38(t) tanks. These Czech tanks were employed during the French campaign. In particular, the Pz.38(t) tank was widely used by *Panzer-Regiment 25*, *Panzer-Regiment 204* and *Panzer-Regiment 10*. The German *Sicherungsdivisionen* (Security Divisions) and other rear-area units were also equipped with Czech weaponry. This included rear-area divisions and second-line units employed in the East. The Germans supplemented their arsenal with Czech small arms due to shortages of standard German weapons.

As far as German divisions which contained a high proportion of Sudeten Germans, we know in particular that the *262. Infanterie-Division* (2nd Wave – created in March 1939), with its garrison town being Brünn (Brno), was one such formation. Another division which included many Sudeten German conscripts and cadre staff from the Sudetenland and Czech Protectorate was the *297. Infanterie-Division.* This division was formed in early 1940 and headquartered in Moravia. The *371. Infanterie-Division* was partially raised in Austria and Moravia, with significant numbers of Austrians, but also a large proportion of Sudeten Germans. Three *Sicherungsdivisionen* (security divisions), employed in the East, also contained a good number of ethnic Germans from the Sudetenland. These included *201. Sicherungs-Division, 203. Sicherungs-Division,* and *221. Sicherungs-Division.* However, these security divisions included many of the older-age *Volksdeutsch* from Czech lands. Finally, based on strict racial qualifications, *SS-Division 'Das Reich'* and *SS-Division 'Totenkopf'* included Sudeten Germans among their early recruits, especially during the period 1940–2. Sudeten Germans also joined police units. The ethnic German *Selbstschutz* in the Sudetenland remained active, but included more men of the older age group.

Alsace-Lorraine

Background to the Region

Before 1648, the regions of Alsace and Lorraine were a patchwork of semi-independent lordships, bishoprics and imperial cities within the framework of the Holy Roman Empire. However, when the Thirty Years' War ended in 1648, these two provinces were handed over to the French in gratitude for France's help in the war. Even though France was 95 per cent Catholic, it had assisted the Protestants because the French king opposed the Holy Roman Emperor. The provinces remained in French hands until 1871, when they were absorbed by Imperial Germany after the Franco-Prussian War. The French never forgave the Prussians (Germans) for taking these two provinces. After the First World War ended, Alsace and Lorraine returned to French rule.

Like all border regions, several languages were spoken in the provinces of *Elsäs* (Alsace) and *Lothringen* (Lorraine). The principal languages of course, were French and German. However, in rural areas and small towns, *Elsässisch* (Alsatian) was also spoken. *Hochdeutsch* (High German) was likewise used and was more common than Alsatian. High German was the vernacular of most ethnic Alsatians. It was also a Germanic dialect and part of the Alemannic group (like Swiss-German). The official language, however, was French, especially in urban areas like Strasbourg. French was used in education, religion, and administration. To a lesser degree, Yiddish was spoken by Alsatian Jews, especially in the urban centres like Strasbourg and Colmar. After the German occupation of course, German became the official language.

In Lorraine (especially the *Moselle département*), the main languages included *Plattdeutsch/Lothringer Platt* (Lorraine Franconian), which was a west-central German dialect, specifically Moselle Franconian. It was spoken in north-eastern Moselle, near the German border. This dialect was very similar to the dialects of the Saarland and Luxembourg. French was the official language and was more dominant in central and southern Moselle. High German was less common, but was taught or imposed during the German occupation. Minority languages in Lorraine included Yiddish, as in Alsace, as well as Polish and Italian – especially in the mining towns of Lorraine. Those languages represented the Polish and Italian immigrant community of miners. These two communities (Polish and Italian) had migrated to Lorraine looking for jobs during the late nineteenth and early twentieth centuries.

The Manpower Pool

It was therefore quite understandable that in the French regions of Alsace and Lorraine, there existed a significant ethnic-German population. In 1940, the total population of Alsace – containing the *Bas-Rhin département* (with its *préfecture* at Colmar), and *Haut-Rhin département* (with its *préfecture* at Strasbourg) had perhaps around 1,200,000 people. There, the majority of the population was ethnic-German-speaking Alsatians, particularly in the rural areas. A rough estimate of ethnic Germans and German-speaking population was perhaps 90–95 per cent of the population. These people lived in many areas, especially Bas-Rhin and Haut-Rhin. While linguistically and culturally Germanic, not all of these identified politically as German. In fact, many felt culturally distinct or loyal to France. In Lorraine, the estimated population in 1940 was some 825,000 people.

There were three *départements:* Meurthe-et-Moselle (with its *préfecture* at Nancy), Meuse (with its *préfecture* at Bar-le-Duc), and Moselle (with its *préfecture* at Metz) – the *Moselle département* was annexed by Germany in 1940. Out of 825,000 people, around 350,000 were ethnic German or German-speaking. These people were mostly concentrated in the north-eastern part of the region. Lorraine, therefore, had a more mixed German-speaking population which was significant, but less dominant than in Alsace. The combined ethnic-German / German-speaking population in both provinces was just over 1,322,000. In demographic terms, typically about 20–25 per cent of a population is male and between ages 18–45 (military age). The military-age population eligible for service in the *Wehrmacht* in Alsace and Lorraine was as follows:

Table 1. Ethnic-German Males of Military Age in Alsace-Lorraine

Region	Estimated *Volksdeutsch*	Estimated Military Age Males (18–45)
Alsace	Around 1,100,000	235,000
Moselle	Around 350,000	70,000
TOTAL	About 1,450,000	305,000

Not all of these were conscripted or volunteered, but this was the pool of potential manpower from the regions. After the annexation of these provinces in 1940, Germany began recruiting young men from Alsace and Moselle starting in 1942, under a conscription policy known to the locals as *Malgré-nous* (against our will). Alsatians and Lorrainers were now subject to *Wehrpflicht* (conscription – mandatory military service). By 1945, around 135,000 men from Alsace and Lorraine had been conscripted into the *Wehrmacht* and / or *Waffen-SS*. The *Volksdeutsche Mittelstelle* (VoMi) and the local *Gestapo* handled political vetting and forced recruitment of these men. The majority of these men served in the *Heer,* while around 13,000 served in the *Waffen-SS*.

While conscripts from Alsace and Moselle were scattered across many units, a significant number of Alsatian and Lorraine conscripts were employed in certain *Heer* and *Waffen-SS* divisions. After the war, almost all of the forcibly conscripted Alsatians and Lorrainers testified that they were forced to serve in the German military under threat of retaliation against their families. The following German infantry divisions (especially from the 7th and 9th Waves) had a significant number of men from Alsace and Lorraine:

- *257. Infanterie-Division*
- *268. Infanterie-Division*
- *294. Infanterie-Division*
- *361. Infanterie-Division*

These four divisions were reinforced between 1943–4 with conscripts from Alsace-Lorraine. These divisions were mostly deployed on the Eastern Front, often in high-casualty sectors. Many were taken prisoner in Ukraine (1943–4) and later, in Poland (1944–5). As a result, many *Malgré-nous* fell into Soviet captivity. It is estimated that around 40,000 conscripts from Alsace and Lorraine were taken prisoner and sent to Soviet POW camps, of whom around 25,000 died. On the Western Front a minority of conscripts were sent to France in 1944 to defend against the Allied invasion. Units with Alsatian conscripts were scattered throughout Normandy, Brittany, and the Vosges. After France was liberated and the war ended, many *Malgré-nous* were misunderstood or even prosecuted in France for 'collaboration' despite having been forcibly conscripted. For example, the 'Bordeaux Trial' in 1953 triggered a national debate.

In that year, twenty-one Alsatians were put on trial for war crimes committed at Oradour-sur-Glane while they had been serving under the *2. SS-Panzer-Division 'Das Reich'*. Most of the accused claimed they had been forced to join the *Waffen-SS-* under threats to their families. After a major public outcry in Alsace, they were pardoned in 1954, but the stigma persisted for decades. Another *Waffen-SS* division that contained a sizable number of ethnic Germans from Alsace and Lorraine was the *16. SS-Panzergrenadier-Division 'Reichsführer-SS'*. This SS division was formed in late 1943 and was mostly active in Italy. The men from Alsace and Lorraine were concentrated in the support and logistics part of the division. The *'Reichsführer-SS'* Division, alongside units of the Italian Fascist *'Brigate Nere'*, took part in a massacre at Sant'Anna di Stazzema. On 12 August 1944, men from the *'Reichsführer-SS'*, with the help of the Italian paramilitary *Brigate Nere,* murdered some 560 local villagers and refugees, including over 100 children. Afterwards, the bodies were burned using flamethrowers.

The Annexed Polish Territories

The Invasion of Poland

On 1 September 1939, there were an estimated one million-plus ethnic Germans living in Poland.[7] During the campaign, accusations arose that Poles were killing ethnic-German Poles in revenge for the German invasion. After the conquest of Poland, however, only about 5,437 Polish citizens of ethnic-German ancestry were positively identified as having died from acts of persecution. Another 45,000 were unaccounted for or otherwise missing.[8] By the end of the war, about 400,000 ethnic

Germans who had been considered Polish citizens before 1 September 1939 ended up serving in the *Wehrmacht* in one capacity or another. The ethnic-German communities in Poland had organised a 'self-defence' force which (in theory) it could use to protect these ethnic-German communities in Polish territory from just that type of retaliation.

Figure 1. The map depicts those Polish lands that were to be annexed and absorbed into the Reich. (Author's line drawing)

These Polish citizens of German extraction very quickly came to the aid of the invader. When the war began, several SS '*Sonderkommandos*' had been created for employment in Poland. These SS and police forces each contained a list of persons that they were supposed to kill. In essence the Third Reich was trying to kill off the Polish leadership (the intelligentsia included) so there would be no-one who could organise resistance to the Nazi occupation. For example, *Teilkommando Bromberg* (Bydgoszcz) entered that city with the intent of killing certain persons on their list. The SS unit was assisted by 370 members of the German Army, 150 men of the *Nationalsozialistisches*

Kraftfahrkorps (NSKK – National Socialist Motor Transport Corps), eighty policemen, and 150 ethnic Germans from the Bydgoszcz *Selbstschutz*.[9] What happened in Bydgoszcz was repeated hundreds of times, all over Poland.

Figure 2. The newly created Military Districts from Polish Territories. (Author's line drawing)

The next step in the German plan for Poland was the annexation of large tracts of land – some of which had belonged to Imperial Germany before 1918, and other territories that Germany claimed were rightfully theirs. This annexation of land required the displacement of the Polish population living on those lands. The plan was to leave these lands for Poles of ethnic-German origin and to bring in Reich Germans in order to colonise the region and make it a permanent part of the Reich by Germanisation of the region. Of the approximately nine million Polish citizens living in the regions annexed by Germany, approximately 560,000 were already earmarked for evacuation to the so-called

Generalgouvernement (General Government, hereafter referred to as the GG). The GG had been created using Polish territory not earmarked for absorption into the Reich. The GG was considered rump Poland. This forced deportation began almost from the start of the war.

Between 1–16 December 1939 80,000 Polish citizens (both Jews and non-Jews) were sent to the GG. By 1 May 1940, the following people had been killed or sent to the GG from the *Wartheland* region and surrounding areas:[10]

1. From East Prussia: 30,000 Jews
2. From Silesia: 24,000 Jews
3. From Danzig-West Prussia (Jews and non-Jews): 40,000
4. From the newly created *Reichsgau Wartheland* (Jews and non-Jews): 90,000
5. People killed in the annexed territories: 45,000
6. People killed in the GG: 7,000
7. Grand Total: 236,000.[11]

Of the above figure, 52,000 were killed and 186,000 were forcibly evacuated from territories annexed by Germany.[12] By the end of 1940, at least 325,000 people from the annexed Polish lands had been expelled and forced to resettle in the GG. Upon the Nazi invasion and occupation of Poland in 1939, the German authorities sought to identify and count ethnic Germans across various annexed and occupied areas. The estimates below are based on Nazi census data, German administrative records, and post-war studies. In 1941, the estimated number of *Volksdeutsch* in occupied Polish regions numbered between 856,000 to 970,000 divided into the following regions:[13]

Table 2. Estimated Number of Ethnic-Germans in Annexed Polish Lands, 1941.

REGION	**Estimated *Volksdeutsche***	**Total *Volksdeutsche* and Pure German**	**Comments**
Reichsgau Wartheland	450,000–500,000	500,000–600,000	See Figure 2
Reichsgau Danzig-West Preussen	140,000	120,000–150,000	See Figure 2

REGION	**Estimated *Volksdeutsche***	**Total *Volksdeutsche* and Pure German**	**Comments**
Oberschlesien	230,000	200,000–300,000	East of pre-1939 border
General gouvernement	25,000	25,000–30,000	Nazi-occupied administrative region, 1939–45
Regierungsbezirk Zichenau	11,00–15,000		Annexed to East Prussia
Bialystok	25,000–35,000	10,000–12,000	Not annexed. Administered as an *eigenständiger Bezirk* (separate district)

The numbers in Table 2 show the total long-established ethnic-German Polish population in these regions and districts. The Nazis divided ethnic Germans outside the Reich into categories for recruitment purposes. Category I included *Volksdeutsche* with German citizenship or *Reichsdeutsche* – considered fully German, eligible for full *Wehrmacht* service.

Category II were *Volksdeutsche* with partial German cultural ties who were eligible for service in the *Wehrmacht* after screening or special approval. Category III were ethnic Germans with weak ties, often in mixed marriages or assimilated populations, which limited eligibility, and were employed mostly in auxiliary roles or labour service. Category IV were not fit or not considered for military service, and were thus excluded from service in the *Wehrmacht*. These men were often used for civil or labour tasks.[14] Many of the ethnic Germans from these regions resented being forcibly inducted into the *Wehrmacht*. The following table was created using demographic models of the time – roughly 20–25 per cent of a given population being military age males, i.e., ages 17–45. The availability of military-age men from these *Volksdeutsche* populations were as follows:[15]

Table 3. Draft-Age Ethnic-German Males by Region

Region	Estimated Draft-Age Males (17-45)	*Wehrmacht* Draft Eligibility Estimate (17–45)	Comments
Reichsgau Wartheland	100,000–125,000	85,000–110,000	See map
Reichsgau Danzig-West Preussen	28,000–35,000	23,000–30,000	See map
Oberschlesien	46,000–57,500	35,000–46,000	East of pre-1939 border
General gouvernement	5,000–6,250	2,000–3,000 (mostly auxil-iary or labour)	Nazi-occupied administrative region, 1939–45
Regierungsbezirk Zichenau	2,200–3,750	1,500–2,500	Annexed to East Prussia
Bezirk Bialystok	5,000–7,850	2,500–4,000 (mostly auxiliary or labour)	Not annexed. Administered as an *eigenständiger Bezirk* (separate district)

During the war, there were certain German divisions with high numbers of *Volksdeutsche* from Polish territories. Several units had notable concentrations of Polish ethnic Germans, especially those formed or replenished in or from areas of occupied Poland. In the *Heer* (Army), the divisions included the following units:

48. Infanterie-Division – This division was formed in November 1943 in Ostend, West Flanders from the *171. Reserve-Division.* It had a strong presence of ethnic-German Poles throughout its ranks.

68. Infanterie-Division – Known to have included a substantial number of *Volksdeutsche* from *Oberschlesien* (Upper Silesia).

75. Infanterie-Division – Partial recruitment from annexed Polish territories.

371. Infanterie-Division – Included men from the *Warthegau* and Silesian *Volksdeutsche.*

One *Waffen-SS* unit, the *14. Waffen-Grenadier-Division der-SS 'Galizien' (ukrainische Nr. 1)*, also included ethnic Germans from Poland. Though this *Waffen-SS* division was Ukrainian in name and majority composition, some ethnic Germans from south-eastern Poland served in the division, especially from Volhynia and Galicia. Eventually, some of these men served in its ranks or were transferred to other *Waffen-SS* units.

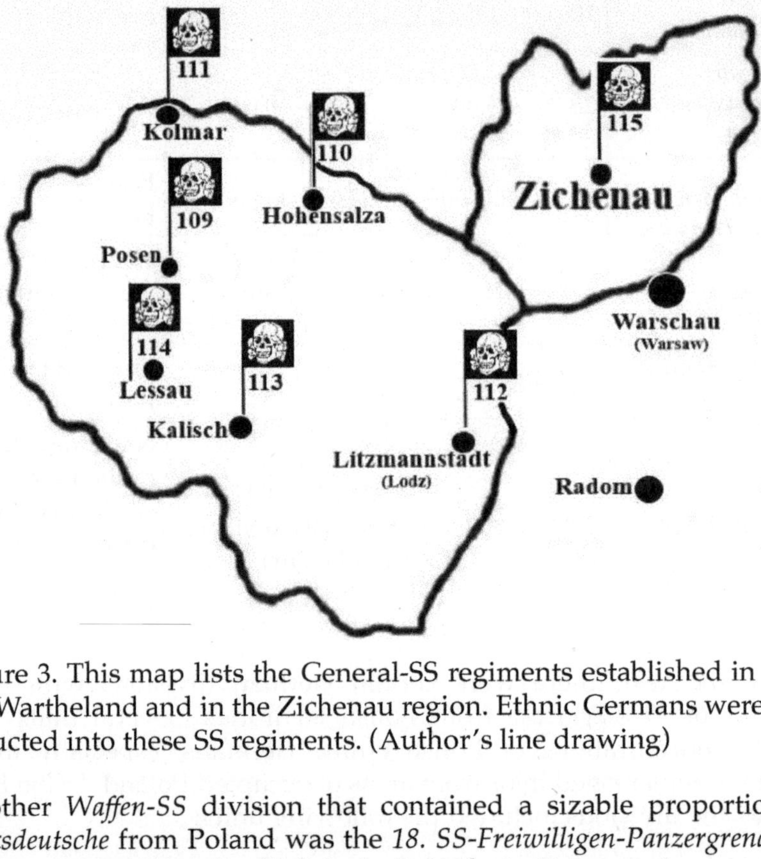

Figure 3. This map lists the General-SS regiments established in both the Wartheland and in the Zichenau region. Ethnic Germans were also inducted into these SS regiments. (Author's line drawing)

Another *Waffen-SS* division that contained a sizable proportion of *Volksdeutsche* from Poland was the *18. SS-Freiwilligen-Panzergrenadier-Division 'Horst Wessel'* which included ethnic Germans from various Polish territories, especially those resettled. The *5. SS Panzer-Division 'Wiking'* contained ethnic-German volunteers from Poland who were listed as Category I conscripts. In the case of these early pure ethnic Germans from Polish lands, most were volunteers and were not drafted. This was true during the period 1939–42. Finally, numerous *Schutzmannschaft* battalions and *SS-Polizei* regiments in Poland and the occupied East drew heavily from ethnic-German manpower in

Poland. The following is a regional breakdown by year of estimated conscription (drafted or volunteered) of *Volksdeutsche* from Nazi-occupied Polish territories, focusing on military-age males, from 1939 to 1945, and sorted by region and year. This includes those sent into the *Wehrmacht, Waffen-SS, Ordnungspolizei,* and several auxiliary services.[16]

Table 4. Estimated *Volksdeutsche* Conscription by Region and Year (Poland, 1939–1945)[17]

Region	**1939–1941**	**1942**	**1943**	**1944**	**1945**	**Total**
Warthegau	15,000	18,000	20,000	15,000	5,000	73,000
Danzig-West Preussen	8,000	10,000	11,000	9,000	3,000	41,000
Oberschlesien	10,000	12,000	14,000	10,000	3,000	49,000
General gouvernement	8,000	9,000	10,000	7,000	2,000	36,000
Zichenau	2,000	2,500	3,000	2,000	1,000	10,500
Bialystok	1,500	2,000	2,500	2,000	500	8,500
Baltic & Galician ethnic Germans, forcibly resettled in annexed Polish territories.	12,000	10,000	8,000	6,000	1,000	37,000
Total[18]	56,500	63,500	68,500	51,000	15,500	255,000

During the war, *SS-Gruppenführer* Gottlob Berger noted in internal memos from the period 1942–4 that the *Volksdeutsche* from Poland represented one of the largest recruitment reservoirs of ethnic Germans outside the borders of the pre-war Reich. For example, the *SS-Ersatzkommando* (SS replacement commands) in Łódź and Danzig processed thousands of *Volksdeutsche* annually from these areas. As far as what percentage of the Polish *Volksdeutsche* served in which particular branch of the *Wehrmacht,* we know that approximately 50 per cent served in the *Heer* (Army), 20–25 per cent served in the *Waffen-SS,* 10–15 per cent served in the *Ordnungspolizei* and *Sicherheitsdienst,* as well as the *Sonderdienst,* and 10–15 per cent were employed in labour and construction units. Many of the men who served in the police and

SS/SD units served as auxiliaries in occupied zones or as ghetto or concentration camp guards.

Between 1939 and 1941 military service was done largely on a voluntary basis and was limited to DVL Categories I and II. Ethnic Germans resettled from the Baltics and from the Bukovina/Bessarabia regions were also inducted into military service during this time. The year 1942 was the beginning of general conscription in the annexed Polish territories. Drafts now extended to DVL Category III. The year 1943 was the peak of ethnic-German conscription from Polish territories annexed by Nazi Germany. Men and older boys from 17–45 were drafted in large numbers. The period 1944–5 saw a declining recruitment pool. *Volkssturm* units in the period 1944–5, specially around Upper Silesia and Poznań, included tens of thousands of late-war conscripts aged 16–60, many from DVL Categories II–IV. It was during this period that boys as young as 16 (sometimes 15) and men as old as 60 (sometimes as old as 65) were drafted into *Volkssturm* or last-ditch battalions. These late-war units were often poorly trained and possessed low morale.

In *Oberschlesien* (Upper Silesia), the *Volksdeutsche* were often assigned to 'mixed companies' or had segregated platoons within larger units. Units with high *Volksdeutsche* personnel often had lower morale and higher desertion rates – especially when DVL Category III men were involved. SS recruitment drives from 1942 onward deliberately targeted DVL I–III for both front-line and auxiliary roles, especially when 'German-blood' was confirmed. As for which specific German units contained a large percentage of ethnic Germans from Poland, the following divisions were known to have contained large numbers of *Volksdeutsche* from the occupied Polish territories:

Table 5. German formations with a sizable number of *Volksdeutsche* from annexed Polish territories.

Heer	Region	Notes
68. Infanterie-Division	*Warthegau & Silesia*	Replacement drafts from the Silesian and Lodz regions; some companies were heavily composed of *Volksdeutsche* from these areas.
75. Infanterie-Division	*Warthegau, Danzig-West Preussen*	Included battalions with DVL I–III conscripts, especially after 1942.

Heer	**Region**	**Notes**
88. Infanterie-Division	*General gouvernement*	This division was replenished using Volksdeutsche from the central Polish districts, especially around the city of Lublin.
371. Infanterie-Division	*Warthegau*	This division was formed in 1942, partially with *Volksdeutsche* recruits from Posen (Poznań) and Litzmannstadt (Łódź).
541. Volksgrenadier-Division[19]	*Warthegau & Silesia*	Contained many Category III conscripts. Later linked to *Division Nr. 606.*[20]
Infanterie-Ersatz-Regiment 254	*Danzig-West Preussen*	Several replacement battalions were fed with DVL recruits from across Poland.
Grenadier-Ersatz und Ausbildungs-Regiment 491	*Danzig-West Preussen*	Several replacement battalions were fed with DVL recruits from across Poland.
Grenadier-Ersatz und Ausbildungs-Regiment 121	*Warthegau*	Several replacement battalions were fed with DVL recruits from across Poland.
Reserve-Grenadier-Regiment 68	*Warthegau*	Several replacement battalions were fed with DVL recruits from across Poland.
Grenadier-Ausbildungs-Regiment 32	*Warthegau*	Several replacement battalions were fed with DVL recruits from across Poland.
Reserve-Grenadier-Regiment 208	*Warthegau*	Several replacement battalions were fed with DVL recruits from across Poland.
5. SS-Panzer-Division 'Wiking'	*Warthegau, Silesia & General gouvernment*	Especially early war volunteers. Some Polish *Volksdeutsche* in artillery and pioneer units.

Heer	**Region**	**Notes**
10. SS-Panzer-Division 'Frundsberg'	*Warthegau*	Contained some DVL Category I/II conscripts, especially after 1943.
18. SS-Freiwilligen-Panzergrenadier-Division 'Horst Wessel'	*Warthegau, Galicia, Danzig*	Included large contingents of *Volksdeutsche* who had been settled on Polish lands from Bessarabia and the Baltics states.
Transport-Begleit-Regiment 'Posen'	*Warthegau*	Employed escorting motorised transport columns of supplies and equipment.
SS-Polizeiregiment 23	*General gouvernement*	Formed with a sizable number of *Volksdeutsche,* often assigned to anti-partisan operations.
SS-Polizeiregiment 25	*General gouvernement*	Formed with a sizable number of *Volksdeutsche,* often assigned to anti-partisan operations.
Polizei Schützen-regiment 34	*Bialystok*	Formed with a sizable number of *Volksdeutsche,* often assigned to anti-partisan operations.
Polizei Schützen-regiment 35	*Warthegau*	Formed with a sizable number of *Volksdeutsche,* often assigned to anti-partisan operations.
Schutzmannschaft battalions	*General gouvernement*	*Schutzmannschafts-Bataillone 202, 203, 204, 205, 206, 207 und 208.* Employed as guards or in anti-partisan operations
Hilfspolizei units	*Warthegau, Zichenau, General gouvernement* and *Danzi-West Preussen*	Local DVL conscripts or volunteers used in ghetto and security roles. These included not only the auxiliary police of the *Sonderdienst,* but *Wach* (Guard) and *Landesschützen* (regional defence) battalions (too numerous to list).

Figure 4. General-SS regiments in the region of Danzig-West Preussen. (Author's line drawing)

The **Selbstschutz** *and* **Sonderdienst**

Most ethnic-German Poles had been drawn initially into the *Selbstschutz* (Self-Defence) set up shortly after the collapse of Polish resistance along the lines of the Nazi *SA* – the *Sturmabteilungen*, or Storm Trooper battalions. Governor Hans Frank had ordered the creation of the *Selbstschutz* so that the *Volksdeutsche* community in Poland could serve:

> Himmler had authorised the German Order Police headquarters to establish locally based *Selbstschutz* units in the annexed western territories of Poland. For the Government General, he appointed an SS and *Selbstschutz* commander, subordinate to the Higher SS and Police Leader [*Höherer SS- und Polizeiführer* – HSSPF] for the Government General, *SS-Obergruppenführer* Friedrich-Wilhelm Krüger. Between November 1939 and April 1940, some 12,600 ethnic-German men were recruited into *Selbstschutz* units under command of the SSPF for each of the four districts of the Government General.[21]

The *Selbstschutz* eventually numbered about 45,000 ethnic-German Poles between the ages of 18 and 40. The effective date of activation for the *Selbstschutz* was 30 November 1939. We know some of the commanders of the *Selbstschutz*, but the list is not complete. The *Selbstschutz* commander for the Lublin District was *SS-Standartenführer* Walter Gunst. By December 1939 a *Selbstschutz* battalion made up of five companies was established there. Counting all officers, NCOs, and enlisted men, the strength of the battalion was somewhere between 800 and 1,000 men.[22] The *Selbstschutz* were also directly implicated in the persecution of the Jews. On 22 April 1940 *SS-Gruppenführer* Odilo Globocnik, the head of the *SS- und Polizeiführer Lublin* command, ordered that the *Selbstschutz* be used in an additional capacity. They were to guard the labour camps that held the Jewish forced labourers. the *Selbstschutz* would eventually guard a total of six camps containing approximately 2,700 Jewish labourers. These had been put to work on regulating the Bug River by the *Wasserwirtschaftsinspektion* (Water Economy Inspectorate) for the Biala-Podlaska District.[23]

Figure 5. The cuff band of the ***Sonderdienst*** was worn on the lower left sleeve of the field blouse. (Author's line drawing)

In April 1940 Hans Frank ordered the *Selbstschutz* officially disbanded and the following month he decreed the establishment of the *Sonderdienst* (Special Service), which was to become Frank's special police in Poland. The basic unit in the *Sonderdienst* was the *Sturm*, which contained thirty men and was equal to an American platoon of the Second World War. A *Sturmkompanie* contained four *Sturm* and was thus roughly the size of a small company. A *Sturmbataillon* (Assault Battalion) contained three or four *Sturmkompanie*.

Table 6. Estimated Distribution of *Volksdeutsche* by DVL Category and Year

Year(s)	Category I	Category II	Category III	Category IV
1939–40	100 per cent volunteers	Mostly volunteers	None yet conscripted	Not used
1941	70 per cent volunteers, and 30 per cent conscripted	Increasing conscription	Small numbers in labour units	Excluded
1942	85 per cent Mostly conscripted	Widespread drafting	Start of forced conscription	Excluded or interned
1943	100 per cent Fully conscripted	Fully conscripted	Forced conscription expanded	Some recruits were monitored or reviewed
1944–5	Few remaining	Last reserves conscripted	Drafted *en-masse*, including minors	Some were pressed into *Volkssturm* or labour units

Governor Hans Frank employed these locally-raised ethnic-German troops as guards for civil and military buildings and installations, among their many duties. Frank's control of the *Sonderdienst* ended in August 1942 when *Reichsführer-SS* Heinrich Himmler ordered that the *Sonderdienst* be assigned to the control of *SS-Obergruppenführer* Friedrich-Wilhelm Krüger.[24] One large-scale employment of the *Sonderdienst* while under Frank's control occurred on 11 June 1942, when a special round-up of Jews took place in Tarnow. The city had a pre-war Jewish population of around 25,000. This amounted to about 45 per cent of the city's total population. The operation was so large that the security services sought assistance from the local police as well as the district police. A company of *Waffen-SS* troops, commanded by *SS-Hauptsturmführer* Klienow, that was stationed at *SS-Truppenübungsplatz Debica,* also participated.

The *Sonderdienst*, the *Baudienst* (Polish Labour Service), and several employees of the Tarnow labour exchange all took part as well. The round-up of Jews in Tarnow continued from 11–19 June 1942. The Nazis and their accomplices gathered about 3,000 of the town's Jewish population in the market square. Panic set in as some of the Jews in there realised what was about to happen. In desperation, hundreds tried to escape. In the bedlam that ensued, about 3,000 men, women, children, and old folks were murdered in the streets and in the town's Jewish cemetery, where many had taken refuge. Those who didn't try to run away were taken out of the town to a forest near the village of Zbylitowska Góra, about six miles south-west of Tarnow. It was there that another 7,000 Jews were shot to death and dumped into a shallow grave.

Nord-Schleswig

After the First World War, as part of the Treaty of Versailles and related plebiscites, Denmark regained territory that had previously belonged to Imperial Germany. The Germans annexed the region of Schleswig (Slesvig in Danish), which had been part of the Kingdom of Prussia and then Imperial Germany since 1864, after the Second Schleswig War. In 1920 the region was divided after a plebiscite. The northern part of Schleswig voted to reunite with Denmark, so it was transferred from Germany to Denmark. This area was known as Northern Schleswig (*Nordslesvig* in Danish). The southern part of Schleswig remained under German control. This border adjustment restored Denmark's sovereignty over parts of Schleswig that had been lost in the nineteenth century. The estimate of the ethnic-German population in Northern Schleswig in 1940 was some 20,000 people. These *Volksdeutsche* were the minority who chose to stay despite the territory transferring to Denmark.

Under Danish rule the German minority in Northern Schleswig was officially recognised as a national minority with cultural and linguistic rights, but Denmark remained sovereign over the region throughout the Second World War, given that Nazi Germany did not claim northern Schleswig as being a part of Germany. As for the ethnic-German community of *Nord-Schleswig*, since the Third Reich had not annexed the region, there was no compulsory conscription into the German armed forces. However, some ethnic Germans volunteered or emigrated to Germany and joined the *Wehrmacht* voluntarily, most of them opting to join the *Waffen-SS*, which was recruiting many *Volksdeutsche* outside of Germany's border.

Estimates vary but sources suggest around 1,100 ethnic Germans from Northern Schleswig served in the German military – most in units of the *Waffen-SS*.[25] The two principal *Waffen-SS* formations where a good number of ethnic Germans or pure Germans who lived in Northern Schleswig could be found, was the *5. SS Panzer-Division 'Wiking'* – originally a *motorisiert* (motorised), then a *panzergrenadier* (armoured infantry) division, before officially becoming a panzer division in October 1943. The other was the *11. SS-Freiwilligen-Panzergrenadier Division 'Nordland'*. Almost all of the Germans who lived in Northern Schleswig spoke both German and Danish. This ability to speak Danish was the reason why these men were sent to either the *'Wiking'* or *'Nordland' Waffen-SS divisions* – units that contained a good number of Danish volunteers. For this reason, it only made sense for the *SS-Hauptamt* (SS Main Office), specifically its *Amt II* department, to assign these men to these specific *Waffen-SS* units.

Luxembourg

Luxembourg was invaded on 10 May 1940, but as early as 8 September 1940, volunteers from Luxemburg were already joining the German armed forces. On that date 425 men (out of 507) were inducted into a *Freiwilligen-Bataillon Luxemburg* (Volunteer Battalion Luxemburg), which was to serve as an auxiliary police force for the German *Gendarmerie*. The Germans renamed it *Polizei-Ausbildungs-Bataillon (L)*, where 'L' stood for 'Luxemburg'. Almost as quickly however, a resistance movement was established and came to be known as the *Patriotes Independents*. They were soon referred to simply as *'PI-Männer'* (PI-Men).[26] Once military conscription became mandatory, men from Luxembourg found themselves in just about every branch of the German Armed Forces. In fact, some Luxembourg men eventually found their way into *Reserve-Polizeibataillon 101*, which has become infamous for its actions in Poland during the war.[27] In July 1940, Nazi Germany formally annexed Luxembourg into the German Reich as part of the *Gau Moselland*. As a result, it lost its sovereignty and was administered as a German province until liberation in late 1944.[28]

The annexation was not recognised by the Allies and was resisted by the majority of the Luxembourg population.[29] Initially, ethnic Germans in Luxembourg could volunteer to serve in either the *Luftwaffe*, *Kriegsmarine*, *Heer* or *Waffen-SS*. In addition, if the volunteer was too old to serve in combat, there were other ways to serve, such as factory guards at German-run factories or important facilities, or even as policemen. Beginning in 1942, compulsory conscription was instituted, and included non-German Luxembourgers. This recruitment was resisted by many young Luxembourg men. In total, some 12,000 Luxembourgers served.[30] Of that number, around 3,500 were ethnic Germans from Luxembourg who served in the German military in one capacity or another. The remaining 8,500 men were non-German Luxembourgers, recruited under Nazi conscription policies. Many Luxembourgers resisted conscription, fleeing to neighbouring countries, or joining the resistance movement.

The *11. SS-Freiwilligen-Panzergrenadier-Division 'Nordland'* included many volunteers and conscripts from smaller Germanic countries and ethnic-German minorities, including Luxembourgers. However, the most prominent unit with Luxembourgish recruits was the *SS-Sturmbrigade 'Wallonien'*, which was primarily Belgian Walloons but also had some Luxembourgers mixed in due to geographic proximity and recruitment overlaps. The initial batch of Luxembourgers served in *Infanterie-Bataillon 373*. This was a unit composed principally of Belgian-Walloons which had been sent to the Eastern Front in February 1942, after it had undergone training. Initially assigned to a Romanian unit, *Infanterie-Bataillon 373* would serve almost exclusively under the command of *100. Jäger-Division* (*17. Armee*). In late 1942, more Luxembourgers were sent to this battalion, given that the unit suffered heavy losses and in early 1942, the Germans could not find sufficient recruits in Belgium to replace its losses. In June 1943 what remained of *Infanterie-Bataillon 373* became the basis for *SS-Sturmbrigade Wallonien* – a new *Waffen-SS* formation made up principally of Belgian volunteers.[31] Luxembourgers however, also served in the *Waffen-SS* under the *11. SS-Freiwilligen-Panzergrenadier-Division 'Nordland'* as early as 1941. Post-war research shows Luxembourgish volunteers were often assigned based on training needs and available slots rather than nationality-specific units. The lack of a Luxembourgish unit reflects Luxembourg's small size and population.

Chapter 3

GERMANIC VOLUNTEERS AND THE CRUSADE AGAINST BOLSHEVISM

Norway

Pre-War Fascism in Norway: The Partiet Nasjonal Samling

The *Partiet Nasjonal Samling* (NS) was established on 17 May 1933 (Norwegian Constitution Day) by Vidkun Quisling, who had been the Norwegian defence minister, and Johan Bernhard Hjort. The party was Fascist, strongly nationalist, anti-communist, and explicitly modelled on Italian Fascism and German National Socialism. The symbol of the party was a golden sun cross on a red background. The structure of the party was highly centralised with Quisling as *fører* (leader), mirroring the *Führerprinzip*. Membership before 1940 was estimated at about 2,000–3,000 active members by 1939. The party was tiny compared to mainstream Norwegian political parties. However, because of the centralisation, it was well organised. Before the German invasion on 9 April 1940, the activities of the *Partiet Nasjonal Samling* were relegated to propaganda through its newspaper *Fritt Folk*. Recruiting efforts yielded small numbers of Norwegians who wished to join the party. For the most part, Norwegians didn't seem to be interested in living under a dictatorship.

The party contained a paramilitary-style group called the *Hirden*, like the Italian Fascist *Camicie nere* (Blackshirts) and the Nazi *Sturmabteilung* (SA, Stormtroopers). The party also included a youth wing called the *Ungdomsfylking*. Before the war, the *Nasjonal Samling* party maintained close ties with Nazi Germany. In fact, Vidkun Quisling met with Hitler in December 1939. The purpose of the meeting was to discuss a potential German-backed coup in Norway.

Although this never materialised, the *Partiet Nasjonal Samling* served as the nucleus of the collaborationist regime established after the German invasion of 9 April 1940. The NS never had mass electoral support – garnering only about 2 per cent of the vote in the election of 1933. Three years later, in the election of 1936, it garnered even less than 1 per cent. Apart from *Nasjonal Samling,* there were smaller, less formal groups and associations who were sympathetic to a Nazi victory.

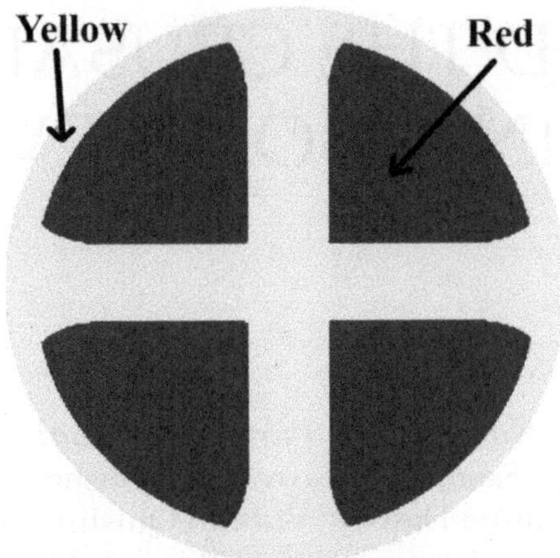

Figure 6. The symbol of the ***Nasjonal Samling*** party was a golden (yellow) sun cross on a red background. (Author's line drawing)

One was the *Den Germanske Forening* (The Germanic Society), a pro-German cultural organisation, which attempted to foster ties between Norwegians and the Third Reich. The *Nasjonal Samling* also contained cultural and sports clubs, which were often mere fronts for Norwegian Nazi propaganda and recruitment. There were also Germanophile circles within the Norwegian Army officer corps. This was small but notable. Some Norwegian officers admired German military efficiency, though most remained loyal to the King and government. There was also the Norwegian-German Friendship Society which was established earlier, in the 1930s to promote 'Nordic' unity. This society occasionally hosted lectures and events with German diplomats geared to promote cooperation between Nazi Germany and Norway.

The Reason for the German Invasion of Norway

When war broke out in Europe on 1 September 1939 Norway declared its neutrality. It remained officially neutral during the early phase of the Second World War, following the precedent it had kept during the

First World War. The key strategic issue was iron ore from Sweden – vital for German armaments. In summer, ore could be shipped through the Baltic, but during winter the Baltic ports iced over. In winter, the ore was transported by rail to the Norwegian port of Narvik, which remained ice-free year-round, and from there shipped south along Norway's coast through the protected Norwegian territorial waters to Germany. Britain wanted to stop this trade without provoking neutral Norway into outright hostility. From late 1939 into early 1940, Royal Navy vessels began shadowing and intercepting German ships within Norway's three-mile territorial limit. This was a violation of Norway's neutrality under international law.

A significant escalation of tension between the United Kingdom, Norway and Nazi Germany was the '*Altmark* Incident' (16 February 1940), where the German tanker *Altmark*, carrying British POWs from the *Graf Spee*, was traveling south through Norwegian waters. A British destroyer, HMS *Cossack*, entered Norwegian waters, boarded the ship near Jøssingfjord, and freed the prisoners. This was a direct breach of Norway's territorial sovereignty. Prior to this incident, the British admiralty had proposed laying naval mines on Norwegian waters. This proposal had been made as early as December 1939. The British codeword for mining Norwegian waters was called Operation Wilfred. The plan was to force German ore carriers into the open sea, where the Royal Navy could intercept them.

In March 1940, British warships sometimes pursued or checked German vessels close to the Norwegian coast – often testing Norway's ability (or willingness) to enforce neutrality. Germany wanted to protect its supply of iron ore at all costs. The Third Reich made formal protests to Norway, which in turn protested to both the United Kingdom and Nazi Germany regarding the violations of its neutrality. However, these protests were largely diplomatic formalities without real enforcement measures. The closest that the Norwegian government came to siding with the Germans was to occasionally escort belligerent ships near Norwegian waters, in order to assert Norway's neutrality.

However, in the *Altmark* case, Norwegian escorts allowed the ship to proceed without searching it for POWs – thus giving Britain a propaganda argument that Norway was turning a blind eye to German use of its waters. The Nygaardsvold government in Oslo feared that decisive action against either Britain or Germany would provoke an invasion by either side, or the loss of its neutrality and sovereignty. As a result, enforcement of neutrality was inconsistent and cautious, satisfying neither side. Hitler's reasoning for *Unternehmen Weserübung* (the German invasion of Norway) was multi-layered. First, Hitler claimed that Germany needed to secure iron ore supply. Second, he wanted to protect the port of Narvik, where Germany's iron ore travelled through during the winter. He also wanted to protect the route from Narvik to Germany from British interference.

By doing this Germany could avoid dependence on the vulnerable Baltic shipping route in the winter. Hitler also argued that conquering Norway would offer strategically located air and naval bases in order to prosecute the war against Britain. Further, Norway's long Atlantic coastline would give Germany submarine and air bases much closer to British shipping lanes. Control of Norwegian fjords and airfields could extend German reconnaissance and bomber reach over the North Atlantic. Finally, Hitler believed that it was just a matter of time before the United Kingdom would completely ignore Norwegian neutrality. Finally, after Germany invaded the USSR, the Baltic Sea became more dangerous on account of Soviet warships and submarines based principally in Leningrad.

The *Altmark* Incident and German intelligence on British planning, such as Operation Wilfred and Plan R 4 (the proposed occupation of Norwegian ports), convinced Adolf Hitler that the British might land troops in Norway to cut off the iron ore route. Admiral Erich Raeder, the *Kriegsmarine* commander-in-chief, pressed Hitler on the urgency of beating the British to the punch in Norway. He argued that if Britain moved first, Germany's strategic position in Scandinavia and the North Sea would be critically weakened. Finally, there were also political factors that led Hitler to invade Norway. Norway's weak military preparedness and reluctance to offend Germany made Hitler believe a rapid, surprise occupation could succeed with minimal resistance. The potential to sway Sweden toward closer cooperation (or at least secure its ore deliveries) was also a consideration.

Meanwhile, between December 1939 and January 1940 French and British planners debated cutting the German iron ore supply via Norway. The *Altmark* Incident indicated that Norway could not effectively enforce its own neutrality. The Nygaardsvold government's protests lacked teeth, reinforcing the perception of weakness. Combined with intelligence on Allied plans, this tipped the balance toward a pre-emptive German strike to secure both the iron ore lifeline and strategic bases before Britain could act. It was in February 1940 that Hitler ordered that plans be formulated for a possible invasion of Norway. Meanwhile, in March 1940 the United Kingdom had finalised plans for Operation Wilfred. Hearing of this, Germany accelerated the launching of *Unternehmen Weserübung*. This operation was initiated in the early morning hours of 9 April 1940, when Germany launched the simultaneous invasion of Denmark and Norway.

Fear of a 'Fifth Column'

Prior to the start of the war on 1 September 1939, the small Fascist *Nasjonal Samling* party was not considered a threat by the Norwegian government. Of course, once Nazi Germany began its road of European conquest, Norwegian (and British) intelligence became concerned about the possibility that pro-Nazi Norwegians could infiltrate ports, shipping companies, and radio communications facilities in advance of a German invasion. Quisling's 1939 Berlin meetings with Hitler and Joachim von Ribbentrop and his December 1939 broadcast accusing the Norwegian government of plotting with Britain, were seen as open alignment of the *Nasjonal Samling* party with German interests. The Germans planned *Unternehmen Weserübung* in part assuming that Quisling's *Nasjonal Samling* party could help neutralise any resistance. In reality, the NS had too little popular support to play a decisive role in the invasion itself. Therefore, before the German invasion, the only significant pro-Nazi political party in Norway was the *Nasjonal Samling,* but it was electorally weak and marginalised. There were, however, small pro-German cultural associations and a few German-sympathising individuals in business and the military. After the invasion, the German used the NS by making it the sole legal party under German occupation. It was thus that eventually Quisling's name would become synonymous with treason.

Quisling Takes Over

On the day of the German invasion (9 April 1940), Vidkun Quisling, leader of the *Nasjonal Samling,* declared himself head of a new Norwegian government in a radio broadcast. The German command did not initially oppose this brazen move and instead decided to use Quisling. On 15 April, only six days after allowing Quisling's claim to be the new Prime Minister of Norway, Adolf Hitler ordered him effectively removed from office. There were several reasons why this occurred. Fundamentally, Quisling had severely overestimated both his influence and the support for his movement within Norway to the Führer. He had assured Hitler that, despite the *Nasjonal Samling*'s modest membership of approximately 15,000 Norwegians, there were 'at least two or three hundred thousand' people in Norway who were broadly sympathetic to his cause, and who would rally in support his government at any moment. However, this 'support' never materialised. Moreover, Quisling had claimed that King Haakon VII would acquiesce to the German occupation and that the general public would remain passive. These assurances quickly proved unfounded.

Internally, Quisling faced opposition from influential figures within the Nazi regime itself. Led by Foreign Minister Joachim von Ribbentrop, an anti-Quisling faction succeeded in persuading Hitler that Quisling, far from facilitating Germany's objectives, was alienating the Norwegian population and exacerbating tensions under the occupation (which he actually was). Rather than stabilising the situation, his presence was contributing to unrest. The majority of Norwegians saw his act as treason. Compounding matters, Quisling had begun to act unilaterally, disregarding the authority of German military officials such as General Nikolaus von Falkenhorst and attempting to govern Norway as though he held full sovereign control. This presumptuous behaviour, coupled with his political miscalculations, ultimately led to his marginalisation by the German leadership.

On 15 April 1940, the German dictator appointed Josef Terboven as the official Nazi authority in Norway. Terboven became *Reichskommissar* for Norway and governed the country as the de facto head of the occupation administration. At this time, Vidkun Quisling remained politically active but without real power. This situation however, changed in the late winter of 1941/42. On 1 February 1942, with Hitler's approval, Quisling was appointed 'Minister President' of Norway under German occupation. This gave him nominal control of a collaborationist government, but the actual authority in Norway remained with Terboven and the occupation forces. No one was fooled by this charade, and the majority of Norwegians continued to view Quisling and his supporters as traitors to their country.

Internal Security

During the occupation, the Germans allowed for the creation of an internal security force that could operate within Norway, and whose focus would be fighting the Norwegian Resistance, repression of opposition, and enforcement of Nazi control, and finally, policing duties. This is how the *Statspolitiet* (STAPO, State Police) was formed in 1941. At peak strength: this force never amounted to more than 1,200–1,400 personnel. However, it proved to be a reliable tool of control for the Germans. These men also took part in the deportation of Jews – notably, the 1942 deportation to Auschwitz. The *Statspolitiet* also worked closely with the Gestapo. It took part in raids and operations against the Norwegian resistance. The *Statspolitiet* was both feared and hated, for they very quickly gained a reputation for brutal interrogation techniques and torture. Many of the men who served in the *Statspolitiet* came from the ranks of the *Hirden* – the paramilitary force of the *Partiet Nasjonal Samling*. At its peak strength (1943–4) the *Hirden* contained some 8,000 men.

The Ordenspoliti *and* Sikkerhetspoliti

With Vidkun Quisling's blessing and under the tutelage of the Germans, the Norwegian police force was re-organised in May 1941 to reflect a more pro-Nazi stance. The *Statspoliti* was 'cleansed' of 'undesirable' members and divided into two main sections in July 1941: (1) the *Ordenspoliti* (Order Police) and (2) *Sikkerhetspoliti* (Security Police). This purge began in December 1941 after a new Norwegian Minister of Police, Jonas Lie and his Chief of the State Police, Colonel Konrad Sundlo, were appointed. This also resulted in the former dark blue uniform of the pre-war Norwegian police being discarded in favour of a grey-green one, based on Germany's *Ordnungspolizei*.[1] In March 1942 these Norwegian police dress regulations were instituted. The tunic was open-necked to show a white shirt and black tie. The collar tabs were green bearing a heraldic lion holding an axe facing towards the tie. A special medal was produced to award those Norwegian police members who served on the Eastern front. It sported a Christian cross with the Norwegian *Hirden* 'sun wheel' at its centre.

The *Sikkerhetspoliti* was overseen by Karl A. Marthinsen, who led both the *Statspolitiet* and the *Sikkerhetspoliti* under the Nazi-controlled police apparatus in occupied Norway, while the *Statspolitiet* had about 350 officers and focused on political crimes, sabotage, espionage, and assisted in implementing anti-Jewish policies. The new *Ordenspoliti* were grouped into six known police companies as follows: *Politikompani 1* (Oslo); *Politikompani 2* (Oslo); *Politikompani 3* (Oslo); *Politikompani 4* (Trondheim); *Politikompani 5* (Lofoten); and *Politikompani 6* (Narvik). It is possible that more police companies could have existed. These included *Politikompani 8*, based in Bergen, and *Politikompani 7*, stationed in Mosjoen.

Two of these Norwegian police companies, *Politikompani 2* and *Politikompani 3*, saw some service with the *6. SS-Gebirgs-Division 'Nord'* in northern Finland in 1942.[2] Another company, under the command of *SS-Sturmbannführer* Jonas Lie, saw service in the *SS Legion Norwegen*.[3] This unit was attached to the German 2. *SS-Infanterie-Brigade (motorisiert)* in the Leningrad sector of the Russian Front in 1942. One of the higher Police commanders of the *Ordenspoliti* and a close friend of Vidkun Quisling was Major Ragnvald Hvoslef, an ex-Norwegian Army officer who was Police Chief for South Varanger province in the region of Finnmark.

Major Ragnvald Hvoslef died on 8 August 1944. It is estimated that the Norwegian *Sikkerhetspoliti* contained around 500–600 members while the *Statspoliti* as the *Ordenspoliti* was officially called, could count on 1,200–1,500 men. The total strength of the Norwegian SS on 30 September 1944 was 1,247 of which 330 were fighting with the *Waffen-SS*, while 245 were in the *Ordenspoliti* and 511 in other units, including the *Sikkerhetspoliti*, about which very little is known. We do know that there was a Gestapo unit made up of Norwegian *Sikkerhetspoliti* men stationed in Trondheim called the '*Sonderabteilung Lola*'.

Sonderabteilung Lola ('Rinnan band') and its Role

In spite of its title, the unit was not a battalion and never totalled more than sixty to seventy men. However, it was an effective Gestapo unit and caused the deaths of many Norwegian Resistance fighters. Its specialty was infiltrating Resistance groups. The unit was led by *SD-Hauptsturmführer* Henry Oliver Rinnan. After the war, Rinnan was tried for treason and executed in 1947, alongside eleven other members of his unit. Although formally operating under the German *Sicherheitsdienst* (SD) in Trondheim, *Sonderabteilung Lola* included many operatives from the Norwegian *Sikkerhetspoliti*. This unit, commonly known as the Rinnan gang, comprised about 50–60 Norwegian informants and agents, many with prior *Waffen-SS* or *Sikkerhetspoliti* affiliations. Led by Henry Rinnan, the group infiltrated Norwegian Resistance networks under false pretences, using so-called 'provocation operations' to entrap members by pretending to be sympathetic to the Resistance; once trust was established, they would arrest and/or hand individuals over to German authorities for interrogation, torture, or execution.

From September 1943, Rinnan's gang operated out of a fixed base at Jonsvannsveien 46 in Trondheim (later infamously called *Bande-Klosteret*), which housed cells and torture chambers in its basement. The group's operations spanned central Norway, particularly Trøndelag, Møreog Romsdal, and Nordland, with ambitions to expand into Oslo. Hundreds were tortured, more than eighty were killed, and the gang was not above executing its own members on suspicion of disloyalty. In the post-war legal purge, up to forty-one members were prosecuted. Ten men – including Rinnan – were executed; the women received long prison terms (later commuted for many). Several key figures include Ivar Grande, Rinnan's second-in-command, who was assassinated by the resistance in December 1944, and Ruth Johanne Rognes, who served as a translator for the group and later married a German officer after the war. *Sonderabteilung Lola*'s penetration of Resistance networks across central and northern Norway shows a far greater footprint than was perhaps previously assumed. The severity of post-war punishments reflects the gang's notoriety and the broader impact of Norwegian-perpetrated wartime atrocities.

The *Hirdens Bedriftsvern* (Factory Guard)

The *Hirden* – the Norwegian National Socialist militia – contained seven regiments. In March 1941, the *Hirden* was awarded official police powers.[4] *Hirden* members could now arrest Norwegian citizens at will. As such it was an auxiliary police force to the *Ordenspoliti* and *Sikkerhetspoliti*. A year later, in March 1942 volunteers from the *Hirden* created a battalion of factory guards, which was called the *Hirdens Bedriftsvern*, or HBV. The uniform of the HBV was the German field grey uniform, which was supplied by the German Army. Norwegian *Ordenspoliti* insignia was worn except that they wore black shoulder straps and a cuff band.[5] The HBV could be considered a part of the *Ordenspoliti*, but one which limited itself to guarding factories and warehouses.

The Uniform of the Norwegian Police and Security Police

The *Ordenspoliti* uniform had a preponderance of green and grey-green as compared to the *Sikkerhetspoliti* uniform which was German field grey and whose black collar tabs had the letters 'SP' in silver in place of the lion emblem collar patch of the *Ordenspoliti* NCOs or the gold oak leaf collar tabs for *Ordenspoliti* NCOs or the gold oakleaf collar tabs for *Ordenspoliti* officers. A Norwegian Army helmet, black boots and brown leather belt and pouch completed the uniform. The peaked cap was the type used by the pre-war Norwegian Police but had the added green cloth cap band of the *Ordenspoliti* to further distinguish the uniform from the uniform of the *Sikkerhetspoliti*, as well as woven and straight patterns, depending on rank. The chin strap and peaked cap were both made of black leather. The shoulder straps of the *Ordenspoliti* were also manufactured from green cloth as compared to the *Sikkerhetspoliti* which wore black shoulder boards with silver piping. The main armament carried by the Norwegian collaborationist police would have been the 6.5mm Krag-Jörgensen rifle of Norwegian manufacture.

The Road to Pro-German Military Service

After 9 April 1940, the German military occupation quickly marginalised all political parties except the *Nasjonal Samling*. These pre-war networks became the foundation for Norway's collaborationist apparatus. In order to secure his collaborationist government, Vidkun Quisling very quickly ordered the creation of a security force that could protect the interest of his party and that of the German occupiers. This turned out to be the *Statspolitiet* (State Police). The *Statspolitiet* was staffed largely with NS members and pro-German sympathisers. Its principal tasks were to handle political policing, arrest any would-be resistance members. To this end, the *Statspolitiet* worked closely with the German *Gestapo*. The storm troopers of the *Nasjonal Samling* party – the *Hirden* (Quisling's political militia) initially became a ceremonial force employed at important gatherings and celebrations. It later became an armed force and was eventually used in anti-partisan operations.

The *Germanske SS Norge* was established in May 1941 from a core of radical NS members and pro-German recruits. It was the Norwegian branch of the *Germanische SS*, a network of SS units created in several occupied and collaborationist countries to recruit 'racially suitable' volunteers for Nazi Germany's war effort. They were also to serve as the ideological and political extensions of the SS in those nations. It was formally modelled on the German *Allgemeine-SS*, but placed under the control of *Reichskommissar* Josef Terboven and the *SS Hauptamt*. This was part of Heinrich Himmler's plan to build a 'Greater Germanic Reich' by integrating 'Germanic' peoples – including Norwegians, Danes, Dutch, and Flemings – into the SS system.

Many early recruits of the *Germanske SS Norge* came from the ranks of the *Nasjonal Samling* party. The commanders of the *Germanske SS Norge* included Jonas Lie, the Norwegian police chief who was also a full-fledged SS officer, and Leif Schøren. The organisation had its own ranks, uniforms, and insignia, closely resembling those of the German *Allgemeine-SS* but with Norwegian national symbols. Membership in the *Germanske SS Norge* was small. The organisation could count on perhaps only a few hundred men at most. Service in the *Germanske SS Norge* was voluntary. Like the *Allgemeine-SS*, the *Germanske SS Norge* was organised into local *Standarten* (regiments) based mainly in Oslo and other major cities.

One of the primary functions of the *Germanske SS Norge* was to encourage and facilitate volunteer enlistment of Norwegians into the *Waffen-SS* – notably *SS Division 'Wiking'* and later *SS Division 'Nordland'*. It also served propaganda and ideological work by disseminating Nazi racial ideology, Germanic unity concepts, and anti-Communist propaganda through its rallies, publications, and public appearances. The *Germanske SS Norge* was also employed in police and security matters. Members sometimes aided German security forces, especially the *Sicherheitsdienst*, and more specifically, the *Gestapo*, in arresting Resistance members or guarding prisoners. They also served in a ceremonial and political role. They always appeared in parades, propaganda films, and official events as a showpiece of 'Norwegian-German brotherhood'.

While both were pro-Nazi, the *Germanske SS Norge* was directly tied to the SS hierarchy in Germany, whereas the *Nasjonal Samling* was a Norwegian political party. This sometimes caused friction. For example, Quisling wanted full control over all collaborationist groups, but Berlin kept the *Germanske SS Norge* under Himmler's command to ensure ideological purity and loyalty to the Reich. As the war turned against Germany, recruitment dried up. By late 1944, it existed mostly in name only, with members absorbed into police units or the *Waffen-SS*. After the German capitulation in May 1945, members were arrested by Norwegian authorities. Many faced imprisonment, loss of civil rights, or long-term social stigma.

1. SS-Freiwilligen-Legion Norwegen *(1941–3)*

Established in June 1941, right after Germany invaded the Soviet Union, it was sponsored by the *Nasjonal Samling* party and the *SS-Hauptamt* as a way to bring Norwegian volunteers into the *Waffen-SS*. The unit's creation was heavily tied to propaganda about the 'European crusade against Bolshevism'. Officially, enlistment was 'voluntary', but Nazi propaganda in Norway portrayed it as a patriotic duty. The initial force formed from these Norwegian volunteers numbered roughly 1,200–1,500 men in the initial wave of recruits. The Norwegian recruits trained in Germany, at Sennheim (Alsace) and later at Fallingbostel.

This Norwegian SS contingent was initially under *SS-Hauptsturmführer* Arthur Quist, who was Norwegian. *SS-Freiwilligen-Legion Norwegen* was sent to the Eastern Front in February 1942, and was attached to the SS *'Wiking'* division. It operated as a reinforced infantry battalion within the division, and saw heavy fighting in eastern Ukraine and later in the summer and autumn of 1942, in the Caucasus. After the Stalingrad debacle, the reinforced battalion continued to serve in the *'Wiking'* division, taking part in the retreat in eastern Ukraine in early 1943. By mid-1943, losses and dwindling enlistments led to the disbandment of the Legion. Survivors and re-enlistees were absorbed into other SS formations – especially the new *SS-Panzergrenadier-Regiment 'Norge'* within *11. SS-Freiwilligen-Panzergrenadier-Division 'Nordland'*. This SS division was also to contain many Danish and Dutch volunteers.

SS-Skijäger-Bataillon 'Norge' *(1943–5)*

By mid-1943, the original *SS-Freiwilligen-Legion Norwegen* was being wound down. Many veterans' enlistments had expired, and the unit had suffered heavy casualties on the Eastern Front. Heinrich Himmler still wanted to keep a distinct Norwegian *Waffen-SS* presence, partly for propaganda and partly to tap the 'Germanic' manpower pool for winter and mountain warfare. At the same time, the Finnish front and the northern sector of the Eastern Front required specialised troops capable of operating in Arctic and sub-Arctic terrain. Late in 1943 volunteers for this new specialised force came from the disbanded *SS-Freiwilligen-Legion Norwegen* and the NS party's *Hirden* paramilitary wing. New Norwegian recruits were also attracted by the elite nature of this new *Norwegian-SS* unit (ski troops). Training took place in Oberwischau (today Vișeu de Sus, in Romania) and other *Waffen-SS* winter warfare training facilities. The unit was officially designated *SS-Skijäger-Bataillon 'Norge'* – a battalion-sized formation trained in ski warfare, reconnaissance, and mountain warfare. This specialised battalion was subordinated to the *SS-Führungshauptamt* (SS-FHA, SS Leadership Main Office) for recruitment and training.

However, operational control varied depending on the front. It was initially assigned to *20. Gebirgsarmee* in Finland for Arctic warfare duties. The battalion contained many *Waffen-SS* officers who were Norwegian, but also included some German officers as well. The cadre of the battalion was composed of experienced Eastern Front veterans from the Norwegian-SS Legion. The battalion was sent to the far north, operating along the Finnish-Soviet front. It engaged in patrols, reconnaissance and small-scale raids across snow-covered terrain. This Norwegian-SS ski battalion often worked alongside German *Gebirgsjäger* and Finnish ski troops. Their tasks included disrupting Soviet ski patrols, guarding key passes and supply routes in winter, performing long-range reconnaissance patrols in deep snow and forested areas. After Finland signed the armistice with the USSR in September 1944, German forces in northern Finland were forced to withdraw. The withdrawal of German forces from Finland was code-named *Unternehmen Birke* (Operation Birch). The battalion, as well as the rest of *20. Gebirgsarmee,* withdrew into northern Norway.

SS-Skijäger-Bataillon 'Norge' was then ordered redeployed to the Baltic area, where it was increasingly used as a standard infantry unit. By late 1944, it had been absorbed into the *11. SS-Freiwilligen-Panzergrenadier-Division 'Nordland'*, specifically as part of *SS-Panzergrenadier-Regiment* 23 *'Norge'*. Once it was absorbed into the *'Nordland'* division, the battalion ceased to exist as a separate ski unit. The remaining Norwegian troops fought in the Courland Pocket, then along the Oder River in 1945 in defence of the German capital. In mid-April 1945 survivors of the SS *Nordland* division retreated into Berlin, where elements of the former *Skijäger* contingent fought in the final battles in late April-early May 1945. Most surviving Norwegian *Waffen-SS* personnel surrendered to the Soviets, with many spending years in captivity before being repatriated to Norway to face trial and imprisonment. By 1945, about 6,000–6,500 Norwegians had served in German uniform, most in *Waffen-SS* formations, and almost all of them came through or were influenced by these pre-war and early occupation period networks.

Denmark

Pre-War Nazis in Denmark: The DNSAP

In 1930, the *Danmarks Nationalsocialistiske Arbejderparti* (DNSAP, Danish National Socialist Workers Party) was founded by Frits Clausen. The DNSAP was modelled directly on German Nazism – anti-communist, nationalist, anti-Semitic, and loyal to Adolf Hitler's vision of a racially pure Europe. The Party used the Swastika and similar uniforms/ imagery to the German Nazi Party. The DNSAP, like the Norwegian *Partiet Nasjonal Samling*, never achieved significant electoral success. In the 1939 Danish parliamentary election, it only received some 1.8 per cent of the vote, and in 1943, its support peaked at 2.1 per cent, winning three seats out of 149 in the Danish parliament. It had some support in northern Jutland, where Frits Clausen was from, but was broadly unpopular elsewhere.

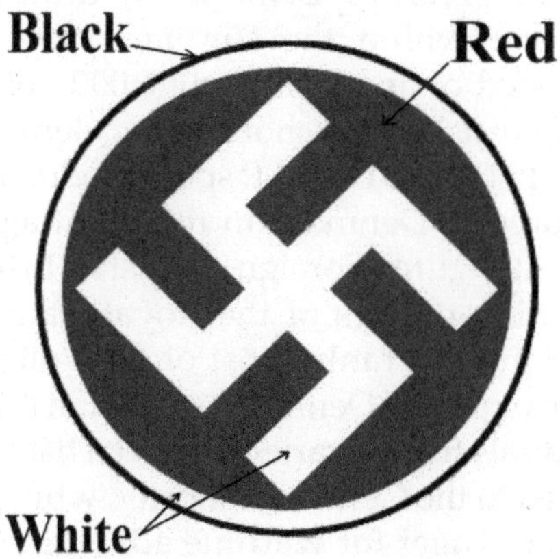

Figure 7. The insignia of the DNSAP – a white swastika on a red background and a white outer circle. (Author's line drawing)

After Germany occupied Denmark on 9 April 1940, the DNSAP hoped to become the ruling party, similar to Quisling's *Nasjonal Samling* in Norway. However, Hitler chose to maintain Denmark's constitutional monarchy and existing government (at least until 1943), sidelining the DNSAP. Hitler did this because he realised that there was no strong public support for the DNSAP. It was thus that Clausen and his Danish Nazi Party remained politically marginalised even under German occupation. In November 1940, the Germans once again tested the waters in Denmark by sponsoring a 'March of Unity' that would be organised by the DNSAP, but it failed to gain traction with the broader population. There were several other, smaller fascist or ultranationalist groups which existed in Denmark in the 1930s, but none rivalled the DNSAP in visibility. Some focused more on anti-communism than racial ideology. Many of these small parties faded by the early 1940s or were absorbed by the DNSAP. Although the pre-war Danish government was retained, the Danish government and business sectors continued to trade extensively with Germany, especially with regard to foodstuffs (particularly butter, meat and dairy products), agricultural goods, raw materials and manufactured goods, including parts useful for the German war effort. Danish industry was allowed to continue operating, provided it supplied the German military, which many Danish companies did, though some did so under pressure. Danish labour and firms were involved in construction projects, including working on defensive fortifications like building part of the Atlantic Wall.

The Freikorps Danmark

The *Freikorps Danmark* (*Frikorps Danmark* in Danish) was a Danish volunteer infantry unit within the German *Waffen-SS*, active from 1941 to 1943. It consisted of approximately 6,000 volunteers during its existence. The unit was established shortly after Germany's attack on the Soviet Union in June 1941. The DNSAP spearheaded the creation of this force that would represent Denmark in the 'fight against Bolshevism'. A Danish government figure, Foreign Minister Erik Scavenius, later sanctioned it, permitting officers of the Royal Danish Army to enlist while retaining their present rank. Most of the volunteers were either supporters of Nazism or part of Denmark's German minority, though the unit attracted individuals from a variety of social backgrounds. Roughly 1,500 recruits belonged to the German minority, while many others were politically motivated or eager for wartime adventure. Danish historian Bo Lidegaard notes that civilian attitudes toward volunteers were intensely hostile:

> The relationship between the population and the corps was freezing cold . . . legionnaires on leave time and again came into fights with civilians meeting the corps' volunteers with massive contempt.[6]

The first commander was *SS-Obersturmbannführer* Christian Peder Kryssing, appointed in mid-1941. Despite not being a Nazi, he was selected, though ideological disagreements led to his replacement in early 1942. Christian Frederik von Schalburg, a Danish-Russian aristocrat loyal to Nazi ideology, succeeded him. He was killed in early June 1942 during the battle to relieve the Demyansk Pocket. Briefly thereafter, command passed through *SS-Sturmbannführer* Knud Børge Martinsen (promoted to *SS-Obersturmbannführer* on 18 February 1943), then *SS-Sturmbannführer* Hans Albert von Lettow-Vorbeck, before Martinsen took the helm again until the unit's dissolution in mid-1943. Training for the approximately 1,000–1,200 volunteers began in July 1941 near Hamburg. By September, the formation was deployed to Poland as *Freikorps Danmark*. Through its operational front-line service, the *Freikorps Danmark* never exceeded 1,500–2,000 men at any one time. Throughout its history, approximately 6,000 men served, of which seventy-seven were officers with the rank of captain or higher.

The unit saw severe action in the Demyansk Pocket (1942) and later fought near Novgorod, Jelgava (Latvia), the Battle of Velikiye Luki, and other front-line engagements. Casualties were said to have been extremely high in early battles, especially at the battle for the Demyansk Pocket, reportedly losing up to 78 per cent of its strength in 1942. Additionally, in their book *Danish Volunteers of the Waffen-SS: Freikorps Danmark 1941-43*, authors Lars Larsen and Jens Pank Bjerregaard provide photographic evidence and accounts of *Freikorps Danmark*'s participation in the killing of Soviet prisoners of war. One account describes an incident where a Jewish individual was dragged behind a building and killed by members of the unit. This reflects the broader pattern of atrocities committed by German forces on the Eastern Front. Sources cite involvement in atrocities, especially against civilians and prisoners of war, including reports of the shooting of captured Russians and suspected participation in anti-Jewish killings and partisan-mopping operations.[7] Between March and April 1943, the remnants of the *Freikorps Danmark* was withdrawn from combat and sent to Grafenwöhr Training Camp in Bavaria. The formation was officially disbanded on 6 May 1943. Its remnants were restructured into a new unit: *SS-Panzergrenadier Regiment 24 'Danmark'*, which was to serve in a new *Waffen-SS* division: *11. SS-Freiwilligen-Panzergrenadier-Division 'Nordland'*. After the war, over 3,000 former Danish *Waffen-SS* volunteers were prosecuted by Danish courts under retroactive legislation, often receiving sentences around two years' imprisonment, despite some having left Denmark with nominal government support.

The Schleswigsche Kameradschaft

After Germany's defeat in the First World War, a referendum was ordered to see if the people of that region of Schleswig wished to remain as part of Germany. Southern Schleswig-Holstein decided to remain a part of Germany, but northern Schleswig did not. The Germans that remained in northern Schleswig-Holstein now found themselves becoming Danish citizens. These were the core of supporters who welcomed the German invasion in 1940 and became members of the Danish Nazi Party. In 1943 many of these ethnic-German Danes joined the *Schleswigsche Kameradschaft* which some have characterised as the Danish Nazi Party version of the Hitler Youth. They numbered about 1,761 members in 1943. In the Danish General Election of March 1943, the Danish Nazi Party, which Danes and ethnic-German Danies could join, won only 43,267 votes. This small voting block only gained them three seats in the Danish Parliament.[8]

The *Schleswigsche Kameradschaft* served more as a cultural or ideological youth group, aligning younger ethnic Germans in Denmark with Nazi values – but not as a policing entity and with no documented role in recruiting for the *Schalburgkorps*. The *Schalburgkorps*, by contrast, was an active paramilitary organisation under German SS control, involved in security operations, suppression of resistance, and collaboration with German police forces – but its recruitment did not formally derive from groups like the *Schleswigsche Kameradschaft*, although most likely, some ethnic-German members of the *Schleswigsche Kameradschaft* found their way into the *Schalburgkorps* or the *Hilfspolizei* (Hipo) forces. The *Schleswigsche Kameradschaft* appears to have been a German minority youth or student organisation active in North Schleswig (*Sønderjylland*), which is the region of southern Denmark bordering Germany. Multiple archival photos indicate they held gatherings such as placing a commemorative wreath on 9 November 1941 in Sønderborg, a 'führer gathering' on 21 June 1942 at a camp school operated by *Deutsche Jungenschaft Nordschleswig*, which featured flag-raising ceremonies and rifle drills. These activities suggest they functioned similarly to *Hitler Jugend*-style groups among the ethnic-German minority in Danish territory. They likely focused on ideological indoctrination, camaraderie and paramilitary-style exercises, but not a formal university student corps or university-based '*Kameradschaften*' associated with the *Nationalsozialisticher Deutscher Studentbund* (NSDStB, National Socialist German Students' League). There is no evidence that the *Schleswigsche Kameradschaft* performed police functions. Their documented activities – ceremonial events, rifle drills, summer camps – were typical of youth groups. There are no records indicating involvement in policing, security missions, or enforcement.

There is also no indication in the sources that the *Schleswigsche Kameradschaft* was directly involved in recruiting for the *Freikorps Danmark*, *Schalburgkorps*, *Hilfspolizei* or any other paramilitary/

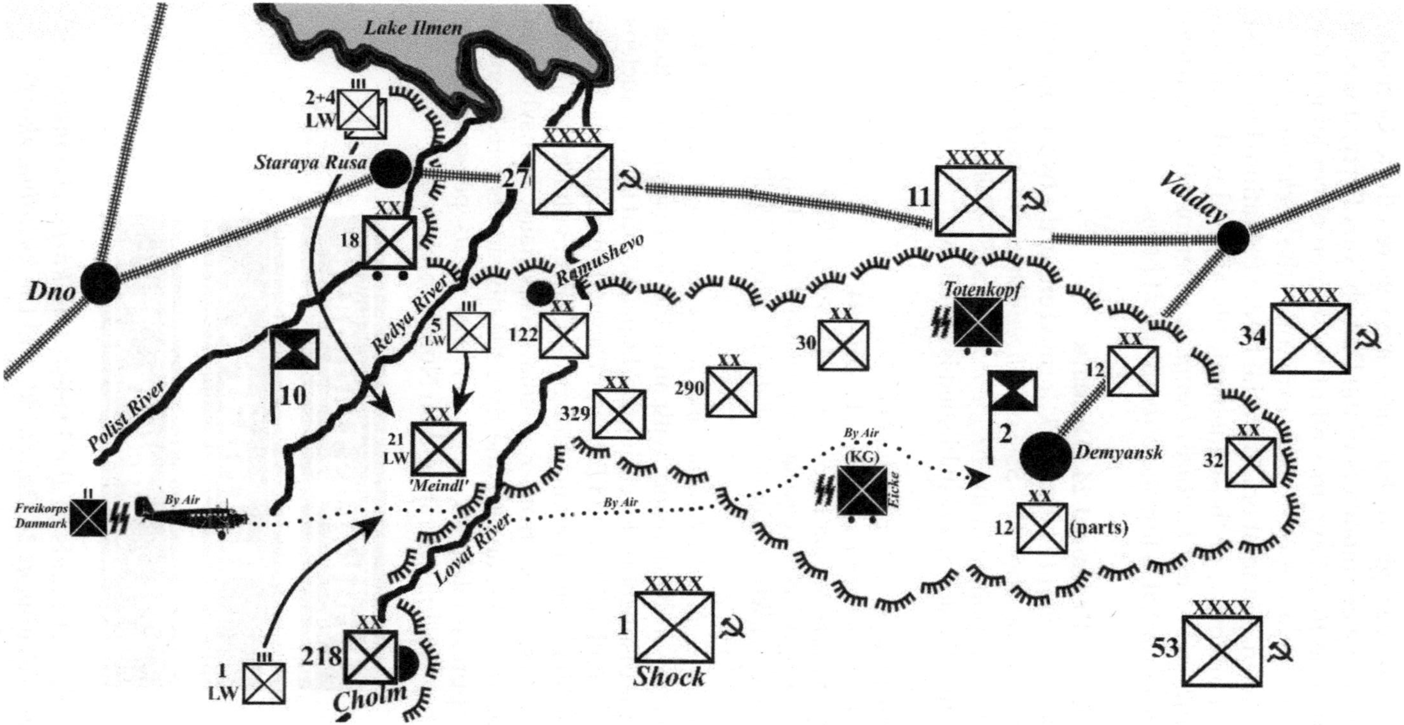

Figure 8. The Demyansk Pocket in early June 1942. ***Freikorps Danmark*** was flown into the pocket in jU 52 transport planes, and employed under ***SS-Infanterie-Division 'Totenkopf' (motorisiert)*** (Author's line drawing)

security unit. However, given that these men were ethnic Germans and a good number were members of the Danish Nazi Party, it would be naïve for anyone to believe that all of these men never joined the aforementioned organisations. For example, the *Schalburgkorps*'s recruitment focused on members from the DNSAP, National Socialist milieu, German minority, or those ideologically aligned with Nazism or anti-Communism. Many *Freikorps Danmark* veterans who returned from the Eastern Front also formed a recruitment basis.

SS-Panzergrenadier Regiment 24 Danmark

SS-Panzergrenadier-Regiment 24 'Danmark' formed one of the two armoured infantry regiments of the *11. SS-Freiwilligen-Panzergrenadier-Division 'Nordland'*, itself a component of the *III. (germanisches) SS-Panzerkorps*. The lineage of how the division was established is as follows:

1. *Kampfverband Waräger* – February 1943
2. *Germanische-Freiwilligen-Division* – February 1943
3. *SS-Panzergrenadier-Division 11 (Germanische)* – April 1943
4. *11. SS- Freiwilligen-Panzergrenadier-Division Nordland* – July 1943
5. *11. SS-Panzergrenadier-Division Nordland* – 22 October 1943[9]

SS-Panzergrenadier-Regiment 24 'Danmark' was established in July 1943 during the creation of the division, with an authorised strength of three battalions and the distinction of wearing the *'Danmark'* cuff title. Its nucleus came from the recently disbanded *Freikorps Danmark*, though it was never exclusively Danish in composition. Alongside Danish volunteers, a large proportion of *Volksdeutsche* from Romania – especially Transylvanian Saxons – joined its ranks, and by the time the division entered combat in late 1943, approximately 75 to 80 per cent of its personnel were *Reichsdeutsche* or *Volksdeutsche* rather than Nordic foreigners.[10]

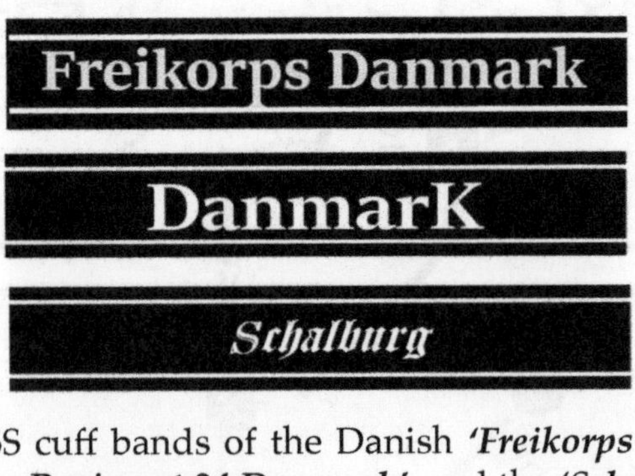

Figure 9. The SS cuff bands of the Danish ***'Freikorps Danmark', 'SS-Panzergrenadier-Regiment 24 Danmark'***, and the ***'Schalburgkorps'***. (Author's black & white drawing)

The regiment's first operational deployment occurred in September–October 1943, when it participated in anti-partisan operations in the Banija region of Croatia, operating in and around Hrastovica, Sisak, Glina, and Petrinja. In December 1943 it was transferred to the Eastern Front, where it joined the division west of Leningrad, on the westernmost edge of the Oranienbaum Pocket. During the summer of 1944, it played a significant role in the defence of the Narva front, particularly during the battles on the Tannenberg Line, where its anti-tank company fought in key defensive positions, including the Orphanage and Grenadier Hills.[11] The regiment subsequently took part in the retreat through the Baltic States, fighting in Riga and withdrawing into the Courland Pocket before being evacuated by sea from Libau (Liepāja) to Stettin.

In early 1945, *SS-Panzergrenadier-Regiment 24 'Danmark'* was committed to the fighting in Pomerania and later retreated into Berlin with the remainder of the SS Nordland Division. By April 1945, when *SS-Brigadeführer* Gustav Krukenberg entered Berlin with a battalion of the French *33. Waffen-Grenadier-Division der-SS 'Charlemagne'*, as well as both the '*Danmark*' and '*Norge*' SS regiments – both of which were reduced to about battalion strength.[12] The '*Danmark*' regiment fought in Neukölln, then in the defence of the city centre and Tiergarten, continuing until the final collapse of organised resistance in early May. Survivors either surrendered to Soviet forces or attempted to break out westward. Over the course of the war, approximately 6,000 Danes served in the *Waffen-SS*, though not all in the '*Danmark*' regiment. Many of those who served in '*Danmark*' had seen earlier service in the *Freikorps Danmark* before its dissolution in May 1943.[13]

Internal Politics

The initial German police involvement in Denmark came by way of the German embassy in Copenhagen, which initially limited its staff to observing the daily events of their newly occupied country. One of these German officials was *SS-Oberführer* (later *SS-Brigadeführer*) Paul Kanstein, who was designated as the *Polizei Attaché* in the embassy. Initially, Kanstein only had a passing interest in the Danish police force which was left intact after the occupation. This changed slowly as this *Sicherheitsdienst* general would eventually try to influence (unsuccessfully) the Danish police to take a more pro-German stance. In a strange twist of fate, Kanstein became involved in the 20 July 1944 bomb plot to kill Hitler.

The conspirators had offered him the post of *'Chef der Sicherheitspolizei'* if the attempt on Hitler's life had been successful. After the bomb plot failed, he was implicated in the attempt on Hitler's life. From 8–9 August 1944, he was personally interrogated by Gestapo chief, Heinrich Müller and *Reichssicherheitshauptamt* (RSHA – Reich Main Security Office) head, Ernst Kaltenbrunner. Although suspected of being part of the plot, he was ultimately released, supposedly due to intervention by Interior State Secretary and *SS-Obergruppenführer* Wilhelm Stuckart. This decision greatly upset Kaltenbrunner. After the war ended, Kanstein was interned by Allied authorities for several years. He went through a denazification process *Spruchkammerverfahren* (Denazification Tribunal Proceedings), with a final report completed in 1949. Following that, he was deemed *entnazifiziert* (denazified) and allowed to return to civilian life. He lived out his remaining years in his hometown, passing away in 1980 or 1981.

In the summer of 1943, Kanstein and many of the German staff assigned to Denmark were relieved from their posts due to the growing Danish unrest and the apparent lack of control over events in that country. The Germans had been quite aware of the dislike by the majority of Danes towards the small pro-Nazi Danish National Socialist Party. This fact alone kept the small Danish Nazi Party in check in spite of attempts in some German circles, most notably elements in the German SD, to force King Christian to appoint Danish Nazis to the government. Joachim von Ribbentrop, the German Foreign Minister and Hitler both opposed this idea. The majority of the members of the small Danish Nazi Party were primarily located in the northern part of the region of Schleswig-Holstein.[14]

The General Strike of July–August 1943

From 9 April 1940 until the summer of 1943, Denmark experienced an unusually lenient occupation compared to other Nazi-controlled countries. The Danish government was allowed to remain in place. The Danish police and army continued to operate, though under certain restrictions. Censorship existed, but daily life was relatively undisturbed compared to occupied Poland, France, or Norway. However, by 1943, this arrangement was breaking down because of German military setbacks – especially the defeats at Stalingrad and in North Africa. These defeats boosted Danish morale and helped to increase Danish Resistance activity.

In mid-1943, sabotage, particularly of the railways, shipyard destruction, and attacks on factories that were serving the German war effort increased sharply. These attacks were led by communist and nationalist resistance groups in the country. Public resentment had also increased due to rationing, economic hardship, and the presence of German troops all of which were further intensified by anti-occupation sentiment.

Berlin demanded harsher measures be taken in Denmark, including the death penalty for sabotage, tighter censorship, and mass arrests. In late July and early August 1943 sabotage activity intensified, especially in Odense, Esbjerg, Aalborg, and Copenhagen. Workers began wildcat strikes over wages and food shortages, often escalating into anti-German demonstrations. German troops opened fire in several incidents, killing and wounding protesters – all of which inflamed public anger. By mid-August the major population centres, including Copenhagen, were near insurrection. The first erupted in Odense (Funen Island), and quickly spread to other cities. Street battles occurred between demonstrators and German forces. Factories shut down, as thousands of Danish workers joined the strikes in solidarity. Resistance groups took the opportunity and coordinated with striking workers to sustain unrest. In response, the Germans issued an ultimatum on 28 August 1943. The German plenipotentiary in Denmark, Dr. Werner Best, told the Danish government that if sabotage and unrest continued, he would declare a state of emergency and impose a curfew, ban public assemblies, crack down on resistance leaders and strikers, and introduce the death penalty for sabotage.

The Danish government did not heed Werner Best's warning, arguing that these measures violated the constitution. On 29 August 1943, the Danish government resigned *en-masse* rather than comply with the German demands. King Christian X then openly suspended cooperation with the Germans. As a result, the Germans were forced to follow through on their threat, and imposed martial law in Denmark. Immediately, Danish army units were disarmed, and the Danish navy scuttled thirty-two of its ships in Copenhagen harbour, in order to prevent the Germans from seizing them. The Germans actually had a plan to capture the ships (*Unternehmen Safari*), but the rapid action of the Danish naval officers prevented this operation from taking place. The Danish police remained intact for the moment, but would be disbanded in September 1944 when they were finally deemed too unreliable. The 'model occupation' which the Germans had boasted about as the ideal of what an occupied country could hope for, ended. Thus began a harsher phase of German rule in Denmark. However, now that the Danish government was clearly out of the picture, the Danish Resistance gained more legitimacy among the wider Danish population. The August events indirectly set the stage for October 1943, when the Germans attempted to arrest Denmark's Jews.

The Jews of Denmark

Between 1940 and 1942, the Germans attempted to tread lightly in Denmark, trying not to ruffle too many feathers. This included leaving the roundup of Denmark's Jews until 1943. Another reason for the delay was because the Danish government refused to implement anti-Semitic laws, allowing Danish Jews to be largely protected. However, when the Germans imposed martial law in August 1943, this changed. In October 1943, German authorities attempted to deport Danish Jews. The Nazi move to arrest Denmark's Jews began on the night of 1/2 October 1943. The Nazi plan to move against Denmark's Jews was finalised in September 1943. The plan was ordered by Werner Best, the German plenipotentiary in Denmark, following Berlin's instructions to begin deportations. However, Best covertly tipped off Danish politicians and the Danish resistance, and the German maritime attaché, Georg Ferdinand Duckwitz, warned Jewish leaders. Because of these warnings, the vast majority of Denmark's 7,200–7,300 Jews managed to escape across the Øresund Strait to neutral Sweden, leaving only about 470 Danish Jews to be captured and deported to Theresienstadt. The people that saved over 7,000 Danish Jews by smuggling them to safety in Sweden included ordinary Danes as well as the Danish Resistance. It was a rare and remarkable success story in occupied Europe.

SS-Obergruppenführer Werner Best was a high-ranking SS officer and a senior official in the RSHA before being posted to Denmark in November 1942. Best's main mission in Denmark was to keep the occupation relatively calm so that Denmark could continue supplying Germany with food and agricultural products without tying down additional German troops. By late 1943, after the August uprising and general strike, tensions were already high. Best needed to obey the orders from Berlin, to round up Denmark's Jews, but he likely knew that a mass arrest of Jews would inflame the Danish public, strengthen the Resistance, and cause unrest – making his job that much harder. Best was not opposed to Nazi racial policy in principle, but in Denmark he adopted a 'pragmatic collaboration' approach. He sometimes manoeuvred to slow or soften Berlin's harsher orders when he thought they undermined occupation goals.

He may have also seen Denmark as a potential bargaining chip in a post-war scenario, wanting to avoid being remembered as the man who destroyed the 'model protectorate' image. Finally, Best may have also calculated that if Germany lost the war, he could claim that he aided in saving Jewish lives – thus avoid possible prosecution. This actually proved to be the case when in 1948 he was tried and sentenced to death for his actions in Denmark. Three years later, in 1951, his death sentence was commuted to 12 years in prison by the Danish king, after political debates and lobbying – partly because of the argument that he had indirectly helped save Denmark's Jews in 1943.

As for the motives of Georg Ferdinand Duckwitz – the German maritime attaché – Duckwitz had been part of the Nazi Party in the early years, but had become disillusioned with the regime. By 1943, he maintained good relations with Danish politicians, business leaders, and even the Danish Resistance. He may have been motivated by personal morality. Duckwitz was strongly opposed to anti-Semitic persecution. Historical evidence suggests his motives were largely humanitarian rather than strategic. In fact, we know that he actively sabotaged Nazi orders. He directly informed Danish Social Democratic leaders of the planned deportations, who then passed the warning to the Jewish community and the resistance. Duckwitz then travelled to Sweden ahead of the arrests to secure Sweden's agreement to accept Danish Jews. This was a decisive move in making the mass escape possible.

While some collaborators helped the Germans identify Jews, the majority of Danes rejected this. While some Danes actively collaborated and a few supported the Nazi cause out of ideology or self-interest, most of the Danish population did not. In fact, public opinion shifted dramatically against Germany, especially after 1943, when the Danish government resigned rather than accept further German demands, Danish resistance grew more organised and active. It was at this time (1943) that the German occupation became harsher and more repressive. Although Danish society had been deeply divided about the war, over time support for Nazi Germany waned in favour of widespread resistance and humanitarian defiance, most famously seen in the rescue of Danish Jews in 1943.

Policing Denmark under Nazi Rule: the **Schalburgkorps** *and* **Hilfspolizei**

When Germany occupied Denmark on 9 April 1940, the Danish police was officially left intact under Danish authority as part of the 'model protectorate' arrangement. However, the Germans quickly created supplementary paramilitary forces under pro-Nazi leadership to act alongside, and eventually bypass, the Danish police. Danish Nazi Party members were encouraged to join newly created German-backed units.

This included the *Freikorps Danmark* (for military service on the Eastern Front) and later the *Schalburgkorps* (a home-front SS police/military unit). The *Statspolitiet* (State Police) was also expanded in 1941–2 with men sympathetic to the occupiers, many trained in Germany. During the August 1943 general strike and wave of sabotage, the regular Danish police refused to crack down effectively on strikers and resistance members. German authorities – particularly SS and police chief Günther Pancke – decided the existing police was unreliable and began systematically replacing it with collaborationist forces directly under German SS control.

The Schalburgkorps

The *Schalburgkorps* was named after a fallen Danish volunteer, Christian Frederik von Schalburg. On 27 February 1942 *SS-Sturmbannführer* von Schalburg arrived at the headquarters of the *Freikorps Danmark*, which at the time was located in Treskau. He had previously served on the staff of the *SS-Infanterie-Division Wiking (motorisiert)*. On 1 March 1942 he assumed command of the *Freikorps Danmark*. On 8 May Schalburg and part of the Danish *Waffen-SS* battalion were transported into the Demyansk Pocket in Junkers Ju 52 transports. The battalion was assigned to *II. Armeekorps*, and operated under the *SS-Infanterie-Division 'Totenkopf' (motorisiert)*. On 2 June 1942, while trying to rally his men, who appeared to waver under a Red Army attack, he was killed by fragments from a Soviet artillery shell.[15] His replacement as the new commander of the *Freikorps Danmark* was likewise killed just two days after assuming command of the battalion.

In February 1943, while *SS-Sturmbannführer* Knud Børge Martinsen was on leave, he established what would become the Danish version of the German SS. This was done with the support and assistance of the SS command in Denmark. The *Schalburg-Korps*, also known as *Schalburgkorpsets* or *Schalburg Corps*, became a pro-German paramilitary unit. The formation was divided into two main groups. Group I comprised the regular, uniformed soldiers, and was initially organised into three *Infanteriekompagni* (infantry companies) and a *Kanonkompagni* (light artillery or infantry-gun company). The *Kanonkompagni* alone contained about fifty men. Group II was made up of the civilian or political arm, known as the *Dansk Folkeværn* (Danish People's Defence), which provided moral and financial support. Based on historical estimates, the overall force size by the winter of 1943, appears to have been around 1,000 men. The *Schalburgkorps* was officered by many Danish officers who had seen combat service in the *Waffen-SS*.

From 1943 to 1945, the *Schalburgkorps* became the main Danish collaborationist paramilitary force during the German occupation. Previously, it was the *Freikorps Danmark* that represented the main pro-German force created from Danish volunteers. As stated previously, the *Schalburgkorps* was created in April 1943, after the *Freikorps Danmark* was withdrawn from the Eastern Front and disbanded in 1943. The Germans wanted to keep a loyal, armed Danish unit for security and counter-Resistance operations inside Denmark. One of its most nefarious members was *SS-Hauptsturmführer* Carl Værnet, the unit's medical officer. Later in the war, Værnet became infamous for experiments performed at Buchenwald concentration camp. The *Schalburgkorps* was organised with the help and sponsorship of the *SS-Hauptamt* (SS Main Office) and was supported financially and logistically by both the German occupation authorities in Denmark and the Danish Nazi Party (DNSAP). It was intended as both a recruitment pool for the *Waffen-SS* and a domestic paramilitary force to combat Danish resistance activities.

For recruits, Martinsen turned to the DNSAP, as well as former members of the *Freikorps Danmark* who had opted not to form part of *SS-Panzergrenadier-Regiment 24 'Danmark'*, which was a regiment of Danes that was to be part of a new *Waffen-SS* division: *11. SS-Freiwilligen-Panzergrenadier-Division 'Nordland'*. He also obtained a good number of men from the *Nye Danmark* Party – a new right-wing party that was not that dissimilar to the DNSAP. From the *Nye Danmark* Party, Martinsen acquired the entire 700-man stormtrooper force (called the *Landstormen*) of this political party. From these men, he created an initial uniformed section of 200 men (*Gruppe I*) and non-uniformed section of 500 men (*Gruppe II*). Later, the uniformed section would be enlarged to some 400–500 men. The official date of the establishment of the *Schalburgkorps* was 19 June 1943. The mission of the *Schalburgkorps* was quite straightforward. It was tasked with supporting the occupation, combating the Danish resistance, and performing security and police duties.

However, very soon after its establishment, a personal squabble broke out between Martinsen and the SS command when the Germans appointed Poul Sommer to lead *Gruppe I* without the approval of Martinsen. For some reason, Martinsen detested Sommer. Sommer's military background was just as good as Martinsen's, although he was a decorated fighter pilot, not an infantry officer. Sommer had served as a pilot in the *Luftwaffe* in North Africa and in Russia. Before he was detached from the *Luftwaffe*, he had been promoted to *Hauptmann* (captain). Martinson had held the rank of major in the *Waffen-SS*.

Leadership of the *Schalburgkorps* initially went to *SS-Sturmbannführer* Knud Børge Martinsen. Then Martinsen threatened to resign because the Germans had appointed *Hauptmann* Poul Sommer to lead the uniformed section (*Gruppe I*) of the *Korps*. It was then that *SS-Hauptsturmführer* Tage Læssøe assumed brief command of the *Schalburgkorps* after Martinsen resigned his position.

During his brief tenure, Læssøe became known for organisational efficiency and close ties to German-SS leadership. Martinsen later returned to command the *Schalburgkorps* when the German SS command relented and relieved Sommer of his command of *Gruppe I. SS-Hauptsturmführer* Jørgen Bitsch was the final commander before dissolution of the *Schalburgkorps* in early 1945. German SS liaison officers were assigned to oversee operations, maintain SS doctrine, and coordinate with Gestapo and RSHA. They ensured the *Schalburgkorps* would be aligned with German security and ideological goals. As to who in the SS was supporting Sommer, we know that during the summer months of 1943, Werner Best initially envisioned Poul Sommer as the leader of the *Schalburgkorps*. However, these plans remained throughout October, indicating a possible shift or delay in the appointment process. According to a study on Nazi ideology among Scandinavian National Socialist intellectuals, Martinsen's speech at the Schalburg School in Birekröd highlighted the tension between Danish and German perspectives on the purpose of the organisation.[16] It became increasingly clear that the *Germanische Leitstelle* and its chief, Bruno Boysen, aimed to establish a Danish SS Corps that would be completely subordinated to the SS. This ideological conflict suggests that Martinsen may have had reservations about the leadership and direction imposed by the SS.

The *Schalburgkorps* was generally despised by the majority of the Danish population. Almost immediately upon the creation of the *Korps*, members began to get killed. The first assassination, carried out on 30 August 1943, was that of Carl Henrik Clemmensen. However, his death was not actually performed by the Danish Resistance. He actually died at the hands of three fellow members of the *Schalburgkorps*, including Flemming Helweg-Larsen and Søren Kam. Carl Henrik Clemmensen was a Danish newspaper editor and also a member of the *Schalburgkorps*. However, Clemmensen was apparently opposed to some of the decisions made by the newly established *Schalburgkorps*. Because of his reservations about the leadership, Clemmensen was perceived as a threat or, at the very least, as a dissenter within the unit. He is a perfect paradigm of the internal brutality that lay within the power-politics in a collaborationist paramilitary group.

The *Hilfspolizei* (Hipo)

The replacement forces included the *Hilfspolizei* (Hipo). The *Hilfspolizei* was established after the Germans disarmed and arrested 1,960 members of the Danish regular police on 19 September 1944, deporting most to Buchenwald and Neuengamme concentration camps. From October 1944 onward, HIPO members, who were mostly Danish Nazis, as well as *Schalburgkorps* veterans, or recruits lured by high pay and privileges took on policing duties. The strength of the *Hipo Korps* was never more than 700 men, of which 550 were stationed in Copenhagen. Initially however, it numbered 350 men. The duties of the *Hilfspolizei* encompassed all of the regular duties that police performed but also included anti-sabotage patrols, raids against Resistance safe houses, guarding important buildings, and working with Gestapo.

Command of the Hipo was entrusted to *SS-Sturmbannführer* Knud Børge Martinsen. Martinsen also briefly served in leadership roles in Hipo after the integration of the *Schalburgkorps*. Another member was *SS-Obersturmführer* Jørgen Bitsch, who was active in the *Hilfspolizei* leadership, coordinating anti-resistance activities. The Hipo was under direct SS and Gestapo control. The commander in overall control of all security forces in Denmark was the *Befehlshaber der Sicherheitspolizei und des SD in Dänemark* (BdS). From 1940 to 1942 this post was held by *SS-Gruppenführer* Wilhelm Rediess and *SS-Brigadeführer* Günther Pancke, who was also the *Höhere SS- und Polizeiführer Dänemark*. In addition to leading the SD, Rediess was the first senior SS and police leader in Denmark. He played a significant role in organising German security forces and suppressing early resistance efforts. *SS-Brigadeführer* Günther Pancke succeeded Rediess and served as BdS from 1942 until the end of the occupation.

He intensified repression and coordinated closely with Danish collaborators, including the *Schalburgkorps* and *Hipo Korps*. Pancke oversaw the expansion of the Gestapo and the crackdown after the 1943 strikes and sabotage campaigns. The head of the *Sicherheitsdienst* in Denmark was effectively the top security official for the German occupation administration, responsible for intelligence gathering, counter-insurgency, and political policing. The BdS worked closely with the German military command, the *SS-Hauptamt*, and the RSHA in Berlin. He directed operations involving Danish collaborationist units, like the *Schalburgkorps* and the *Hilfspolizei*. Rediess and Pancke therefore, were instrumental in suppressing the Danish resistance movement.

The *Schalburgkorps* and *Hilfspolizei* took over from the disbanded Danish police after the 19 September 1944 mass arrest of police officers.

Both acted as the primary paramilitary police force in Denmark for the remainder of the occupation. They were responsible for the violent suppression of the Danish Resistance, including infiltration of Resistance cells, torture of captured Resistance men, and executions. Both coordinated closely with the German SS, Gestapo, and *Waffen-SS*. The *Schalburgkorps* and *Hilfspolizei* (Hipo) operated under RSHA supervision, especially *Amt IV* (Gestapo) and *Amt VI* (SD). The *Befehlshaber der Sicherheitspolizei und des SD in Dänemark* (BDS) had direct command authority over these forces. German SS units provided training, weapons, intelligence, and political direction. Danish collaborators – DNSAP and *Schalburgkorps* leaders – acted as local intermediaries but ultimate control was in the hands of the Germans.

Chapter 4

WESTERN EUROPEAN VOLUNTEERS AND THE CRUSADE AGAINST BOLSHEVISM: FRANCE AND SPAIN

The *Légion des Volontaires Français contre le Bolchevisme*

After the collapse of the French Third Republic, France was divided between an occupied and unoccupied region. The unoccupied region was controlled by a new French government which was led by Marshal Philippe Petain. This government was headquartered in the city of Vichy. It is from there that the term 'Vichy France' came from. In the occupied zone, the Germans established their security apparatus.[1] When the Soviet Union was invaded on 22 June 1941, the Germans began a propaganda campaign throughout Western Europe, painting the invasion of the USSR as a noble crusade against Bolshevism. In France, as elsewhere in Western Europe, volunteers came forward to join this 'crusade'. These were mostly individuals who supported a Nazi victory. Some believed that France could only move forward as a nation if it cooperated with Germany. Hatred of communism and the Stalinist regime rounded out the principal reasons why these men joined.

The *Légion des Volontaires Français contre le Bolchevisme* (LVF) was established in July 1941 as a French collaborationist military formation.[2] Officially designated as *Infanterie-Regiment 638 (verstärkt)* – the 638th Infantry Regiment (reinforced) – within the German Army, the LVF was composed primarily of volunteers drawn from far-right political movements in France, including Jacques Doriot's French Popular Party and Marcel Déat's National Popular Rally. These volunteers were ideologically committed to combating Bolshevism and supporting Germany's military objectives on the Eastern Front.[3]

Although the Vichy regime maintained formal neutrality, it tacitly approved the LVF's formation, reflecting the ambiguous position of the Vichy government vis-à-vis collaboration.[4] Initially, the LVF was limited in size, numbering roughly 1,000 men when first deployed to the Eastern Front in late 1941.[5] The regiment eventually numbered some 2,300 to 2,500 men. In the autumn of 1941, it was formally integrated into the *Wehrmacht* as *Infanterie-Regiment 638 (französiches)* and attached to the veteran *7. Infanterie-Division* for operations in the central sector of the front. The unit took part in the Battle of Moscow in November and December 1941, where it sustained severe casualties and demonstrated only limited operational effectiveness.[6]

The regiment's baptism of fire came during the Battle of Bobr, a relatively small but symbolically important clash that occurred in November 1941 near Smolensk, in the midst of the larger Moscow campaign. A French *Kampfgruppe,* deployed alongside German forces, was called upon to resist a Soviet armoured counter-attack. Despite their inexperience, the French volunteers managed to help repel the assault, destroying a number of Soviet tanks, largely with the aid of German anti-tank weapons. The encounter, however, was costly. The French contingent lost forty-one men killed in action, a figure which carried great weight for such a newly raised and politically sensitive formation.[7]

For the Vichy authorities, Bobr quickly became a propaganda touchstone, celebrated as evidence of France's supposed renewed 'crusade' against Bolshevism. In military terms, however, the engagement exposed the regiment's weaknesses. The LVF lacked both the cohesion and training of a German line unit, and its morale and endurance suffered severely under the rigours of the Russian winter. By the spring of 1942, following months of exposure, disease, and desertion, the regiment had been reduced to fewer than 700 combat-effective men. Thereafter, the 638th Infantry Regiment ceased to operate as a unified combat regiment in front-line engagements. The remnants were withdrawn for reorganisation, with the surviving battalions largely relegated to rear-area duties, particularly in anti-partisan warfare, rather than being employed in the front line. In the subsequent years, the LVF was primarily engaged in anti-partisan operations (*Bandenbekämpfung*) in occupied Belarus and Ukraine. An example of these were *Unternehmen Ankara I* and *II,* which took place in central Russia.

Unternehmen Ankara I und II: *26 December 1942–21 January 1943*

Ankara I and *II* were local anti-partisan drives in the Bryansk–Orel–Gomel triangle of central Russia that were planned and executed by *221. Sicherungs Division* between 19–24 December 1942, and 17–21 January 1943. The division's subordinate units carried out these two local operations, which only garnered a total of thirty-two dead guerrillas.[8] As such the operations were deemed failures. The forces employed included: *Ost-Bataillon 604* (604th Eastern Battalion), the *3. Kompanie* (3rd Company) of *Sicherungs-Bataillon 791* (791st Security Battalion), under *Sicherungs-Regiment 36* (36th Security Regiment),[9] the *III. Bataillon* of *Infanterie-Regiment 638 (verstärkt)* – the (French) 638th Infantry Regiment (reinforced), and *I. Bataillon* of *Polizeiregiment 8* (8th Police Regiment). At this time, the order of battle for *221. Sicherungs Division* was as follows:

CO: Major-General Karl *Freiherr* von Lersner
Ia: Lieutenant-Colonel Helmuth Kreidel (July 1942–September 1943)
- 350. *Infanterie-Regiment* (reinforced)
  - I. *Bataillon*
    - 1. Company
    - 2. Kompanie
    - 3. Kompanie
    - 4. (MG) Kompanie
  - II. *Bataillon*
    - 5. Company
    - 6. Company
    - 7. Company
    - 8. (MG) Company
  - III.*Bataillon*
    - 9. Company
    - 10.Company
    - 11.Company
    - 12.(MG) Company
- *I. Abteilung der 221. Artillerie-Regiment*
    - 1. Battery
    - 2. Battery
    - 3. Battery

Wachbataillon 701 (renamed *Sicherungs-Bataillon 791* 28 June 1942)
1. Company
2. Company
3. Company
4. Company

Nachrichten-Abteilung 824
I. Battalion of Police Regiment 8
1. Company
2. Company
3. Company
4. Company

1. und 2. Schwadron der Kavallerie-Abteilung 221

45. Landesschützenregiment
I. Battalion
1. Company
2. Company
3. Company
4. Company

II. Bataillon
5. Company
6. Company
7. Company
8. Company

III. Battalion
9. Company
10.Company
11.Company
12.Company
13.Company[10]
14.Company[11]

221st Supply Forces
(350th Divisional Supply Leader)
Eastern Troops in the division (as of 5 September 1943):
221. Ost-Kompanie
221. Ost-Reiter-Squadron
350. Ostversorgungskompanie
930. Ost-Sicherungs-Kompanie
45. Ost-Sicherungs-Kompanie

Figure 10. The area of operations for ***Ankara I*** and ***Ankara II*** in relation to its location to the city of Bryansk. The LVF employed one to two battalions for these two anti-partisan operations. (Author's line drawing)

The main component that took part in *Ankara I* and *II* was not just *221. Sicherungs-Division,* but also a part of the *286. Sicherungs-Division.* That part was the *36. Sicherungs-Regiment,* which had been established in June 1942 using *Sicherungs Bataillonen 642, 555 und 794* – the 642nd, 555th, and 794th Security Battalions.[12] The attention of *221. Sicherungs-Division* in December 1942 seemed to be focused on where the partisan problem seemed the worst: the north-eastern Mamayevka Forest sector while *Ankara I* and *Ankara II* both targeted the localities of Nivnoye, Lugovka, Catolino, Zhirkovka (Shirkovka), Khotimsky (Chochimsk):[13]

> The 221st Security Division's view of the Ankara operations, conducted in the north-eastern sector of the division's jurisdiction primarily by the 36th Security Regiment, was that the operations' purpose was to pacify the area, not plunder it. The regiment ordered that quota levels be strictly observed in the requisitioning of livestock, horses and produce, so as to ensure that the subsistence level be maintained. The 221st itself was even more unequivocal; there was to be no unbridled exploitation, even in those villages which had not achieved the necessary quota. For Ankara II, requisitioning was in most cases restricted, again, to collecting quotas from inhabited villages; only in the case of abandoned villages was the requisitioning to be more thorough and all-encompassing. Much of the livestock and foodstuffs procured in Ankara II, it seems, was not plundered from villages, but was in fact picked up when the partisans abandoned it. Moreover, the division imposed a total ban on the burning of villages for the duration of Ankara II. This may well have been a direct response to excesses committed during Ankara, for which the division had allowed the burning of villages 'under certain circumstances'.[14]

These missions often involved harsh reprisals against civilian populations suspected of assisting Soviet partisans, a practice that contributed to the unit's controversial reputation.[15] In mid-1942, efforts by the Vichy government to exercise greater oversight led to the temporary rebranding of the LVF as the *Légion Tricolore,* intended to align the unit with ostensibly French national interests.[16] However, this reorganisation was largely symbolic; the LVF remained under German command and continued its service on the Eastern Front with little change in operational focus.[17] The French volunteers followed a pattern familiar to several other foreign contingents in the *Wehrmacht,* whose political symbolism far outweighed their actual battlefield effectiveness.

The LVF's final major engagements occurred during the Soviet summer offensive of 1944, known as Operation Bagration. Facing overwhelming Soviet forces, German authorities withdrew the LVF to Germany, where roughly 400 survivors were formed into an ad hoc *kampfgruppe* tasked with delaying Soviet advances.[18] Following this engagement, the LVF was officially disbanded on 1 September 1944, with its remaining personnel incorporated into the *Waffen-SS*, forming the nucleus of the *SS-Freiwilligen-Sturmbrigade Frankreich*.[19]

SS-Freiwilligen-Sturmbrigade Frankreich

Formation, Training, and Deployment

The creation of the *SS-Freiwilligen-Sturmbrigade Frankreich* marked a significant evolution in *Waffen-SS* recruitment policy. For much of the war, Himmler's elite military organisation had adhered to a rigid racial doctrine, admitting only 'Germanic' volunteers from countries such as the Netherlands, Norway, and Denmark. By mid-1943, however, the catastrophic manpower losses on the Eastern Front, coupled with the *Wehrmacht*'s urgent need to bolster its combat strength, compelled Berlin to reconsider its position. On 22 July 1943, an official decree authorised the enlistment of French nationals into the *Waffen-SS*, opening the way for the formation of an all-French unit under SS control. Recruitment was carried out primarily in the former unoccupied zone (*zone libre*) and, to a lesser extent, in German-occupied northern France.

The response from collaborationist circles, particularly among members of the *Milice* security police, university youth, and various fascist leagues, was substantial, with approximately 3,000 men volunteering in the initial intake.[20] A sizable number of men from the LVF also opted to remain in the fight by joining this new French-SS brigade, like Fascist reporter Christian de La Mazière.

Training for the new formation took place in two main phases. Basic instruction occurred at Sennheim in Alsace (present-day Cernay), where recruits were subjected to German drill, physical conditioning and political indoctrination. Instructors were drawn from veteran *Waffen-SS* personnel, including Germans, Dutch, and Flemish volunteers, ensuring that training was carried out in strict accordance with SS standards. Orders were given in German, and uniforms bore no French insignia – a deliberate effort to subsume national identity into the transnational 'SS community'. Selected officer candidates attended the *SS-Junkerschule* at Bad Tölz in Bavaria,[21] while non-commissioned officer aspirants trained at Posen (Poznan) in occupied Poland.[22]

Employment

By 30 June 1944, the unit had achieved an official strength of 1,688 personnel, including 30 officers, 44 NCOs, and 1,614 enlisted men. Under the command of *SS-Obersturmbannführer* Paul-Marie Gamory-Dubourdeau, the Brigade was organised into five infantry companies, each commanded by a French SS officer such as Henri Joseph Fenet. Gamory-Dubourdeau had served in the French colonial forces during the First World War. He retired from the French Army in 1928. Eight years later, in 1936, he joined the *Parti populaire français* (French Popular Party) – a rabidly anti-Semitic and ultra-nationalistic political party that could best be described as a mixture of Fascism and Nazism.

In late July 1944, a reinforced battalion – comprising 18 officers and approximately 1,000 other ranks – was dispatched to Galicia on the Eastern Front. There, the French SS volunteers were attached to the *18. SS-Panzergrenadier-Division 'Horst Wessel'* and engaged in bitter defensive fighting against the Red Army in the Sanok-Mielec sector. Casualties were severe: at least 130 men were killed and more than 660 wounded in a matter of weeks, including heavy officer losses. By late August 1944, fewer than 150 combat-capable soldiers remained, and the Brigade effectively ceased to exist as an independent fighting unit.[23] In September 1944 what remained of the brigade was sent back to Germany to Neweklau for reorganisation. There the survivors of *SS-Freiwilligen-Sturmbrigade Frankreich* were merged with recent recruits for a new French-SS formation, *Waffen-Grenadier-Regiment der SS 57 (französisches Nr. 1)*, which was currently being organised into a new French SS formation at brigade level: *Waffen-Grenadier-Brigade der SS 'Charlemagne' (französische Nr. 1)*.

Thus, some of the French volunteers who had served in the *Legion des Volontaires Français contre le Bolchevisme* (LVF) since 1941, and some members from the *SS-Freiwilligen-Sturmbrigade Frankreich*, together with new recruits, helped to create the *Waffen-Grenadier-Brigade der SS 'Charlemagne' (französische Nr. 1)*. This French SS brigade would be expanded in early 1945 into the 33. *Waffen-Grenadier-Division der SS 'Charlemagne' (französische Nr. 1)*. However, the peak strength of this 'division' was a mere 7,340 men – more akin to the strength of a reinforced brigade than a division-sized formation. This final iteration of French SS volunteers would go on to fight in the East Pomeranian campaign and, most famously, a battalion of French-SS volunteers took part in the Battle of Berlin during April-May 1945, where small remnants resisted in the government quarter until the capitulation of the city.[24]

From French Collaboration to Volunteers in the German Armed Forces

The history of French collaborationist forces is important because they not only served to assist the Germans in controlling France, but later on, when France was liberated, many of these pro-German Frenchmen withdrew into Germany in order to avoid the retribution that was sure to befall them. Many ended up with the remnant Vichy government in Sigmaringen, Germany. There, they were asked to volunteer yet again – this time for a newly-raised French SS formation. A third of the *Milice* militiamen, around 1,800 to 2,000, enlisted in the forming SS division *'Charlemagne'* which was being established at this time. Another third – made up of the older men or men unfit for combat – left to work in German factories. Members of the Franc-Garde also volunteered for the French SS division. For this reason alone, their story needs to be told.

The origins of the *Milice* date back to the *Service d'ordre Legionnaire* (SOL) which was created by Joseph Darnand in 1941 and operated in unoccupied France.[25] The SOL had the 'blessing' of Vichy Interior Minister Joseph Darnand and his Interior Secretary Pierre Pucheu. Initially the formation was a patriotic organisation but in reality, it was geared to promote Petain's version of a Fascist New Order in France. In fact, a month after Germany invaded the unoccupied southern zone in France (November 1942), Adolf Hitler met with Pierre Laval. This meeting occurred on 19 December 1942. Hitler basically told Laval that Germany was not satisfied with the reliability of the French police and that the Vichy government should create a brand-new police force, whose loyalty would not be questioned.[26] Laval did not waste any time, speaking with Darnand in early January 1943 and proposing to use the SOL to create the *Milice.* On 31 January 1943 a decree changed the title to *La Milice.* The headquarters of the organisation was in Vichy. Initially, the *Milice* was to have a table of organisation strength of 29,000 members, although its membership remained around 25,000 militiamen throughout its existence, meaning that those number of volunteers went through the ranks as full or part-time *Milicien.*[27] While many members were part-time *Milicien,* there was a permanent armed barracks police force within the *Milice* called the *Franc-Garde.* The *Franc-Garde* therefore, was the armed wing of the *Milice.* It was established in June 1943.

It was organised into tiers of generic formation names rather than numbered battalions:

- *main* (one chief + four men)
- *dizaine* (10–15 men, a combat group)
- *trentaine* (30man section, one per provincial capital)
- *centaine* (100–120man company, in regional capitals; 'mobile' or 'normal')
- *cohorte* (300–360man battalion)
- *centre* (900–1,080-man regiment, made up of multiple *cohortes*)

In early 1944, there was a *cohort* stationed in the town of Vichy, and a *centaine* each in the cities of Lyon, Marseille and Toulouse. In addition, there was a *trentaine* section in each of the forty-five southern departments of Metropolitan France. While the strength of the *Milice* never exceeded more than 15,000 men at any one time, the strength of the *Franc-Garde* peaked at just under 4,000 men by June 1944. Some sources differ as to the number of active *Franc-Garde* members.

These estimates range from 1,700 to as many as 6,000 active members.[28] Although the *Milice* had been ordered created by the Germans, they did not trust the French enough to initially arm the *Milice* in January 1943. This now came back to haunt the Germans as militiamen began to be assassinated by the French underground. In fact, during the summer of 1943, the Maquis had received specific orders from British intelligence regarding the *Milice*: 'They are unarmed, hit them now! They have nothing to shoot back with.' The *Milice* lost seventy men before the Germans realised they had better arm them or they would lose more volunteers. In April 1943 permission was granted for selected Vichy French political and military movements to parade openly, and in September 1943 the SS allowed the *Milice* to establish training camps in order to train members in policing matters. In this way, an initial batch of 600 *Miliciens* began training under SD officers.[29] Joseph Darnand's post as second in command of the *Milice* was titled as either 'Executive Commander of the *Milice*' or 'National Chief of the Milice'.[30] In addition to the *Franc-Garde,* the *Milice* had two other departments- the *Avant Garde Milicienne* (Milice Youth Section), and '*Les Miliciennes*' (Milice Women's Section).

While the youth sections were later tapped for volunteers in the *33. Waffen-Grenadier-Division der-SS 'Charlemagne'*, and the female members were used in a support role, the bulk of the fighting was performed by the *Franc-Garde*. Within the *Franc-Garde*, you had the *Franc-Garde Permanente* and the *Franc-Garde Non permanente*. The *Franc-Garde Permanente* was the 'permanent' (quartered in barracks) troops and the *Franc-Garde Non permanente* was the part-time volunteer force. The insignia of the *Milice* was the letter 'Gamma' in the Greek alphabet. It had been chosen since this Greek letter in the zodiac was represented by the Ram, a symbol of power. In addition, the Ram symbol in the zodiac also stood for spring in the seasonal year. Thus, in one fell swoop, the *Milice* use of the Gamma letter was meant to represent power year. Thus, in one fell swoop, the *Milice* use of the Gamma letter was meant to represent power associated with rebirth and strength.[31]

When the Allies landed in Normandy on 6 June 1944, the *Milice* was put on alert. Seven days later, on 13 June a general call-up of all active and part-time volunteers was announced. A total of 6,695 *Miliciens* heeded the call-up. Of this number, 4,740 were part-time volunteers while 1,955 were the full-time *Franc-Garde*. It appears then, that only a small number of the estimated 25,000–29,000 *Miliciens* who served at one time or another heeded the call-up. An average of three men out of four decided it was time to either seek anonymity or to join the *Maquisards* in the hope that their collaboration would go undetected. Before 6 June 1944, about 100,000 French citizens collaborated in one way or another with the Germans. On 7 June 1944 these people suddenly declared they were for General De Gaulle and tried to blend in. After the Allied invasion of France, the Germans found it wise to transfer the Vichy government to Alsace-Lorraine, near the pre-war Franco-German border. But by late summer that region was also threatened by the Allied advance.

At the end of August 1944 about 6,000 surviving *Miliciens* and 41,000 of their dependents (who feared retribution by association) withdrew from Belfort, France.[32] Their arrival in Alsace-Lorraine had been dramatic. The local French population (that part which had not been deported in 1940), had initially greeted the *Milice* as friends and liberators, but upon realising that these men were not Free French troops, their praise and waving had turned to shouts of insults or looks of disapproval. Many in the *Milice* had mistreated their countrymen horribly. For their crimes, many *Miliciens* which were caught by the FFI and civilian population in general, were destined to suffer terrible and gruesome torture before being killed.

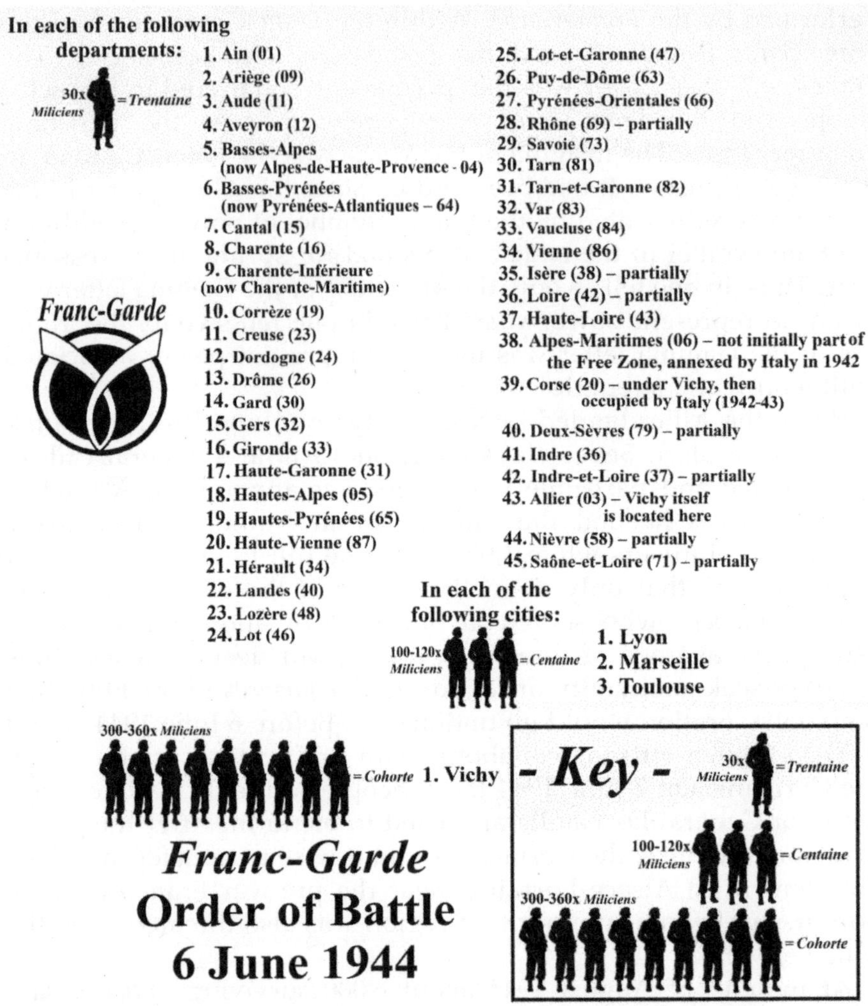

Figure 11. The *Franc-Garde* Order of Battle for 6 June 1944. (Author's line drawing)

One *Maquisard* kept a diary of the actions of his partisan unit. He wrote how he witnessed the horrors perpetrated on a captured *Milicien* in July 1944. His account says it all:

> Aged twenty-nine, married three months ago, made to saw wood in the hot sun wearing a pullover and jacket, made to drink warm salted water, ears cut off, covered with blows from fists and bayonets, stoned, made to dig his grave, made to lie in it, finished off with a sharp blow in the stomach from a spade, two days to die.[33]

Most women who collaborated with the Germans got off a lot easier. They were stripped of their clothes in public and their heads were shaved. In many cases a Swastika was either painted or carved into their foreheads. In the most extreme cases, women were also killed. After having withdrawn from many regions of France, *Milice* militiamen and other collaborators converged in the area of Belfort. It was there that the Vichy government in exile was now located. Most of the *Milice* had been operating in what had previous to November 1942, been the unoccupied zone in southern France. Some *Milice* were operating in the northern region of France, but the overwhelming number were in the south. When the call-up had come on 13 June 1944, 415 *Franc-Garde* came from the north, while 1,540 *Franc-Garde* were moving from southern France. They now followed Marshal Philippe Petain, who was a virtual prisoner of the Germans by now, as well as other Vichy leaders. They all withdrew from Belfort for Sigmaringen, Germany where the Vichy government in exile was to be relocated.[34]

They travelled through Mulhouse, Struthof, and Ulm. Of the 6,000 *Milicien*, about 2,500 were deemed physically fit and were sent to join the forming French 33. *Waffen-Grenadier-Division der-SS 'Charlemagne'*, while 400 more remained at Sigmaringen and became the 'palace guard' for Marshal Pétain.[35] Joseph Darnand kept 250 men as his personal bodyguard. He left with this small force for northern Italy on 12 March 1945. Darnand attempted to escape into Switzerland but was captured by Italian partisans at Tirano. He was tried by a French court and executed on 10 October 1945. Many other *Miliciens* were executed at the end of the war. Those who were spared lived because by then the anger and thirst for revenge by the Free French had been basically quenched. Those lucky enough not to be killed were given the choice of being jailed or to serve in Indochina as part of the *Légion étrangère française* (French Foreign Legion). In cases where a *Milice* member was judged to have collaborated more closely with the Germans, he was either killed or, in some rare instances, allowed to join the *Légion étrangère*. All those who were given a choice, chose service in the Legion, either in Indochina or in France's African possessions. Many died there serving in the French Foreign Legion. A good number were killed at the battle of Dien Bien Phu in 1954.

Other French collaborationist forces eventually contributed members to the SS '*Charlemagne*' Division. One was the *Police Allemand*, which was established in 1941. The *Carlingue*, as they were more commonly known, was led by Pierre Bonny, a former French police officer. Later, Henri Lafont and Pierre Loutrel, both professional criminals, took over its operations.[36] The group was based at 93 rue Lauriston, in Paris. The term '*Police Allemand*' actually came from the manner in which these French operatives of the *Gestapo* would announce themselves. When approaching a suspicious person who needed to be questioned, or whether they were knocking on the door of a suspect's apartment, they would always announce themselves as '*Police Allemand*!' ('German Police!'). The *Carlingue* operated under the direction of the German *Sicherheitsdienst* (SD). Specifically, under the *Gestapo* which was an integral part of the German SS and police forces that helped to control France and fought the partisans.

Another pro-German force which eventually contributed volunteers for the French SS division, was the *Selbstschutzpolizei* – which was born from an idea by *SS-Gruppenführer* Karl Oberg in the spring of 1943. As stated earlier, German official permits for pro-German Frenchmen to bear arms were severely restricted. Oberg had the idea to group those Frenchmen who wanted to defend themselves into a *Selbstschutz* (self-defence) formation. Of course, this new unit would not be under the control of the Vichy government, but would be run directly by the German Sipo and SD command. At the same time the German police needed more and more French volunteers to assist them in the fight against the growing resistance. In the spring of 1943 Karl Oberg ordered *SS-Standartenführer* Dr. Hermann Bickler to organise what would become the French '*Selbstschutzpolizei*' (Self Defence Police).[37] Hermann Bickler was an Alsatian lawyer who was born in Germany in 1904. He later became a French citizen after 1918, when the province of Alsace was returned to France.[38]

After July 1944 the *Selbstschutzpolizei* was dissolved. Some full-time members eventually enlisted in the *8. Kompanie / II. Bataillon / Brandenburger-Regiment 3 / Division 'Brandenburg'*.[39] This included Jacques Dugé de Bernonville, the former French commander of the Taverny School.[40] The majority of the Frenchmen at the Taverny School followed the withdrawal of the German Army from France in the late summer of 1944 and eventually joined the French 33. *Waffen-Grenadier-Division der-SS Charlemagne* that was in the process of forming at *Truppenübungsplatz Wildflecken,* located in the Rhön Mountains of Bavaria. Some of the bolder members chose to remain behind the Allied lines to try and provide intelligence. At the end of the war, few members of the *Selbstschutzpolizei* were caught and tried, even though the FFI had infiltrated two of its members into the organisation in 1944 and these two men had actually seized the negatives of most of the *Selbstschutzpolizei* identity cards.[41]

Another group turned out to be the Bezen Perrot group, which was named after Abbot Jean-Marie Perrot, a prominent Breton priest and cultural figure who promoted Breton identity and independence for Brittany. Abbot Jean-Marie Perrot was assassinated in 1943 by members of the French Resistance, who viewed Breton independence as divisive and contrary to the interests of France. The group was driven by Breton nationalism, not simply pro-German sympathies. Its members believed that supporting the Nazi regime would help achieve independence for Brittany from France. The Bezen Perrot group was the military faction of the BNP. Perrot and his group were seen as a threat, so the Maquis assassinated him on 12 December 1943.

The origins of the Bezen Perrot military unit comes from the creation of the *'Lu Brezhon'* ('Brittany Army') which was declared in October 1943. That declaration is what likely prompted the French Resistance to target the Abbot for assassination. The 'army' initially had twelve members and later was raised to some eighty or ninety men. Initially, there was talk of establishing a *'Bretonische-Waffenverband der SS'* (Breton Group of the Armed SS), but there were such small numbers of volunteers that the Germans decided to scrap the plan. This is rather odd, given that the British Free Corps, raised by the SS, never exceeded more than two to three-dozen men (British, Irish, Canadian and South African). The SS even took the time and trouble to create a *Waffen-SS* cuff band for this English-speaking unit. It was the only *Waffen-SS* cuff band that was written in English. The words 'British Free Corps' were written in silver thread on a black cloth background.

So why would the SS take the time and trouble to nurture three dozen traitors from the United Kingdom and its Commonwealth, and ignore almost three times the number of Breton separatists? The answer is that for propaganda purposes, it was more worthwhile to see an Englishman wearing the uniform of the *Waffen-SS* than a Breton separatist. In the end, the 80–90 or so volunteers were armed and clothed by the local SD command. Another source however, states that only around seventy men were serving in the Bezen Perrot Group.[42] Of these, sixty-five were between the ages of 18 and 25. During the initial stages of the German occupation (1941–2), the Bezen Perrot group operated under the auspices of the local German *Feldgendarmerie* (military field police) unit of *Feldkommandantur 148*. This military government staff was led by *Oberstleutnant* Baron von Gebsattel.[43] In April 1943 the group was taken over by the local KdS command under *SS-Obersturmbannführer* Hartmut Pulmer. Pulmer, who had been born on 9 November 1908, was 35 years old in 1943.[44]

In July 1944 the 1st Section of the Breton of the Sipo/SD command was located in Brest, while the 2nd Section was located in Rennes. Both sections were withdrawn and eventually reached Alsace-Lorraine but not before many of its members had deserted, since they felt that their interests lay in Brittany and not in Alsace-Lorraine or Germany. What was left of the force was initially transferred to the *Abwehr* under the *Brandenburg* commandos, and later, under *SS-Obersturmbannführer* Otto Skorzeny's commando force. Skorzeny assigned them to *SS-Jagdverbände Südwest*. The initial unit these men joined was *Streifkorps-Südfrankreich*. In the summer of 1944, the unit was stationed at Alès, Cévennes, France.

In September 1944 it was still located there. It included the 8th 'Legionary' Company, which consisted of 180 Spanish and French volunteers, among them, some Bretons. The unit was eventually transferred to north-western Italy and fought Italian partisans on the French-Italian border until January 1945. It then carried out deep reconnaissance behind the lines of the 7th US Army in the Black Forest region. It was finally withdrawn to Austria, where it was to join up with the other *SS-Jagdverbände* in Linz. However, that plan failed to materialise. *SS-Jagdverbände Südwest* ended the war in the region of Bressanone (Brixen), in the province of South Tyrol. After the liberation of France, many members of the Bezen Perrot fled, were arrested, or were tried and convicted for collaboration.

Le Corps Franc Français was created using remnants of volunteers from the Bordeaux section of the MSR, or *Mouvement Social Révolutionnaire* (Social Revolutionary Movement), a staunchly anti-Semitic, anti-Freemason, anti-communist and anti-Anglo-Saxon political party whose bulk of its members returned to Marcel Deat's RNP party: *Rassemblement National Populaire* (National Popular Rally). The unit was created in 1943 by André Besson, whose nom de guerre was Besson Rapp. The local *Abwehr* unit, which was headed by *Hauptmann* Gartner, supported the *Corps Franc Français*. The unit was later loosely tied to the SD, since it had absorbed all *Geheime Feldpolizei* (GFP) units in 1942 and the entire *Abwehr* in August 1944. In fact, the unit assisted *Geheime Feldpolizei-Gruppe 644* quite effectively against the local communist partisan units. The force was never larger than 90–100 men. When the withdrawal to Germany was ordered, André Besson was recuperating from shrapnel wounds. In Alsace, the group was integrated into the 33. *Waffen-Grenadier-Division der-SS 'Charlemagne'*.

The Connection of the *Brigade nord-africaine* with the Free India Legion

At the beginning of 1944 Henri Lafont (a.k.a. Henri Chamberlain) contacted Mohamed el-Maadi, who was a former French colonial captain, and proposed the creation of an organisation called *La Légion nord-africaine*. Mohamed el-Maadi was rabidly anti-communist and was an active member of the secret French Army organisation, *La Cagoule*. Members of this group had taken part in assassinations of important left-wing politicians and newspaper editors during the period of the Third Republic and into the Vichy French period. The more than 300 Arabs chosen for this battalion were grouped into platoons and were dressed in the uniform of the *Milice*. The men of the battalion initially operated in the region of the Dordogne, although it is known that the *Première Compagnie* (1st Company) and *Troisième Compagnie* (3rd Company) also operated in Montbéliard.[45]

In July 1944 the *Brigade nord-africaine* was reformed and soon disbanded because of desertions by Arabs within the unit. The reason for the desertions was that it was clear the war was turning against the Germans. Some of its former members travelled to Germany with Capitaine el-Maadi, while others joined the *Freies Indien Legion* (Free India Legion). The India Legion was the *Infanterie-Regiment 950 (indisch)* of the German Army, which was now making its way towards the relative safety of southern Germany. The Arab companies were now basically reduced to the size of platoons of perhaps twenty-five to thirty volunteers each. Each platoon was named as a section. Desertions continued throughout the withdrawal and by the time the remnants of *Brigade nord-africaine* reached Grenoble, on their way north to the German border, barely thirty Arabs remained within the unit. All except one of the French SS second lieutenants who had served in the battalion ended up joining the *33. Waffen-Grenadier-Division der-SS 'Charlemagne'*.

33. Waffen-Grenadier-Division der SS 'Charlemagne'

The *33. Waffen-Grenadier-Division der SS 'Charlemagne' (französische Nr. 1)* was one of the most unusual foreign formations of the late-war *Waffen-SS*. One of the most interesting and honest accounts of this division was published in 1972 by a former French volunteer in the division, who had been a journalist before the war and during the German occupation of France. Christian de La Mazière's *The Captive Dreamer* provides insight into the ideological motivations of French volunteers in the *Waffen-SS*. Drawing upon his own experience in the *'Charlemagne'* division, de La Mazière emphasises anti-communist and nationalist convictions as central to his enlistment.[46] These motivations, while deeply personal, reflect broader trends among French collaborators who perceived the German war effort as aligned with their political and cultural aspirations. By situating his narrative within both personal and collective experience, the memoir allows historians to examine the interplay of individual conviction, social environment, and historical circumstance in shaping the decision to volunteer.

Composed predominantly of French volunteers, its existence was the result of the consolidation of earlier collaborationist units that had fought for Germany since 1941. The most prominent of these was the LVF, created under Vichy auspices and attached to the German Army on the Eastern Front.[47] As stated previously, the LVF served with the *7. Infanterie-Division* in the Moscow sector from 1941–2, later seeing combat in the Smolensk region and enduring severe attrition. By 1943, manpower losses and political friction between Vichy officials and the *Waffen-SS* led to the creation of the *8. Französische SS-Freiwilligen-Sturmbrigade*, an elite but small contingent trained and equipped directly by the SS.[48] This brigade fought in Galicia in 1944, suffering heavy casualties during Soviet summer offensives.

When German forces began their general withdrawal from Eastern Europe in the summer of 1944, the remnants of both French formations, along with other collaborators evacuated from Belgium, France, and the Netherlands, were concentrated in West Prussia. In September 1944, Heinrich Himmler ordered the formal amalgamation of these forces into the *Waffen-Grenadier-Brigade der SS 'Charlemagne'*.[49] The name *'Charlemagne'* deliberately invoked the memory of the medieval Frankish emperor, who was just as much Germanic as French, suggesting a supranational European mission in the struggle against Bolshevism. The consolidation took place at training camps such as Greifenberg and Wildflecken, where German cadres attempted to standardise training and rebuild cohesion.

Organisation and Manpower

In reality, the brigade's resources were modest. Its manpower fluctuated between 4,000 and 7,500,[50] but these numbers masked shortages in experienced NCOs, artillery, armour, and motor transport. In February 1945, Himmler approved its elevation to *33. Waffen-Grenadier-Division der SS 'Charlemagne' (französische Nr. 1)*.[51] The division comprised two infantry regiments – *Waffen-Grenadier-Regiment der SS 57* and *58* – each of two battalions. As far as the battalion-sized supporting units that a German division would have, such as a communications battalion, anti-tank battalion, reconnaissance battalion, etc. none were ever supplied. Instead, only company-sized units were established:

SS-Artillerie-Abteilung 33 (three light field batteries of 75mm artillery)
SS-Panzerjäger-Abteilung 33 (two companies supplied with the hand-held *Panzerfaust*)

SS-Pionier-Kompanie 33 (engineer company)
SS-Nachrichten-Kompanie 33 (communications company)
SS-Feldersatz-Kompanie 33 (field replacement company)

SS-Brigadeführer Gustav Krukenberg was appointed divisional commander, while *SS-Oberführer* Edgar Puaud, the senior French officer, remained as a symbolic figurehead.[52] Ideological composition varied: some were committed fascists or convinced anti-communists, others political opportunists, and some seeking refuge from post-liberation justice in France.[53]

The Strategic Situation in Pomerania

The division's first operational assignment coincided with one of the *Wehrmacht*'s most desperate strategic crises. In January 1945, the Red Army launched the Vistula-Oder Offensive, shattering German Army Group A and advancing to the Oder River. Simultaneously, Marshal Konstatin Rokossovsky's 2nd Belorussian Front drove northward, threatening to cut off German Army Group Vistula in Pomerania.[54] This sector, anchored on the Baltic coast, was vital for maintaining lines of retreat from East Prussia and protecting the naval base of Stettin. By February, Soviet spearheads under Generals Bagramyan and Chuikov were converging on the Pomeranian heartland, forcing the Germans into a series of improvised countermeasures. Army Group Vistula, commanded by Heinrich Himmler and later *Generaloberst* Gotthard Heinrici, deployed the ephemeral *11. Panzerarmee* (also referred to as *11. SS-Panzerarmee*) – under *Generaloberst* Felix Steiner – in an attempt to stabilise the front.[55] Among the divisions rushed into this collapsing sector was the newly-formed *'Charlemagne'*, assigned to defensive positions east of Belgard and Hammerstein.[56]

Counter-attack at Arnswalde

At this time, Felix Steiner's *III. SS-Panzerkorps (germanisches)* was elevated from a corps to an army-level command and redesignated as the *11. SS-Panzerarmee*. Steiner assumed command of ten divisions, the majority of which existed largely in name only, with little time available to adequately organise his staff. Operational conditions were critical: ammunition stocks were low, fuel supplies were severely constrained, and air support was entirely absent.

The counteroffensive was deployed along a 30-mile front and organised into three primary groups. The Eastern Group, the weakest component, comprised the *163. Infanterie-Division* and *281. Infanterie-Division*, along with the *Führer-Grenadier-Division*. Collectively designated *Korpsgruppe Munzel* after its commander, their objective was to secure the flank and advance toward Landsberg on the River Warthe.

The Central Group, under *Generalleutnant* Martin Unrein, incorporated Steiner's former command, the *III. (Germanisches) SS-Panzerkorps*. Its composition included the *11. SS-Freiwilligen-Panzergrenadier-Division 'Nordland'*, a battlegroup of the forming *27. SS-Freiwilligen-Grenadier-Division 'Langemarck'*, the *Führer-Begleit-Division*, and the Dutch *23. SS-Freiwilligen-Panzergrenadier-Division 'Nederland'*, which, though small, had recently been elevated to divisional status. This group's mission was to drive southward, seize Arnswalde (modern-day Choszno), and prepare for further advances. One of the strongest divisions in Steiner's command was the *'Nordland'* Division, whose tank battalion contained thirty Panther tanks and thirty assault guns.

Completing the counter-attack formation was the Western Group, represented by *XXXIX. Panzerkorps* under *General der Panzertruppen* Karl Decker. Its composition included *Panzer-Division Holstein*, the *10. SS-Panzer-Division 'Frundsberg'*, the *4. SS-Panzergrenadier-Division 'Polizei'*, and Leon Degrelle's *28. SS-Freiwilligen-Grenadier-Division 'Wallonie'*, also recently redesignated as a division. This group was tasked with flank security, as with the Eastern Group, but additionally served to exploit and reinforce any breakthroughs achieved by the Central Group. Opposing Steiner's hastily assembled 'army' were five large Soviet formations, notably the experienced 1st and 2nd Guards Tank Armies, the 3rd Shock Army, the 47th Army, and the 61st Army, presenting a formidable resistance to the German counteroffensive.

Combat in Pomerania

The French SS entered combat in mid-February 1945 against elements of the Soviet 19th Army and 3rd Guards Tank Corps, supported by massed artillery.[57] The disparity in strength was overwhelming. Soviet armoured spearheads penetrated thin German lines, and *'Charlemagne'* was committed piecemeal to plug gaps, often fighting alongside ad hoc *Volkssturm* units and retreating *Wehrmacht* remnants. Krukenberg's men showed notable skill in close-range anti-tank fighting, knocking out several Soviet T-34s with the hand-held single-shot *Panzerfausts*, but the tactical successes could not alter the operational reality.[58] By 26 February, Soviet encirclement was complete. Attempts to break out toward Kolberg and the Baltic coast were met with heavy fire; entire French companies were overrun.[59] Many of those captured were summarily executed by Soviet troops, while others perished during the breakout attempts through snow-covered forests. Only around

2,500 men – less than a third of the division's initial strength of 7,340 – reached German lines.[60]

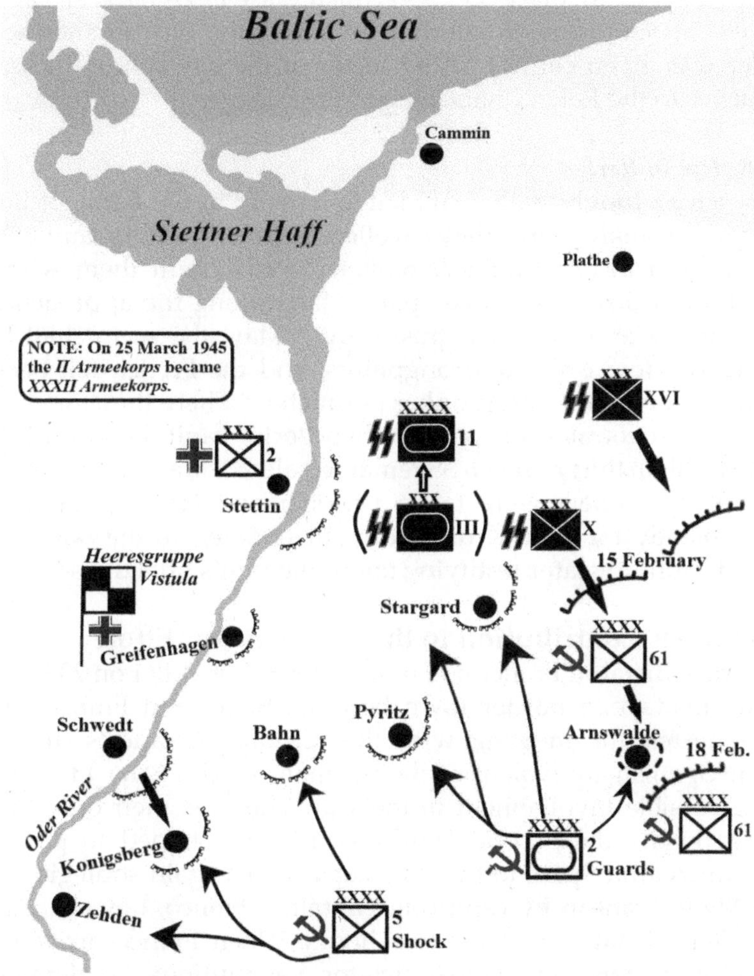

Figure 12. The military situation in Western Pomerania in mid-February 1945. (Author's line drawing)

Retreat and the Berlin Decision

In March 1945, the survivors were regrouped in Neustrelitz. The division was no longer combat-capable in any conventional sense. At this stage, Krukenberg volunteered a select detachment of roughly 350 men for the defence of Berlin.[61] Transported by rail and truck, they arrived in the capital in mid-April, just as the Soviet 1st Belorussian and 1st Ukrainian Fronts began encircling the city. In an ironic twist of fate, these French, Spanish, Dutch, Danish and Norwegian SS volunteers would help defend the *Reichstag* from the Red Army. Krukenberg was initially ordered to place *11. SS-Freiwilligen-Panzergrenadier-Division 'Nordland'* in south-eastern Berlin, to guard the city in that sector. He later was given control of the sector of the city centre, including approaches to the Reich Chancellery.[62]

Final Battle in Berlin

The French SS fought with remarkable ferocity in the Battle of Berlin. Operating in small teams, they excelled in street fighting, ambushing Soviet armour at close range.[63] Soviet records credit them with the destruction of dozens of tanks, particularly along the approaches to Hermannplatz and Friedrichstrasse. By 1 May, the sector had been reduced to a few isolated strongpoints, and the French fell back to the Chancellery and Führerbunker perimeter.[64] There they fought like fanatics, often counter-attacking. When Berlin capitulated on 2 May 1945, fewer than thirty French SS remained alive.[65] Many were executed upon capture; others were taken prisoner and later transferred to French custody for trial. Krukenberg surrendered to the Soviets but survived captivity, later testifying about the unit's final days.[66]

The Spanish Contribution to the German War Effort

The Spanish dictator, Francisco Franco, met Adolf Hitler on 23 October 1940 at Hendaye, a border town between Spain and France. Hitler had requested the meeting with the '*Caudillo*' (Franco's unofficial title, the Spanish equivalent of the German word '*Führer*') to discuss Spain's possible involvement in the war. This was their only formal meeting during the Second World War. Hitler hoped to persuade Franco to commit Spain to the Axis cause and to gain strategic access to the Mediterranean by capturing Gibraltar. Franco, however, made the German dictator wait for two hours. When Franco arrived and the meeting began, the Spanish dictator was cautious. He demanded extensive territorial and economic concessions, including control over parts of French North Africa and Gibraltar. The negotiations ultimately proved inconclusive, with neither leader willing to fully compromise, leaving Spain officially neutral for the remainder of the war. The only concession Hitler was able to obtain from the *Caudillo* was permission for Spaniards to join the campaign in Russia. After the meeting, Hitler was reportedly overheard saying he would rather undergo a root canal than negotiate with Franco again. What Hitler did not know, however, was that a month before the meeting, the head of the *Abwehr*, Admiral Wilhelm Canaris, had contacted Franco and warned him that

Germany was likely to lose the war. Armed with this warning, Franco made the meeting as difficult as possible, ensuring that no meaningful agreement could be reached.

The Spanish contribution to the German war effort was a unique manifestation of the complex political and ideological ties between Francoist Spain and Nazi Germany. It was also an accommodation that Francisco Franco felt he had to make in order to partially placate the German dictator. Following the Spanish Civil War (July 1936–March 1939), in which Franco's Nationalist forces received substantial support from Nazi Germany and Fascist Italy, Spain remained officially neutral during the Second World War. However, a combination of ideological affinity, anti-communism, and personal loyalty to the Axis prompted the Spanish government to allow volunteers to fight alongside German forces against the Soviet Union. The most prominent formation of Spanish volunteers was the *250. Infanterie-Division (spanische)*, commonly known as the *División Azul* (Blue Division). Formed in 1941, shortly after *Unternehmen Barbarossa*, the division was composed primarily of Spanish Army veterans, Carlists, and fervent anti-communist volunteers.

Deployed to the Eastern Front, the division was assigned to *Heeresgruppe Nord*, operating near Leningrad. Contemporary accounts describe the Spaniards as fierce and often fanatical fighters, noted for their tenacity under harsh conditions. They participated in both defensive and offensive operations, including the gruelling winter campaigns of 1941–2, and earned a measure of respect from their Soviet opponents for their determination and resilience in combat. Despite their battlefield effectiveness, Spanish involvement on the Eastern Front created political complications. By 1943, the Franco regime grew increasingly wary that prolonged Spanish participation could provoke Allied retaliation, particularly as the war began to turn against Germany. On 20 October 1943, Madrid ordered the withdrawal of the *División Azul.*

The majority of the volunteers returned home, although some opted to remain in German service. To accommodate these committed volunteers, the Germans authorised the creation of a smaller unit, the *Legión Azul* (Blue Legion). This force never exceeded 2,200 men, of whom roughly 1,500 were infantry. It was organised into two battalions with supporting elements and participated in covering the German retreat from the Leningrad Front. The Legion faced the same harsh conditions and fierce Soviet opposition as their predecessors, although their numbers and operational impact were significantly reduced. By the summer of 1944, the *Legión Azul* was disbanded, reflecting both the diminishing utility of foreign volunteer units and Spain's continued caution in exposing its citizens to the risks of the wider war.

Nevertheless, a handful of dedicated Spanish volunteers were retained under *Waffen-SS* control. These die-hards were reorganised into two small companies, the *Spanische-Freiwilligen-Kompanie der SS 101* and *102*, and integrated into German command structures. Their service culminated in the final defence of Berlin in April 1945, where approximately fifty Spanish survivors took part in the desperate battle for the city. These volunteers fought alongside the *11. SS-Freiwilligen-Panzergrenadier-Division Nordland*, defending the Reichstag and government sector against overwhelming Soviet forces. Their presence in Berlin marked the symbolic, albeit tragic, endpoint of Spain's contribution to the German war effort.

The story of the Spanish volunteers illustrates the intersection of ideology, loyalty, and pragmatism in the Second World War. Though Spain maintained official neutrality, the regime allowed anti-communist Spaniards to participate in one of the war's most brutal theatres, creating a small but notable contingent within the *Wehrmacht* and *Waffen-SS*. Their service was both admired and criticised: admired for battlefield courage and steadfastness, yet criticised for the political compromises and human costs involved. The volunteers' experiences reflect broader patterns of foreign volunteerism in the German war effort, where ideological affinity and personal conviction drove men to fight far from home, often with limited recognition or reward.

Chapter 5

WESTERN EUROPEAN VOLUNTEERS AND THE CRUSADE AGAINST BOLSHEVISM: BELGIUM AND THE NETHERLANDS

Belgium

While the number of Norwegian and Danish collaborators who aided the Germans in the Second World War can be counted in the thousands, those who were citizens of Belgium, Luxemburg and The Netherlands and supported the German military were in the tens of thousands! In Belgium alone where the two predominant ethnic groups were Flemings and Walloons, about 38,000–39,000 citizens were found guilty of 'taking up arms against Belgium'. Of this number, about 3,000 could not be prosecuted since they had been killed fighting on the Eastern Front.[1] By 1943 about 20,000 Belgians were serving in the *Wehrmacht* in one capacity or another. The German Army had a great deal more to do with the occupation of Belgium than did the German Order Police. In fact, the post of *Befehlshaber der Ordnungspolizei Brüssel* (Supreme Commander of the Order Police – Brussels) was not even created until August 1944 when *Oberst der Schutzpolizei* Willi Wolter assumed this post but only held it until September 1944 before the Western Allied advance made the post irrelevant.[2]

Wolter later went on to lead the *Befehlshaber der Ordnungspolizei Alpenland* post a month later. The German Security Police (Sipo) and Security Service (SD) were represented in Belgium early as 1940. The first commander of the SD and Sipo was the former leader of the *Stapoleitstelle Düsseldorf*, Dr. Kurt Hasselbacher. However, Hasselbacher was killed in the summer of 1940 during an anti-partisan operation in Belgium. It is important to note that the collaborationist forces raised in Western Europe were created and/or supported by various factions of the German *Wehrmacht*, SS, and Police. In some instances, some organisations were run by the German Army instead of the Order Police, but nevertheless these auxiliary units had police duties and performed as police forces rather than as regular army units.

For example, the German military commander in Belgium-North France, *General der Infanterie* Alexander von Falkenhausen, created the *Hilfsfeldgendarmerie* (Auxiliary Field Police) in the beginning of 1942.[3] The purpose of this organisation was to recruit Belgians in order to augment the German Army field police (*Feldgendarmerie*) and secret field police (*Geheime Feldpolizei*) units in that part of occupied Europe. They were to assist the German Army police forces. The Germans recruited hundreds of volunteers from one of the two principal right-wing political parties which catered to either the Walloon or Flemish population. Hundreds of Rexist militiamen joined the *Hilfsfeldgendarmerie*. These men were members of the *Christus Rex*, or Christ the King (Walloon) Party. The commander assigned to control these Belgian *Hilfsfeldgendarmerie* volunteers was *Oberst der Schutzpolizei* Dr. Oskar Lossen.

The Rexists

The Rexist movement emerged in Belgium during the early 1930s under the leadership of Léon Degrelle, a former Catholic journalist and publisher. Initially, Rexism was conceived as a socially conservative, corporatist and Catholic nationalist movement, drawing inspiration from the Papal encyclicals *Rerum Novarum* and *Quadragesimo Anno* as well as from authoritarian movements elsewhere in Europe. The party's name derived from its publication *Christus Rex*, which served as a vehicle for Degrelle's moralistic critique of the Belgian political establishment. In its formative years, Rexism appealed to a broad swathe of right-leaning Catholics, conservative middle-class voters, and certain rural constituencies disillusioned with parliamentary democracy.

Rexism's ideology during this early phase was not explicitly fascist in the Italian or German sense, but it shared common ground with other authoritarian Catholic movements such as Portugal's *Estado Novo*. Degrelle envisioned a moral and political renewal of Belgium, grounded in Christian values and hierarchical order, and initially expressed loyalty to King Leopold III. Electoral successes in 1936 –

when Rexists secured over 10 per cent of the national vote – was the party's high-water mark. However, political miscalculations, including Degrelle's confrontational rhetoric toward the Catholic hierarchy and his overreach in challenging established elites, led to a rapid erosion of electoral support by 1939. By the eve of the Second World War, Rexism had largely transitioned from a competitive political party into a marginal yet radicalised political sect.

Radicalisation and Shift Toward Collaboration

The German invasion of Belgium in May 1940 provided the Rexist movement with a new political opening. Degrelle, who had been briefly imprisoned by the Belgian authorities during the invasion as a suspected pro-German sympathiser, sought to reposition Rexism as a loyal collaborator of the occupying power. Ideologically, Rexism began shedding its earlier emphasis on Catholic corporatism in favour of an increasingly overt embrace of fascist and National Socialist principles. The party aligned itself with the German vision of a 'New Order' in Europe, emphasising anti-Communism, authoritarian governance, and ethnic nationalism.

This ideological realignment also entailed a re-evaluation of the Belgian national question. Whereas pre-war Rexism had stressed Belgian unity under the monarchy, wartime Rexists became more accommodating toward the German policy of exploiting Flemish-Walloon divisions, seeing in it an opportunity to marginalise political rivals and expand their own influence in Wallonia. The German authorities, while often sceptical of Rexism's effectiveness, nonetheless saw utility in supporting the movement as a counterweight to other collaborationist factions, particularly in occupied Wallonia. As part of its wartime transformation, the Rexist movement established paramilitary organisations designed to serve both as instruments of political control and as auxiliaries to German security forces.

The Belgian Resistance had begun operations as early as the autumn of 1940, but its activities had increased in 1941 as more and more Belgian patriots joined it. One such example was a young woman, Yvonne de Ridder Files, whose husband had managed to get out of Belgium in the late summer of 1940 on the last train authorised by the Germans which travelled through France and Spain, and reached Portugal. From there her husband made his way to the United States. In the meantime, Yvonne de Ridder Files continued to work for her father in Amsterdam, when in 1941 she was recruited into the *Groupe Général de Sabotage de Belgigue*, the General Sabotage Group of Belgium, or Group G as the people in this Resistance cell called themselves. As the Belgian Resistance asserted itself, the Germans turned more and more to collaborationist groups as a source of support.[4]

The most prominent of these was the *Formations de Combat*, which functioned as a party militia responsible for propaganda enforcement, intimidation of political opponents, and limited policing duties under German supervision. In 1941, this evolved into the *Garde Rexiste*, a uniformed force modelled on fascist militias in Italy and Germany. The *Garde Rexiste* not only patrolled localities but also played a role in anti-resistance operations, often working in concert with the German *Sicherheitspolizei* and *Sicherheitsdienst*. Members were armed, trained, and in some cases deployed in operations against the Belgian underground. These paramilitary structures served both as a political symbol of the movement's commitment to the German cause and as a practical mechanism for ensuring Rexist dominance in occupied local administrations.

Infanterie-Bataillon 373

Beyond its activities in policing and propaganda, the Rexist movement actively promoted military collaboration with Germany, portraying enlistment in the *Wehrmacht* or the *Waffen-SS* as both a crusade against Bolshevism and a means of securing Belgium's place within the post-war *Neue Ordnung* (New Order). Léon Degrelle himself would later achieve notoriety as an officer of the Waffen-SS on the Eastern Front with the *Légion Wallonie*, yet the Rexist organisation also played a central role in facilitating enlistment into regular German Army formations. One notable example of this was the recruitment campaign that led to the formation of *Infanterie-Bataillon 373* (373rd Infantry Battalion), a *Wehrmacht* unit composed largely of Walloon volunteers from Belgium. This battalion, numbering several hundred men, was deployed to the Eastern Front, where it conducted security and rear-area operations in the German-occupied Soviet Union. Degrelle volunteered for service in this formation, refusing a commission and enlisting as a *Landser* (private). His personal bravery and charismatic leadership eventually earned him a commission, enhancing his stature both within the unit and in collaborationist circles.

The motivations of these Walloon volunteers were diverse, ranging from ideological anti-Communism and pan-European idealism to opportunism and the pursuit of social prestige through service under German command. By 1943–4, Rexism had completed its transformation from a pre-war Catholic nationalist protest movement into an explicitly collaborationist organisation integrated into the German occupation system. Its political apparatus functioned as an administrative adjunct to the occupiers; its paramilitary branches served as instruments of repression against the Resistance; and its recruitment mechanisms supplied manpower to both the *Waffen-SS* and *Wehrmacht* formations such as *Infanterie-Bataillon 373*.

This multifaceted collaboration, however, did not yield enduring political authority. As Germany's position in Western Europe deteriorated in 1944, the influence of the Rexist movement declined rapidly. Following the liberation of Belgium, many of its adherents faced violent reprisals, while Degrelle fled first to Germany and subsequently to Spain. The movement collapsed entirely in the post-war period, discredited by its close association with Nazi occupation and repression. The trajectory of Rexism thus offers a revealing case study in the radicalisation of interwar authoritarian movements under foreign occupation – demonstrating how ideological pliability, opportunism, and organisational adaptation could transform a marginal political party into an active instrument of external domination.

The creation of *Infanterie-Bataillon 373* – later redesignated as the *Légion Wallonie* (Walloon Legion) – marked a significant stage in the evolution of Rexist collaboration. In August 1941, approximately 860 French-speaking Belgians, predominantly Walloons, departed for Germany to join the *Wehrmacht;* of these, some 730 were members of the Rexist movement, underscoring its decisive role in the mobilisation effort. Degrelle, as party leader, played a pivotal role in this process. In late July 1941, he publicly declared his intention to volunteer for the Walloon Legion, thereby seeking to inspire broader enlistment among his followers. Despite his lack of military training, Degrelle was accepted into the unit and joined the contingent that left for Germany in August 1941. After completing their training, the volunteers were dispatched to the Eastern Front, where they participated in combat operations against Soviet forces.

The Walloon Legion adopted the Cross of Burgundy as its insignia – a symbol intended to evoke the historic Burgundian heritage of Wallonia and to articulate an ideal of a renewed, unified Walloon identity within a German-dominated Europe. The Legion's campaigns on the Eastern Front were marked by heavy casualties and the brutal realities of front-line warfare. The recruitment of Belgian volunteers for *Infanterie-Bataillon 373* thus epitomised the Rexist movement's metamorphosis from a political organisation into a direct participant in the Nazi war effort. Through this militarisation and the establishment of paramilitary structures, Rexism sought to demonstrate its loyalty to the German cause and to secure its relevance in the envisioned postwar order.

On 20 February 1944, Degrelle was awarded the Knight's Cross of the Iron Cross with Oak Leaves – one of Nazi Germany's highest decorations for valour. His conduct on the Eastern Front earned him widespread admiration within German circles, and Adolf Hitler reportedly remarked that if he ever had a son, he would wish him to be like Degrelle– an extraordinary expression of esteem from the *Führer* himself.

In Waffen-SS *Service*

In late 1942, Heinrich Himmler, head of the SS, declared the Walloons to be a Germanic race, facilitating their incorporation into the *Waffen-SS*. On 1 June 1943, the unit was restructured and renamed the *SS-Sturmbrigade Wallonien* (SS Assault Brigade Wallonia), marking its transition from the *Wehrmacht* to the *Waffen-SS*. This reorganisation involved severing ties with the Rexist movement and establishing new organisational structures, such as the *Entre'ide Nationale-Socialiste* (National Socialist Welfare), to replace previous Rexist welfare organisations. Several high-profile assassinations of members of the Rexist Party occurred in Belgium. One was the killing of Jules Memeire, a mid-level Rexist official in Wallonia, by Resistance fighters in 1943, due to his active role in recruiting volunteers for the German military and organising propaganda. Another prominent assassination was that of Edmond de Goeyse. Though less well-known than Leon Degrelle, de Goeyse held the local administrative authority under the German occupation and was assassinated by members of the resistance in late 1943. Then there was Louis Collard, who was a Rexist and administrative functionary who coordinated forced labour conscriptions, who was assassinated in 1944. Other, lower-level to mid-level officials of the regional police and administration who had collaborated with the German occupation authorities were targeted for assassination; especially those assisting in rounding up Jews, conscripting workers, or providing intelligence on Resistance movements, were assassinated or severely attacked.

Combat Engagements and Expansion

The *SS-Sturmbrigade Wallonien* was first deployed to the Eastern Front in November 1943, participating in the Dnieper-Carpathian Offensive in Ukraine. The brigade's most notable engagement occurred during the Korsun–Cherkassy Pocket in February 1944, where it fought alongside the SS Division 'Wiking'. The unit suffered significant casualties, with estimates indicating up to 70 per cent losses. In October 1944, following the Allied liberation of Belgium, Degrelle managed to have the brigade upgraded to division status, forming the *28. SS-Freiwilligen-Grenadier-Division Wallonien*. The new division, however, was understrength, numbering fewer than 4,000 men. To bolster its ranks, additional volunteers were recruited, including Rexist refugees and members of the NSKK. Despite these efforts, the division remained considerably below full strength throughout its existence.

Final Campaigns and Disbandment

In early 1945, the *28. SS-Freiwilligen-Grenadier-Division Wallonien* was deployed to defend Pomerania. The division participated in the Battle of Stargard on 5 February 1945, and subsequently engaged in operations along the Oder River. By the end of February, the division had been reduced to approximately 700 men and suffered further heavy losses during a failed attack on Soviet positions. In the aftermath, some survivors were evacuated to Denmark. In May 1945 Degrelle met with Himmler in Plön but received no further orders, so he fled to Norway. The remaining personnel of the division surrendered to the British Army at Lübeck to avoid capture by Soviet forces. Degrelle did not remain in Norway long. He took a plane and flew from Norway to Spain. His plane crash-landed but he survived. He asked for, and received, political asylum in Francoist Spain. He lived there, totally unrepentant for his actions during the war. In the 1960s Leon Degrelle sneaked back into Belgium to attend his oldest daughter's wedding. He appeared at the reception in a white Spanish Falangist uniform, with SS insignia sewn on. He gave his daughter away in marriage while a church full of astounded guests looked on. Whereupon he managed to get back to Fascist Spain before the authorities could apprehend him. He died in exile on 31 March 1994 in Malaga, Spain.

The Flemish

The nation of Belgium in many ways, is the mirror image of Ireland. Whereas Ireland is a nation of one people divided by two faiths (Catholicism and Protestantism), Belgium is a nation of two people, united by one faith (Catholicism). Racially speaking, Belgium is divided amongst these two principal ethnic groups: the Walloons, who are closer to the French and speak their language, and the Flemish who constitute more than half of the population and speak Flemish, a Germanic dialect.

The *Verbond van Dietsche Nationaal-Solidaristen* (*Verdinaso*), or Union of Dutch National Solidarists, was founded on 6 October 1931 by Joris van Severen, along with Jef François, Wies Moens, and Emiel Thiers. Emerging from the broader Flemish Movement, Verdinaso initially advocated the creation of a 'Greater Netherlands' *(Dietschland)*, unifying Flanders with the Netherlands, and adhered to an authoritarian, corporatist ideology known as *Nationaal-Solidarisme* (National Solidarism). By the mid-1930s, the party shifted toward a more Belgian corporatist vision, inspired by Catholic social teachings and foreign models such as Portugal's *Estado Novo* and France's *Action Française*. Explicitly anti-parliamentarian, *Verdinaso* opposed both communism and liberal capitalism and harboured anti-Semitic and anti-Masonic sentiments. It also established a military wing, the *Dietsche Militanten Orden*.

In 1931, in an effort to broaden the party's appeal, Van Severen asserted that the Walloon population shared a common Frankish heritage and could be incorporated into the arcadian *Dietsche Volksstaat* that *Verdinaso* sought to establish. This marked a significant ideological shift from the party's prior anti-Belgian stance, with members now instructed to greet one another with the Nazi salute. While some Flemish members rejected this volte-face and left the party, the majority accepted the change, contributing to an increase in membership. According to David Littlejohn, *Verdinaso* enjoyed particular popularity among intellectuals, university students, and, to a lesser extent, members of the Belgian aristocracy.[5]

The *Dinaso Militie* was founded in 1932–3 as *Verdinaso*'s first uniformed paramilitary wing. The purpose of *Dinaso Militie* was to protect meetings, enforce internal discipline, serve as a visible symbol of strength. The early leadership structure of the *Dinaso Militie* was not as formalised as the later DMO. Rather, local commanders managed street-level operations. The *Dinaso Militie* (DM) was organised along military lines, with its principal function being the facilitation and protection of *Verdinaso* meetings. Inevitably, this brought the formation into frequent violent confrontations with political adversaries. From late 1933 onward, the Belgian authorities implemented restrictive measures against the DM, including police searches and municipal prohibitions on public marches and drills. On 29 July 1934, the enactment of the *Loi sur les milices privées* (Law on Private Militias) rendered such paramilitary organisations illegal, prompting Joris Van Severen to formally dissolve the DM.

Several months later, at *Verdinaso*'s Third Diet in Tielt, the *Dinaso Militanten Orde* (DMO) was established as its successor. Although retaining much of the DM's organisational structure, the DMO abandoned overtly military features – such as storm caps and batons – in favour of a more legally permissible and politically palatable emphasis on propaganda.

During this period, the role of Jef François within the DMO grew steadily in importance. Following a dispute with Edward 'Ward' Missoorten, who subsequently withdrew from the movement in the spring of 1936, François assumed command. Under his leadership, the DMO evolved into a disciplined propaganda apparatus, with door-to-door dissemination of literature and organised propaganda marches forming its core activities. In the same year, François expanded the organisation's manpower through the creation of the *Reserve Militanten Orde* (RMO), composed partly of *Verdinaso* cadre members and deployed primarily for large-scale propaganda events. This initiative increased the militant ranks by approximately 200, augmenting the DMO's existing force of between 400 and 500 active members. In 1937, *Verdinaso* established its own paramilitary faction, the *Dinaso Militanten Orde* (Dinaso Militant Order). Members were recognised by their distinctive green shirts. The organisation adopted several symbols and practices associated with contemporary fascist movements – such as political uniforms, the Roman salute, and the *Führerprinzip*. The militia was initially named *Dinaso Militie*, later renamed to *Dinaso Militanten Orde* around 1934. Jef François became party leader following the death of Joris Edmond Eduard Van Severen in Abbeville, May 1940.

***Reserve Militanten Orde* (RMO)**

The RMO was an auxiliary formation established by Jef François in 1936 as part of *Verdinaso*'s paramilitary apparatus. Its creation served several purposes. First, it hoped to augment membership. The RMO incorporated approximately 200 additional militants drawn from *Verdinaso*'s cadre pool, supplementing the 400–500 active members of the *Dinaso Militanten Orde* (DMO). Second, it sought to expand propaganda for the party. Unlike the original DM, which emphasised strict military discipline, the RMO was primarily used for large-scale propaganda activities, including organised marches, public demonstrations, and distribution of *Verdinaso* literature. Thirdly, the RMO was meant to be a flexible tool. The RMO could be mobilised for high-profile political events or demonstrations where a stronger, more visible presence was required, functioning as a 'reserve force' to support the DMO's core membership. Essentially, the RMO was a propaganda-oriented reserve militia, designed to project the movement's strength and ideological reach without engaging in the more overtly militaristic practices that had drawn government scrutiny in the early 1930s.

The *Vlaamsch Nationaal Verbond*

The *Vlaamsch Nationaal Verbond* (VNV; Flemish National Union) was founded in October 1933 as the primary political expression of Flemish nationalism in interwar Belgium. Its creation was driven by the desire to unify Flemish nationalist activism under a single, structured political party, after a period of fragmentation among smaller nationalist movements. The VNV was established by Staf De Clercq (1884–1942), a prominent Flemish nationalist intellectual and activist. De Clercq had previously been involved with *Frontpartij*, the earlier Flemish nationalist party, and sought to create a more disciplined, authoritarian, and cohesive movement. The VNV's ideological goal was aimed at advancing Flemish autonomy within Belgium, promote Flemish identity and language rights, and advocate a corporatist, authoritarian political structure inspired by contemporary fascist movements in Europe. It was explicitly anti-communist, anti-liberal, and nationalist in orientation. From its inception, the VNV incorporated a political party framework along with a paramilitary wing, designed to protect meetings, enforce discipline, and project strength in public demonstrations – similar to other European nationalist movements of the period.

The VNV emerged from the political vacuum created by the decline of the *Frontpartij* and the perceived inefficacy of smaller Flemish nationalist groups in influencing Belgian politics. Staf De Clercq consolidated several local nationalist organisations and activists under the VNV banner, including later absorption of groups like *Verdinaso* in May 1941. This allowed the VNV to present itself as the dominant Flemish nationalist party during the German occupation. Prior to the German occupation, the VNV participated in Belgian elections, advocating for language reforms, regional autonomy, and nationalist cultural policies. After 1940, under German occupation, the VNV became the main Flemish collaborationist party, providing cadres for auxiliary policing, propaganda, and recruitment into German forces, including the *Algemeene-SS Vlaanderen*.

Algemeene-SS Vlaanderen (General SS Flanders)

The *Algemeene-SS Vlaanderen* was a Flemish collaborationist paramilitary organisation formed during the German occupation. It emerged in 1940–1 as part of the Nazi administration's effort to organise local auxiliary forces from Flemish nationalist movements. The *Algemeene-SS Vlaanderen* included many former *Verdinaso* members, including ex-DMO and RMO personnel, who were merged with the *Algemeene-SS Vlaanderen* after *Verdinaso* was absorbed into the *Vlaamsch Nationaal Verbond* (VNV) in May 1941. The role and function of the *Algemeene-SS Vlaanderen* was to serve as a collaborationist paramilitary formation, conducting security operations, recruitment for German forces, and support of Nazi political objectives in occupied

Flanders. It was not formally part of the German SS but operated under its supervision and ideological guidance.

Members were generally motivated by Flemish nationalism, anti-communism, and authoritarian sympathies. The organisation provided a channel for militants from pre-war groups like *Verdinaso* to continue political and paramilitary activity under the occupation.

Context of the May 1941 Absorption

In May 1941, the *Verdinaso,* along with its DMO and RMO formations, was formally absorbed into the *Vlaamsch Nationaal Verbond* (VNV), the largest collaborationist Flemish nationalist party. Following this merger many ex-DMO / RMO members were integrated into the VNV's paramilitary wing, continuing the propagation of Flemish nationalist ideology. Others joined the *Algemeene-SS Vlaanderen,* aligning more directly with the German occupation authorities and serving in auxiliary or enforcement roles. In essence, the RMO was the internal reserve and propaganda force of *Verdinaso,* while the *Algemeene-SS Vlaanderen* became the external collaborationist outlet for former *Verdinaso* militants under Nazi occupation. A minority of former *Verdinaso* loyalists, unhappy with the collaborationist alignment of the *Vlaamsch Nationaal Verbond,* became politically inactive or joined Resistance efforts.

SS Legion Vlaanderen

After the German invasion of Belgium in May 1940, Flemish nationalist movements saw an opportunity to advance their political goals under the occupation. The *Vlaamsch Nationaal Verbond* (VNV), led by Staf De Clercq, became the primary Flemish nationalist party collaborating with the German authorities. Its paramilitary arm and affiliated structures, including former *Verdinaso* militants, provided a pool of trained, ideologically motivated personnel. The *Algemeene-SS Vlaanderen,* formed around the same time, was a Flemish auxiliary organisation under German supervision. It drew many former members of *Verdinaso*'s *Dinaso Militanten Orde* (DMO) and *Reserve Militanten Orde* (RMO) as well as VNV militants. Its role was to serve as a recruitment and organisational bridge between Flemish nationalist militants and the German SS apparatus. In 1941, the *SS Legion Vlaanderen (Legioen Vlaanderen)* – also known as the Flemish SS Volunteer Legion – was officially established to provide a Flemish volunteer formation for service on the Eastern Front alongside the *Waffen-SS*. The recruitment base for the *SS Legion Vlaanderen* was from the VNV. The VNV controlled much of the Flemish nationalist political infrastructure and had an active paramilitary wing. Many VNV members were motivated by anti-communism, Flemish nationalism, and authoritarian ideology, making them suitable candidates for German service. VNV propaganda emphasised the fight against Bolshevism and portrayed service in the Flemish-SS legion as both a nationalist and ideological duty.

The *Algemeene-SS Vlaanderen* provided pre-existing paramilitary training and organisational discipline. Ex-DMO and RMO militants – veterans of *Verdinaso*'s pre-war militias – were integrated, giving the new Legion a core of experienced personnel familiar with military drill, hierarchy, and propaganda-oriented operations. The German occupation authorities, particularly the SS and the *Waffen-SS* command, coordinated closely with the VNV leadership to ensure a reliable Flemish volunteer force. The *Algemeene-SS Vlaanderen* acted as a liaison and vetting organisation, ensuring volunteers met ideological, political, and military criteria. Both the VNV and the *Algemeene-SS Vlaanderen* framed participation in the Flemish-SS legion as a means of advancing Flemish autonomy and identity while simultaneously fighting Bolshevism. Recruitment campaigns stressed heroism, duty, and the prestige of serving in a *Waffen-SS* unit composed of 'Flemish brothers-in-arms'. The *SS Legion Vlaanderen* became a key vehicle for Flemish collaboration in Nazi military operations, particularly on the Eastern Front. Its formation depended directly on the networks, training, and manpower provided by the VNV and *Algemeene-SS Vlaanderen*. Without these pre-existing political and paramilitary structures, German recruitment of a cohesive Flemish volunteer unit would have been significantly more difficult.

SS-Freiwilligen-Legion 'Flandern'

The *SS Legion Vlaanderen*, also known as the Flemish-SS Legion, was established in November 1941 as a volunteer formation of Flemish-speaking Belgians within the *Waffen-SS*. Its creation was closely tied to pre-existing Flemish nationalist structures, particularly the *Vlaamsch Nationaal Verbond* (VNV) and the *Algemeene-SS Vlaanderen*, which provided both ideological motivation and a pool of trained paramilitary personnel. The VNV, under the leadership of Staf De Clercq, contributed politically committed volunteers, while the *Algemeene-SS Vlaanderen* offered organisational discipline and prior paramilitary experience from former *Verdinaso* formations, including the *Dinaso Militanten Orde* (DMO) and *Reserve Militanten Orde* (RMO). Recruitment emphasised anti-communism and Flemish nationalist sentiment, framing service on the Eastern Front as both a patriotic and ideological duty.[6]

The Legion underwent initial training at a training camp near Milovice, in Bohemia. This was a facility commonly used by the *Waffen-SS* for foreign volunteer units. Training focused on military drill, small-unit tactics, weapons handling, and ideological indoctrination, aiming to prepare Flemish volunteers for the rigours of combat on the Eastern Front while fostering loyalty to the SS and Nazi ideology. Reserve personnel, drawn largely from the RMO, often received abbreviated training before joining the front-line units, reinforcing the Legion's manpower and capabilities. Command of the unit initially fell to *SS-Hauptsturmführer* Michael Lippert, whose tenure was marked by tension with the Flemish volunteers. In April 1942, Lippert was replaced by *SS-Sturmbannführer* Conrad Schellong, a veteran of the *Waffen-SS 'Wiking'* division, who brought greater professional experience and improved relations with the Flemish rank-and-file. Schellong led *SS-Freiwilligen-Legion 'Flandern'* from 14 July 1942 until May 1943.[7] Among notable Flemish members was Reimond Tollenaere, a VNV activist who was killed in the early stages of combat, reflecting the significant human cost borne by the volunteers. Operationally, the Legion was first deployed to the Leningrad sector in November 1941, where it participated in the German siege operations. The unit faced heavy combat and sustained considerable casualties during this period.

In 1942, the Legion was transferred to Ukraine, engaging in defensive and offensive operations near Kiev and Zhitomir, including anti-partisan missions and holding front-line positions under severe Soviet resistance. By December 1943, the Flemish-SS Legion was amalgamated with other Flemish volunteer contingents to form the *SS-Sturmbrigade Langemarck,* later designated the *6. SS-Freiwilligen-Sturmbrigade 'Langemarck'*. This reorganisation increased the unit's strength to over 2,000 men, although continued combat attrition reduced the brigade to roughly 400 men by March 1944. Throughout its existence, the *SS-Freiwilligen-Legion 'Flandern'* exemplified the integration of Flemish nationalist collaborationist movements into the German military structure. Its composition – primarily Flemish volunteers with prior paramilitary experience – combined with ideological training and structured command, allowed it to function as a disciplined, though relatively small, volunteer unit within the *Waffen-SS*. The Legion's formation and operational history illustrate the interconnection between local nationalist organisations, paramilitary experience, and German occupation authorities in mobilising foreign volunteers for service on the Eastern Front.

Flemish and Walloon Guard Battalions

The Christus Rex Party, which was more commonly referred to simply as the 'Rexist Party', was created in 1935 by a newspaper man named Leon Marie Ignace Degrelle. The Flemish population had a similar leader by the name of Jeroom Gustaaf de Clercq, but he was neither as charismatic as Degrelle, nor did he lead the Flemish collaborationists for very long. The 85-year-old de Clercq suffered a heart attack and died on 22 October 1942.[8] In his place, Dr. Henrik Elias assumed the post of leader of the Flemish nationalist *Vlaamsch National Verbond*, or VNV.[9] In total, some 1,300 men served in the *Hilfsfeldgendarmerie*. While initially the Walloon population joined, Flemish nationalists also supplied volunteers for the German guard units which were to help protect German military installations and interests in Belgium (Flemish Factory Guard).

The *Vlaamse Wacht* was formed just prior to the start of the German invasion of the Soviet Union. A few months earlier in April 1941, the *Vlaamse Fabriekswacht* had been created by Christian Turcksin, a VNV member who was also a bar owner. Even though the *Vlaamse Fabriekswacht* implied that its lightly-armed members were factory guards, the real truth was that they were acting as guards for German airfields. The men of the *Vlaamse Fabriekswacht* wore the black uniform of the *Dietsche Militie, Zwarte Brigade*, that is, the militia of the VNV. Because they served the *Luftwaffe*, the unit was under the control of *Luftwaffegaukommando Belgien und Nordfrankreich*. By 1943 the force reached a strength of 3,362 men.[10] This number was about 1,100 men larger than the *Vlaamse Wacht* which contained 2,209 men in 1943.

Because of the short-term contracts of the men serving in the *Fabriekswacht*, about 5,000 men served for a period of time from 1941 to 1944, with the average number of men being 2,500 at any one time. In 1943 the *Vlaamse Fabriekswacht* was re-designated as the *Vlaamse Wachtbrigade*, or simply as the *Wacht Brigade*. In total, the *Wacht Brigade* was divided into four battalions which were stationed in the four principal Flemish towns: Antwerp, Ghent, Leuven, and Brussels.[11] These locations served as the central hubs for the *Wacht Brigade*'s operations, where they were tasked with maintaining order and supporting German authorities during the occupation. In addition to these main stations, local branches of the *Wacht Brigade* were also founded in smaller Flemish cities.

While the Flemish nationalists were creating the *Vlaamse Wacht* and *Vlaamse Fabriekswacht*, the Walloons were also tapped for a guard unit titled the *Garde Wallonne*. Many of the men who joined the *Garde*

Wallonne came from the Rexist Party militia known as the *Formations de Combat* (FC). The men of the FC wore a dark blue uniform. By 1943 the FC membership had been so diluted by the transfer of its volunteers into the *Garde Wallonne* and the *Waffen-SS* that it was disbanded. The *Garde Wallonne* was raised on 6 July 1941. Between 1943 and 1944 the *Garde Wallonne* contained about 1,500 men.[12] Finally, in both the Walloon and Flemish regions there existed the *Erlawacht* (Erla Guard) which was established to guard the Erla-airplane motor factory in Mortsel (near Antwerp) and the *Marine Überwachungstelle Cockerill* at the Cockerill shipyard in Hoboken, also near Antwerp. In total, the *Erlawacht* numbered several hundred members.[13]

These Flemish and Walloon guard units were organised into battalions in 1942. By the end of the year, three Flemish guard units *(Flämische Wachbataillone I–III)* and one Walloon battalion (*Wallonische Wachabteilung*) had been organised. In the winter of 1942/43 these four battalions were renamed as *Westwachabteilungen I–IV*. Two additional battalions were organised in the summer of 1943 when a Flemish and a Walloon railway guard unit were created: *Flämische Eisenbahnwachabteilung* and *Wallonische Eisenbahn-wachabteilung*. These six battalions were renamed once more in November 1943, becoming *Flämische Wachabteilungen I–IV* and *Wallonische Wachabteilungen I–II*. In the autumn of 1944 these six battalions were disbanded due to the Allied advance.

The Belgian Collaborationist Police

On 1 November 1943 the German Military Administration in Belgium-Northern France established the *Zivilfahnungsdienst*, or Civil Search Service. This organisation was formed using members from *De Vlag* and the Rexist movement. Its members were to help track down draft dodgers who were trying to avoid serving in any of the various military organisations which had become mandatory in 1942 and 1943. Several hundred Belgians served in the *Zivilfahnungsdienst* and assisted the German military authorities. Even though Belgium did not have a *Höhere-SS- und Polizeiführer* (Higher-SS & Police Leader) – HSSPF command until 1944 an embryonic one existed since 1 April 1942 when *SS-Oberführer* Richard Jungclaus assumed the post as Himmler's representative in the *Volkstumsfragen.* Some members of the Flemish SS were recruited by Jungclaus in order to work for the Sipo and SD. At first their duties were strictly clerical, but as time wore on and the Germans trusted these men more and more, their duties were expanded to actual field police work which included hunting down

Belgian Resistance members, Allied pilots who had been shot down, and civilians who supported the guerrillas.

In the winter of 1942–3 Flemish *SS-Stormbanleider* Robert Verleben was allowed to organise a platoon of fifty men within the Sipo/SD post in Belgium called the *Polizeizug 1 Verleben.* This unit became infamous throughout Belgium as a tool of the German SD. They were equalled in infamy by the Flemish SD guard that was created by Jungclaus to guard Jews in the Breendonk Concentration Camp and the Mechelen assembly point, which was used to concentrate Jews in one area before transport to death camps in Poland. After the Walloons were given acceptance into the SS in 1943, SS General Jungclaus established '*Verband B*', which had about 400 Rexist members acting as auxiliary police to the SD. In March 1943 the Rexist Party had established an intelligence service known as the *Departement de Securite et d'Information* (DSI). At the beginning of 1944 the *Hilfsfeldgendarmerie* and other Belgian security forces were employed in a large anti-partisan sweep in the Belgian province of Limburg. The Resistance in this region was particularly strong and the guerrilla and anti-guerrilla struggle continued throughout the war.

In July 1944 the DSI became an official part of the Sipo/SD organisation in Belgium. In the autumn of 1944 Heinrich Himmler made the decision to transform the Flemish Langemarck SS Assault Brigade and Wallonien SS Assault Brigade into the 27th and 28th SS Divisions respectively. All possible Flemish and Walloon collaborationist forces were urged, coerced or conscripted en masse into the *Waffen-SS*. Suddenly, 200 Flemings who had been working in the NSKK and several hundred Flemish men working for the *Kriegsmarine* now found themselves in *Waffen-SS* uniform. The *Vlaamse Wacht* as well as the Flemings working for the Sipo/SD now formed a Flemish SS police battalion which was added to the forming Flemish SS division.

Only about 300 protesting Flemish guards from the *Vlaamse Wacht* were released from military service in the *Waffen-SS,* basically because they were considered incorrigible.[14] The Flemish Hitler Youth even formed a battalion of youths to fight in the forming 27th SS Division. But all of these draconian methods resulted in a Flemish 'division' of some 7,000–8,000 men.[15] The *Wallonie (Wallonien)* SS Division had a similar recruiting effort and was only able to form a small brigade which the Germans grandiosely titled a 'division'. In February 1944 *Wehrkreis VI* sent one *Polizei-Wachbataillon* (Police Guard Battalion) and stationed it in the Malmédy-Eupen region of Belgium. In addition, a *Polizei-Landesschützen-Bataillon Belgien* was formed at *Truppenübungsplatzs 'Elsenborn'* and stationed in the Eifel region.

In September 1944 the Allies launched Operation Market Garden – the airborne assault to clear a path to the Rhine River through The Netherlands. In response to this operation, *Wehrkreis VI* sent three *Polizei Wach Bataillonen* (Police Guard Battalions), under the command of *Oberst der Schutzpolizei* Max Daume (from Cologne) to the Eifel region of Belgium as an emergency reinforcement for the West Wall. Post-war records indicate that about 87,000 Belgians collaborated in one way or another with the Germans during the war. Of this number about 4,000 were condemned to death, although some managed to avoid the hangman's noose by escaping to other countries.[16]

The Flemish-SS

The leadership of the Flemish (Germanic) SS changed hands several times during the occupation.[17] Hendrik Elias Lagrou was killed while serving as a volunteer on the Eastern Front with the *Waffen-SS*, while Ward Hermans departed for Germany to broadcast propaganda over Bremen Radio.[18] Command subsequently passed to J.E. de Langhe, Raf van Hulse, and Jef François, formerly of the *Verdinaso* movement. Relations between the Flemish SS and the *Vlaams Nationaal Verbond* (VNV) were marked by open hostility, in contrast to the *Deutscher-Vlaamse Arbeitsgemeinschaft* (Devlag), which supported the organisation without reservation.[19]

A nominal roll dated 30 June 1944 recorded 3,499 members of the Flemish-SS, of whom 501 served in the *Vlaanderen-Korps*. The majority of the remainder were deployed at the front – 1,660 in the *Waffen-SS* and 939 in the NSKK or other German military formations – leaving only 399 members in Flanders, ninety-eight of which were still on probation. Given the imminent liberation of Belgium, significant new recruitment in the subsequent three months is improbable, making these figures a reliable estimate of the organisation's late-war strength.[20]

As in other Nordic countries, the Flemish SS also maintained a body of 'Sponsoring Members' (*Beschermende Leden*) who contributed monthly to SS funds and were entitled to wear a sports badge marked with the initials 'B.L'. and the SS runes. By September 1942, this category comprised approximately 4,200 individuals, including women.

The Netherlands

Anton Mussert and the NSB

Anton Adriaan Mussert (1894–1946) occupies a central place in the history of Dutch fascism and collaboration during the Second World

War. Trained as a civil engineer, Mussert initially worked in the Dutch state infrastructure services, contributing to projects of water management and road construction that reflected the Netherlands' long tradition of technical innovation. His entry into politics in the interwar years was spurred by the widespread economic crisis and the perceived failure of parliamentary democracy to secure national unity. In 1931, together with Cornelis van Geelkerken, Mussert founded the *Nationaal-Socialistische Beweging* (NSB), which quickly established itself as the most prominent Dutch fascist movement. From the beginning, Mussert cultivated a self-image not as a revolutionary destroyer of the state, but rather as a disciplined engineer-politician who sought to 'rebuild' Dutch society on authoritarian and nationalist lines.[21]

Figure 13. Although the NSB was clearly inspired by German example, it strove to impress the Dutch people with its patriotism. It adopted a red and black triangle which incorporated the national device of Holland - a lion rampant ona shield of horizontal orange/white/blue. (Author's black and white drawing)

The NSB drew inspiration from German National Socialism and Italian Fascism but sought to adapt these models to Dutch circumstances. Its ideology centred on a combination of radical nationalism, corporatism, authoritarian governance, and, eventually, anti-Semitism. During the early 1930s, the NSB rejected the fragmentation of Dutch politics into denominational 'pillarized' structures (Catholic, Protestant, socialist, and liberal blocs) and instead advocated for a unitary state led by a strong leader. Mussert presented himself as that leader, carefully cultivating a personality cult modelled loosely on Mussolini and Hitler. The movement's early propaganda emphasised Dutch cultural unity, the preservation of national traditions, and a rejection of parliamentary compromise. Unlike the German National Socialists, the NSB initially avoided overt racial anti-Semitism, which helped it win modest electoral success in the mid-1930s.[22]

By 1935, the NSB had grown into a movement with tens of thousands of members, reaching its electoral peak during the provincial elections of that year when it secured nearly 8 per cent of the vote. This success alarmed mainstream Dutch parties and prompted a campaign of political and social isolation against the NSB. At the same time, Mussert began to embrace increasingly radical and openly pro-German positions, partly in response to the rise of Nazi Germany as a hegemonic power in Europe. By the late 1930s, the NSB had shifted closer to Hitler's ideological programme, formally adopting anti-Semitic positions and aligning itself with the idea of a 'New Order' in Europe. This radicalisation eroded much of the NSB's earlier popular support, particularly as many Dutch citizens remained deeply attached to constitutional monarchy and parliamentary traditions.[23]

The German invasion and occupation of the Netherlands in May 1940 fundamentally altered Mussert's political trajectory. Whereas many Dutch political parties were banned, the NSB was permitted to continue under strict German supervision. Mussert quickly pledged loyalty to Adolf Hitler and presented himself as the natural leader of a 'renewed' Netherlands within the Nazi-dominated European order. However, his influence was always circumscribed by the German occupation authorities, who distrusted his reliability and preferred to retain ultimate power in the hands of *Reichskommissar* Arthur Seyss-Inquart and the SS apparatus. Mussert was accorded the honorary title of *Leider van het Nederlandse Volk* (Leader of the Dutch People) in 1942, but this was largely a symbolic gesture designed to bolster German control rather than grant him real authority.[24]

The NSB itself was gradually transformed under occupation conditions. While retaining its formal identity, it became increasingly integrated into German-led organisations such as the *Waffen-SS* and other collaborationist paramilitary structures. Young Dutch volunteers were recruited from NSB circles into the *Waffen-SS*, where they served on the Eastern Front, most notably in units like the *SS-Freiwilligen-Legion Niederlande* and later the *23. SS-Freiwilligen-Panzergrenadier-Division 'Nederland'*. The NSB's paramilitary wing, the *Weerbaarheidsafdeling* (WA), became a crucial instrument of intimidation and repression, frequently assisting the German police and SD in persecuting Jews, political dissidents, and members of the Resistance. Through these developments, the NSB lost much of its earlier character as an autonomous political party and functioned instead as a reservoir of manpower and legitimacy for the occupiers.[25]

Despite his ambitions, Mussert remained a marginal figure in the German power structure. Unlike Vidkun Quisling in Norway, he was never installed as head of a collaborationist government, nor was he granted control over state institutions. The German occupiers preferred a colonial-style administration, in which the Netherlands was ruled directly from Berlin through Seyss-Inquart, rather than through a puppet regime. This reality deeply frustrated Mussert, who envisioned himself as the *Führer* of a Dutch National Socialist state. Nonetheless, he continued to propagate the idea of a future incorporation of the Netherlands into a Greater Germanic Reich, portraying the Dutch as racial kin of the Germans. His rhetoric emphasised shared 'Germanic' heritage and suggested a destiny in which the Netherlands would abandon its independence to become a constituent part of a continental empire.[26]

By the final years of the war, the NSB had become synonymous with collaboration and betrayal in the eyes of the Dutch population. Its members participated in the repression of resistance fighters, the rounding up of Jews for deportation, and the enforcement of German economic exploitation. Mussert's own credibility diminished further as German defeats mounted, and his promises of a 'New Order' rang increasingly hollow. In May 1945, with the collapse of Nazi Germany, Mussert was arrested and placed on trial for treason. His trial attracted widespread attention in the newly liberated Netherlands, where public anger against collaborators was at its peak. He was convicted and executed by firing squad in The Hague on 7 May 1946, a fate that symbolised the broader reckoning with collaboration in the post-liberation Netherlands.[27] Mussert's legacy is one of failure and discredit. He began as a nationalist engineer seeking to modernise Dutch politics but ended as a collaborator subordinated to German power. The NSB, which once aspired to become a mass movement, collapsed under the weight of its compromises with the occupiers and its complicity in crimes against the Dutch people. In retrospect, Mussert's trajectory illustrates the limits of indigenous fascist movements in occupied

Western Europe, where local leaders often found themselves reduced to auxiliaries of the German state rather than autonomous rulers. His fate also symbolised the broader reckoning with collaboration that shaped post-war Dutch society and politics.

SS-Freiwilligen-Legion 'Niederlande'

The *SS-Freiwilligen-Legion 'Niederlande'* was created in 1941 in the aftermath of the German invasion and occupation of the Netherlands. Its origins were bound up with the broader SS policy of mobilising 'Germanic' volunteers from occupied North-west Europe for the war against the Soviet Union. Heinrich Himmler and the *SS-Führungshauptamt* portrayed this recruitment effort as the foundation of a future 'Germanic empire', in which Dutch, Flemish, Danish, and Norwegian contingents would take part as racial kin of the Germans. In the Netherlands, the pro-German NSB under Anton Mussert provided organisational and political support for the recruitment campaign, which began shortly after *Unternehmen Barbarossa* in June 1941. Dutch propaganda stressed both the ideological battle against Bolshevism and the promise of preserving national honour within a supranational Germanic framework, although the German authorities never intended to grant the Dutch any real autonomy within the *Waffen-SS*.

The Legion was officially formed in July 1941 as the *Legion Niederlande*. Early recruits included members of the NSB, Dutch fascist youth organisations, and men motivated by a mix of ideology, economic pressure, and opportunism. Training initially took place in Germany, including at camps in Hamburg and later at Debica in occupied Poland, where the Legion was organised as a regiment-sized formation of around 2,000 men under German officers and Dutch SS volunteers. The Dutch volunteers were formally part of the *Waffen-SS*, though the unit retained the 'Legion' designation in order to appeal to nationalist sentiments and to suggest a degree of separation from direct German control. In terms of deployment, the Legion was committed to the Eastern Front in late 1941, attached to the 2. *SS-Infanterie-Brigade (motorisiert)*, a unit comprised largely of foreign volunteer legions. It was first engaged in combat near Novgorod and Leningrad during the winter campaign of 1941–2. The conditions were exceptionally harsh, and the Dutch volunteers suffered from inadequate training, severe cold, and high casualty rates. By the summer of 1942 the Legion had been rebuilt and returned to the front, taking part in defensive operations south of Lake Ilmen and along the Volkhov front. Its combat reputation was mixed; while some reports praised the determination of individual companies, German officers frequently criticised the unit's cohesion and effectiveness, particularly under conditions of sustained combat.

The Legion was withdrawn from the front in 1943 after suffering heavy attrition. It was subsequently disbanded in its original form, and surviving personnel were transferred to the newly created *4. SS-Freiwilligen-Panzergrenadier-Brigade 'Nederland'*, which would itself later form the nucleus of the *23. SS-Freiwilligen-Panzergrenadier-Division 'Nederland'*. This reorganisation reflected the SS's policy of consolidating smaller national legions into larger, more permanent *Waffen-SS* divisions. By this point, the 'Legion' concept had outlived its propaganda usefulness, and the German command preferred to absorb foreign volunteers into divisions modelled more closely on German standards. The combat history of the *SS-Freiwilligen-Legion 'Niederlande'* is thus relatively brief but illustrative of the larger dynamics of collaboration and foreign recruitment in the *Waffen-SS*. Formed in 1941 as a politically symbolic unit under the auspices of the NSB and the SS, it endured the severe attritional warfare on the Eastern Front, where its limited training and experience led to heavy losses. Its eventual dissolution and absorption into larger *Waffen-SS* formations underscored both the failure of the independent 'legion' model and the determination of the German leadership to continue mobilising Dutch manpower within the *Waffen-SS* framework. The Legion's legacy remained controversial in the Netherlands after the war, where participation in the *Waffen-SS* was broadly associated with collaboration and treason, despite the variety of motives that had driven men to enlist in 1941.

4. SS-Freiwilligen-Panzergrenadier-Brigade 'Nederland'

Following the dissolution of the *SS-Freiwilligen-Legion 'Niederlande'* in 1943, surviving Dutch volunteers were reorganised into the *4. SS-Freiwilligen-Panzergrenadier-Brigade 'Nederland'*. This reorganisation reflected a shift in German strategy: the *Waffen-SS* sought to consolidate smaller national volunteer formations into larger, more combat-effective units capable of front-line operations on the Eastern Front. The brigade retained a predominantly Dutch composition but was now integrated more fully into the German SS command structure, with a mixture of Dutch officers and German cadre providing leadership. Its formation coincided with a period of intense attritional warfare on the Eastern Front, where manpower shortages, severe casualties, and logistical difficulties demanded a reorientation of all foreign volunteer units into more standardised brigades. The 4th Brigade

Members of the Italian-SS Battalion 'Debica'. It was deemed ready for battle in February 1944. The battalion eventually became the Fusilier Battalion of the *Waffen-Grenadier-Brigade der SS (italienische Nr. 1)*. The brigade was employed against the partisans. In the autumn of 1944, it was expanded to division level. (*Photo courtesy of the Adriano Marco Navarese collection*)

A *Plastun* (Cossack infantryman) on coastal watch duty. Notice he is wearing the insignia of the Russian Army of Liberation on his left sleeve. (*Bundesarchiv*)

A Turkestani volunteer from central Asia. The top of the arm patch reads 'Biz Alla Bilen' (We are with God). The bottom of the patch simply reads 'Turkistan'. (*Bundesarchiv*)

The leader of the so-called Indian National Army, Subhas Chandra Bose, seen here with the commander of *Infanterie-Regiment 950 (indisches)*, *Oberstleutnant* Kurt Krappe. In the background, we see a truck full of Indian volunteers. In 1942 Chandra Bose was transported by submarine to Japanese-held territory. With his assistance, the Japanese raised four divisions of volunteers made up of Indians, men from Burma (today's Myanmar), and other Southeast Asians. The Japanese employed these divisions in their attempted invasion of the Indian subcontinent. (*Bundesarchiv*)

German and Indian members of *Infanterie-Regiment 950 (indisches)*. (*Bundesarchiv*)

A closer view of the men and uniforms of *Infanterie-Regiment 950 (indisches)*. (*Photo courtesy John M. Miller*)

Two members of the Arab Parachute Company dance, while other German and Arab paratroopers look on. The Germans raised an Arab paratrooper company in Tunisia. In April 1945, members of this company served as part of *9. Fallschirmjäger-Division* along the Oder front, defending Berlin. (*Bundesarchiv*)

Cossack cavalrymen of the pro-German *1. Kosaken-Kavallerie-Division* in Yugoslavia, 1944. (*Bundesarchiv*)

Members of a Lithuanian *Schutzmannschaft* battalion, circa 1942. In the background you can see three German *Ordnungspolizei* men (one is an officer). (*Bundesarchiv*)

Not Germans, but Belarusian volunteers, circa 1943. (*Minsk State Archives*)

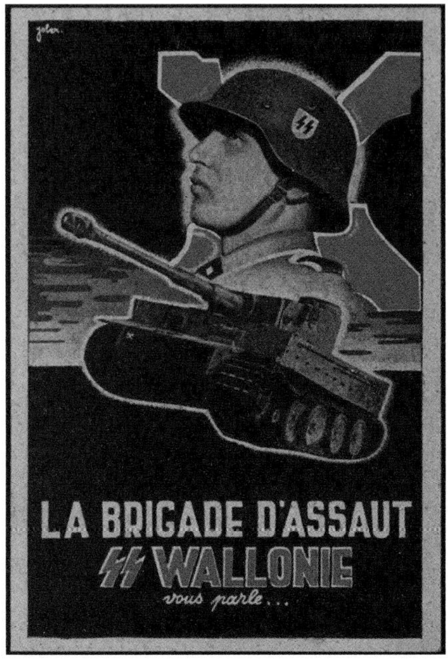

A recruiting poster for the Wallonien SS Assault Brigade. (*Royal Military Museum (Brussels)*).

General der Artillerie Paul Bader, the commander of the *Wehrmachtbefehlshaber in Serbien* headquarters, inspects the *Russisches Kavallerieregiment 1*, of the *Russisches Schutzkorps Serbien* (Russian Guard Corps in Serbia), circa 1942. (*Author's collection*)

Inspection of the *Russisches Schutzkorps Serbien* in 1942. In the background we can see several trucks, a motorcycle and a French Hotchkiss H-35 tank armed with the 37mm SA 18 gun (SA 38 - 1939 version) The Russian Guard Corps acquired five such small tanks and employed them against the partisans. (*Author's collection*)

An elderly volunteer belonging to the Russian Guard Corps. He appears to be a member of the *Russisches Kavallerieregiment 1*. (*Author's collection*)

Members of the *13. Waffen-Gebirgs-Division der SS 'Handschar'* take time for a photograph, some time in 1944. (*Bundesarchiv*)

An obviously posed propaganda photograph of three Bosnian Muslim members of the SS *'Handschar'* mountain division. The man in the middle is 'reading' a pamphlet titled 'Islam and Judaism'. (*Bundesarchiv*)

A German officer stands next to a Belgian policeman. After the Nazi occupation of Belgium, the Germans created a central authority to supervise the *Gendarmerie* (*Rijkswacht*) as well as the municipal police, placing it under the control of the *Militärverwaltung* (German Military Administration). (*Author's collection*)

A member of the Belgian SS brigade, some time in 1943. (*Bundesarchiv*)

Members of the French *Milice* marching. The *Franc-Garde*, the armed wing of the *Milice*, was primarily equipped with British weapons such as the Lee-Enfield No. 4 Mk I rifle, the Sten submachine gun – which was relatively inexpensive to produce – and the Mk I Bren light machine gun (shown here). Many of these French *Miliciens* later served in the French SS Division *'Charlemagne.'* (*Archives nationales*)

Two members of *Verstärktes Infanterie-Regiment 638 (französisch)*. (*Archives nationales*)

French *Milice* parade near the *Arc de Triomphe* in Paris, 1944. (*Archives nationales*)

Members of the Sudetenland *Volksdeutsche* defence force, the *Sudetendeutsche Freikorps*. (*Bundesarchiv*)

Members of the staff of the *Druzhina-SS Brigade*. Notice the mixture of German SD and Russian personnel. When the brigade mutinied in 1943, most of the German cadre staff were killed. (*Author's collection*)

Colonel Vladimir Boyarsky. In 1943 he was assigned to inspect battalions serving under turncoat General Andrei Vlasov's Russian Army of Liberation (ROA). In April 1945, when the ROA moved to aid Czech patriots in the Prague Uprising, Boyarsky was among the officers sent to the capital to coordinate efforts. There he encountered a group of Czech fighters who had already placed themselves under the authority of a Red Army captain. A heated argument broke out, during which the captain mocked Boyarsky's patriotism. Boyarsky, stung by the insult, struck the officer across the face. The act sealed his fate: he was immediately seized, strung up, and hanged on the spot. His death, however, did not prevent the ROA from continuing to fight alongside the Czech insurgents for several days. (*Author's collection*)

Ethnic-German Slovenians who joined the *Wehrmannschaft*, a self-defence force created in late 1941. (*Museum of Modern History, Ljubljana*)

Members of the *Wehrmannschaft* observe a fellow member with a Mauser C96 Broomhandle semi-automatic pistol with detachable wood stock. (*Museum of Modern History, Ljubljana*)

Rifle practice was also required of the members of the *Wehrmannschaft*. (*Museum of Modern History, Ljubljana*)

Members of the pro-German Slovenian *Domobranci*, some time in 1943. (*Museum of Modern History, Ljubljana*)

The Germans provided newspapers and magazines to keep the morale of the foreign volunteers as high as possible. This is the 28 September 1944 issue of *Slovensko Domobranstvo*. (*Museum of Modern History, Ljubljana*)

Members of the *Schalburg Korps* wearing the field grey uniform of the German military. On their right collar tab, they wear the *Sonnenrad* – the sun wheel swastika emblem. On 19 September 1944, the Germans arrested some 2,000 Danish police, sending them to Neuengamme and Buchenwald concentration camps. This was done because the Germans considered the Danish police unreliable in fighting the Resistance. Eliminating so many policemen in one fell swoop had repercussions. Even though the *Schalburg Korps* assumed police duties, crime actually increased. Locals had to organise ad-hoc street patrols to protect property and person. *(Danmarks Fotografiske Museum)*.

Members of the pro-German *Schalburg Korps*. One person is wearing the uniform of a *Waffen-SS* sergeant, while the rest are wearing the black uniform. As Danish volunteers returned from service on the Eastern Front, many were encouraged to join the *Schalburg Korps*. (*Danmarks Fotografiske Museum*)

On the far left of this photograph is the commander of the *Höherer SS- und Polizeiführer 'Nord'*, *SS-Obergruppenführer* Wilhelm Rediess. To the right of him is Vidkun Quisling, to the right of Quisling is Josef Terboven, the *Reichskommissar* for Norway. To the right of Terboven, wearing glasses, is *SS-Brigadeführer und Generalmajor der Polizei* Franz Wilhelm Seiß, the *Befehlshaber der Ordnungspolizei* (BdO) in Norway. They are inspecting pro-German Norwegian police who are standing at attention. (*Norges Hjemmefrontmuseum*)

was organised along *Panzergrenadier* lines, incorporating mechanised infantry elements intended to provide mobile support for armoured formations, although in practice shortages of vehicles and equipment limited its operational mobility.

The *4. SS-Panzergrenadier-Brigade 'Nederland'* saw combat primarily on the Eastern Front, participating in defensive operations against the advancing Red Army during 1943–4. Its deployments included holding sectors along the Volkhov River and areas surrounding Novgorod, regions familiar to many of the veterans from the original Legion. Combat reports highlight mixed performance: while individual Dutch companies occasionally demonstrated courage and initiative, German commanders frequently criticised the brigade's limited cohesion, lack of experience in sustained mechanised warfare, and occasional failures under pressure. By mid-1944, as Soviet offensives intensified, the brigade suffered severe casualties and was withdrawn for refit, its survivors forming the nucleus for a larger divisional formation to better utilise Dutch manpower in accordance with SS organisational standards.

23. *SS-Freiwilligen-Panzergrenadier-Division 'Nederland'*

This transition led directly to the formation of the *23. SS-Freiwilligen-Panzergrenadier-Division 'Nederland'*, officially established in late 1944. The division represented the culmination of German efforts to mobilise Dutch volunteers within the *Waffen-SS* framework: it combined survivors of the *4. SS-Panzergrenadier-Brigade 'Nederland'*, conscripts drawn from Dutch collaborationist organisations, and a small number of newly recruited volunteers. Its structure adhered more closely to the German SS divisional model, including two *Panzergrenadier* regiments, supporting artillery, reconnaissance and anti-tank battalions, though like many late-war formations, it was chronically understrength in both manpower and equipment. Despite these limitations, it was designated a 'division' for propaganda purposes, signalling both the SS's commitment to Dutch volunteerism and the symbolic importance of maintaining Dutch national contingents within the *Waffen-SS* hierarchy.

Operationally, the *23. SS-Freiwilligen-Panzergrenadier-Division 'Nederland'* was committed to battles against the Red Army in western Pomerania and along the Oder River in early 1945. While in western Pomerania, it operated under the *III. (Germanisches) SS Panzerkorps*. It later withdrew to the Oder River under Army Group Vistula. It ended the war fighting in Berlin. The Dutch SS division fought its last battle defending the Nazi capital in April 1945. By then the unit had been reduced to regiment in size (at best). Combat effectiveness was uneven, reflecting both the inexperience of many new recruits and chronic shortages of armoured vehicles, heavy weapons, and trained officers. The division's final engagements were largely characterised by rearguard actions, local counter-attacks, and attempts to maintain cohesion under the collapsing German military situation.

The legacy of both the *4. SS-Panzergrenadier-Brigade 'Nederland'* and the *23. SS-Freiwilligen-Panzergrenadier-Division 'Nederland'* was complex. While initially framed as an opportunity for Dutch volunteers to assert their loyalty to Germany or to engage ideologically in the fight against Bolshevism, the formations increasingly incorporated coerced conscripts and those motivated by material needs or survival in a wartime environment. Both units suffered heavy casualties, and many veterans faced post-war prosecution in the Netherlands for collaboration and service in the *Waffen-SS*. In historical memory, they are remembered less for combat achievements than for their association with German occupation policies and the broader moral and political questions surrounding Dutch collaboration. Their evolution from the Legion through the brigade to the division illustrates the adaptive use by the SS of foreign manpower and the ways in which national volunteer formations were absorbed, restructured, and ultimately committed to the German war effort, often under extremely adverse circumstances.

34. SS-Freiwilligen-Grenadier-Division 'Landstorm Nederland'

The *34. SS-Freiwilligen-Grenadier-Division 'Landstorm Nederland'* was one of the last *Waffen-SS* formations created during the Second World War and reflected both the radicalisation of Dutch collaborationism and the military desperation of the Third Reich in its final year. Its origins lay in the *'Landwacht Nederland'*, a paramilitary militia established in the occupied Netherlands in March 1943 under German supervision. Initially, this force was conceived as a kind of gendarmerie or auxiliary police, designed to combat growing Resistance activity and to serve as an internal security formation. The *Landwacht* recruited largely from the ranks of the NSB and its youth movement, as well as other pro-German collaborators. Its early tasks included manning roadblocks, guarding food depots, assisting the *Sicherheitspolizei* in roundups, and intimidating the civilian population. As such, the *Landwacht* quickly earned a reputation for brutality, and its members were loathed by the Dutch public.[28]

By late 1943, the German authorities began to militarise the *Landwacht* more systematically. The formation was renamed *'Landstorm Nederland'* in November of that year and reorganised as a *Waffen-SS* unit, though at first it retained a hybrid status between a police and military formation. Heinrich Himmler and SS recruiters viewed it as a way of mobilising Dutch manpower at a time when resistance activity was intensifying and the *Wehrmacht* was suffering catastrophic losses on the Eastern Front. Many members were conscripted, while others were drawn by ideological loyalty to Mussert's NSB and by promises of pay or protection. In this sense, the *Landstorm* functioned both as a paramilitary arm of the collaborationist party and as a manpower reservoir for the *Waffen-SS*. Its recruitment methods, however, often generated resentment, as many Dutch men found themselves pressured or coerced into service.[29]

Throughout 1944, the *Landstorm Nederland* was gradually expanded and committed to combat operations within the Netherlands. Its tasks ranged from anti-partisan sweeps and reprisals against civilians to defensive battles against advancing Allied forces. The unit was deployed during Operation Market Garden in September 1944, when it fought against British and Polish paratroopers in the Arnhem sector. Although poorly trained and equipped, *Landstorm* units managed to delay Allied advances in several sectors, largely under the direction of German SS and *Wehrmacht* officers. Their performance was uneven: while individual units fought with determination, the formation as a whole lacked cohesion and suffered heavy casualties.[30]

In December 1944, the formation was formally elevated to divisional status and designated as the *34. SS-Freiwilligen-Grenadier-Division 'Landstorm Nederland'*. Despite this title, it was in reality a division in name only. Its manpower strength never approached that of a full *Waffen-SS* division, and its equipment was deficient. The division was organised around two grenadier regiments, supplemented by small artillery and support units, but many of its sub-units were understrength. The designation was part of the late-war German practice of inflating unit titles in order to project an image of strength that did not correspond to operational realities. Nevertheless, the division represented the culmination of efforts to transform Dutch collaborationist auxiliaries into a regular *Waffen-SS* field formation.[31]

During March and April 1945, the 34th SS Volunteer Grenadier Division *Landstorm Nederland* functioned primarily as an understrength territorial defense formation deployed in the central Netherlands, where it occupied positions along the Grebbe Line, the Betuwe region, and the southern approaches to the Veluwe. It operated as a collection of small infantry battlegroups assigned to static defensive duties. Its principal mission was to delay any Allied advance, protect German lines of communication, and maintain internal security within the occupied territory. By this stage of the war morale had deteriorated. The division also absorbed a number of late-war recruits, including men drawn by the catastrophic conditions of the Hunger Winter of 1944–5, who enlisted to secure regular rations, avoid deportation for labour service in Germany, or simply improve their chances of survival. It remained confined to the Netherlands throughout its existence and ultimately surrendered alongside other German forces in the country during the capitulation of 4–5 May 1945. Beyond its battlefield role, it took part in anti-Resistance operations. These activities, combined with its visible service under the *Waffen-SS*, cemented its image as one of the most reviled collaborationist units in Dutch memory.[33]

With the collapse of the Third Reich in May 1945, remnants of the *34. SS-Freiwilligen-Grenadier-Division Landstorm Nederland* surrendered to Allied forces between 4–5 May 1945. Many of its members were subsequently interned and tried by Dutch authorities for treason, collaboration, and war crimes. The trials revealed the extent of their involvement in repressive measures against the Dutch population, and numerous former *Landstorm* members received long prison sentences. Some of its officers were executed. In the post-war Netherlands, '*Landwacht*' and '*Landstormer*' became synonymous with betrayal and brutality, encapsulating the degree to which domestic collaboration could align itself with Nazi power structures.[34]

In retrospect, the *34. SS-Freiwilligen-Grenadier-Division 'Landstorm Nederland'* illustrates both the limits and the extremity of Dutch collaboration under German occupation. It never achieved the status of a genuine combat division but nonetheless played a visible role in both repression and late-war defensive operations. Its formation demonstrates how the German occupation authorities sought to transform auxiliary militias into formal *Waffen-SS* units, often inflating their designation for propaganda purposes. At the same time, its unpopularity among the Dutch population underscores the deep divide between collaborators and the majority of the population, a divide that shaped post-war memory and justice. The *Landstorm*'s trajectory, from police auxiliary to SS division in name, embodies the fusion of ideology, coercion, and desperation that characterised Nazi collaborationist projects in occupied Western Europe.

The Hongerwinter *as a Recruiting Incentive*

The *Hongerwinter* of 1944–5 was one of the most devastating episodes of the German occupation of the Netherlands. From September 1944 to May 1945, after the failure of Operation Market Garden and the Allied advance stalled at the rivers, and a Dutch railway strike, the German authorities cut off food and fuel shipments to the still-occupied western provinces. As a result, between 18,000 and 22,000 Dutch civilians are estimated to have died of starvation, with countless others suffering from malnutrition, disease, and extreme privation. Given this desperate context, the question of whether some Dutchmen may have joined the German armed forces as a means of survival is both plausible and important.

The Hunger Context and its Plausibility

As a result of the German embargo, rations in the densely-populated western provinces plummeted to between 400 and 800 calories per person per day, with some cities dipping below 600 calories, clearly insufficient for survival. More than 20,000 Dutch civilians died of starvation or related causes during this period. People resorted to eating tulip bulbs, sugar beets, even pets, and scavenged wild plants just to stay alive. It is historically plausible that individuals, especially young men in desperate circumstances, might have viewed service in the *Wehrmacht* or *Waffen-SS* as a way to secure food, clothing, and shelter. Military service guaranteed rations and regular meals at a time when civilians in the occupied Netherlands faced near-starvation. This phenomenon was not unique to the Dutch: in other occupied countries, including Belgium, France, and parts of Eastern Europe, some late-war volunteers for German units were motivated less by ideology than by sheer survival.

Given this extreme context, it is historically plausible that some individuals looked to enlist in German military forces – such as the *Waffen-SS Landstorm Nederland* – not out of ideology, but for more tangible survival benefits such as:

1. Regular rations and warmth, compared to near-starvation at home
2. Relative protection from the acute deprivation plaguing civilians
3. Avoidance of forced labour or death due to hunger

For the Netherlands specifically, most scholarship emphasises political or ideological motivations (Dutch fascism, nationalism, anti-communism, or the appeal of German victory earlier in the war) as central to the earlier waves of volunteering between 1940 and 1943. However, by late

1944 the situation had changed: Germany was losing the war, the Dutch NSB was in disarray, and recruitment appeals were far less successful. The Germans launched frantic campaigns to recruit for the *Waffen-SS* and the *Landstorm Nederland*, often resorting to coercion, press-ganging or the threat of forced labour in Germany. Historians such as Loe de Jong (*Het Koninkrijk der Nederlanden in de Tweede Wereldoorlog*) note that by late 1944 and early 1945, the number of genuine volunteers had collapsed, and that the majority of Dutchmen entering German service did so under duress, or as part of forced conscription measures. Yet within this group, it is certainly plausible that some men weighed the possibility of starvation at home against the relative security of a soldier's ration, and thus 'volunteered' as the lesser of two evils.

There are scattered references in Dutch post-war testimonies and German records that hint at survival as a motivation. Some late-war recruitment propaganda explicitly promised warm meals, boots, and regular pay – a clear signal that the Germans themselves were aware that material incentives, not ideology, were the only effective draw by 1944–5. In certain cases, young men rounded up for labour service (*Arbeitseinsatz*) chose to enlist in German-controlled Dutch formations rather than risk starvation or deportation to labour camps under dire conditions. Open appeals failed, and German authorities turned to increasingly desperate efforts to fill ranks – often with men seeking food or protection rather than ideological alignment. Evidence of this includes:

1. Recruitment propaganda that highlighted material incentives – food, shelter, pay – as motivators.
2. Some labour service conscripts choosing military service over forced labour in camps, likely driven by basic survival instincts.
3. Parliamentary and personal records (though sparse) indicating late-war enlistees weighed starvation against enlistment.

Conclusions

While there is no large body of documented cases where Dutchmen explicitly stated 'I joined to avoid starving', the context of the *Hongerwinter* makes it highly plausible that survival needs influenced some late-war enlistments. The combination of food scarcity, German recruitment drives, and coercion created conditions in which the line between volunteerism and compulsion blurred. In this sense, it is historically reasonable to say that a subset of Dutch enlistments in late 1944 and early 1945 were motivated less by ideology and more by desperation for food and survival, even if the archival record does not always capture this motive in explicit terms.

29. Waffen-Grenadier-Division der SS (italienische Nr. 1)

Italy assisted Nazi Germany as an Axis allied country beginning in June 1940, when Mussolini declared war on France and the United Kingdom. Even after the Fascist Grand Council ousted Mussolini from power, with Italy suing for peace in September 1943, the Germans managed to use the Italians once again by rescuing Mussolini (who had been imprisoned) and taking him to northern Italy, where, under German auspices, he rallied what Italian fascists still supported him and created the *Repubblica Sociale Italiana* (RSI – Italian Social Republic) which existed from 1943–5. The Germans even lent him a hand and helped to organise four Italian divisions that would serve as the backbone of the RSI. In addition, numerous independent RSI regiments and battalions were created. In November 1943 the Germans established the *SS-Freiwilligen-Legion,* but soon was renamed *1. Sturmbrigade Italienische Freiwilligen-Legion*. Three battalions of this Italian SS unit fought at Anzio beach. Up until then, the collar tabs of the Italian SS were on a red background (instead of the established black collar tabs). Because of their good performance at Anzio, Himmler declared that they could now wear the black collar tabs. In the autumn of 1944, the decision was made to expand the brigade to a division. Its formation took place in northern Italy, mainly in the area of Lake Garda and the Veneto, drawing from volunteers of the RSI.

In December 1944 it reached a strength of around 15,000 men. The division's primary employment was anti-partisan warfare in northern Italy during the last months of the war. Its units were spread across Veneto, Friuli, and South Tyrol, where they fought against Italian Resistance formations, often alongside German police, security, and *Wehrmacht* units. It engaged in sweeps, reprisals, and security operations rather than conventional front-line battles. When the German front in Italy collapsed in April 1945, the division retreated northward toward the Alpine regions. Some elements attempted to fight their way into Germany, while others surrendered locally. A large portion of the division was captured by partisans before reaching Allied lines, and many of its members were executed in reprisal for their collaboration with the Germans. Only a fraction managed to surrender formally to the Western Allies in late April and early May 1945.

Chapter 6

THE 'PROPAGANDA LEGIONS' 1941–1945, PART 1

Introduction

During the Second World War, the German armed forces, particularly the *Waffen-SS*, established a series of volunteer legions drawn from populations outside of Europe, including the Middle East, South Asia, Central Asia and the Caucasus. Units such as the Arab *Infanterie-Bataillon 845*, the Indian *Infanterie-Regiment 950*, the *Osttürkischer Waffenverband der SS* and the *Kaukasischer Waffenverband der SS* were raised with the ostensible goal of mobilising foreign manpower to support the German war effort. These formations were generally composed of volunteers motivated by a complex mixture of anti-Soviet sentiment, anti-British nationalism, personal opportunity or coercion, reflecting the opportunistic and ideologically selective nature of German foreign recruitment. Recruitment was often facilitated by German propaganda emphasising shared enemies or 'common civilisation' narratives, while ideological indoctrination was limited, and German officers retained tight operational control over unit deployment and activities.

Despite their official status as military units, the operational impact of many of these volunteer legions was minimal. Their combat deployments were usually confined to rear-area security, anti-partisan operations or limited defensive engagements, and in many cases their contributions were sporadic or symbolic rather than tactically decisive. High attrition rates, inadequate training, poor equipment and language barriers further restricted their battlefield effectiveness. In practice, these units rarely altered the course of campaigns or significantly reinforced German front-line forces, and their military role remained largely peripheral in the broader context of the *Wehrmacht* and *Waffen-SS* operations.

Nevertheless, these volunteer formations played a disproportionate role in the German propaganda apparatus. They were extensively photographed, filmed, and documented in magazines, newsreels and recruitment posters, serving as vivid symbols of supposed international support for the Third Reich. The visual representation of diverse, global volunteers – Arabs, Indians, Turkestanis, Caucasians and others – was used to project the image of a cosmopolitan, ideologically unified anti-Bolshevik coalition, reinforcing the narrative that the German war effort enjoyed the sympathy or active support of peoples around the world. In many cases, the photographs and film served less to document military action than to construct an image of legitimacy and prestige for Nazi audiences and foreign observers.

The contrast between the real and the propagandistic roles of these units highlights the extent to which the Third Reich relied on symbolic capital to supplement military power. Units such as the Arab *Infanterie-Bataillon 845* or the Indian *Infanterie-Regiment 950* existed simultaneously as armed formations and as living propaganda tools, their importance measured more by the images they produced than by their operational outcomes. A case in point is the Indian *Infanterie-Regiment 950,* which provided the Germans with the ability to say that Germany was fighting for Indian self-determination. However, militarily speaking, the Indian *Infanterie-Regiment 950* never fired a single shot in anger. Towards the end of the war, as weapons and munitions became scarce, Adolf Hitler discovered (during a military conference in 1945), that just about every man in the Indian infantry regiment possessed two weapons. Hitler wryly commented that the Indians could turn thousands of prayer wheels, but were wasting weaponry that was much-needed by actual combat formations.

Even as these volunteers faced harsh conditions, logistical neglect and sometimes suspicion from their German superiors, their presence was leveraged to produce the illusion of broad international collaboration with Nazi objectives, serving to inspire both domestic audiences and potential foreign recruits. In sum, the story of these esoteric volunteer legions underscores a recurrent pattern in German foreign recruitment: units raised from non-European populations were often militarily marginal yet propagandistically valuable. Their existence reflects both the ideological ambitions of the SS and *Wehrmacht* to construct a transnational anti-Bolshevik coalition and the practical constraints of late-war manpower shortages. By examining the dual function of these formations – as minor combatants and major visual symbols – historians can better understand the intersection of military policy, ideology, and propaganda in the Third Reich, and the ways in which the image of a global 'volunteer crusade' was cultivated even when substantive operational impact was negligible.

Paper Tigers: *Infanterie-Regiment 950*

During the Second World War the Allies and Axis made every effort to raise troops from North Africa, the Middle East and Asia. The Allies were the most successful since they basically controlled these regions for all or most of the war. Axis attempts to raise troops from these regions proved to have mixed results due to numerous reasons. First, they never reached Iraq, Persia (Iran), Palestine, India, and other Middle Eastern countries and territories. Attempts to raise Arab units in Libya, Tunisia and Morrocco proved too little, too late. Secondly, political insensibilities at the outset (i.e. German arrogance) also played a role in delaying the mass recruitment of Arab and other peoples of Africa and the Middle and Far East. Finally, Allied military gains in North Africa ended German efforts to correct their earlier mistake almost as soon as recruitment and arming of these peoples had begun. By May 1943 North Africa was in complete allied hands. The Germans only partly managed to train and form a few Arab battalions, most of whose men were captured when the Axis surrendered in Tunisia.

Just as the North African campaign was drawing to a close, a new formation, made up mostly of Indian Hindus and some Muslims was being organised inside Nazi Germany. The unit, officially titled the *Infanterie-Regiment 950 (Indisches)* (950th Indian Infantry Regiment) in the German Army rolls, would eventually become known as the 'Indian Legion' or 'Springing Tiger Legion'. This last reference was to its distinctive arm patch showing a leaping tiger with the Indian national colours in the background and the words 'Free India' inscribed on the top part of the patch. The regiment was formed and organised along regular German Army lines, although its actual aim was actually for propaganda purposes. Its appearance on the scene had taken about a year, since construction of the Indian regiment had begun in earnest in 1942. By the time the unit was ready, there was absolutely no chance that the German forces would ever reach India, and thus employ the regiment as a spearhead for their countrymen to rally around. But 1943 had brought some great reversals in German fortunes and Germany needed to show the world that many peoples were rallying to her cause. The Indian Legion fit this need nicely. In 1943 the majority of the Muslim and Hindu world was still dominated and controlled by the British, a fact which many of these indigenous peoples resented greatly. The Germans realised this all too well.

Nationalism was just beginning to show itself fully in these Third-World regions, and the peoples of these countries were trying to assert themselves. It was common therefore, that anti-colonialism (and therefore, anti-British) feelings ran high, especially among the intelligentsia and the less well to do, as is often the case. Only those directly benefited by English colonial occupation desired for a continuance of the status quo. These feelings were most extreme in Iraq, Iran, Palestine, and finally but not least, India where the independence movement had already begun even before the Second World War.

Indian or Arab expectations of being 'liberated' from the British had been pretty much dashed with the defeat of Friedrich Paulus' *6. Armee* at Stalingrad and Rommel's *Afrika Korps* at El Alamein. Pretences had to be kept however, and the German propaganda department had orders to continue to try and undermine Allied relations with the Arab and Indian world. Within this purpose, it's no small wonder that the only shots fired in anger by the Indian Legion turned out to be in self-defence and against French *Maquisards*. Ironically enough, the French were trying to rid themselves of the German occupiers, much like the majority of Indians were trying to get rid of their British occupiers. This incident occurred in 1944, as the Indian Legion made a withdrawal from southern France.

Origins of the Indian Legion

The man most responsible for raising of the Indian Legion was Subhas Chandra Bose, an Indian lawyer and former leader of the Indian National Congress. Bose wanted India to be free as much as Mahatma Gandhi did. This was where both men agreed. However, in all other respects he was the complete antithesis of Gandhi, who supported Indian independence through non-violent methods. Bose was willing to take up arms for his ideals and principals. He had been an ardent supporter of Indian independence for a long time and was well known like Gandhi. Bose, a Hindu, and the Mufti of Jerusalem (Haj Amin al Husseini), who was a respected Muslin leader, had been equally instrumental in fomenting anti-British sentiment in their respective regions. Both men not only cited nationalistic reasons for siding with Nazi Germany, but also offered religious reasons for hoping for an Axis victory. It wasn't so much what the Nazis had to offer them, as much as what the Arabs and Indians would get rid of due to that Nazi victory.

An old Arab proverb states that the enemy of my enemy is my friend. It seems that Bose, as well as other leaders with the same aspirations and background, took this proverb to heart. After traveling through

Afghanistan, Bose crossed the frontiers of what was still neutral USSR and headed towards the German Reich. He arrived in Germany in the beginning of 1941. Bose soon established an office in the heart of Berlin and began to campaign for German recognition of an 'Indian Provisional Government' in exile. Soon the Germans offered Bose and his newly-created 'Centre for a Free India' the status of a provisional government. Bose himself was made 'president of the provisional government of Free India'. This worked hand in glove with Germany's (and Bose's) attempts to undermine the British Empire. Bose's staff grew quickly and soon he was putting out an Indian language newspaper for the Indian community in Europe. He soon expanded this to a radio show that was directed not only at Indians and Arabs in Europe, but in North Africa and the Middle East as well. His themes were always the same: magnifying the negative aspects of British colonial rule while explaining the benefits of an Axis victory. To long oppressed Muslims and Hindus, his arguments seemed to make sense.

It wasn't long before Bose and his adherents were calling for the establishment of the Indian Liberation Army. The first Indian recruits were actually taken into the ranks of the German Army before Bose ever touched foot on German soil. As early as 1940 the German *Abwehr* (Secret Service) had begun recruiting Indian volunteers into their commando regiment (later a division) – the Brandenburg formation. Most of these early volunteers had been rich or well to do privileged Indian university students who had been studying in Germany. Actual recruiting for the 'Indian Liberation Army' began in earnest in September 1941. The initial recruits came from Indian students, businessmen and exiled Indians hiding from the British authorities.

The number of Indians recruited from German universities proved to be a trifle: just ten had volunteered. To this number were added five former Indian POWs who had served in the British Army in North Africa and had been captured. It was with this small group of men that Bose began his newspaper and radio show. In December 1941, Bose made a trip to a German prisoner of war camp, which was located near the town of Annaberg. The camp was home to a large percentage of Indian prisoners of war. These men were rather surprised to see Bose, whom many of them had heard about back home, walking without hindrance. It impressed them that an Indian was allowed to travel freely within Germany. Bose saw this and took the opportunity to explain in great detail his reasons for being in Germany and his desire for an Axis victory over the British. He played heavily on any nationalistic tendencies which he perceived in any recruit. Before he left on the following day, he had won over 100 new volunteers to his cause. He told them that Britain's chokehold over India would end with an Axis victory. It was therefore their duty as Indians and as nationalists, to aid the Germans

Even though the Nazis espoused their theories of the superiority of the Germanic race, to Bose and Rashid Ali al-Gaylani, and all the other non-Germans who rallied to the *Hakenkreuz* (Swastika), it was enough for them that the Germans were fighting Communism, the Jews, French rule or British hegemony. 'The enemy of my enemy is my friend.' That was an adage that became a dictum in the minds of these men. Many would pay with their lives for this, during and after the war. Britain, Bose argued, had used India and her people for the enrichment of the British Empire. Her army had abandoned them to their fate in German POW camps. In all of this, Indian blood was still being spilled in order to keep the English status quo. These were arguments that eventually won Bose an additional 600 volunteers from another POW camp, this one near Frankenberg. By August 1942 these 700 initial recruits had been sent to a new training camp. This camp was specifically erected for the Indian volunteers near Kingsbrook near Dresden, Germany.

Employment of the Regiment

During September 1942 the Indian Legion was accepted into the ranks of the German *Wehrmacht* as *Infanterie-Regiment 950 (indisches)*, or the 950th (Indian) Infantry Regiment. Initially the unit had two battalions. Each battalion was composed of five infantry companies apiece. Even for 1943 German standards, the Indian regiment was magnificently armed and manned. Two years later, as the Third Reich lay in ruins and Hitler was reduced to scratching for arms with which to arm his last German levies, he would complain bitterly about the fact that foreign units were armed with more than one weapon, while German formations were left searching for First World War leftovers or foreign hand-me-downs. In November 1942 its order of battle was as follows:

I. *Bataillon, Infanterie-Regiment 950 (indisches)*
   1. *Kompanie – Vier Infanteriezüge*
   2. *Kompanie – Vier Infanteriezüge*
   3. *Kompanie – Vier Infanteriezüge*
   4. *Kompanie (schwer) – Maschinengewehr Kompanie – Vier Maschinengewehrzüge*
   5. *Kompanie (schwer)* – 1 x 50mm PAK (*Panzerabwehrkanone*), 1 x 150mm *Infanteriegeschütz, Ein Pionierzug und Drei Infanteriezüge*

II. Bataillon, Infanterie-Regiment 950 (indisches)
- *6. Kompanie – Vier Infanteriezüge*
- *7. Kompanie – Vier Infanteriezüge*
- *8. Kompanie – Vier Infanteriezüge*
- *9. Kompanie (schwer) – Maschinengewehr Kompanie Vier Maschinengewehrzüge*
- *10. Kompanie (schwer)* – 1 x 50mm PAK (*Panzerabwehrkanone*), 1 x 150mm *Infanteriegeschütz, Ein Pionierzug und Drei Infanteriezüge*

Total number of volunteers: 2,593
Divided as follows:
1,503 Hindu volunteers
516 Sikh volunteers
497 Muslim volunteers
77 'other' volunteers
Total: 2,593

An additional recruiting drive from the POW camps netted an additional 907 men so that by April 1943 the total strength rose to 3,500 men. This number was equivalent to the size of a small brigade. It was in April that the regiment and its two reinforced infantry battalions were sent to Beverloo in Holland where they were attached to the *16. Luftwaffen-Felddivision.* This too had only recently arrived on the Dutch coast a month before. The Indians were now relegated to guarding a part of Hitler's Atlantic Wall. It was during this time that the regiment experienced its first serious problem. A rebellion broke out within its ranks.

Most of the 170 men of the *3. Kompanie, I. Bataillon* had refused to comply with the order to transfer to Holland. The Germans took great care to settle the situation without causing much harm on the morale of the Indians, but in the end, 47 out of the 170 had to be court-martialled and sent back to POW camps. On 31 August 1943 the regiment was ordered moved further south and became attached to the German *344. Infanterie-Division,* which was on garrison duty around the south-western French city of Bordeaux, by the Bay of Biscay region. By 17 September the transfer was completed, although the *II. Bataillon* did not quite fit itself in until 7 October, when its Headquarters' Company reached the town of Montalivet. *Infanterie-Regiment 950 (indisches)* now received the newly created *III. Bataillon,* and would remain in this region until the beginning of its withdrawal from France in late June-early July 1944. By late 1943 the order of battle looked like this:

Table 7. The Indian Legion, Autumn 1943

Infanterie-Regiment 950 (indisches)	
1.-5 Kompanie	*I. Bataillon*
6.-8. Kompanie	*II. Bataillon*
9.-12. Kompanie	*III. Bataillon*
13. Kompanie (Infanteriegeschütz)	
14. Kompanie (Panzerabwehrkanonen)	
15. Kompanie (Pionier)	
Ehrenkompanie (Honor Guard Company)	

When the *344. Infanterie-Division* withdrew from Bordeaux and was sent to Berck in the Pas de Calais, in the region of *15. Armee,* the Indian Legion remained behind. The *159. Infanterie-Division* replaced the *344. Infanterie-Division* in and around Bordeaux and the Bay of Biscay. The *Infanterie-Regiment 950 (indisches)* was now attached to this new formation. This occurred on 8 January 1944. Thirteen days later, on 21 January the regiment was officially enrolled in the 'Indian National Army'. This was not the fantasy or machinations of some Axis propaganda machine, but a reality that the Japanese Army had brought to fruition. The story dates back to December 1942, when the British Army in Burma and Mayala was in retreat. It was in the northern Malayan town of Alor Star that Major Iwaichi Fujiwara of the Imperial Japanese General Staff interviewed a Sikh POW officer. The officer's name was Major Mohan Singh. Singh agreed to set up a special unit for Indians, Burmese, and Thai volunteers who opposed British and French control of their lands.

Figure 14. The arm patch of the Indian Legion: a springing tiger on a shield background using the national colours (from top to bottom) of orange, white and green. (Author's black and white drawing)

Bose, who was then in Germany, had realised by then that the prospect the Germans would ever reach India was nil. He therefore decided to make a special trip to Japanese-held territory. To Bose, it now seemed that the Japanese had produced a sizeable force that could truly become the core of an Indian Liberation Army. He now hoped to become the titular head of that fledgling army. The battle cry of this new Indian and East Asian force was 'Asia for the Asiatics', which conveniently left the Japanese in the equation.[1] This phrase had been uttered by other pro-Japanese collaborationist forces throughout the Empire of Japan and was obviously part of a calculated propaganda campaign by the Japanese. To the credit of the Japanese, this new force would eventually number some 33,000 men split into three divisions. These three divisions would fight alongside Japanese troops although their morale was always low and their ranks thinned by desertions.

It was into this 'Indian National Army' that *Infanterie-Regiment 950 (indisches)* was officially and ceremoniously inducted in early 1944. However, this decision, geared for its propaganda purposes, and possibly to raise the morale of the volunteers, did not have the desired effect. By late 1944 it was apparent to the whole world that the Axis were going to lose the war. German propaganda photographs of Indian volunteers in German uniform brought little hope to ordinary Indians that Germany would free them from British rule. As a result, the reason why the Germans had allowed the regiment to be raised – for propaganda purposes – no longer existed. There were no plans to transfer the regiment to Burma, where the Indian National Army was fighting. It had taken special preparations just to carry Subhas Chandra Bose and a small staff by submarine to Japanese-held territory.[2] There was no question that a surface vessel could make it past Allied fleets. By 1944 the German submarine force was also in retreat. It was thus decided that the regiment had to remain in Europe. To the Germans, disbanding a full-strength combat unit in 1944 seemed heretical. In addition, the ever-present chance of an Allied invasion seemed to loom ever closer, and the German Army in France needed every man possible to man the Atlantic Wall.

The spring of 1944 proved uneventful for the men of the *Infanterie-Regiment 950 (indisches)*. However, one particularly motivated company within the Regiment, the *9. Kompanie,* requested to be posted to the Italian front in early May 1944. Surprisingly, the commander of the regiment, *Oberstleutnant* Kurt Krappe, approved the transfer, believing that the unit was the best and most motivated company in the Legion. Three officers, two of whom were German and one Indian, *Leutnant* Jaswat Singh Bindra, led it. One of the German officers was named *Leutnant* A. Opitz.[3] The company had an authorised strength of 199 NCO's and enlisted men, which was almost double the principal strength of a German front-line company by 1944 standards. By 26 May 1944 the *9. Kompanie* was located in the Mailla Mountain range, just south of Chieti. It later moved to Pescara where it was attached to the *Fusilier Bataillon* of the *278. Infanterie-Division.*[4]

The company was employed against the British 5th Corps and Polish 2nd Corps. Specifically, Bindra requested that the unit be placed against any British and Indian Allied formation. It eventually confronted and fought a British formation and elements of the 8th Indian and later the 4th Indian Division. This occurred in late May and throughout June 1944. Towards the end of June, the unit was pulled from the front lines and used for anti-partisan sweeps in and around the rear area of the German Gothic Line. During these operations, the company lost no men. In July the unit withdrew to Pesaro, south of Rimini, then to Pistoia and La Spezia. It remained in Ravenna in the autumn of 1944 performing security duty between the Ravenna-Ferrara Road and rail line until April 1945 when the front line collapsed. In this month eight to ten Indian volunteers in the *9. Kompanie* were wounded near Comacchio due to an enemy strafing attack. Shortly afterwards the company was caught by advancing allied forces and forced to surrender.

Meanwhile, garrison duty in France had proved relatively easy for the Legion's volunteers, and many of the men had the opportunity of going on short furloughs to Paris and other parts of France. This included scenic tours and the chance to meet or purchase female companionship and drink – things that were very important for soldiers. This all chnaged, however, when the Allies landed on Normandy on 6 June 1944 and began the invasion of France. Acting on the orders of British SOE operatives, the French *Maquisards* went into action all across France. The region of Bordeaux was no exception. It was in June that the first Indian volunteers from the regiment were lost to French guerrilla forces. In July 1944 the Indian regiment was finally ordered withdrawn from France. It was decided not to commit the regiment since the consensus within the German cadre staff was that the regiment would collapse from desertions and low morale.

The withdrawal of the regiment finally cost about forty Indian lives to French guerrilla attacks before they reached Dijon, a staging area on their withdrawal into Germany. The Free French Forces of General de Gaulle took Dijon itself in early September 1944. Worse still for the regiment, during the withdrawal from France, about 250 Indian volunteers had either surrendered or deserted to the French guerrillas. The morale of the Indian regiment was at an all-time low. Defeat loomed in the background and the volunteers knew it. For those men who surrendered, their pragmatism proved fatal to some of the Indian turncoats. Of the 250 who tried their lot with the French, some 29 were shot outright, while the rest were handed over to the British Army for punishment.[5]

On 8 August 1944 at Heuberg, the Indian regiment was transferred into the ranks of the *Waffen-SS*. Like the Cossacks of the German Army, this transfer proved to be only a 'paper' formality. Heinrich Himmler had been placed in charge of the Replacement Army after the attempt on Hitler's life on 20 July 1944. This allowed him the added leverage to acquire almost all of the foreign volunteer formations in the *Heer* into his private SS kingdom. Another force that was inducted into the *Waffen-SS* for supply, support and payment purposes was the *Serbisches Freiwilligen-Korps*. Like the Cossacks and the Indians, their uniform did not change. The title of the regiment changed one more time. The unit was now to be known as *Indische Legion der SS*.[6] Some SS officers were indeed assigned to the regiment, but *Heer* (Army) officers and army uniforms remained in use, with the exception of the SS officers now placed on staff. The officer roster for the Legion looked as follows on 6 March 1945:

> Commander: *SS-Standartenführer* Kurt Krappe, born on 15 July 1899, and promoted to his SS rank on 1 November 1944.
> IIa (Operations Officer): *SS-Obersturmführer* Hellmuth Starcke, born on 28 October 1905, and promoted to current rank on 1 October 1942.
> *I. Bataillon* CO: *Hauptmann* Adolf Scharwachter, born on 3 December 1914, and promoted to current rank on 1 February 1944.
> *II. Bataillon* CO: *Hauptmann* Karl Hamerl, born on 24 October 1917, and promoted to current rank on 1 December 1944.
> *III. Bataillon* CO: *Hauptmann* Hans Kutscher, born on 14 December 1911, and promoted to current rank on 1 August 1944.
> *Ersatz und Ausbildungs Bataillon* CO: *Hauptmann* Theodor Glodig, born on 27 May 1895, and promoted to current rank on 22 November 1940.[7]

The SS High Command had plans to eventually outfit the entire unit in SS uniforms. In fact, proof that this even began to take shape did not come out into the public eye until the summer of 1995, when David Littlejohn published a small but important article regarding this matter.[8] In it he revealed for the first time that indeed at least one SS officer in the Indian Legion had worn a right collar tab that had been designed by the *Waffen-SS* specifically for the *Indische Legion der SS*. It was the head of a tiger on silver thread, with the characteristic black cloth background that was so typical of the collar tabs of all *Waffen-SS* units.[9] The *Indische Legion der SS* went into relative obscurity from the autumn of 1944 until it was brought out in a conversation which occurred at Hitler's headquarters during a conference held on 24 March 1945. This was about six weeks before the end of the war. During this palaver Hitler became frustrated when told that not enough weapons were available for the new units that were being formed. When told that some foreign units had been armed before German ones, he complained that certain foreign formations were 'resting all the time and never fighting!' The transcript of the conversation is, in my opinion, a fitting end-piece to the story of the Indian volunteers:[10]

Hitler: '. . . I can't raise German divisions because I don't have any weapons. I'd rather just raise a German division and give it all those weapons.'
General Wilhelm Burgdorff: 'The Indian Legion!'
Hitler: 'The Indian Legion is a joke. There are Indians who can't kill a louse, who'd rather let them be eaten up. They won't kill Englishman either. I consider it nonsense purposely to put them opposite the English. Why should the Indians be braver in our service than they were under Bose in India? They used Indian units under Bose's leadership in Burma for the purpose of freeing India from the British. They ran away like a bunch of sheep!
Why should they be braver here? I think that if we used the Indians to turn prayer mills or for something of that sort, they would be the most indefatigable soldiers in the world. But to use them for a real death struggle is ridiculous. How strong are the Indians? But it's all nonsense. If you have the surplus of weapons, such jokes for propaganda purposes are entirely irresponsible.'
SS-Sturmbannführer Johannes Göhler 'The Indian Legion has a strength of 2,300 men.'
Hitler: 'We would be doing them the greatest favour if we told them that they don't have to fight anymore.'
Göhler 'They have 1,468 rifles, 550 pistols, 420 submachine-guns, 200 light machine-pistols . . .'
Hitler: 'Just imagine, they have more weapons than men. Some of their people must carry two weapons.'
Göhler '. . . Twenty-four heavy machine guns, 20 medium mortars, 4 light howitzers, 6 light infantry howitzers, 6 anti-tank guns, it doesn't say what kind, 700 horses, 81 vehicles, 61 passenger cars, 5 motorcycles, 12 prime movers, of which 11 are ready for use.'
Hitler: 'What is the Indian Legion supposed to be doing?'
Göhler 'I can't say. They've been resting for quite some time.'
Hitler: 'But they've never been in battle!'
Göhler 'No.'

> Hitler: 'A unit which is in a rest area should, in my opinion, be a unit that has seen heavy fighting and is being refreshed. These outfits of yours are always refreshing and never fighting!'

Indeed, the unit was considered such a joke that when *SS-Oberführer* Heinz Bertling was appointed to command it in August 1944,[11] he failed to show up for his command out of lack of interest! In the end, *Oberstleutnant* Kurt Krappe was given the rank of *SS-Standartenführer* and continued to command the unit. In May 1945, after a failed attempt to cross over into neutral Switzerland, the Indian volunteers and German cadre staff quietly turned themselves over to US Army and French units. It was during this time that apparently some Indian volunteers were shot by French forces for having committed some crimes in France. The rest were eventually turned over to the British for punishment. So ended the history of the Indian Legion. In the end, they owned up to their springing tiger emblem by being 'paper tigers'. Their propaganda value however, should not be minimised.

Arab and North African Volunteers in the German Armed Forces, 1941–1945

Sonderstab F was initially established with the strategic objective of supporting the 1941 Iraqi uprising against British forces. Although the effort to mobilise the Iraqi Army failed, the framework laid the groundwork for Germany's later attempts to recruit Arab volunteers into the *Wehrmacht.* By 1942, these volunteers were deployed only temporarily in southern Russia during *Fall Blau,* serving alongside German units in the Caucasus campaign. Units such as *Sonderverbänd 287,* including both German and Arab personnel, were assigned to the left flank of the *1. Panzerarmee* near Kuma and the Nogaye Steppe. Their employment was limited by the short duration of operations and the eventual retreat of the German Army from the Caucasus, yet these early deployments allowed the Germans to test their ability to integrate Arab recruits into mobile formations, while also providing experience for future operations in North Africa.

In North Africa, the Germans organised several specialised battalions composed of Arabs and North Africans. The first of these was the *Deutsch-Arabisches Ausbildungs Bataillon,* or German-Arab Training Battalion, which trained volunteers in infantry tactics, guerrilla warfare and, in some cases, parachute operations. By late 1942, the battalion had been sent to Tunisia, where it began recruiting local volunteers under the supervision of *Oberstleutnant* Meyer-Ricks and *Hauptmann*

Schober. The battalion eventually evolved into the *Deutsche Arabisches Infanterie Bataillon 845*, which became operational under *Sonderstab F*, which was now being referred to as *Generalkommando z.b.V. F.*

The 845th was structured with four primary companies and, at its peak, numbered approximately 1,200 men, although some 2,200 men eventually passed through its ranks. Volunteers came from a wide array of regions: Tunisians, Moroccans, Algerians, Egyptians, Syrians, Iraqis, Lebanese and desert Arabs such as Senussi and Tuaregs. A smaller contingent of Arab paratroopers was trained alongside German *Fallschirmjäger* units in Tunisia. That Arab parachute company eventually performed operations on the Eastern Front and in the defence of Berlin in 1945 under *9. Fallschirmjäger-Division*. Five German ex-Foreign Legionnaires were often attached to each company as NCOs, ensuring that operational standards were maintained despite the diverse backgrounds of the recruits.

The battalion's operational record in Greece illustrates both the potential and limitations of these formations. In 1945 the battalion was assigned to the German *41. Festungs-Division*. The *Deutsche Arabisches Infanterie Bataillon 845* conducted anti-partisan operations against the 2nd ELAS Division in the Helicon Mountain range and along the Gulf of Corinth. In April 1944, the battalion participated in a coordinated attack with 3,000–4,000 German and Italian troops, advancing from landing points at Zaltsa and Ayii Saranda Bay toward Kyriaki, Distomo, and Chostia. Despite facing steep terrain, determined partisan resistance and harsh weather, the battalion distinguished itself in both combat and rearguard operations. Accounts from officers such as *Hauptmann* von Voss highlight both the bravery and the cultural challenges presented by the Arab volunteers. Incidents of individual initiative, such as rescuing fellow officers across rivers, demonstrated adaptability and courage, while disciplinary challenges reflected cultural differences and the psychological stresses of prolonged conflict. These stories, often anecdotal, paint a nuanced picture of a unit that was both unconventional and effective within its limited scope.

During the retreat through the Balkans in late 1944, the battalion continued to provide rearguard coverage, delaying partisan advances while German forces withdrew toward Yugoslavia. The unit suffered attrition from combat, harsh conditions and desertions. The same occurred along the Oder River in 1945 among parachute-trained volunteers who joined *Fallschirmjäger-Regiment 25* under *Major* Gerhard Schacht. Nonetheless, the remaining battalion elements participated in operations in Bosnia-Herzegovina and Syrmia, ultimately being captured near Zagreb in April 1945. The Arab recruits were detained in

POW camps under Yugoslav control and released after approximately one year, returning to their countries of origin.

The Germans also organised a second Arab battalion in Austria at the Döllersheim Training Area, designated *II. Bataillon der Deutsch Arabische Infanterie-Bataillon 845*. Though it never reached the front in full strength, it trained volunteers in infantry and guerrilla tactics and included an Arab parachute company, highlighting the emphasis placed on specialised training for select recruits.

While German commanders occasionally employed these volunteers in front-line operations, the overall military contribution was minimal. Roughly 6,000 Arab and North African volunteers served under German command between 1941 and 1945, alongside additional recruits under Vichy French authority. The limitations were clear: shortages of weapons, uniforms and experienced officers, combined with the small size of the units and the short duration of their deployment, constrained operational effectiveness. Their combat value was limited to localised engagements, rearguard actions, and anti-partisan campaigns rather than strategic operations. Yet, their symbolic and political significance outweighed their battlefield performance. German propaganda exploited the presence of Arabs in *Wehrmacht* uniforms, portraying the Third Reich as a champion of Arab independence and a liberator from Anglo-French colonial rule. Newsreels, photographs and internal reports emphasised the Arab volunteers' commitment, cultivating the image of a broader anti-imperialist coalition aligned with Germany. In this sense, the volunteers served as a tool of political influence, lending weight to propaganda narratives and bolstering the Reich's claim of pan-Arab support.

The campaign in Tunisia during early 1943 marked the high point of Arab recruitment under the Germans. Within weeks, five battalions – approximately a small brigade – were raised under difficult wartime conditions. These units freed German forces for front-line service while simultaneously providing a political and symbolic presence in North Africa. Had strategic conditions been different – had the Middle East fallen to Axis control, or had Germany possessed sufficient resources – the potential for larger Arab formations may have been realised. In reality, the battalions remained small, strategically marginal, and largely symbolic, serving primarily as a propaganda instrument rather than a decisive military force.

In conclusion, Arab and North African volunteers in the German Armed Forces exemplify the intersection of military necessity and political imagination. While their combat impact was minimal, their symbolic value was significant. They offered the Reich the illusion of a pan-Arab coalition and allowed German propaganda to project influence in distant regions, amplifying perceived Axis support. The envisioned pro-German Arab army remained unrealised, but its presence – however limited – reflected the broader strategic and political ambitions of Nazi Germany in the Middle East and North Africa.

Summary of Units, Movements, and Commanders

The principal Arab and North African formations raised by Germany between 1941 and 1945 consisted primarily of the *Deutsche Arabisches Infanterie Bataillon 845* and the German-Arab Training Battalion, along with several smaller North African battalions formed in Tunisia. The German-Arab Training Battalion was initially organised at *Truppenübungsplatz Döberitz* and later partially deployed to Stalino in southern Russia under *Sonderstab F.* It comprised three battalions: *I.* and *II. Panzergrenadier Bataillone*, which entered combat in the Caucasus, and *III. Bataillon*, the German-Arab training unit, which would later be sent to the Mediterranean theatre. Commanded at the corps level by *General der Flieger* Helmuth Felmy, the unit included hundreds of Arab volunteers recruited locally in North Africa as well as from Arabs living in occupied Europe.

The *Deutsche Arabisches Infanterie Bataillon 845*, formally organised at Döllersheim in Austria in 1943, initially contained four companies and numbered approximately 1,200 men. It trained volunteers in basic infantry tactics, with emphasis on fighting guerrillas. Its first operational deployment occurred in Tunisia under the supervision of *Oberstleutnant* Meyer-Ricks and *Hauptmann* Schober. Several Arab battalions were regionally recruited from Moroccans, Tunisians, and Algerians, while a smaller number of Egyptians, Syrians, Iraqis, Lebanese, and desert Arabs were also incorporated. The Arab parachute company, attached to Major Witzig's *Fallschirmjäger-Pionier-Bataillon*, later saw combat on the Eastern Front during the defence of Berlin in 1945.

Following the North African campaign, the 845th was transferred to Greece, where it fell under the command of the *41. Festungs-Division*. It participated in anti-partisan operations in the Helicon Mountains and the Peloponnese under the supervision of local company commanders such as *Hauptmann* von Voss. During the retreat from southern Greece through the Balkans, the battalion provided rearguard coverage in Macedonia, Bosnia-Herzegovina and Croatia, sustaining losses but maintaining cohesion and morale despite harsh conditions and partisan attacks. A second battalion, *II. Bataillon der Deutsche Arabische*

Infanterie-Bataillon 845, was raised at Zwettl near Döllersheim in September 1944 and underwent training before being dissolved in January 1945, with its men redistributed to reinforce the original 845th.

As previously stated, several smaller North African battalions, recruited in Tunisia, served under German supervision for rear-area security and construction tasks, freeing German combat troops for front-line service. These units were typically organised into three infantry companies and a heavy weapons company. German officers and NCOs led them. Each battalion numbered between 500 and 700 men each. Although they were rarely employed in direct combat, they performed guard duties along the coast, protected supply depots, and maintained order in liberated areas. The German-Arab recruiting network, centred in Paris and Tunisia, also provided intelligence support and facilitated the creation of new companies whenever local volunteers came forward.

Overall, these units were limited in size and scope. While *Deutsche Arabisches Infanterie-Bataillon 845* remained the most significant formation, the combination of logistical constraints, training limitations, and the overstretched Axis front prevented the creation of a fully operational Arab or North African corps. Nevertheless, the strategic vision behind these units – whether in Russia, North Africa, or the Balkans – underscored Germany's attempt to leverage local support for both military and propaganda purposes. German commanders recognised the tactical value of their Arab and North African recruits, especially in guerrilla warfare, rearguard actions and the protection of lines of communication. The political and symbolic significance of their presence, however, far exceeded any direct military effect.

Note: For a full history of the Arab and North African volunteers in the German Army, please refer to *Hitler's Muslim Allies: German Army and Waffen-SS Islamic Volunteers, 1941-1945* by Frontline Books (an imprint of Pen & Sword), 2025.

Chapter 7

THE 'PROPAGANDA LEGIONS' 1941–1945, PART 2

The *13. Waffen-Gebirgs-Division der SS 'Handschar'*: Propaganda Triumph, Military Mediocrity

On 10 February 1943, Adolf Hitler formally approved the creation of a Muslim *Waffen-SS* division, and three days later, Heinrich Himmler directed *SS-Gruppenführer und Generalleutnant der Waffen-SS* Artur Phleps, commander of the ethnic-German *7. SS-Freiwilligen-Gebirgs-Division 'Prinz Eugen'*, to raise the unit. Phleps, himself an ethnic German from Romania, was assisted by NCOs and officers from the *'Prinz Eugen'* division to organise the new formation, initially referred to as the *Kroatische SS-Freiwilligen-Division* (Croatian SS Volunteer Division). By 19 February, Phleps had begun establishing a formation staff, and shortly thereafter, a meeting was held between Ante Pavelić, the Croatian fascist *Poglavnik* (Leader), Phleps and *SS-Brigadeführer* Konstantine Kammerhofer, Himmler's representative in Croatia.

Pavelić, though outwardly compliant, was furious that thousands of his subjects were to be conscripted into a foreign military organisation without his consent. Recognising his dependence on German and Italian military support, however, he acquiesced but sought to undermine the effort covertly. His first action was to demand that the new SS formation bear the title *'SS Ustaše Division Hrvatska'* to assert some nominal control, a request initially granted but later ignored by the Germans. Pavelić then warned Croatian Muslims that enlisting in the *Waffen-SS* would result in either service in the Croatian Army or imprisonment, a tactic which effectively stalled recruitment.

Despite Himmler's order for substantial funding, by March and April 1943 the number of recruits was far below target. Investigations revealed that the Croatian regime's active sabotage was the principal cause. Himmler's outrage prompted Kammerhofer to remind Pavelić of Croatia's strategic vulnerability and reliance on German support, and the recruiting campaign resumed. However, the damage had been done: recruitment lagged, and by July 1943, only enough recruits had been gathered for formal training to begin. The division was then given its first official title, *Kroatische SS-Freiwilligen-Gebirgs-Division*, and later *Handschar*, referencing the scimitar, a curved, single-edged sword traditionally associated with Muslim soldiers.

Special accommodations were made for the predominantly Bosnian Muslim recruits. They were permitted to practice Islam, and the division established imams and mullahs for each regiment, alongside religious schools in Göttingen and Dresden for training clergy. The right collar tab of the uniform featured a swastika and scimitar, while the left denoted rank. The officer corps, however, remained predominantly German or ethnic German, including officers from Hungary who served as interpreters. These arrangements reflected the Germans' attempts to balance ideological racial doctrines with pragmatic military needs, though tensions between German officers and Muslim recruits were inevitable.

Training proceeded initially in France to prevent Croatian interference and partisan disruptions. Herbert von Obwurzer, appointed in April 1943, initially oversaw recruitment and formation but was replaced in August by Major Karl Gustav Sauberzweig, who joined the *Waffen-SS* voluntarily and assumed full command. Tensions within the unit were exacerbated by discriminatory treatment, compounded by communist agents spreading rumours that the division would fight the Western Allies. This misinformation, coupled with forced conscription, led to the first *Waffen-SS* mutiny in history on 16–17 September 1943 in Villefranche-de-Rouergue. There, the 1,000-man engineer battalion rebelled, killing twenty German officers and NCOs. Reprisals were swift: fourteen ringleaders were executed, 825 soldiers were sent to Dachau concentration camp, and a replacement unit was established for penal service in Russia.

By October 1943, the division had 21,065 personnel, including 360 officers, 1,931 NCOs, and 18,774 enlisted men. It was redesignated as the *13. SS-Freiwilligen-Bosnien-Herzegowinen-Gebirgs-Division (Kroatien Nr. 1)*, with regiments renumbered to reflect non-Germanic status: *Waffen-Gebirgsjäger-Regiment der SS 27 (kroatische Nr. 1)* and *Waffen-Gebirgsjäger-Regiment der SS 28 (kroatische Nr. 2)*. A German press release in January 1944 emphasised the division's role in combating Bolshevism and highlighted the spiritual support of the Mufti of Jerusalem, though no mention was made of the mutiny or recruitment difficulties.

The division returned to Bosnia in February 1944, where it was assigned to the German 2. *Panzerarmee* alongside the *392.* (*Kroatische*) *Infanterie-Division*, the *42. Jäger-Division*, and the *Panzergrenadier-Division Brandenburg*. Its headquarters was initially in Vinkovci, later moving south of Brcko. The division participated in operations against partisan forces, including *Unternehmen Osterei* (Operation Easter Egg) in April 1944, targeting the 3rd Proletarian Corps, and *Unternehmen Maibaum I* (Operation Maypole I) later that month, focusing on remnants of the 17th Partisan Division north-east of Sarajevo. Operational control alternated between *V. SS-Freiwilligen-Gebirgskorps* and direct orders from *2. Panzerarmee,* while the *Handschar* SS division coordinated alongside the *7. SS-Freiwilligen-Gebirgs-Division 'Prinz Eugen'*.

Combat operations were costly. By September 1944, the division had suffered 7,000 casualties, including approximately 3,000 desertions, averaging roughly 1,000 men lost per month. Losses reflected both operational intensity and low morale, exacerbated by conscription, German mistreatment, and prior communist agitation. Despite being ostensibly raised to defend their homeland, the Bosnian Muslim recruits exhibited minimal enthusiasm, and overall combat effectiveness remained mediocre. This was not what Heinrich Himmler had hoped for. Instead of raising a ferocious anti-communist and anti-Semitic SS division made up of Muslims, he got a mediocre division with little desire to fight.

Efforts to raise a second Muslim SS division, *Kama,* were hampered by similar recruitment challenges. *Handschar*'s men, equipment, and sub-units, including the *13. SS-Aufklärungs-Abteilung* and *SS-Flak-Abteilung 13,* were partially diverted to form the new division, further weakening *Handschar*. Subsequent anti-partisan operations in July and August 1944 – *Vollmund* (Full Moon), *Unternehmen Fliegenfänger* (Operation Flycatcher), and *Unternehmen Hackfleisch* (Operation Mincemeat) – continued to erode the division's strength. By December 1944, total personnel had dwindled to 12,793, prompting the decision to disband the division. Remaining German and ethnic-German elements were reconstituted as *Kampfgruppe Handschar,* reinforced by 3,000 naval personnel, but the division itself ceased to function as a coherent formation.

The trajectory of the *13. Waffen-Gebirgs-Division der SS Handschar* illustrates the limits of Nazi propaganda in translating ideological and logistical efforts into effective military performance. From the outset, the division was a product of both German opportunism and Croatian obstructionism. Pavelić's covert sabotage, the communist infiltration and mutiny, and the structural inadequacies of the officer corps all contributed to substandard operational performance. Even the Mufti of Jerusalem's symbolic presence and the extensive accommodations granted to the Muslim recruits – religious observances, dietary considerations, specialised insignia, and schools – were insufficient to overcome fundamental flaws.

Ultimately, the division's formation served the Nazis more as a propaganda coup than a combat asset. It allowed Joseph Goebbels and the German press to display ostensibly loyal Muslim volunteers aligned with the Reich, bolstering the image of SS internationalism and ideological reach. In reality, the unit's effectiveness was severely limited by desertions, poor morale and leadership deficits. Even as late as 1944, the Germans struggled to recruit additional personnel, and the disbandment of *Handschar* marked the failure of the *Waffen-SS* to capitalise on Bosnia's manpower. The *Handschar* Division, therefore, stands as a historical example of the gap between Nazi ideological ambition and practical military reality: while it provided propaganda value and temporary operational support, the division never achieved the strategic significance its creators had envisioned. The *13. Waffen-Gebirgs-Division der SS Handschar* lasted less than a year in combat – from March to December 1944. Its history underscores the complexity and pitfalls of raising foreign volunteer units under coercion and ideological manipulation. Its story is one of propaganda success and operational mediocrity, highlighting how political, cultural, and human factors can frustrate even the most meticulous military planning. The *Handschar* division may have existed on paper as a symbol of Nazi reach, but its battlefield record and internal dysfunction reveal the inherent limitations of forced multinational formations in sustaining effective combat power.

The *Kaukasischer Waffen-Verbände der SS:* Propaganda Over Combat

As Germany's fortunes declined in 1944–5, the Third Reich turned increasingly to pragmatic military expediency, raising units from non-Aryan volunteers to supplement its depleted forces. Among these was the *Kaukasischer Waffen-Verbände der SS*, a Caucasian SS cavalry brigade formed from Muslim volunteers of the Soviet Union. The brigade never saw combat, but its story illustrates the Nazi approach: a unit more valuable for propaganda than battlefield utility. The formation emerged from the Volunteer Cadre Division in France, created to supply trained men to eastern volunteer battalions, Russian and Cossack units, and even the *162. (Turkestanische) Infanterie-Division*. By early 1944, France housed the divisional headquarters in Lyon, administering five regiments segregated by nationality. In late 1944,

General Andrei Vlasov of the Russian Liberation Army attempted to assert control over all Soviet volunteers, but Caucasian leaders insisted on autonomy, recognising Vlasov only as head of a Russian movement.

The SS cavalry brigade was commanded by *SS-Standartenführer der Reserve* Arved Theuermann, a Russian-born ethnic German with extensive military experience in the Tsarist Army, the Baltic *Landwehr*, and later Nazi paramilitary organisations, including the SA and SS. Theuermann's selection reflected his language skills and prior service in the Caucasus under the SS & Police command. Assisting him was *SS-Obersturmbannführer* Walter Blume, tasked with organising regimental commanders, including *Waffen-Obersturmbannführer der SS* Israfil Bey (Azerbaijanis), *Waffen-Obersturmbannführer der SS* Kutschuk Ulagaj (North Caucasians), *Waffen-Obersturmbannführer der SS* Michael Pridon Zulukidse (Georgians), and *Waffen-Obersturmbannführer der SS* V. Sarkisjan (Armenians). Each regiment contained two cavalry battalions, though some sources suggest the North Caucasian and Georgian regiments may have included a third battalion.

Training was conducted primarily by replacement battalions of the *8. SS Kavalleriedivision 'Florian Geyer'* and *22. SS Freiwilligen-Kavalleriedivision 'Maria Theresa'*. By late 1944, regiments were in northern Italy, notably Paluzza, with the brigade's strength roughly 4,800–5,000 men, plus approximately 2,000 dependents. Many volunteers arrived from German POW and labour camps, with SS estimates suggesting tens of thousands of potential Caucasian recruits, though attrition through desertion, death, or reassignment reduced the effective pool. Individual officers highlighted the unit's unique composition. Ulagaj, a Circassian, had served in the Tsarist and Albanian armies and volunteered for the Germans in 1944, rescuing Tscherim Soobzokov, a Circassian who had avoided execution after deserting a German battalion, by offering him a position in the brigade. Prince Zulukidse, a Georgian, had fought in multiple anti-Bolshevik campaigns, served in the Vichy French Army, and trained Georgian volunteers in the SS.

Bey's records are sparse, but he commanded Azerbaijani volunteers and survived the war with his family. Despite the formal structure, the brigade never achieved combat readiness. By early 1945, it remained stationed in northern Italy, still in the process of formation, untested against either the Red Army or the Western Allies. Individual battalions occasionally participated in minor security duties, but the unit as a whole was largely administrative. Notably, in late April 1945, Prince Zulukidse surrendered the *III. Kavallerie-Abteilung* to Italian partisans – a battalion exceeding the official organisation – underscoring confusion and the largely symbolic nature of the brigade. The post-war experience of brigade members, particularly Soobzokov, reflects the broader context of non-German SS volunteers. While interrogated decades later for alleged war crimes, evidence confirms that the brigade never engaged in combat or atrocities. Its primary function was to demonstrate, for propaganda purposes, the alleged willingness of Caucasian peoples to join the German cause against the Soviets. In sum, the *Kaukasischer Waffen-Verbände der SS* was emblematic of late-war SS formations: meticulously organised on paper, staffed by experienced officers and motivated volunteers, yet lacking any meaningful military impact. Its value lay in propaganda – highlighting the diversity of anti-Soviet volunteers – rather than battlefield contribution. Militarily, the brigade was not worth the effort required to raise it, but politically, it provided a symbolic win for the Third Reich in the desperate final months of the Second World War. In spite of this, the Germans intended to employ the brigade had the war lasted longer, but its combat value would have been insignificant.

Note: For a full history of the *Kaukasischer Waffen-Verbände der SS*, please refer to *Hitler's Muslim Allies: German Army and Waffen-SS Islamic Volunteers, 1941-1945* by Frontline Books (an imprint of Pen & Sword), 2025.

The *Waffen-Gebirgsjäger-Brigade der SS (tatarische Nr. 1)*

Origins

This unit originated from early Crimean Tartar volunteer auxiliary companies raised in the Crimea in late 1941. Opposition to the Soviet regime among Muslim populations in the USSR – including Uzbeks, Kazaks, Kirghiz, Crimean Tartars and Caucasian peoples – predated the German invasion. Many émigrés, such as Mustafa Chokai, Osman Khoja (Togan), Kayum Khan, and Crimean intellectuals Jafar Krimer and Cafar Seydahmet, sought regional independence rather than a restoration of the Romanov monarchy. They distrusted all Russian governments, whether communist, monarchist or democratic, and resisted inclusion in Vlasov's *Komitet osvobozhdeniya narodov Rossii* (KONR – Russian Liberation Army), with few non-Russian ethnic groups accepting significant roles. German promises of self-determination stirred these populations into cooperation. Alfred Rosenberg's *Ostministerium* helped organise independence committees, though these were largely symbolic. Hitler initially intended to depopulate Crimea of Tartars, but Himmler advised postponing this until after the war to avoid alienating pro-German locals.

Early Volunteer Units

The first Crimean volunteers were organised in October 1941 under the auspices of the German *22. Infanterie-Division*. These units were created as local militias, lightly armed and tasked with village policing. By January 1942, the SD began forming Tatar self-defence companies in key towns such as Karassubasar, Simferopol, and Yalta. These companies expanded into six, and eventually eight, battalions under SD guidance before being transferred to *Ordnungspolizei* (Order Police) administration:

Schutzmannschaft-Bataillonen 147–154

These units served primarily as anti-partisan forces, with nationalist leaders viewing them as the nucleus of a potential Crimean army.

Forming the **Waffen-Gebirgsjäger-Regiment der SS (Tatarische Nr. 1)**

In March–April 1944, remaining effective Tartar battalions were consolidated into a three-battalion SS mountain regiment under German command. The regiment first saw action on 11 April 1944 at Dzahankoy, supporting Romanian defences alongside the 10th and 19th Romanian Infantry Divisions. By 14 April, Axis forces had retreated to Barangar south of Simferopol. The regiment later defended positions north of Simferopol and was withdrawn to Romania in early May 1944. During this evacuation, Germany managed to rescue 36,000 Germans, 3,800 POWs, 16,000 Eastern Legion volunteers, 1,600 Crimean civilians, and 9,600 Romanians. Post-war Soviet accounts estimate 15–20,000 Crimean Tartars served in German forces, though the actual number was closer to 5,000.

The **Waffen Gebirgs-Brigade der SS (Tatarische Nr. 1)**

Himmler instructed *SS-Brigadeführer* Konrad Hitschler to supply 200 ethnic-German *Ordnungspolizei* members for the formation of the Tartar SS brigade. *SS-Sturmbannführer* Dr. Heinz Thumstäder served as brigade medical officer. The brigade also included auxiliary *Hilfswilliger* support personnel. By 20 September 1944, authorised strength was 3,434 men (67 officers, 440 NCOs, 2,927 enlisted men, 614 auxiliaries), but actual strength was 2,421 (11 officers, 191 NCOs, 2,219 enlisted men), including 1,097 *Volksdeutsche*. Morale was low, affected by the withdrawal from Crimea, awareness of Germany's strategic decline and poor administration. Defections had already occurred among Tatar volunteers, some of whom had served in the *1. Ostmuselmanisches SS-Regiment* in Belarus.

In late 1944, the brigade was disbanded and reformed as a two-battalion regiment within the *Osttürkischer Waffenverband der SS*. Earlier plans to absorb the Kalmyk Cavalry Corps were abandoned due to opposition from German officers and Kalmyks; the latter were transferred to the Kosaken-Kavallerie-Korps in 1945. The Tartar regiment retained two infantry battalions of four companies each, along with a regimental anti-tank company and an infantry gun company. The unit moved to *SS-Truppenübungsplatz Kurmark*, near Frankfurt, in mid-to-late December 1944. Ethnic Germans remained at Kurmark to reinforce other *Waffen-SS* units. While the brigade's combat effectiveness was limited, it served as both a propaganda tool and a localised defensive force. Its formation illustrates German reliance on non-Russian volunteers from the Soviet Union, though chronic low morale, administrative mismanagement, and Germany's deteriorating strategic position undermined its operational value.

Note: For a full history of the *Kaukasischer Waffen-Verbände der SS*, please refer to *'Hitler's Muslim Allies: German Army and Waffen-SS Islamic Volunteers, 1941-1945'* by Frontline Books (an imprint of Pen & Sword), 2025.

The *Osttürkischer-Waffen-Verbände der SS*

Toward the end of 1943, the SS-FHA, in cooperation with the RSHA, began plans to raise a Turkic Muslim SS division. Himmler, impressed by the fighting prowess of Turkic volunteers – who had resisted to the last man at Stalingrad and distinguished themselves in the Caucasus and near Kharkov – endorsed the project. Key proponents included Dr. Reiner Olzscha, a physician in the SS fascinated by the East, and Major Andreas Meyer-Mader, a German Army officer experienced in commanding Turkic battalions and familiar with Eastern cultures through prior service in China. Meyer-Mader transferred into the *Waffen-SS* in order to obtain a post leading Turkic troops. The Germans sought to harness Turkestani resentment toward Stalinism, given the Soviet suppression of religion, language, and personal freedoms. Approximately 50,000 Turkestani men fought for Germany, with 12,000 wounded and only around 3,000 deserting – mostly to anti-German partisan forces rather than the Soviets.

In November 1943, Meyer-Mader met with Himmler, who then sought the endorsement of the Grand Mufti of Jerusalem, Haj Amin al-Husseini, to lend religious and political legitimacy to the division. Meyer-Mader was appointed head of the proposed *Muselmanische SS-Division Neu-Turkistan*, promoted to *SS-Obersturmbannführer* effective 1 January 1944. Meetings in December 1943 and January 1944 finalised the recruitment plan, drawing men from the disbanded *Turkestanisches Infanterie-Bataillonen 450, 480, I./94*, and the unit began assembling near Poniatowa, Poland, with divisional headquarters in Lublin and training at Trawniki. By mid-January 1944, Meyer-Mader had recruited about 3,000 men from Turkestan, Azerbaijan, Kirghiz, Uzbek, and Tadzhik populations, forming the *1. Ostmuselmanisches SS-Regiment*. Volunteers were motivated variably by religious loyalty, political persuasion, or the desire to escape harsh POW camp conditions. Notable volunteers included *Waffen-Untersturmführer der-SS* Alichan Kuliev, a former Red Army officer who had survived multiple campaigns and POW imprisonment before joining the regiment.

Shortages of uniforms and equipment slowed formation. In February, the regiment moved to Belarus for further training and anti-partisan duties. Meyer-Mader was killed by a partisan sniper in March 1944, and command passed to *SS-Hauptsturmführer* Billig, an alcoholic whose drunken, violent handling of internal unrest – including the shooting of seventy-eight suspected mutineers – severely demoralised the regiment. Emil Hermann succeeded Billig in late April 1944, briefly restoring order before being removed. By July, the regiment had been attached to the notorious *SS-Sturmbrigade Dirlewanger*, known for brutal criminal elements, and participated indirectly in anti-partisan and garrison duties. Himmler remained intent on creating an eastern Muslim SS division. By October 1944, with insufficient recruits to form a full division, he ordered the establishment of the *Osttürkischer Waffenverband der SS* a formation designed to consolidate all available Turkic volunteers – including Turkestani, Volga and Ural Tatars, Crimean Turks, and Azerbaijanis – under SS-FHA supervision. Harun-el-Raschid Bey, formerly Wilhelm Hintersatz, a German officer who had converted to Islam in the First World War. Hintersatz was liaison to the Grand Mufti when he was offered the post of commander.

By the end of 1944, the *1. Ostmuselmanisches SS-Regiment* was reorganised in Slovakia. Battalions were divided along ethnic lines – Turkestani, Azerbaijani, and Idel-Ural Tartars – with regimental staff and five rifle companies per battalion. Political interference from the RSHA, proposing eventual transfer to Vlasov's Russian Liberation Army, conflicted with the Turkestani National Committee's goal of independence, fomenting resentment and eventually leading to mutiny. On Christmas Eve 1944, *Waffen-Obersturmführer der-SS* Gulam Alimov led approximately 450–500 men of the *I. Bataillon* to desert, with around 200 joining the Slovak partisans. *SS-Standartenführer* Harun-el-

Raschid Bey was blamed for failing to prevent the mutiny and was removed in February 1945, with *SS-Hauptsturmführer* Furst assuming command.

Following the mutiny, the *Osttürkischer-Waffen-Verbände der-SS-* underwent reorganisation. The Azerbaijani regiment was transferred to the *Kaukasicher-Waffen-Verbände der-SS* in Italy, the Idel-Ural battalion became part of *SS-Waffengruppe Idel-Ural,* and the *I.* and *II. Bataillon* formed *SS-Waffengruppe Turkistan. SS-Waffengruppe Krim* was created using the disbanded Tartar units, and maintained a separate anti-tank and artillery company. By mid-1945, the formation remained largely a training unit. Its final location may have been Austria, though some sources suggest northern Italy, with no confirmed combat involvement before Germany's surrender in May 1945. The *Osttürkischer-Waffen-Verbände der SS* was notable for its diverse Turkic composition and distinctive cuff band which was green-and-white, contrasting with typical *Waffen-SS* black cuff bands. Its strategic value lay mainly in propaganda, symbolising supposed global support for the Nazi cause, while its operational significance was minimal, with morale and cohesion repeatedly undermined by poor leadership, political interference, and desertion.

Note: For a full history of the *Osttürkischer Waffenverband der SS* please refer to *'Hitler's Muslim Allies: German Army and Waffen-SS Islamic Volunteers, 1941-1945'* by Frontline Books (an imprint of Pen & Sword), 2025.

Chapter 8

1941–1942: ATTRITION IN THE EAST. ENROLMENT OF NON-ARYANS BEGINS

Introduction

When Hitler's forces invaded the Soviet Union in the early morning hours of 22 June 1941 the German dictator expected a Blitzkrieg campaign of perhaps six to eight weeks. The *Oberkommando der Wehrmacht* (OKW, German Armed Forces High Command) was not as optimistic, and had planned for a campaign of six months. Although the Red Army had been dealt a serious blow when its officer corps had been purged in the 1930s by a suspicious and often paranoid Joseph Stalin (dictator of the USSR), it was by no means a crippling blow to the Red Army. True enough, the Soviet armed forces had been given a bloody nose during the Winter War with Finland (1939–40), but it had survived those heavy losses (it could afford to) and had gone on to force the Finns to sit down at the 'negotiating' table and eventually cede lands to the USSR which were claimed by Stalin. The sheer numbers of men which the Soviet Union could field and the vastness of the country were her two greatest assets. The third was the weather. These three main factors, augmented by a strict and draconian communist system, is what stopped the Nazi Blitzkrieg from totally overrunning the country in 1941 and 1942. German arrogance and stupidity were the 'fourth' factor.

The large stretches of land were used to wear down the invading Axis armies. Not only was the vastness of the countryside physically exhausting to the men and machines, but psychologically it also had an effect on them, for no matter how many thousands of kilometres were conquered, there always seemed to be another steppe, or another forest or city to capture. Additionally, the Soviets would also give up ground in order to gain time in which to regroup and reorganise their forces and to bring their industrial might to a full war footing. The Red Army was able to organise and even expand their officer corps while at the same time develop new tactics. In effect, the Soviet armed forces underwent a dramatic reconstruction and reorganisation while fighting for its life. This remarkable feat was accomplished virtually without any outside assistance. Land and manpower were also exchanged for new and improved military equipment, which was just beginning to filter into the combat units, to arrive in sufficient quantities to make an appreciable difference. One such example was the Soviet T-34/76 tank, with its superb, sloping armour, dependable and deadly (for its time) 76mm AT gun, and wide tracks (excellent for traversing mud). This vehicle was later superseded by the T-34/85, possibly the best Soviet medium tank design of the war.

In the very same way, when it was deemed unadvisable to give up territory, the Soviet riflemen were then sacrificed by the tens of thousands in order to slow down and delay the invaders. Mass infantry wave attacks were simple (and costly), but the Soviet High Command could afford the losses while the Axis forces suffered psychologically from the apparent indifference to life. No matter how many Russians you killed, there always seemed to be twice that number to take their place. A nation of 170,000,000 people (170.6 million to be exact) could afford this kind of sacrifice. Every year, Russia's poor 'highways' (basically unpaved roads) would turn to quagmire as soon as the autumn rains began. The only significant paved highway in European Russia before the war was the Moscow–Minsk highway, which had been completed just before 1941. The lack of proper roads turned out to be a logistical nightmare – one which was sure to wear down the best-built German vehicles, using up petrol and spare parts at an amazingly high rate. Adding to the problem was Russia's rail system, which employed a wide track gauge that was 1.524m (5ft) wide. This gauge was wholly incompatible to the European standard, which was 1.435m (4ft 8in) wide. That meant that the invaders were faced with having to convert every foot of Russian rail to the European model – a painstaking and slow process. Thus, every single piece of railway track in captured Soviet territory had to be changed to accommodate European trains, otherwise the Axis forces would have had to use the very limited number of captured Russian trains, and that was not logistically possible for an invading army of almost some 4.8 to 5 million men (including German and Axis allied troops).[1]

What eventually happened was that the German engineers would work to change the Soviet tracks into the European standard, but supplies reaching the German fronts had to depend on captured Soviet trains, railways and rail nets after certain points behind the lines (German railway engineers were never able to fully convert the tens of thousands of kilometres of Soviet rail to the European version). The growing partisan menace, which always targeted rail lines, kept these German and Axis allied engineer units tied down trying to patch up the rail lines, thus denying their use at extending the rail lines. 'General Winter', always a Soviet ally, also played a crucial role in stopping the Axis advance. While the Germans captured 3,350,639 men in the 1941 campaign season, the Germans themselves lost 35,875 who were listed as either becoming prisoners or listed as 'missing' during the same period. However, there were exactly 133,620 frostbite cases in 1941 alone and a total of 775,078 casualties of all types during the same period.

As can be seen, the usually severe weather of the Soviet Union was coupled with wholly inadequate logistical planning for a winter campaign since Hitler had deemed that it was unnecessary. This neglect to prepare for a winter war would cause grievous losses from frostbite and other related deaths in the German Army in the first winter of the war in Russia. While the Soviet Union could afford to lose hundreds of thousands of men, this was not the case with the Germans. Germany's 80,000,000 inhabitants were not the bottomless pit of manpower that the USSR seemed to be. In fact, General Franz Halder estimated that by the spring of 1942, the German Army in the East would be faced with a manpower shortage of some 625,000 men. German arrogance and ignorance of the Soviet peoples, an attitude that for the most part permeated from the highest echelons and filtered on down to the lowest ranks was the 'fourth' factor which contributed to the decisive defeat of the Nazi invasion. The heady and seemingly quick victories of 1939–41 added to the problem, since constant success tends to make one self-centred, overly confident, and arrogant. I believe that this social factor was the primary reason why the Germans and their Axis allies were not able to defeat the Soviet Union.

Granted, there were those 'enlightened' Germans in a position of command who could affect the relationship with the Russian population locally, but they were few and far between, and could not stop the racist and economically exploitable policies that the Germans carried with them into the Soviet Union. The Nazi *Einsatzgruppen* also had a terrible and negative effect on the Soviet population. While the leading elements of the *Wehrmacht* were offered bread and salt by the throngs of cheering Ukrainian citizens, and greeted by cheering Soviet citizens elsewhere in European Russia, the SS killing units would follow in their wake, leaving a horrible impression on those very same Soviet people who welcomed the German invader. There were those in the Soviet Union – hundreds of thousands if not millions – who detested communism, or Joseph Stalin's brand of communism. Millions of Soviet citizens suffered under this regime and resentment simmered just underneath the surface. In the Ukraine for example, Soviet collectivisation methods and bureaucratic incompetence, coupled by Stalin's willing indifference to human suffering, had caused a great famine in the 1930s in what was the 'bread basket' of the Soviet Union. In fact, Stalin had artificially created the famine to punish the Ukrainian people for resisting collectivisation. Millions died as a result, and is one of the least known but more infamous chapters in the history of the Stalinist era. The famine was so widespread and great that cases of cannibalism were a common occurrence. Parents were afraid to leave their children alone at home, for fear they would be taken and eaten. Many were.

The Soviet 'Gulag' was introduced on a grand scale and with the help of L. P. Beria, the 'General Commissar of State Security', Stalin was able to kill or imprison millions of his fellow countrymen. The terror of the knock in the middle of the night was not a Nazi monopoly, but also existed in Stalin's Russia. Recent objective Soviet studies have concluded that during Joseph Stalin's reign, about 20,000,000 Soviet citizens perished. This morbid tally sheet has only been rivalled by Adolf Hitler. Is it any wonder then, that when the Germans and their Axis allies finally turned their attention to eliminating the Soviet Union (and Stalin's regime as a consequence), so many hundreds of thousands of Soviet citizens and soldiers rallied to the side of the invaders?

Adding to the respect which most Soviet peoples had towards Germany was her brief occupation of the Baltic States and the Ukraine in the First World War. Additionally, there was a large immigrant group of Germans who had settled in the lower Volga River region, with its capital at Petrovsk. The local Russians had nothing but praise for the 'Fritzes'. In addition, we must also scrutinise Soviet propaganda about Nazi Germany, as it was disseminated to the Soviet peoples during the 1930s. Most, if not all of it was derogatory and negative. The Nazis, it went, were the scourge of the working man and of communism. To the millions of Russians and other peoples living under the tyranny of Stalinism, these state-sponsored propaganda messages, aired repeatedly on the radio and in the newspapers served only to reinforce their respect and admiration towards a German regime which seemed to be the 'boogie-man' of the Stalinists. When that 'boogie-man' finally called, they naturally and innocently welcomed him with open arms. It was thus that during the first eight months of the campaign, the Germans threw away a terribly valuable and strategically decisive card. General Ernst Köstring, who led Eastern troops during the Second World War, put it succinctly:

> We Germans, owing to our lack of reason and limitless appetite, inability, and ignorance, have lost the greatest capital that can exist in the fight against Bolshevism. In the imagination of countless Russians, we have thrown the picture of European culture into the mud.[2]

One can only wonder how much different the outcome in Russia might have been, had the Germans adopted a more moderate policy in the East. Of course, from the very narrow perspective of National Socialist policy, this was not a possibility. The noted German historian Hans Werner Neulen hit the nail on the head when he described the reason why Germany was not able to win the 'hearts and minds' of other peoples to their side during the Second World War:

> A 'European Carta' should have guaranteed the prosperity, sovereignty and freedom of all nations under Axis control, but the National Socialists committed to the ways of terror & unforgiveness turned down this project. National Socialist Germany, the leading power of the Axis, was totally unfit for the role of mediator. The daring exploits of the German tank divisions through Europe had not been followed by an inspiring or universal theory or doctrine combined with propaganda of the superiority of Germans might have attracted a minority in Europe, but were extremely useless for an ideology of integration into a European federation of states because they denied the equality of nations and designed a racist hierarchy as the New Order of Europe. There was no place for Jews and Slavs in this vague 'New Order'. Not all Slavs were destined for extermination, but they could not expect a special place in 'New Europe'.[3]

How many more Eastern volunteers would have come forward to join the ranks of the Axis in order to defeat Stalin and Stalinism is open to conjecture. Certainly, most scholars will agree that the numbers would have been much higher. What makes the study of the foreign volunteer movement so fascinating and incredible is the sheer vastness of the numbers of Eastern troops that served on the side of the Axis in spite of the inept and callous manner in which these initially enthusiastic and willing volunteers were treated. The brutally exploitive manner in which the Germans ruled the occupied Eastern territories was another reason why Nazi Germany could not win the support of the majority of the Soviet population. It was thus that in the first year of the Russo-German conflict the Germans lost the one key to defeating Stalin and communism: the support of the Soviet population. But of course, it was impossible for the Nazis to have treated their subject peoples as equal partners in a new Europe. This was especially true in Eastern Europe where the so-called *untermenschen* (subhumans) lived. It was simply not in the Nazi psyche to do so. Their own racist and exterminationist policies would prove to be their undoing.

That many were disillusioned and felt betrayed, there is no doubt. Many mutinied, deserted or switched sides as a result, but most continued to serve a regime which, for no other possible reason, apparently seemed the 'lesser of two evils' to them. Certainly, we cannot categorise the overwhelming majority of these Eastern troops as racists or ardent National Socialists, although anti-Semitism was a common inducement, which had been inculcated into their minds by hundreds of years of tradition and the occasional '*pogrom*' by the ruling Tsars. What seems incomprehensible about the Eastern volunteer movement is that hundreds of thousands of Soviet citizens joined, even after experiencing Germany's inept handling of this valuable 'resource' (i.e. the Eastern volunteers and the populace as a whole), and they continued to serve the Third Reich. A document (dated '24 January 1945') from the Ministry for the Eastern Occupied Territories (located in Berlin) listed the indigenous military and semi-military units up until that time as follows:

Table 8. Estimated Number of Indigenous Volunteers from the USSR Serving in the German Armed Forces as of 24 January 1945.

Armed Lithuanian Units	36,800
Armed Latvian Units	104,000
Armed Estonian Units[4]	10,000
Russian Military Units	10,000
SS-Waffengruppe 'Krim'[5]	10,000
Caucasian Units:	
Estimated Reserves of Turks & Tartars from the Idel-Ural Mountains Region[6]	45,000
Cossack Units[7]	70,000
Armed Armenian Units	7,000

Armed Azerbaijani Units	31,000
Armed Georgian Units	19,000
Total Caucasian Volunteers:	109,000[8]
Kalmyck Cavalry Corps	5,000
Armed North Caucasian Units	7,000
Byelorussian (White Russian) Military Units	19,000
Ukrainian Military Units	75,000
Grand Total Number of Eastern Volunteers Serving in the German Armed Forces	373,800
Russian Army of Liberation (ROA)	300,000
Grand Total Number of Volunteers From the USSR	748,800

This figure of 748,800 Eastern volunteers by January 1945 is very significant because it shows us that even at that late stage in the war, the Germans still possessed about three-quarters of a million Soviet citizens in its armed forces. According to one memorandum by Caucasian leaders, of the estimated 100,000+ volunteers from the Caucasus region, the following fifteen battalions were serving in France and the Low Countries in mid-1944:[9]

- *Georgische Infanterie-Bataillon 795* (795th Georgian Infantry Battalion) – Cherbourg, France
- *Georgische Infanterie-Bataillon 797* (797th Georgian Infantry Battalion) – Near La-Haye-du Poys in Graneville, France
- *Georgische Infanterie-Bataillon 798* (798th Georgian Infantry Battalion) – Near St. Nazaire, France.
- *Georgische Infanterie-Bataillon 799* (799th Georgian Infantry Battalion) – Near Perygeux, France.
- *Georgische Infanterie-Bataillon II/4* (Georgian Infantry Battalion II/4) – In the Albi-Castre region of France
- *Georgische Infanterie-Bataillon I/9* (Georgian Infantry Battalion I/9) – In the Albi-Castre region of France
- *Nordkaukasisches Infanterie-Bataillon 800* (800th North Caucasian Infantry Battalion) – Normandy, France
- *Nordkaukasisches Infanterie-Bataillon 803* (803rd North Caucasian Infantry Battalion) – In Holland
- *Nordkaukasisches Infanterie-Bataillon 804* (804th Azerbaijani Infantry Battalion) – Temporarily in France
- *Nordkaukasisches Infanterie-Bataillon 807* (807th Azerbaijani Infantry Battalion) – Near St. Raphael, France

- *Nordkaukasisches Infanterie-Bataillon 812* (812th Armenian Infantry Battalion) – In Holland
- *Nordkaukasisches Infanterie-Bataillon 822* (822rd Georgian Infantry Battalion) – Zandwort, Holland
- *Nordkaukasisches Infanterie-Bataillon 823* (823 Georgian Infantry Battalion) – Island of Guernsey, England
- *Nordkaukasisches Infanterie-Bataillon 835* (835th North Caucasian Infantry Battalion) – Normandy, France
- *Nordkaukasisches Infanterie-Bataillon 836* (836th North Caucasian Infantry Battalion) – Normandy, France

Another source mentions a figure of 900,000 to 1,000,000 Eastern European troops under the banner of the Swastika during the summer of 1944. This was the time when *Reichsführer-SS* (National Leader of the SS) Heinrich Himmler began supporting a 'National Liberation Army' under Russian turncoat, Andrei Andreivich Vlasov.[10] This same source listed these Eastern volunteers as having the following numbers of troops as of October 1944:

Table 9. Estimated Numbers of Volunteers from the USSR Serving in the German Armed Forces as of October 1944

Armed Lithuanian Units	27,000
Armed Estonian Units	One SS division
Caucasian Peoples: Armenian, Azerbaijani, Georgian, and North Caucasian Units	110,000
Armed Tartar Units	35,000
Armed Latvian Units[11]	Two SS divisions
Belarusian Military Units	One SS division
Ukrainian Military Units	220,000
Armed Turkistan Units	110,000
Cossack Units	82,000
Kalmyck Cavalry Corps	29 squadrons

Granted, the majority of these men had probably lost any illusions about the true nature of the Nazi regime, but they had likely reconciled themselves to having joined the 'losing side' and accepted, with a sense of fatalism, that the die had been cast and that nothing could alter their apparent *fait accompli*. Most also knew what awaited them if Stalin and his henchmen got hold of them. Not all of these Eastern volunteers went willingly to join their German allies in a Teutonic '*Götterdämerung*'. Beginning in 1942, there were numerous instances of individual or mass desertions, defections, and mutinies. There were many reasons for this, mostly German-created, since the policies that were in place in the occupied Eastern territories were so unbearable and harsh, that they were like recruiting posters for the Soviet partisans. One author even noted that the Soviets had bragged that Erich Koch, the *Reichskommissar* for the Ukraine, had done more for the Soviet cause (because of his ruthlessness) than a dozen partisan brigades could have achieved. Treatment of the Soviet peasantry (whether Russian, Ukrainian, etc.) was abysmal. The introduction of conscription of the Russian populace in 1942 for forced labour in German factories was the last straw. Another author put it thusly:

> The harder the German administration bore down upon the country, the greater became the number of partisans. In particular, the conscription to Germany of Eastern workers that commenced in the summer of 1942, drove thousands of men into the arms of the partisans and finally brought about the result that, for all practical purposes, partisan warfare was being waged by the entire Russian population.[12]

The partisans were only too happy to point out the many negative aspects of the German/Axis occupation. Additionally, beginning in late 1942 and increasing in intensity, they could also point to one irrevocable and non-argumentative fact: the German retreat. As a result of these Nazi military reversals the reliability of some of the Eastern volunteers began to come into question. A partisan leaflet, distributed throughout the rear of the German occupied Eastern territories, shows us to what extent the guerrillas used psychological warfare to try and sway these volunteers. The leaflet quotes some figures which are hard to believe, like the claim that Soviet partisans killed 300,000 Germans, but the assertion of the devastating Allied bomber offensive and the coming of a second front were true:

> For two years the Red Army, the heroic partisans and the entire Soviet people have been engaged in a life-and-death struggle against the German Fascist hordes . . . The Soviet partisans, the avengers of the people, have destroyed more than 300,000 of Hitler's monsters; they have derailed at least 3,000 trains, destroyed more than 3,000 bridges. Simultaneously our mighty allies England and America by striking destructive blows with their air forces against the industrial centres of Germany and Italy are preparing to establish the second front. Come to your senses! There is still time. Come over confidently, singly or in groups to the side of the Red Army or the Soviet partisans.[13]

Pragmatism on Account of Necessity

The door to the recruitment of Eastern volunteers officially 'creaked' open in October, 1941 when General Keitel (with Hitler's reluctant consent) issued an order for Russian prisoners of war to be utilised by the German Armed Forces for railway construction. This apparent 'about face' on this matter occurred mainly due to the realisation that the Soviet Union would not be defeated in six months, but it was the mounting German losses on the field that was the *raison d'être* for Hitler's apparent reversal. By the time that the Führer had 'consented' to this, the numbers of possible volunteers had already been reduced considerably. During the planning stages for *Unternehmen Barbarossa*, the German General Staff had estimated that the *Wehrmacht* would capture around 800,000 Soviet soldiers. Accordingly, they had gone about preparing for this estimated number. Little did they realise that the first six months of the campaign alone they would have to house, feed, and guard 3,350,639 men. This was another of those so-called 'logistical nightmares' that the Germans encountered during their campaign in the East. Tens of thousands of Soviet POWs died of malnutrition, ill treatment, exposure to the elements, diseases spread by poor sanitary conditions and overcrowding.

Little or no effort was put forward initially to try and ease this suffering. National Socialist ideology had been officially taught in Germany since 1933, so the Nazis had enough time to try and convince the German people of the inferiority of the Slavic race. It would seem plausible then, that given this attitude towards the Soviet people, little care was given to preserving captured Soviet soldiers. As an example, one of these POW camps, *Stalag 350* established in July 1941 just outside of Riga, Latvia was supposed to hold a maximum of 6,000 Russian prisoners. Yet by the late summer of 1941 the camp was beset by 80,000 POWs. Of these 80,000 prisoners, only around 50,000 were still alive by June 1942 or roughly one year later. This overcrowding problem prevailed all across the Eastern Front. *General der Flieger* Karl Kitzinger, who was in charge of POW camps in the Ukraine, estimated that he was losing around 2,500 prisoners per day.

Another example was the statistical figure of 100,000 captured Turkistan soldiers who, as Soviet citizens, were serving in the Red Army. Of this 1941 figure only 6,000 were still alive by the spring of 1942. It would appear that their Asiatic features had not helped them very much. The Christian peoples of the Caucasus fared a bit better – thus 'only' about half of the Georgian POWs under German care died during the first winter of the war. The Germans themselves have often described these POW camps as 'frightful' and one passage in a book describes the horror which one German officer encountered when visiting a Soviet POW transit camp, in Stalino on 26 January 1942:

> In the gallery where students once sat, almost fleshless skulls were raised here and there. They stared at Herre like so many death masks The camp commandant came up to him. 'Have you found what you were looking for, Major?' The look in his eyes was a blend of bafflement, self-righteousness, and uneasiness But Herre looked past him to a group of weeping Russian women who were standing outside the gate; they were vainly trying to throw a few cold potatoes and pieces of bread to the prisoners.[14]

The camps were so bad, that they bring up another point, and that is the desire for survival. The point cannot be overlooked that when the Germans began to recruit these Russian volunteers, many of them joined, if only to escape the slow death that awaited them in these camps. What percentage of those that joined fell into this category? No one really knows, for the reasons why they joined were so diverse, as I have tried to explain. The point is that given all of these conditions – the mostly arrogant attitude of the Germans towards the Soviet people, their exploitive policies in the East, their killing spree behind the lines, their ill-treatment of Soviet POWs and other short-sighted policies – caused such irreparable damage to the Eastern recruiting effort, that it's a wonder that it managed to start at all. It must be said that the hatred of Stalin and Stalinism was the primary reason why Soviet citizens sided with the invaders.

Recruitment Begins

As mentioned before, the order of October 1941 allowed for the 'official' recruitment of Russian POWs and other volunteers for use by the Germans on the Russian railways. Indeed, by 1 January 1943 the total number of German employees working on the Soviet rail system (in one capacity or another) was 111,899 but total natives working on the same rail system stood at an amazing 633,935 men and women.[15] Some German commanders, extremely short-handed of able-bodied men, did not stop their employment of native volunteers by complying strictly with the order of October 1941, with its very limited clause on the use of Eastern volunteers. Many took it upon themselves to use these men as cooks, drivers, work crews, interpreters, messengers, etc. Some particularly bold officers even went so far as to arm these native volunteers to act as village or town guards, and eventually even to act as security behind the German lines against Partisan attacks.

These volunteers were considered auxiliaries and became known as '*Hilfswilliger*' ('*Hiwis*' for short, which literally meant 'willing helpers').[16]

An example of just exactly how thinly spread were the German rear-area forces, is given by examining *Korück 582,* which was the local Army Rear Area military government, organised into region, district, town and village – all under the direct control of the German Quartermaster General for the Eastern Front. The *Korück*s were responsible for all matters of supply, administration, and security in the combat zone. This latter duty meant that they were ultimately responsible for defending against guerrilla attacks. *Korück 582*'s area of responsibility encompassed 6,900 square miles of territory behind the *9. Armee* lines in the region of Army Group Centre. It contained more than 1,500 villages, in addition to collective farms. Yet, for all of this area, the *Korück* could only count on sixteen companies of about eighty-five men each, or a total of 1,400 men to act as guards for POW rail lines, headquarters personnel, town garrisons, etc. This work left only about 300 men for employment in anti-partisan operations.[17]

The recruitment of these native troops into the auxiliary services, rear-area formations, and combat divisions of the German Army began at various times and in various stages and sizes. For example, the *134. Infanterie-Division,* which had apparently begun to recruit native volunteers on an equal footing as early as 1941, was made up of 50 per cent Russian and other Soviet volunteers by late 1942.[18] The *113. Infanterie-Division* began to organise *Hiwis* in the summer of 1942.[19] An order dated 8 August 1942 called for the raising of *Hiwis* and eventually formed the following units: *Ukrainische Hunterschaft Feldgendarmerie Trupp 113* (Ukrainian Century Field Police Company 113), and *Kriegsgefangen Pioneer Kompanie der Pioneer Bataillon 113* (POW Engineer Company, Engineer Battalion 113).[20]

When the *113. Infanterie-Division* was surrounded and eventually destroyed in the Stalingrad Pocket, these auxiliary units also ceased to exist. As early as the summer of 1941 some German divisions began to recruit native volunteers for what initially were non-combat duties behind the front lines. Eventually, each German division would contain a pre-determined number of *Hilfswilliger* within the framework of the Divisional TO&E (table of organisation). This number varied, but was usually around 3,000–4,000 men. A 1944 estimate averaged that there were perhaps between 600,000 and 1,400,000 *Hiwis* serving in German units in Russia. This equals to around 20 per cent of the German 'divisional' strength on the Eastern Front at the time. So, by 1944, roughly one soldier in five which was wearing the field grey uniform of the *Wehrmacht* in the USSR was a native volunteer! As mentioned earlier, mass recruitment of the native population began in earnest in the autumn of 1941, but most of these early recruitments were illegal, since many German commanders were actually arming these volunteers and allowing them to fight either in the front or against the growing Soviet partisan menace. One German commander described it thusly:

> Everything I have been doing is illegal. There are no regulations for my men. No recognised ranks, no uniforms, no official pay, no clothing. No decorations. No German soldier will salute a Russian whom I have chosen to appoint an officer. Where opportunists are concerned, what motivates them is the belief that we are going to win. But the genuine volunteers are not with us for such reasons. How will both groups react when the war goes badly and they realise we are not meeting them halfway, not treating them as real allies?[21]

How would they react? This was the question most German officers did not want to have answered, for deep inside they knew what the consequences would be. They all held their breaths, prayed, and hoped that a change in policy from the top would soon come and repair the damage that had already been done, but like so many wasted chances and opportunities, the spectre of Soviet citizens in Nazi uniform proved to be at best an expedient that failed, and not a certain and concrete foreign policy, geared to undermine the support for Stalin and the Communists by offering the Soviet people true autonomy and freedom. By the time the Germans finally came around to supporting a 'Russian Liberation Army' in 1944 that opportunity had turned into a mere illusion.

The Experimental Units

There were several independently-raised Russian formations which were the idea and development of individual German officers (in cooperation with local Russian leaders) which surfaced in the autumn of 1941 and spring of 1942. In December 1941 a certain German *Leutnant* von Veltheim established a local 'self-defence' formation in the town of Lokot, just south of the central Soviet city of Bryansk with about 400–500 Russians under the leadership of the town's mayor, Ivan K. Voskoboinkov.[22] After Voskoboinkov was murdered by the partisans in January 1942, command of this unit was handed to his immediate subordinate, Bronislav Kaminski. Kaminski was to lead the formation until almost the end of its existence, enlarging it from a modest battalion of 400–500 men to an entire anti-partisan brigade of five regiments and some 12,000–15,000 men, complete with tanks and artillery pieces.[23] The unit performed with excellent results while it operated in the region where it had been raised, but lost most of its effectiveness when it was forced to uproot themselves and move into areas where it did not possess the support of the local population. German military reversals and their subsequent withdrawals also had an effect on the morale of the formation.

The first experiment with Eastern troops had begun as early as 1939, when the German *Abwehr* – the Secret Intelligence Service of the *Wehrmacht* – had recruited a battalion of Ukrainian volunteers from the Carpathian Mountain region for a battalion-sized unit which would take part in the invasion of Poland. These men had seen earlier service in the very short-lived 'Carpathian' units, formed by Ukrainian nationalists in a bid to create an independent Ukrainian state from the eastern-most end of Slovakia when the Czech government fell.[24] The formation also served propaganda purposes, since it was hoped that Galician Ukrainians, serving in the Polish Army, would be inclined to desert. The *Abwehr*, specifically *Abwehr* Section II (Sabotage and Subversion) of the OKW, under the direction of Erwin Lahousen, assumed responsibility for the organisation and training of non-German military formations. For the Russian campaign, the Germans began to recruit from these Ukrainian nationalists. Work on a Ukrainian 'legion' began as early as the beginning of 1941. The legion contained *Ukrainer) Abwehr-Bataillon 'Roland'* and *(Ukrainer) Abwehr-Bataillon 'Nachtigall'*, trained by the *Abwehr*.

In addition to *Bataillon 'Roland'*, which had been established near Wiener Neustadt, a second Ukrainian unit was created during the winter of 1940/1941 at the Neuhammer training ground near Liegnitz in Silesia. This formation subsequently acquired the designation *'Nachtigall'* ('Nightingale'), a name reportedly derived from the members' proclivity for singing. Compared to *Bataillon 'Roland'*, extant documentation concerning the *'Nachtigall'* unit is more extensive, although much of the available evidence appears applicable to both battalions. Initially, three companies were constituted and subjected to military instruction. According to the testimony of one German officer, the volunteers demonstrated themselves to be 'good, disciplined soldiers', a quality attributed to their earlier service in the Polish peacetime army. The primary function envisaged for these formations was the execution of diversionary and sabotage operations in western Ukraine. To this end, the troops were provided with German uniforms and light infantry weapons, though they were denied the heavy armament typically issued to equivalent German units. As a result, the battalion's equipment was deemed 'at best sufficient for a defensive infantry engagement'. A further consideration influencing the unit's limited armament may have been the OKW's intention to ensure that the battalion could, if necessary, be swiftly disarmed.

The unit was disbanded at the end of the Polish campaign, and its men were employed as policemen and guards in the *Generalgouvernement* (General Government), i.e., that part of Poland not incorporated into the Reich. Many of these men helped to create some *Schutzmannschaft* battalions. It would be from these men, plus a significant number of volunteers from the Ukrainian nationalist OUN-R faction, which would later be used to form the two *Abwehr* volunteer battalions. German staff personnel in the Ukrainian legion included Professors Georg Gerunis, Hans Koch, and Theodor Oberlander – all reserve officers[25] in the OKW. Professor Theodor Oberlander, who would lead the *'Nachtigall'* battalion, would become quite prominent in the field of Eastern volunteers, leading these types of forces throughout the rest of the war.

The *Graukopf Verband*

In the autumn of 1941, in a large industrial plant called Osintorf (not far from Smolensk), another experimental unit was formed from Russian POWs by the *Abwehr*.[26] The Germans unofficially referred to it as the *Graukopf Verband*, or 'Grey Head Formation', after its commander who had greying hair.[27] The Russian commander was Colonel Konstantine Kromiadi.[28] The unit initially had an initial strength of 350–400 men. The formation was intended to be used for special operations behind the Red Army lines.[29] It was formed officially in March 1942.[30] The unit included former Red Army as well as Tsarist Army officers. The known Tsarist officers included ex-Colonel Konstantin Kromiadi, 2nd Lieutenant Igor Zakharov, and Lieutenant Grigory von Lamsdorff, an émigré Russian count. These last two officers had fought in the Spanish Civil War before signing up as interpreters in the *Abwehr*. After the war, these officers would escape the clutches of Stalin's Secret Police. Kromiadi lived out his life in the United States, while Zakharov eventually emigrated to Australia. Count Grigory von Lamsdorff returned to Spain. This unit was organised in late 1941 at Osintorf, a large industrial complex near the village of Osinovka, not too far from the city of Smolensk. The unit was initially organised with the help of Russian émigré officers and was sponsored by the German *Heer* (Army). Even though the unit only contained six battalions, and was therefore the strength of a brigade, it was grandiosely titled the RNNA, or Russian National People's Army.

Although the originators of the unit were Russian émigrés, the majority of the men were ex-Red Army soldiers who had been recruited from the large numbers of German POW camps which had sprung up all across the rear of the advancing German armies. Their uniforms were Russian-style gymnast blouses and trousers, with Tsarist Army epaulets for the officers. Some of the Russian émigré officers who were serving in the brigade had been '*sonderführer*' (special officers) in German commands, basically acting as interpreters. They had volunteered to join the brigade and therefore wore initially German uniforms and insignia. This soon changed when they removed the *Heer* emblems and replaced them with Tsarist-era badges.

The German blouses and trousers were retained, however. The formation proved to be quite effective and the majority of its officers, as well as the German liaison officer, Colonel Rudolf-Christoph *Freiherr* von Gersdorff, wished to commit the six battalions as one whole unit against the Red Army on the front lines. However, in a discussion over the fate of the formation, Field Marshal von Kluge basically stunted the unit's further growth and reliability when he announced that he intended to split up the *Graukopf Brigade* (then numbering an astounding 7,000 men) and send its battalions to serve under separate German commands. Demoralised, the unit was eventually dissolved towards the end of 1943. In 1942, the German *Sicherheitsdienst* had not yet absorbed the *Abwehr,* and was therefore in direct competition with the *Abwehr* to become Nazi Germany's chief intelligence-gathering service. They too also formed their own experimental unit, variously named, but most often referred to as *Druzhina SS Verband*.

The origins of the *Druzhina* SS formation can be traced to February 1942, when a battalion-sized unit was organised and initially stationed in Nevel. At that time, the Abwehr's *Graukopf Verband* possessed a strength of two battalions, of which this formation constituted a part. In March 1942, the *Druzhina* detachment was transferred to Glebokie, where it remained until September of the same year, conducting a series of successful anti-partisan operations. By April 1942, the unit had expanded to a strength of four battalions. The fortunes of the formation began to deteriorate in the spring of 1943. One of its officers, Colonel Gavrilov, together with 110 men, defected to the communist partisans. The most dramatic reversal came on 12 August 1943, when the commander of the *Druzhina SS Verband,* Colonel Vladimir

Vladimirovich Gil – who had adopted the *nom de guerre* I.G. Rodionov – deserted en masse with some 2,000 men, effectively the bulk of the brigade.

Two principal factors contributed to this mass defection. First, the members of the unit had become disillusioned by the harsh and often brutal manner in which the German authorities treated the Russian civilian population, including communities that had initially displayed a degree of sympathy toward the occupiers. Second, by 1943 the changing military situation, with Germany increasingly on the defensive, convinced Rodionov that Germany was likely to lose the war. After joining the Soviet partisans, the former *Druzhina* formation was reconstituted as the '1st Anti-Fascist Partisan Brigade'. Rodionov and many of his men were subsequently killed during a German anti-guerrilla operation in 1944, but the damage had already been done. The large-scale desertion underscored the unreliability of such auxiliary formations, and it contributed to Hitler's decision to abandon further 'experiments' of this kind.

In 1943 so many Eastern volunteer units became so unreliable, that Hitler made the decision to transfer a good number of them to the West. They were exchanged with German battalions from Italy, France and the Low Countries on a ratio of two Eastern battalions (sent west) for one German battalion sent to the Eastern Front. Those volunteers who wished to fight Stalin and communism, now found themselves defending occupied Europe from the Western Allies – people whom these volunteers had no quarrel with. As a result, what morale remained in these people sunk even further. Those Eastern volunteers who had joined to escape starvation in a German POW camp, or because they thought the Germans were going to win, were already demoralised. Now those volunteers who had joined to fight Stalin and Stalinism became similarly disillusioned.

From then on it became common policy and practice to disarm collaborator units which showed the slightest inkling of unreliability, and transfer the so-called 'reliable' units to France, Italy, the Low Countries, Norway, Denmark, and the Balkans. One estimate quotes a figure of about 176 Russian, White Russian, Ukrainian, East Orient, Caucasian and Cossack battalions withdrawn from the Soviet Union and sent to the west in order to prevent these forces from defecting. From September – November 1943 sixty *'Ost'* battalions were exchanged for thirty German battalions. By the end of 1943 the German Armed Forces still possessed a reported 370 *Ost* battalions and an additional 130,000 Eastern volunteers acting as *'Hiwis'* within German divisions.

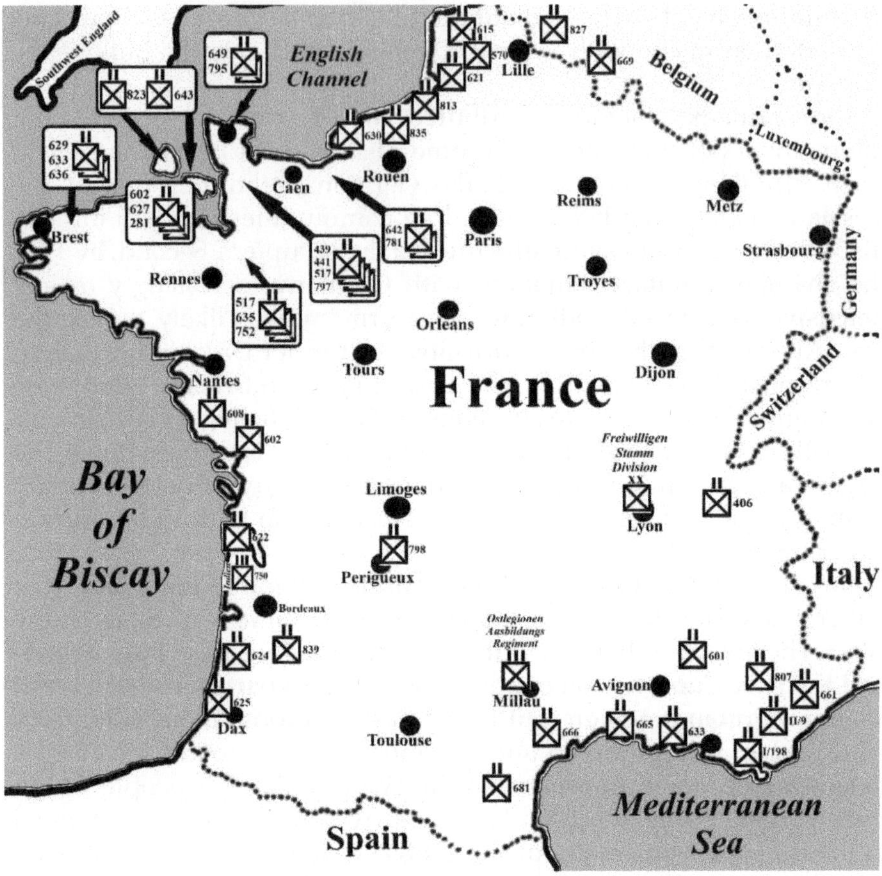

Figure 15. Location of ***Ost-Bataillonen*** (Eastern battalions) in France on 6 June 1944.

This number later changed in June 1944 when 200 *Ost* battalions were available to the *Wehrmacht.* In September 1943 15,000 Eastern troops were transferred to other theatres of war from the Eastern Front. By October thirty-four *Ost* battalions had arrived in the West, with twenty-three more on their way. Between November and December 1943 an additional 25,000 Eastern troops had been shipped out of the Soviet Union. In April 1944 many of these Eastern formations were officially incorporated into these German divisions, becoming either the 3rd or 4th Battalion of a regiment in these German divisions. When the Western Allies invaded France on 6 June 1944, some of these Eastern battalions fought to the bitter end while others simply surrendered or only offered token resistance. In some cases, mutinies broke out, and small wonder, given that these (anti-communist) volunteers were now faced by an 'enemy' with whom they had no quarrel with. Mutinies and defections were not a new phenomenon however, for as early as 1942 they were already a common occurrence.

Kalmyk Volunteers in the German Army, 1942–1945

The recruitment of the Kalmyks into German service was one of the more unusual and little-known episodes of the Second World War. The Kalmyks were a Mongol-speaking, Buddhist people living in the steppe regions along the lower Volga. Their history in the Russian Empire and later in the Soviet Union was marked by tension with the central authorities, as they struggled to maintain their cultural identity and traditions under an often-hostile regime. The collectivisation campaigns of the 1930s, along with brutal suppression of their religion and traditional nomadic ways of life, left scars that were still raw when the German invasion of the Soviet Union began in June 1941. Many Kalmyks had already experienced repression, deportations, and economic hardship, and when German forces entered their homeland in 1942, some saw in the invaders a possible ally against Moscow.

It was in this atmosphere that the Germans sought to organise Kalmyk auxiliaries. Unlike other Soviet minorities who were recruited piecemeal into local militias or police units, the Kalmyks were gathered into what would become a formalised force: the *Kalmykisches Kavallerie-Korps* (Kalmyk Cavalry Corps). The initiative came from *Sonderkommando Dr. Doll,* a German official whose real name was Otto Werba. Werba possessed organisational skills and enthusiasm which turned scattered volunteers into a more coherent body. 'Dr. Doll' promised the Kalmyks that their service would pave the way for autonomy, and he emphasised the shared struggle against Bolshevism. For the Germans, the Kalmyks offered two distinct advantages: they were skilled horsemen well adapted to steppe warfare, and their participation could be paraded as evidence that whole peoples of the Soviet Union were willing to side with the Reich.

By late 1942 the Kalmyk Cavalry Corps was formally established. Its strength has been estimated at between 5,000 and 6,000 men, organised into four cavalry regiments with supporting elements. The Corps was attached to *1. Panzerarmee,* then operating in the Caucasus. There the Kalmyks were employed in reconnaissance, screening operations, and anti-partisan duties. Their knowledge of the steppe terrain, as well as their mobility on horseback, made them useful in theory, but in practice the unit's operations often degenerated into harsh reprisals against civilians. This pattern was common among the various Eastern units in German service, where inadequate supplies, weak discipline and German mistrust combined to blur the line between military action and punitive expeditions.

The collapse of German plans in southern Russia after the defeat at Stalingrad forced the *Kalmykisches Kavallerie-Korps* into retreat. Along with the rest of *Heeresgruppe A* (Army Group A), they withdrew from the Caucasus into the Kuban bridgehead and then further west into Ukraine. Retreat and attrition took a heavy toll. Desertions grew more frequent, and combat losses thinned the ranks. By late 1943 the Corps had shrunk to fewer than 3,000 effectives, reorganised into smaller detachments stiffened by German cadres. Despite Doll's efforts to maintain morale by promising future rewards, the strategic situation made it clear that the Germans could no longer offer the Kalmyks any realistic hope.

Through 1943 and 1944, Kalmyk units were employed mainly in rear-area security operations in Ukraine and later in Poland. They became part of the German response to the growing partisan movements in these regions, and in this role, they earned a grim reputation. Their operations were small in scale, and their actual combat impact on the Eastern Front was minimal, yet their presence served German propaganda needs well. The Corps was frequently depicted as an example of how diverse peoples were rallying to the 'European crusade against Bolshevism'. Posters and newsreels highlighted the exotic appearance of the Buddhist horsemen fighting under German command, turning them into symbols of a supposedly international coalition led by Berlin.

By the beginning of 1945, the Kalmyk Cavalry Corps was a shadow of its former self. Dr. Doll, the unit's founder and main advocate, had been killed in 1944, and his loss affected the morale of the Kalmyk volunteers. The surviving elements were ordered to join the Vlasov Army, but the Kalmyk leaders demanded they be placed with an eastern Turkic formation. The unit was ordered to join a Caucasian cavalry formation of the *Waffen-SS* cavalry which was currently forming in northern Italy. The end of the war brought catastrophe for the Kalmyks. Those captured by the Allies were forcibly repatriated to the Soviet Union under agreements with Moscow. Branded as traitors, many were executed or sent to labour camps. The Soviet regime went even further: in late 1943, well before the war had ended, Stalin had already ordered the mass deportation of the entire Kalmyk population to Siberia and Central Asia, accusing the people as a whole of collaboration. Tens of thousands perished in exile, and the Kalmyk homeland was only reconstituted years later, long after Stalin's death.

In retrospect, the Kalmyk Cavalry Corps offered the Germans good military value for their money. Even after it was forced from its homeland, it continued to perform well against the Red Army partisans. It was only after the death of its beloved commander that morale began to suffer. Its battlefield role for most of the war, was confined largely to reconnaissance and anti-partisan operations. It could not alter the strategic balance on the Russian Front, nor did it provide the manpower or resources to influence the outcome of major campaigns. Its significance lay partially in the realm of propaganda and partly in helping to fight the partisans.

They fought not only in the hope of improving their desperate circumstances under Soviet rule, but also with the belief – fostered by German promises – that service might secure them autonomy. Instead, their association with the Axis brought devastation upon their people, culminating in deportation and exile. The history of the *Kalmykisches Kavallerie-Korps* is thus best understood as both marginal and symbolic. Militarily, it was a footnote in the vast struggle on the Eastern Front, contributing little to the German war effort. Politically and propagandistically, however, it loomed larger than its numbers. The Kalmyks embodied the contradictions of Germany's Eastern policy: the Reich sought to exploit non-Russian resentment of Stalin while simultaneously offering them little real trust or autonomy. For the Kalmyks, caught between two brutal regimes, the war ended in tragedy, leaving their community scarred for generations.

Note: For a full history of the Kalmyk Cavalry Corps, please refer to *Hitler's Muslim Allies: German Army and Waffen-SS Islamic Volunteers, 1941-1945* by Frontline Books (an imprint of Pen & Sword), 2025.

Chapter 9

TAPPING THE BALKANS, PART 1: 1941–1943

The (Slovenian) Ethnic-German *Wehrmannschaft*

Immediately after the defeat of Yugoslavia in 1941, the northern provinces of Slovenia, Gorenjska and Stajerska, and the small Koroska area were incorporated into the Reich as the *Oberkrain* (Upper Carnolia) and *Untersteiermark* (Lower Styria) regions. In keeping with Nazi social and political practice the ethnic German communities in these former Slovene provinces were organised into a paramilitary association, known as the *Heimatbund*. This was supposed to represent the interests of these ethnic Germans, but was basically a means by which the Nazi Party could exert its influence on the ethnic German population. Shortly thereafter, the first militarised unit was raised from the most physically fit members of the *Slowenischer Heimatbund*, and was called the *Wehrmannschaft* (Defence Militia). The *Wehrmannschaft* came into being in the autumn of 1941 and was trained mainly by the SA, or *Sturmabteilung* (storm detachments, the Nazi Party's street soldiers).

The SA provided the organisation, equipment, arms and training for the *Slowenischer Wehrmannschaft* until the beginning of 1942, when the German Order Police and SS took over most of the duties involved with what was now a full-strength battalion. The ranks of the *Wehrmannschaft* changed however, and they kept using the 'SA' rank system. For example, the commander of the initial *Wehrmannschaft* battalion formed was referred to as *SA-Sturmbannführer* Töscher. In April 1942 service in the *Wehrmannschaft* became mandatory for all ethnic Germans living in both newly created provinces. At this time, German census figures showed that exactly 87,400 men were available for call-up in the area of *Untersteiermark* although of this number, only about 25,000 were *Volksdeutsche*. There were an additional 17,592 men given the position as an auxiliary police formation and named '*Wehrmannschaftsbataillon Süd*' (Defence Militia Battalion 'South') in April/May 1942. This unit's ascension as an auxiliary to the SS, Police, and *Gendarmerie* forces in the country was as a direct result of the increase in guerrilla activity.

The *Wehrmannschaft* was gradually expanded over the course of 1942 into two, then three battalions, and by 1943 it was a reinforced regiment with five full-strength battalions. At its height, it contained 6,000+ men. The remaining tens of thousands of potential *Wehrmannschaft* recruits were not called for service, mainly due to their need to tend the crops and to run other sectors of the local economy necessary for the war effort. Many, however, served part-time as '*Selbstschutz*' (self-defence). These were guards stationed in static posts, mostly dependent on where they lived and worked. This began to take shape in 1942, and by May of the same year, there were seven such *Selbstschutz* platoons operating throughout the two provinces. These *Selbstschutz* platoons were made subordinate to the local *Gendarmerie* (rural police) post where they were located. A training company for the first *Wehrmannschaft* battalion was established in Maribor (Marburg), and eventually each battalion was assigned a training company. The 5th Battalion to be formed, named '*Mitte*' (Centre), was simply a grouping together of these various training companies, but this did not occur until late 1943. When formed, this 5th (Training) Battalion was posted to Maribor.

Operations during 1942 by the *Wehrmannschaft* mainly dealt with augmenting the meagre German SS, *Ordnungspolizei* (Order Police), and *Gendarmerie* forces that existed in the two provinces. Patrols and small, brief skirmishes with the Slovenian (communist) guerrillas took up most of the year, but there was one significantly large engagement in which the *Wehrmannschaft* employed, alongside strong German forces, which included *Polizeibataillon 181*. This was launched in the *Oberkrain* (Gorenjska) region, where the Germans employed for the very first time, their newly formed *Polizei-Gebirgsjäger-Regiment 18* (18th Police Mountain Regiment), complete with three rifle battalions, and a police mountain artillery battalion (*Polizei-Gebirgsartillerie-Abteilung*) of three batteries – all of them trained in mountain warfare. This police regiment was actually earmarked for front-line service in northern Finland, but was to receive its baptism of fire against the Slovenian partisans.

The drive was planned to last from June until 27 July 1942. In attendance for this drive were *SS-Obergruppenführer* Dr. Alois

Friedrich Rainer, the *Gauleiter* (Nazi Party District Leader) for Carinthia, and head of the civilian administration for *Oberkrain* and *Untersteiermark; SS-Gruppenführer und Generalleutnant der Waffen SS- und der Polizei* Erwin Rösener, in command of the *Höhere-SS- und Polizeiführer Alpenland* (Higher SS & Police Command 'Alpenland'), and *SS-Oberstgruppenführer and Generaloberst der Polizei* Kurt Daluege, who was the head of the German *Ordnungspolizei*. *Wehrmannschaftsbataillon 'Süd'* was used in company and platoon-sized units to assist each of the police mountain rifle battalions. They not only helped to guide the police units, but also served in such auxiliary roles as interpreters, scouts, and flank protection for the advancing German police units.

Figure 16. The arm band of the ethnic-German Slovenian ***Wehrmannschaft***. A lion rampant inside a white circle on a horizontal white and green background. The arm band was worn on the left sleeve of the field blouse. (Author's black and white drawing)

In July, *Polizei-Gebirgsjäger-Regiment 18,* now deployed in the Upper Krajina region, began the drive. During August, its operations extended to the areas of Blegos, Pokljuca, Jelovica, the Steiner Alps, and the Tucheinartal. At the beginning of September, the regiment advanced through Jelovica, Herzogswald, and St. Valentin (near Moerautsch). In October, its movements encompassed Leermos-Ehrwald, Hammersbach, Greinau, and Kreuzeck, after which the unit devoted the remainder of the month to reorganisation and replenishment. The subject of the attack was the encirclement of the Partisan 2nd Group of Detachments (battalion in size) and the 1st Battalion of the 1st Group of Detachments. Although the drive was to have lasted until July, it continued through August and into September, with *Polizei-Gebirgsjäger-Regiment 18,*

Wehrmannschaftsbataillon 'Süd', and other smaller police, SS, and SD forces carrying the drive through the localities of Blegos, Pokljuka, Jelovca, the Steiner Alps, and Tucheinartal. By 5 September the Slovenian partisans had been pushed back to the Topolsica region, *Polizei-Gebirgsjäger-Regiment 18* moved through that region bordering the Italian/German demarcation area in Slovenia. It was in the Topolsica area that the *Wehrmannschaft* reportedly burnt down the settlements of Smrekovec and Sv. Kriz in the first week of September. The reason given was that these small settlements had provided assistance to the withdrawing guerrillas.

The German command thought that the operation had gone so well that Dr. Rainer held a victory parade in Kranj (Krainburg) on 27 September 1942 and announced that *Oberkrain* (Gorenjska, or Upper Carnolia) had been made 'quiet' at last. It was a boast that would prove premature, for on 23 October 1942 the Partisan 'Pohorje' Battalion attacked the German *Gendarmerie* post at Oplotnica, and destroyed it, also making sure to burn the local Burgermeister's building. In fact, this guerrilla battalion attacked over 100 separate times during the last three months of 1942, before retiring for winter quarters at Trijezebljina Pohurju where it would later be betrayed to the *Wehrmannschaft* and police during the winter of 1942–3. The next significant encounter between the Wehrmannschaft and the guerrillas was the destruction of the 'Pohorje' Battalion during a battle during the night of 7–8 January 1943. The location of the guerrilla battalion's base of operations was given away by pro-German Slovenians during late December 1942. The unit had been raiding local farms and towns for foodstuffs and other supplies needed to keep them operational during the hard winter, and it was one of these farmers, angered by the pilfering, who turned them in to the German authorities.

The operation was quickly prepared by the *Befehlshaber der Ordnungspolizei 'Alpenland'* (Commander of the Order Police 'Alpine Region') and numbered *Einsatzbefehl Nr. 106* (Operational Order Number 106), dated 6 January 1943. The text of the command noted that a strong guerrilla unit of battalion strength had been identified in a region about 20km south-west of Maribor (Marburg), and that a small reconnaissance force, sent in as a *Jagdkommando* (pathfinder unit), had already detected at least thirty partisans encamped in this heavily forested area. The attacking police units were to be split up into four sectors, which would advance into the cordoned area, blocking the withdrawal or destroying any partisans that they encountered along the way until all sector units converged, and the enemy was either killed or captured. The units and assigned for the operation and their sectors were as follows:[1]

Sector I – *Hauptmann der Schutzpolizei* Plecko
4. Kompanie / Polizei-Wachbataillon I Wien
2. Kompanie / Polizei-Wachbataillon Wiesbanden
5. Kompanie / Polizei-Wachbataillon Alpenland
staging area: Leppe
Sector II – *Hauptmann der Schutzpolizei* Kreipel
3. Kompanie / SS-Polizeiregiment 19
Reserve-Gendarmerie-Kompanie Alpenland 1 (motorisiert)
Gendarmerie-Kompanie Marburg
staging area: Osojnka
Sector III – *Hauptmann der Gendarmerie* Winkler
350 men of the *Wehrmacht*
staging area: NW of Jaworski Vrh
Sector IV – *SA-Sturmbannführer* Töscher
Wehrmannschaftsbataillon 'Süd'
staging area: W of Leppe

Accompanying the *Wehrmannschaft* battalion was Franz Steindl, the head of the ethnic-German *Heimatbund* in Stajerska (Styria). The German officer in overall charge of this anti-guerrilla operation was *SS-Standartenführer* Otto Lurker, Chief of the Security Police and SD forces in Styria. The battle began at around 4:30 in the morning, with the German police forces approaching undiscovered. The majority of the guerrilla battalion was caught by surprise as most were sleeping in their wooden bunkers which were partly buried into the ground. After the battle, dozens of bodies littered the snow-covered forest. By 1943 the Slovenian guerrilla menace had increased to such proportions the following localities:

Table 10. *Wehrmannschaft* Self-Defence Battalions in the Spring of 1943

Wehrmannschaft Bataillon	Town/City
Mitte	Maribor (Marburg)
Ost	Maribor (Marburg)
Nord	Bled (Veldes)
West	Kranj (Krainburg)
Süd	Celja (Cilli)

It was in 1943 that the *Wehrmannschaft* battalions were numbered consecutively from I to V as follows:

> *Wehrmannschaft Bataillon Süd* became: *Wehrmannschaft Bataillon I*
> *Wehrmannschaft Bataillon West* became: *Wehrmannschaft Bataillon II*
> *Wehrmannschaft Bataillon Nord* became: *Wehrmannschaft Bataillon III*
> *Wehrmannschaft Bataillon Ost* became: *Wehrmannschaft Bataillon IV*
> *Wehrmannschaft Bataillon Mitte* became: *Wehrmannschaft Bataillon V*

Support for these auxiliary police battalions came in the way of additional police units being sent to the region. In late February or early March 1944, the reinforced *SS-Polizeiregiment 13* made its appearance in the Upper Carinthia (*Oberkrain*) region. *SS-Polizeiregiment 14*, which had been operating out of Ogulin, Croatia since September 1943, was shifted to Upper Carinthia (Upper Carnolia) in February 1944. *SS-Polizeiregiment 28 'Todt'* was similarly sent to the *Oberkrain* region in the same month. In August 1944 the *I. Bataillon* of *SS-Polizeiregiment 25* was transferred to Celje (Cilli). In January 1945 the *I. Bataillon* of *SS-Polizeiregiment 'Alpenvorland'* was transferred to Upper Carinthia. *SS-Polizeiregiment 17* and *Polizeiregiment Nagel* were also transferred to this region in late 1944. In October 1944 *Wehrmannschaft-Regiment Untersteiermark,* along with the thousands of *Selbstschutz* were incorporated into *Regiment Untersteiermark,* along with the thousands of *selbstschutz* were followed the German withdrawal into Austria in late April 1945.

The Slovenian Littoral Guard

On 12 November 1943 a Slovenian Home Guard Lieutenant-Colonel by the name of Anton (Tone) Kokalj, from the western Slovenian province of Primorska, raised a new Slovene collaborationist force called the *Slovenski Narodni Varnostni Zbor* (SNVZ, Slovene National Security Force) in the port of Koper. Colonel Kokalj had received permission to raise this force not only from *SS-Obergruppenführer und General der Waffen-SS- und Polizei* Erwin Rösner – head of the *Höherer SS- und Polizeiführer für SS-Oberabschnitt Alpenland* command — but also from *SS-Gruppenführer und Generalleutnant der Polizei* Odilo Globocnik, who was head of the *Höherer SS- und Polizeiführer 'Adriatisches Küstenland'*. This latter SS command was responsible for the three north-eastern regions of Italy bordering Austria and Slovenia. This area and the Primorska region of Slovenia would be the area where the SNVZ would be employed. Initially and during its entire life span, recruiting efforts for the unit would be hampered by two problems. The first was the fact that the Italian Army had drafted Slovenians into its forces in Africa during their reign over the region.

Figure 17. The Slovenian Littoral Guard SNVC arm patch. It sported a red Viking boat riding a blue ocean, with a white background. The cloth shield was worn on the left sleeve of the field blouse, approximately 1/3 of the way down from the sleeve cap. (Author's black and white drawing)

Many of these Slovenians had been either captured or had surrendered to the British Commonwealth forces there. Later many were recruited for the Royal Yugoslav Army in exile which was being organised inside Yugoslavia. The second problem lay in the fact that by late 1943 the war was clearly turning against the Axis, so recruits were not so forthcoming. The headquarters for the SNVZ was established in Triest, and soon Colonel Kokalj had a few companies of volunteers. Colonel Franc Krenner was able to supply Kokalj with some *Domobranci* officers which would help train the new recruits. In March 1944 an SNVZ Urban Police force was established in the major cities and towns: Kokalj with some *Domobranci* officers would help train the new recruits. In March 1944 an SNVZ Urban Police force was established in the major cities and towns of the Istrian Peninsula.

An SNVZ Rural Police force, *Orozniski Zbor*, was also established almost a year later, in February 1945, but this force never got past the preliminary stages. The numbers of volunteers continued to come in dribs and drabs, but by August 1944 the organisation reached its peak strength of 1,782 men in sixteen rifle companies. These companies were spread out into four regions as shown:

Postojna – Triest Province
Gorica – Gorica Province
Ilirska Bistrica – Rijeka Province
Idrija Province – Rijeka Province

Table 11. SNVZ Urban Police Forces, March 1944

SNVZ Police Unit	Town/City [Slovene – Italian – German]
Triest Kompanie	Triest
Gorz Kompanie	Gorizia – Gorica – Gorz
1. Zug	Pola – Pola – Pula
2. Zug	Koper – Capodistria
3. Zug	Rijeka – Fiume – Fiume
4. Zug	Idrija – Idria – Idria
5. Zug	Postojna – Pustumio – Adelsberg

Initially, these SNVZ rifle companies were spread out amongst the vast countryside, and as a result, possessed no offensive capabilities and only minimal defensive ability. In order to change this and make the SNVZ a more effective anti-partisan force, SS General Globocnik decreed on 27 October 1944 that the SNVZ companies were to concentrate in the region between Postojna and Ilirska Bistrica, where they would be regrouped into four battalions (numbered 1 to 4) which would be controlled by a newly raised SNVZ regimental headquarters. The designation of the regiment was *Slowenisches Küsten-Sturm-Regiment 1* (1st Slovenian Coastal Assault Regiment).

Each SNVZ battalion contained four rifle companies and one heavy weapons company. In December 1944 this SNVZ regiment was moved to an area between Postojna and Idrija and assigned railway security duty and other traffic communication. Their main enemy was the Slovenian Partisan 9th Corps and its 10,000 combatants. The SNVZ Regiment employed three of its four battalions, since the 2nd Battalion was designated as the training unit for the regiment and remained located in the town of Postojna. In February 1945 this 2nd Battalion was re-designated as the *Reservna dezelna bramba* (Reserve Defence Force). Its commander at this time was Major Sinkovec, a *Domobranci* officer who had been assigned to the SNVZ directly from Ljubljana.

By the autumn of 1944 the Slovene 9th Partisan Corps had established a stronghold north-east of Gorizia, and had disrupted rail and road traffic so completely that SS General Odilo Globocnik was forced to launch a major anti-guerrilla operation titled *Unternehmen Adler* (Operation Eagle). The operation was to take place in the Gorizia-Sambasso-Vipacco area. This drive began on 19 December 1944 and would last until the 23rd of the month. Its objective was nothing less than the destruction of the 9th Partisan Corps. A total of a little over 9,000 men were used. The units employed included a variety of formations:[2]

III. Bataillon, SS-Polizeiregiment 10.[3]
5. (verstärkte) Polizei-Panzerkompanie, 121 men containing five T-34 tanks, five Renault R-35 tanks and five Hotchkiss tanks.[4]
III. Bataillon, SS-Police-Regiment 15[5]
Sonder-Bataillon Hein (German mountain troops from the *188. Gebirgs-Division*).
Slowenisches Küsten-Sturm-Regiment 1, with 1,500 men split into four battalions.
Italienisches Polizei-Freiwilligen-Bataillon 'Gorizia' (323 men)
2nd (Italian) Fusilier Battalion, with 260 men.
14th (Italian) Frontier Battalion, with 522 men.
(Italian) Alpine Mountain Regiment 'Tagliamento', with about 3,000 men.
(Italian) Bersaglieri Battalion 'Mussolini' with 569 men.
4th (Italian) National Republican Guard Regiment, with 750 men.
1. Regiment, Serbisches-Freiwilligen-Korps – located in Postojna with 500 men.
Total Strength (by nationality): 1,900 Germans, 1,500 Slovenians, 500 Serbians, and 5,424 Italians. Grand Total: 9,324

As often happened, the number of troops, although substantial, proved to be insufficient to keep the guerrillas from slipping through some openings in the lines, and most of the partisan force was able to escape. In February 1945 the command and control of the SNVZ regiment was disrupted, when Colonel Tone Kokalj was killed in action. While a replacement was sought, *SS-Sturmbannführer* Georg Michalsen assumed command of the regiment, until April when Major Janko Dabeljak assumed control. The next major operation in which the SNVZ regiment took part in was another anti-partisan drive begun in early March 1945 and code-named *Unternehmen Rübezahl* (Operation Mountain Spirit). This time, the Axis forces were trying to destroy the partisan forces in the town of Lokve. This attack was launched by two separate combat groups. The first group, 3,000 strong, was code-named *Unternehmen Zuschneid* (Operation Tailor cut, or Cut-to-Size). This group was made up of three SS police battalions from *SS-Polizeiregiment 10* and the *Slowenisches Küsten-Sturm-Regiment 1*. The second combat group, comprising 2,500 men and code-named *Kampfgruppe Köstermann*, was made up of two battalions of the *Infanterie-Regiment 730* from the *710. Infanterie-Division*, plus a small German/Italian police company and a platoon of engineers. *Unternehmen Rübezahl* was deemed moderately successful, and the town of Lokve and its surroundings was temporarily cleared of guerrillas. On 19 March 1945, a third and final offensive was launched by the *Slowenisches Küsten-Sturm-Regiment 1* and other forces under the command of the *Höhere-SS- und Polizeiführer Adriatisches Küstenland* (Higher SS & Police Leader 'Adriatic Coast'). This operation lasted until 7 April 1945 but was an overall disappointment, since the 9th Partisan Corps was able to once again escape the trap set by the Germans and their Axis allies. *Küsten-Sturm-Regiment 1* remained in the Gorizia area until it surrendered to the advancing British 8th Army in early May 1945.

Creation of the Slovenian Home Guard

Figure 18. Cloth arm shield of the Slovenian Home Guard. A blue eagle inside a shield on a white background. (Author's black and white drawing)

On 10 September 1943 – just two days after the Italian surrender – the Germans attached the former *'Provincia di Lubiana'* (Ljubljana Province), which the Italians had annexed in 1941, to their newly created *Operationszone Adriatisches Küstenland* (Operational Zone Adriatic Coast). This was the military district created by the *Wehrmacht* for administrative and operational control of this north-eastern region of Italy as well as western and central areas of Slovenia. In addition, the SS command created the *Höhere-SS- und Polizeiführer Adriatisches Küstenland* (Higher SS and Police Leader Adriatic Coast). This SS position was given to *SS-Obergruppenführer und General der Polizei* Odilo Globocnik on 13 September 1943.

On 15 September 1943, Friedrich Rainer, *Gauleiter* of *Reichsgau Kärnten* (Carinthia Reichsgau), arrived in Ljubljana, where he conferred with Bishop Gregorij Rožman. During their meeting, Rožman proposed that the city's mayor, General Leon (Lev) Rupnik, a former officer of the Yugoslav Army, be appointed head of the newly established civil administration in the Province of Ljubljana. This administrative restructuring followed the German assumption of authority after the collapse of the Italian occupation in the wake of Italy's armistice that month. Rupnik accepted the proposal and was formally appointed on 20 September 1943. In the same month, the *Slovensko domobranstvo* (Slovene Home Guard) was constituted, drawing its initial manpower from Slovenian collaborationist formations that had previously operated under Italian auspices.

On 24 September 1943 Rupnik organised what he initially referred to as the *Slovenska Domobranska Legija* (Slovene Defence Legion) from some 2,000 former *Milizia Voluntari Anti-Communista* (MVAC – Voluntary Anti-Communist Militia). This legion was quickly organised into three combat battalions. A day later, during the temporary absence of *SS-Obergruppenführer und General der Waffen-SS- und Polizei* Erwin Friedrich Karl Rösener, Rupnik proclaimed himself commander of the Home Guard, though he was quickly displaced once Rösener returned to Ljubljana. On 30 September 1943 the Germans assumed control of this force and quickly renamed it the *Slovensko domobranstvo* (Slovene Home Guard). Although Leon Rupnik retained his rank of Lieutenant-General, and he was given the honorary title of 'Inspector General of the Home Guard', he was nevertheless relegated to running the civilian collaborationist government in Ljubljana. Rösener appointed an ethnic-German named Franc Krenner as commander of the *Slovensko domobranstvo* and given the rank of *Oberst der Polizei* (Colonel of the Police) and assigned actual operational control over the Slovenian Home Guard.

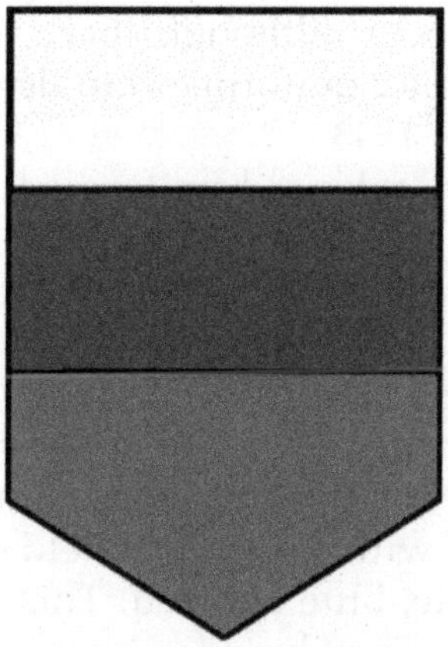

Figure 19. The Slovenian shield, sporting the national colors (white, blue, red). It was worn on the left side of the helmet. (Author's black and white drawing)

Shortly thereafter, on 12 October 1943, Rösener formally appointed *Oberstleutnant* (Lieutenant-Colonel) Franc Krenner as commander of the *Organisationsstab* of the *Slovensko domobranstvo*; Krenner was subsequently promoted to the rank of full colonel on 1 January 1945. To reinforce German control and ensure effective coordination, Rösener also established an *Aufbaustab,* composed of German officers tasked with setting the organisational framework for the Home Guard's headquarters and serving as liaisons between German military units and the Slovene formation. These officers were attached to Home Guard units in an advisory capacity. Both the *Organisationsstab* and the *Aufbaustab* remained directly subordinate to Rösener's command structure. Between 1943 and 1945 the Slovene Home Guard would be expanded greatly.

Leon Rupnik's son, Vuk Rupnik, became a top officer in the Slovene Home Guard. He initially was granted the rank of *Major der Polizei* but he was later promoted to colonel of the police for his bravery in combat. In January 1945 he was awarded the German Iron Cross (1st Class) for leading a battalion of the Home Guard in battle. This initial Home Guard force of 2,000 men was quickly expanded to sixty-three companies, of which forty-three companies were distributed throughout the Slovenian countryside as small garrison outposts, while the remainder was grouped into battalions. The uniform was now changed and the Germans supplied a grey-green blouse and accompanying trousers. This grey-green uniform might have come from ex-Dutch army stocks, although there is ample photographic evidence that German police uniforms were also distributed, especially during the second half of 1943.

The old Italian brown-coloured uniforms (light brown, or tan for officers) were still used, but by the summer of 1944 the Home Guard units were dressed in either grey-green or German police uniforms which were more of a darker green-grey colour. Boot covers were mainly German police style. The Slovenian national eagle was introduced as a cloth insignia in blue against a white background shield. This was worn on the left sleeve. In addition, the Italian helmets were decorated with a painted shield showing the Slovenian national colours of white, blue and red. This shield was painted on the side of the helmets. The shoulder boards were typical German police insignia. The soft cover initially used the triangular metallic cockade with the Slovenian national colours (white-blue-red), but later was changed to an oval cockade.

On 30 September 1943 the Germans assumed control of the 'Slovene Defence Legion', which had been formed just six days earlier, on 24 September by Leon Rupnik. As stated earlier, of the sixty-three companies in existence by the beginning of 1944, forty-three of them were spread out as garrisons, while the remaining twenty companies were formed into combat battalions. It was also in the autumn of 1944 that the Slovenian Home Guard reached its maximum strength of 18,000 men.[6] There were special support companies that were also organised. An Engineer, Communications, Medical, and Construction Company were also raised. The men of the Communications (Signals) Company wore a special metallic insignia on their collars. It resembled two lightning bolts crisscrossing one another.

Table 12. Slovenian *Domobranci* Companies, Winter 1943–1944

Region	Unit	Location	Location	Location
Notranjska (Inner Carnolia)	1st Home Guard Company	Brezovica		
Notranjska	2nd Home Guard Company	Notranje Gore		
Notranjska	3rd Home Guard Company	Borovnica		

Region	Unit	Location	Location	Location
Notranjska	4th Home Guard Company	Borovnica		
Notranjska	5th Home Guard Company	Verd		
Notranjska	6th Home Guard Company	Logatec		
Notranjska	7th Home Guard Company	Rakek		
Ljubljana, then Notranjska	11th Home Guard Company	Ljubljana	Rudnik	Smarje
Ljubljana (Central Slovenia)	12th Home Guard Company	Ljubljana		
Ljubljana	13th Home Guard Company	Polje	Rakek	
Ljubljana	14th Home Guard Company	Polje		
Ljubljana	15th Home Guard Company	Dravlje, Skofljica	Veliki	Gaber
Ljubljana	16th Home Guard Company	Rudnik		
Ljubljana	17th Home Guard Company	Ljubljana	Vrhnika	
Ljubljana	18th Home Guard Company	Ljubljana		
Ljubljana	19th Home Guard Company	Dobrova		
Ljubljana	20th Home Guard Company	Ljubljana		
Ljubljana	21st Home Guard Company	Crna vas		
Ljubljana	22nd Home Guard Company	Skofljica		
Ljubljana	23rd Home Guard Company	Skofljica		

Region	Unit	Location	Location	Location
Dolenjska (Lower Carnolia)	24th Home Guard Company	Velike Lasce		
Dolenjska	25th Home Guard Company	Velike Lasce	Ribnica	
Dolenjska	26th Home Guard Company	Velike Lasce	Grosuplje	Visna Gora
Dolenjska	27th Home Guard Company	Grosuplje		
Dolenjska	28th Home Guard Company	Turjak		
Dolenjska	29th Home Guard Company	Velike Lasce		
Dolenjska	31st Home Guard Company	Novo Mesto		
Dolenjska	32nd Home Guard Company	Grm		
Dolenjska	33rd Home Guard Company	Novo Mesto	Trebnje	
Dolenjska	34th Home Guard Company	Locna		
Dolenjska	35th Home Guard Company	Grm	Trzisce	
Dolenjska	36th Home Guard Company	Kostanjevica	Sv. Ana	
Dolenjska	37th Home Guard Company	Lesnica		
Dolenjska	38th Home Guard Company	Kandija		
Dolenjska	39th Home Guard Company	Novo Mesto	St. Vid	
Dolenjska	40th Home Guard Company	Locna	Dolnji Vrh	
Ljubljana	41st Home Guard Company	Vrhnika		

Region	Unit	Location	Location	Location
Ljubljana	42nd Home Guard Company	Polhov Gradec		
Notranjska	43rd Home Guard Company	St. Jost	Rorjul	
Notranjska	44th Home Guard Company	Rovte		
Notranjska	45th Home Guard Company	Logatec		
Notranjska	46th Home Guard Company	Hotedrseica		
Notranjska	47th Home Guard Company	Idrijska Bela		
Notranjska	48th Home Guard Company	Planina		
Dolenjska	51st Home Guard Company	Bela Cerkev		
Dolenjska	52nd Home Guard Company	Kočevje		
Dolenjska	53rd Home Guard Company	Novo Mesto		
Dolenjska	54th Home Guard Company	Novo Mesto		
Dolenjska	55th Home Guard Company	Trebnje		
Dolenjska	56th Home Guard Company	Šmarješke Toplice		
Dolenjska	61st Home Guard Company	Kočevje		
Dolenjska	62nd Home Guard Company	Kočevje		
Dolenjska, then Notranjska, then Ljubljana	65th Home Guard Company	Ribnica, Zdenska Vas	Ljubljana	Vrhnika
Ljubljana	66th Home Guard Company	Škofja Loka		

Region	Unit	Location	Location	Location
Ljubljana	67th Home Guard Company	Vrhnika		
Ljubljana	71st Home Guard Company	Ljubljana		
Notranjska	72nd Home Guard Company	Postojna		
Notranjska	111th Home Guard Company	Cerknica		
Notranjska	112th Home Guard Company	Pivka		
Dolenjska	113th Home Guard Company	Metlika		
Dolenjska	114th Home Guard Company	Šentrupert		
Dolenjska	115th Home Guard Company	Dolenjske Toplice		

Finally, three Slovene Home Guard artillery batteries were created using captured Italian guns. The 1st and 2nd Batteries were stationed in Ljubljana, while the 3rd Artillery Battery was located at Velike Lasce. The formation of the five Slovene Home Guard combat battalions occurred between September and November 1943. By late September 1943 three battalions were organised. A fourth battalion, complete with a training school was established in November. This training battalion and school were located in Ljubljana. A combat battalion was also organised in November, in the town of Novo Mesto, so by 1 December 1943 the Slovenian Home Guard could count on the following organised battalions:

Table 13. Slovenian Home Guard Battalions, 1 December 1943

Slovenian Home Guard Battalion	Location
Slowenisches Heimatschützen-Bataillon 1	Ljublana
Slowenisches Heimatschützen-Bataillon 2	Vrhnika
Slowenisches Heimatschützen-Bataillon 3	Kostanjevica
Slowenisches Heimatschützen-Bataillon 4	Ljubljana
Slowenisches Heimatschützen-Bataillon 5	Novo Mesto

Oberst der Polizei Franc Krenner established his headquarters on 12 October 1943. He named it the *Organisacijski stab Slovenskega domobranstva* (Organisation Staff of the Slovene Home Guard). On 3 December 1943 Dr. Rainer decreed that henceforth, all Slovenian males were to be made available for compulsory military service in the Slovene Home Guard. By the end of this month the five Home Guard battalions were reorganised and expanded. From now on the battalions would be referred to as *kampfgruppen* (battlegroups), and their size would vary depending on the number of companies assigned at any one time. One of these *kampfgruppen* was led by Major Vuk Rupnik and was initially posted to the main headquarters of the Home Guard in Ljubljana *Grad* (Ljubljana Castle), which overlooks the city. During the winter of 1943–4 the Slovenian Home Guard battalions were reorganised and expanded to include seven *kampfgruppen* (battle groups), with varying numbers of Domobranci companies. These combat groups were organised and located in the following places:

Kampfgruppe 1 (nine companies) – Ljubljana
Kampfgruppe 2 (seven companies) – Skofljica[7]
Kampfgruppe 3 (eight companies) – Novo Mesto
Kampfgruppe 4 (five companies) – Vrhnika
Kampfgruppe 5 (six companies) – Borovnika
Kampfgruppe 6 (two companies) – Kocevje[8]
Kampfgruppe 7 (six companies) – Grosuplje[9]

In Ljubljana, the Home Guard School was reorganised into two school units: 1st Home Guard Battery – Ljubljana. The 2nd School Unit was abolished and disbanded on 15 January 1944. At this time, three Home Guard artillery batteries were also created using captured Italian guns. The batteries were numbered consecutively from 1 to 3 and were stationed as follows:

1st Home Guard Battery – Ljubljana
2nd Home Guard Battery – Ljubljana
3rd Home Guard Battery – Velike Lasce

The month of February 1944 saw a major reorganisation take place in the Home Guard. The seven combat groups were disbanded and reformed into four larger combat groups of regiment-to-brigade in size were established. These new groups were numbered and identified as follows:

Kriegseinheit – This was the ex-1st Group and acted as the Training Unit. It contained nine rifle companies, six training companies, one engineer company, plus the 1st and 2nd Artillery Batteries. This war unit was stationed in Ljubljana.
Kriegseinheit – This was the railway security formation whose headquarters was organised officially on 25 February 1944 in order to safeguard the Ljubljana – Rakek – Postojna Ljubljana – Skofljika – Grosuplje rail line. In order to accomplish this, five armoured trains were supplied by the Germans, who also supplied the Order Police and Rail Police officers to command the Slovenian Home Guard troopers, numbering twelve companies in all. This combat unit had been formed from the former 4th and 5th Combat Groups.
Kriegseinheit – This formation was placed under the control of the *I. Bataillon, SS-Polizeiregiment 14*. This German *Ordnungspolizei* unit was operating in the Upper Krajina region of northern Slovenia in the beginning of 1944. This formation was also responsible for the Mesto area. A special headquarters staff was organised to control these companies and was called the *Zeleznisko vanostno poveljstvo* (Railway Security Headquarters).
Kriegseinheit – This formation included troops who had formerly served in Skofljika, Velike Lasce, and Grosuplje. They had formed the ex-2nd, 6th and 7th (former) *Kampfgruppen*. This combat unit was directly under the control of the Slovene Home Guard Headquarters, but was also available for employment by any local or regional German military headquarters. This unit also included former soldiers from the elite *Heimatschützen Sturmbataillon Kriz* (Assault Battalion 'Kriz'), which had been formed in the autumn of 1943.

This organisation remained the same until mid-May 1944 when the strength of the Slovenian Home Guard had by then reached a strength of some 12,000 men. After the initial success of the storm unit, the Germans decided to expand on the concept by increasing the number of 'storm' battalions from one to four (one under each of the four war units). The initial storm battalion, which had been formed on 26 March 1944, had contained two rifle (later raised to three) and one heavy weapons company. This small but highly flexible and mobile establishment had proven effective in combating the Tito's (Slovenian) partisan units. On 16 May 1944 the whole country was divided into four operational zones, and (as stated above), each contained one *Udarni* (assault) battalion. The assault battalions were now located as follows:

Table 14. Home Guard Assault Battalions, May 1944

Town or City	Province	Assault Battalion
Ljubljana	Ljubljana	*Heimatschützen-Sturmbataillon Nord*
Rakak	Notranjska	*Heimatschützen-Sturmbataillon West*
Grosuplje	Dolenjska	*Heimatschützen Sturmbataillon Mitte*
Trebnje	Dolenjska	*Heimatschützen Sturmbataillon Ost*

Less than two months later, on 5 July 1944 these 'storm' battalions were re-numbered, and a fifth battalion was added as follows:

Table 15. Slovenian Home Guard Assault Battalions, July 1944

New Designation	Old Designation	Town	Province
Heimatschützen-Sturmbataillon 1	*Heimatschützen-Sturmbataillon Nord*	Ljubljana	Ljubljana
Heimatschützen-Sturmbataillon 2	*Heimatschützen-Sturmbataillon West*	Rakak	Notranjska
Heimatschützen-Sturmbataillon 3	*Heimatschützen Sturmbataillon Mitte*	Grosuplje	Dolenjska
Heimatschützen-Sturmbataillon 4	Heimatschützen Sturmbataillon Ost	Trebnje	Dolenjska
Heimatschützen-Sturmbataillon 5	Alarm-Bataillon Schmitz[10]	Ribnica	Dolenjska

As previously stated, by the middle of 1944 the Home Guard had increased dramatically. It could now count on sixty-three rifle companies, and one company each of (a) engineers, (b) communications (signals), (c) medical, and (d) construction. It also contained four artillery batteries: two located in Ljubljana, one at Velike Lasce, and one permanently attached to the armoured trains, of which there were five. *Heimatschützen-Sturmbataillon Nord* used its six training companies to guard the capital of Ljubljana, while its nine rifle companies were responsible for patrolling the valley of the Krka River all the way to Zuzemberk in the Dolenjska district and the area up to the village of Moravce (to the north). The *Heimatschützen-Sturmbataillon Mitte,* with its eleven rifle companies, had the duty of guarding the Ribnica Valley in the Kocevska district and part of the Suha Krajina district.

The *Heimatschützen-Sturmbataillon West* was charged with protecting the Polhovgraj ski, and Dolomiti hills in the Notranjska District. The *Heimatschützen-Sturmbataillon Ost* was to patrol the Dolenjska district with Novo Mesto and the Bela Krajina district. These Home Guard assault battalions were organised in the same manner as the German SS Order Police units. They included three rifle companies and one heavy weapons company, but being formed from native volunteers, were considered much more dangerous to the guerrillas due to their knowledge of the language, peoples'political leanings, and terrain. Heavy battles began to take a toll on the Slovenian Home Guard forces beginning in July 1944. Tito would grant an amnesty later in the summer to all Yugoslav Axis forces that voluntarily laid down their arms and / or switched sides. It was apparent that the Axis forces were now on the losing end of the war, and many former native pro-Axis soldiers in Yugoslavia chose to either desert or defect.

The morale of the Slovenian nationalist forces had been affected adversely when the Western Allies had decided to make amphibious landings on the northern and southern French coast, avoiding the Balkans altogether – save for a few small, token landings on some islands in the Adriatic and Aegean Sea. Faced with the realisation that they could not expect the Western Allies to help them prevent the fall of Slovenia to eventual communist domination, many Slovenian nationalists lost hope and simply gave up the struggle, while only the most fanatical diehards continued to serve alongside the Germans in a last-ditch effort to prevent a communist victory in Slovenia. Yet in spite of these desertions, the Germans were able to maintain at least six Slovenian Home Guard combat battalions in the field, plus a score of other, independent companies, as late as March 1945.

The Germans, who had known all along that the Slovenian nationalists were hoping to be saved by the Western Allies, never fully trusted the *Domobranci*. This became truly evident in December 1944 when the German command decided to attach one *SS Ordnungspolizei* company to each of the Home Guard battalions (with the exception of *Heimatschützen-Sturmbataillon* 2) from *SS-Polizeiregiment 14* and *SS-Polizeiregiment 17* which were then operating in the region.[11] This was clearly done to 'stiffen' the Home Guard and also to keep a closer eye on their activities. Another, more telling incident was found in a German document, dated '14 January 1945' which described how on 30 December 1944 the local SS and Police forces had to disarm the Home Guard garrison at Bistrica. From the report, it seems as though the entire formation was forced to enter Austria, escorted by the German forces.[12]

Other captured documents indicate that the Germans were attempting to split up their collaborationist Axis forces into smaller, more manageable groups and to mingle them whenever possible with German or more reliable Axis troops. For example, on 20 June 1944 in the Trieste region, the town of Aidussina (Adelsberg) was garrisoned by a 49-man *Wehrmannschaft-Selbstschutz* (Self-Defence) platoon, together with 76 men and one officer of the SNVZ *5. Kompanie, II. Bataillon, Slowenisches Küsten-Sturm-Regiment 1*. Another, earlier example involved 100 Germans, 150 Italians, and 50 *Domobranci*.[13] On 7 January 1945 the garrison of Aidussina would change to include 140 'White Guard' troops. These were most likely members of the pro-German *Russisches Schutzkorps* (*Russiches Schutzkorps*). This force consisted of anti-communist 'White' Tsarist exiles who formed a pro-German unit in Yugoslavia in 1941.

Three days later that number would slightly increase to 160 by the arrival of a platoon of twenty 'Nedic' men – the remnants of men from the Serbian puppet government State and Frontier Guard.[14] In Logatec, about 26km east-north-east of Aidussina, another 60 'White Guardists' and 80 'Nedic' men were quartered as of 10 January 1945.[15] A later report about Axis strength in the town of Aidussina (Adelsberg), listed 1,800 Germans, 80 'White Guardists', and between 1,500–2,000 'Nedic' troops. This same report noted an additional fifty 'White Guardists' at Vipava, 6km south-east of Aidussina, and 1,200 'Nedic' men in Prestanek, which lay 6km south-west of Aidussina. Another 5,000–6,000 Axis troops containing German, Italian, and Slovenian troops were in Gorizia (Görz). These and other reports point to the idea that the Germans were trying to stiffen the resolve of the Home Guard by mixing their forces with German or other Axis units. The existence of any Slovenian Home Guard regiments has been denied by post-war Slovenian (communist) sources.

This seems rather self-serving, since it implies that the Germans didn't trust the *Domobranci* enough to allow them to form regimental-sized units, but what they fail to see is that by 1945 they were in desperate straits, so much so that it would have been of little importance to the German command if Slovenian units were grouped into larger formations, so long as they were able to operate more effectively. The first hint of these *Domobranci* regiments comes from a German *'Kriegsgliederung'* schematic report dated 6 March 1945.

Among numerous anti-partisan forces under the various SS and Police commands in Italy, the Austrian frontier and Slovenia, it lists (very clearly) three *Domobranci* 'assault regiments' and thirty *Domobranci* 'defence' companies. Each regiment was carefully drawn, complete with two battalions of Home Guard still contained the following battalions:

Table 16. Slovenian Assault Battalions, March 1945

Date	Old Designation	New Designation
1944	*Sturm-Bataillon 1*	*Sturm-Bataillon 1*
1944	*Sturm-Bataillon 2*	*Sturm-Bataillon 5*
1944	*Sturm-Bataillon 3*	Disbanded March 1945
July '44	*Sturm-Bataillon 4*	*Sturm-Bataillon 2*
Sept. '44	*Sturm-Bataillon 5*	*Sturm-Bataillon 6*
March '45	*Sturm-Bataillon 6*	*Sturm-Bataillon 10*
March '45	New Formation	*Sturm-Bataillon 12*

The first actual mention of these Slovenian Domobran regiments was on 3 March 1945. when the Germans launched *Unternehmen Rübezahl* (Operation Mountain Spirit), an operation aimed at keeping partisan forces away from Trieste. During this drive, the Germans employed the *Slowenisches Küsten-Sturm-Regiment 1,* three German police battalions, two battalions of the 1st Regiment of the *Serbisches-Freiwilligen-Korps* (Serbian Volunteer Corps), parts of the *Russisches Schutzkorps,* the *Infanterie-Regiment 730,* and one company of the *III. Bataillon, SS-Polizeiregiment 10* plus an artillery battery. In addition, *Polizei-Signals-Kompanie 181* which was stationed in Veldes was used. Altogether about 7,000 German and Axis soldiers were employed. The fact that these six battalions were still in existence at a time when the three Home Guard regiments were supposed to have contained altogether six battalions, leads one to conclude that indeed it was possible that the Germans may have authorised the formation of these regiments. In addition, one published source, written by a former Home Guard officer, mentions that four Home Guard regiments (numbered 1 to 4) were in existence and eventually surrendered to British forces in May 1945 at Blieburg, just inside the Austrian border.[16]

We know that on 3 May 1945 the Slovene National Alliance – that is, those nationalist forces that were against a communist victory in

Slovenia – proclaimed Slovenian 'independence', hoping to get Allied protection from the Tito forces. A day later, on 4 May it revived the 'Slovene National Army' which had been planned in July 1943 but had petered out due to a lack of an Allied response. This new 'Slovene National Army', composed of the remnants of the Slovene Home Guard, SNVZ, and the Upper Carnolia Home Defence Force might have decided to create these four Home Guard regiments, but developments were moving too fast for them to have had time to organise these various forces into four regiments in less than a month. In addition, notice that of the sixty or more companies that existed in 1944, thirty remained independent as of March 1945. This leads one to consider that the other thirty were either disbanded, or formed into battalions and (yes) even possibly into regiments. It is more likely therefore, that these regiments (at least three that we can definitely confirm) did in fact exist. German records prove it. Published *Domobranci* memoirs corroborate it, and circumstantial evidence points to it.

The Ethnic-German Serbians of the Banat

The Banat region, a historically multiethnic area in the Kingdom of Yugoslavia, straddling the borders of Serbia, Romania, and Hungary, was home to a significant population of ethnic Germans, known as Danube Swabians – *Volksdeutsche* who had settled there since the eighteenth century.[17] By the early 1940s, this community numbered roughly 120,000 to 130,000 individuals, concentrated in towns such as Pančevo, Vršac and Zrenjanin, as well as in surrounding rural villages.[18] Following the Axis invasion of Yugoslavia in 1941, the Banat came under German occupation, and the local *Volksdeutsche* were soon drawn into the structures of the Nazi regime.[19] The German authorities, seeking to exploit ethnic German populations in the Balkans for military purposes, established recruitment programmes under the auspices of the *Volksdeutsche Mittelstelle* (VoMi), which coordinated the mobilisation of ethnic Germans outside the Reich.[20]

Between 1942 and 1943, approximately 21,000 men from the Banat were recruited into the newly formed *7. SS-Freiwilligen-Gebirgs-Division 'Prinz Eugen'*.[21] While the division was officially designated as a volunteer unit, many of these recruits were subject to significant pressure or indirect coercion.[22] Motivations for joining varied widely; some men were driven by ideological alignment with the Nazi regime and anti-communist sentiment, while others responded to economic incentives or sought to avoid punitive measures for noncompliance.[23] Regardless of motivation, these recruits were trained in mountain warfare in Austria and Germany before being deployed in counter-insurgency operations across Serbia, Montenegro, and later Bosnia.[24] The recruitment of Banat *Volksdeutsche* into the SS *'Prinz Eugen'* division illustrates the complex intersection of ethnicity, coercion, and military mobilisation in the occupied Balkans during the Second World War.[25]

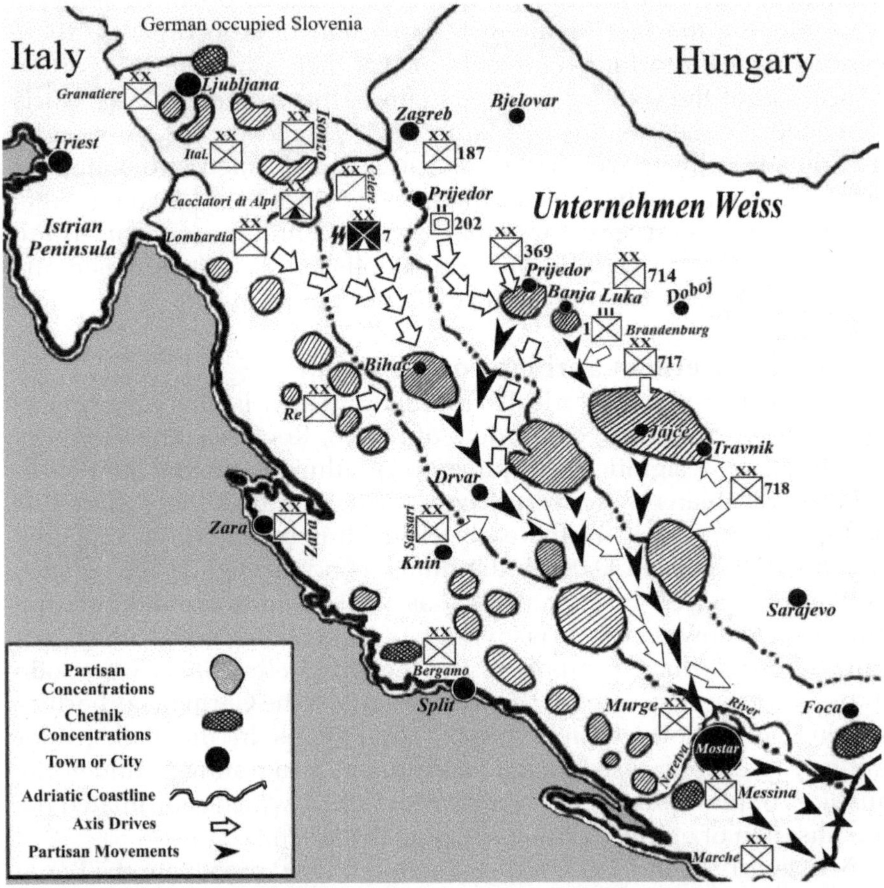

Figure 20. An overall view of ***Unternehmen Weiss*** (Operation White), March–April 1943. (Author's line drawing)

It underscores the role of the Nazi administration in shaping local populations into instruments of its military and ideological objectives, while also revealing the difficult choices faced by ethnic German communities navigating survival, loyalty, and political pressures under occupation.[26]

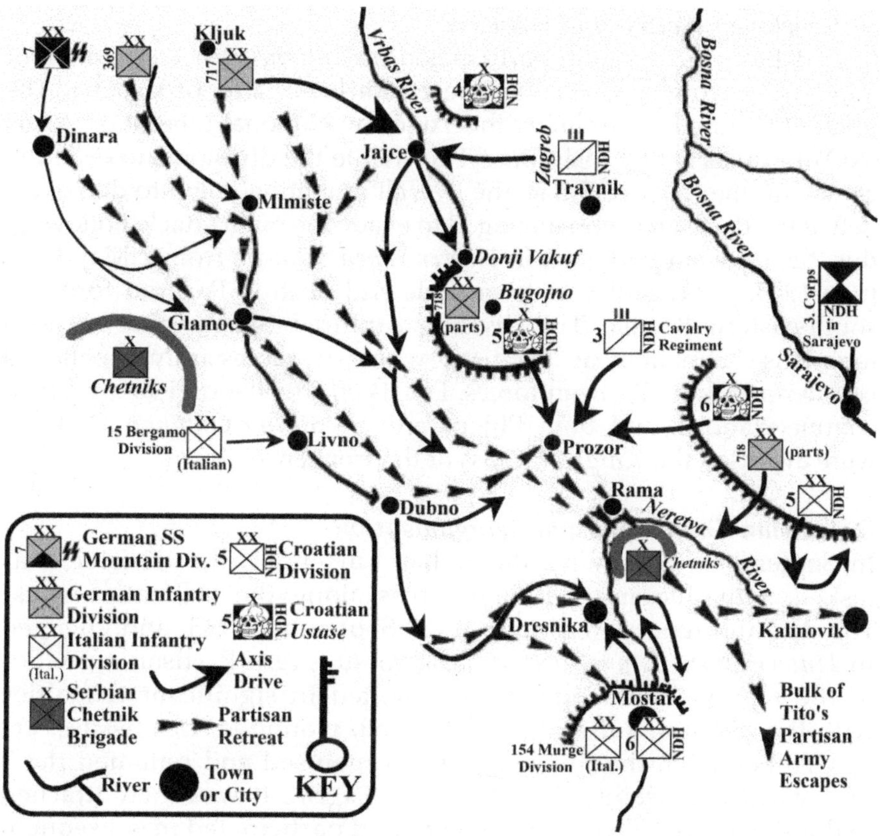

Figure 21. Detail view of Operation White. (Author's line drawing)

Although the *7. SS-Gebirgs-Division 'Prinz Eugen'* was primarily composed of *Volksdeutsche* (ethnic Germans) from the Banat region of Serbia, it also received ethnic Germans from Croatia, Hungary, and even Romania. The division was formed in 1942. Its initial training focused on mountain warfare, preparing it for operations in the rugged terrain of the Balkans.[27] The commander of the division was *SS-Brigadeführer* Artur Phleps, an ethnic German from Romania. In 1941, he left Romania and joined the *Waffen-SS*. He served in the SS *Wiking* Division on the Russian front. The division's first significant combat experience came during *Unternehmen Kopaonik* in early 1943. This operation aimed to suppress Yugoslav Partisan forces in the Kopaonik mountain range. The division, alongside Bulgarian units, engaged in heavy fighting, marking its first large-scale engagement under Phleps's command.

Unternehmen WeiSS- und Schwarz

In mid-1943, the division participated in *Unternehmen Weiss*, a major anti-Partisan offensive in the Zagreb-Karlovac area of Croatia. The operation aimed to eliminate the Yugoslav National Liberation Army (NOVJ) forces led by Josip Broz Tito. While the division succeeded in capturing the town of Bihać, the overall operation failed to decisively defeat the Partisans, who managed to evade the main attack. Following this, the division took part in *Unternehmen Schwarz* from 2 May to 15 June 1943.[28] The goal was to encircle and destroy Partisan forces in south-eastern Bosnia. The division captured Šavnik and engaged in intense combat near Tjentište, where it successfully repelled a counter-attack by Partisan forces. For its efforts, the division received commendations, and both Phleps and *SS-Sturmbannführer* Dietsche were awarded the Knight's Cross of the Iron Cross.

Dalmatian Campaigns and Reorganisation

In September 1943, with the Italian surrender, the division was tasked with disarming Italian forces along the Dalmatian coast. The division reoccupied Split on 29 September 1943, and engaged in *Unternehmen Landsturm*, aiming to suppress Partisan activities in the region. These operations resulted in significant casualties, with the division suffering 1,582 killed, wounded, or missing. On 22 October 1943, the division was reorganised and renamed the *7. SS-Freiwilligen-Gebirgs-Division 'Prinz Eugen'*. It was then attached to the *V. SS-Freiwilligen-Gebirgskorps* and participated in subsequent anti-Partisan operations, including *Kugelblitz* and *Schneesturm*, in Dalmatia.

Battles, Atrocities and Legacy

In January 1944, the division took part in additional counter-insurgency operations under *Unternehmen Waldrausch*. Thereafter, it was deployed in the Seventh Anti-Partisan Offensive (*Unternehmen Rösselsprung*), launched on 25 May 1944 with the objective of decapitating the Partisan leadership (the capture of Tito). As the war progressed, the division continued its operations against Partisan forces in the Balkans. Under the command of *SS-Brigadeführer* August Schmidhuber, the division engaged in rearguard actions during the German retreat from Yugoslavia. During these operations, the division committed several war crimes, including massacres of civilians in Split and Dubrovnik.

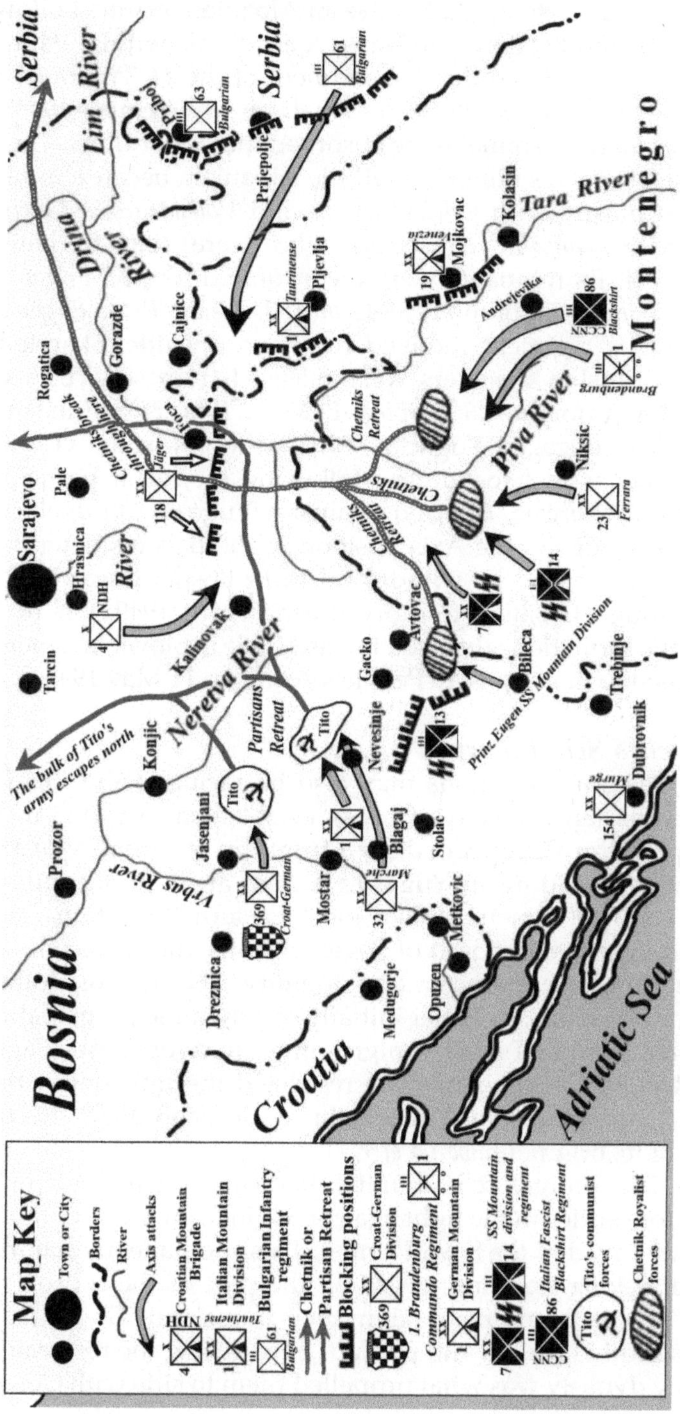

Figure 22. ***Unternehmen Schwarz*** (Operation Black), 2 May to 15 June 1943.

The Germans also attempted to raise an Albanian SS unit. Following widespread demoralisation and mass desertions within its ranks, Heinrich Himmler ordered the disbandment of the *21. Waffen-Gebirgs-Division der SS 'Skanderbeg' (albanische Nr. 1)* on 1 November 1944. The remaining German personnel were absorbed into other units. The 21st SS Division was always nominally ethnic Albanian, because in reality it was staffed mostly with *Reichsdeutsche* and *Volksdeutsche* Germans, including ex-*Kriegsmarine* conscripts who were sent to join the division in 1944. Its remnants were incorporated into *SS-Freiwilligen-Gebirgsjäger-Regiment 14* of the *7. SS-Gebirgs-Division 'Prinz Eugen'*.

Soon after this regiment received the honorary title 'Skanderbeg'. The Albanian Muslim members were released from service in early November 1944. As for the *7. SS-Gebirgs-Division 'Prinz Eugen'*, in January 1945 the division engaged Yugoslav Partisan forces in the vicinity of Otok and Vukovar in Croatia. The following month, it participated in *Unternehmen Wehrwolf*, directed against a Yugoslav bridgehead in the Virovitica sector. As the Axis position in the Balkans deteriorated, the division commenced its withdrawal from Bosnia toward Austria, retreating through Croatian territory during April 1945. On 10 May, elements of the formation advanced toward Celje in Slovenia, where the unit capitulated to the Yugoslav People's Army on 11 May 1945.

The *Russisches Schutzkorps*

Among the Eastern formations may also be included the *Russisches Schutzkorps* (Russian Protective Corps), established in Serbia in 1941. It was composed of volunteers drawn from the community of White Russian émigrés residing in Yugoslavia and, at its peak, numbered approximately 15,000 men. Unlike most Eastern formations, which were predominantly composed of Soviet citizens, the corps possessed a distinctly different character and identity. Its creation followed prolonged negotiations, as Hitler initially opposed the participation of White Russian (former Tsarist) émigrés in military operations against the Soviet Union. Consequently, he restricted the unit's activities to anti-partisan operations in Yugoslavia, a decision that effectively deprived it of its original *raison d'être*.

The Russian émigré community in Yugoslavia had offered themselves for service in the fight against Stalin from the very moment that Germany invaded the Soviet Union. This spontaneous action was the result of a long-standing desire on the part of these pro-Tsarist supporters to see Communism fall in their homeland. Their dream of returning to mother Russia and perhaps even seeing the restoration of the Romanov dynasty was what propelled them to side with Germany.

This action was repeated not only in Yugoslavia, where there was a large Russian émigré community, but also in all other parts of Europe where Tsarist supporters had taken up residence after their departure from Russia once Lenin and the Communists had won the Russian Civil War. These men were the sons and grandsons of officers, and soldiers of the White (pro-Tsarist) Russian armies that fought the Communists. The defeat of the Tsarist forces compelled the survivors of these White armies to flee Russia in order to save their lives lest they and their families should be killed in much the same way as their beloved Tsar Nicholas and his family was murdered. Most of these anti-communists therefore brought their families with them, settling down in numerous European countries, most notably France, Germany and Poland.

To this large batch of White Russian refugees would later be added those men who had fallen from grace in the 'Communist utopia', first in the eyes of Lenin, and later still, Stalin, and had been lucky enough to escape the Soviet Union. Most exiles still hoped to return to their homeland, and from the very beginning of their exile, had begun to organise themselves for that eventuality. Those lucky survivors of the defeated White armies did not perceive the fall of anti-communist resistance in Russia as the end of their struggle. The Western powers had sided with these White Russian forces and had even sent troops, albeit a token force, to defend the ports through which aid was funnelled to the White Russian armies. This gave the Russian émigré community the feeling that Europe was on their side and if the opportunity ever arose, Europe would once again side with the Russian anti-communist elements.

Their dreams of returning to their homeland at the head of a European crusade against Godless communism were heightened by the hope that Europe would eventually throw their lot with them where the exiles would return to mother Russia triumphantly and at the head of a great army. As hard to believe, as this may seem, it was not exactly beyond the realm of possibility in 1920. The reason was that at this time Poland and what was now Bolshevik Russia were locked in a bitter war. Marshal Pilsudski, the Polish leader, was more than willing to take in and assist those Tsarist officers and soldiers who were living in Poland and wished to take up arms against their enemy at home. In this way, some 30,000 of these Russian exiles volunteered to fight for Poland's independence. The Russian forces, which fought against the Reds in Poland, were soon nicknamed the Green Guards. They were fierce fighters and, in many instances, they managed to penetrate the Russian border, making brief incursions into White Russia. One of the founders of the Green Guards was Boris Savinkov.

In 1917, Savinkov had been the political commissar for the Russian 7th Army. He was later appointed by Kerensky to be Assistant Minister of War. When Lenin took control of the interim Russian government, he went about systematically eliminating all of Kerensky's supporters and appointees, making sure to place his supporters in their stead. It was for this reason that Savinkov was accused of the ludicrous charge of being a spy for the French government. He barely escaped Russia with his life. Unfortunately for Savinkov, he was enticed to return to the Soviet Union in an elaborately planned and executed plot to murder him. Lenin had died on 21 January 1924. A power struggle began as to who would take over the reins of power. Joseph Stalin had already positioned himself for the job and his plans included getting rid of any actual or potential enemies. Savinkov was captured during this fluid time period.

This occurred in August 1924 but not before Stalin, who was now just consolidating his power, convinced him that if he would implicate men inside and outside of the Soviet Union, men whom Stalin wanted to eliminate or otherwise neutralise, his life would be spared. Savinkov agreed out of self-preservation, and the Soviet Bolshevik court, first pronouncing his death sentence, magnanimously commuted it to ten years in prison because of the 'completeness and candour' with which Savinkov had agreed to give his testimony. Savinkov had falsely implicated many men who Stalin felt threatened him, all in order to save his own life. Apparently, Stalin had kept his part of the bargain, but strangely enough, Savinkov then committed suicide by hanging himself from his jail cell. Evidently, his 'crimes' against the Soviet people had been so great that he felt he had to take his life. At least this was the fabricated story that was fed to the Russian people.

The end of the Polish-Russian conflict signalled the end of direct and active participation on the part of the anti-communist Russian forces in Poland. The death of Savinkov had not stopped the Green Guards but the end of hostilities did and they were soon forced to disband by the Polish authorities, who now wished to have peace with the communists after they had finally accepted Poland's independence. At this time, numerous members of the now disbanded Green Guards decided to relocate to other parts of Europe. Many of these men settled in the large Russian émigré communities already situated in the capitals of France, Germany, Bulgaria, Czechoslovakia and Yugoslavia. Although the end of the Polish-Russian border war greatly diminished the possibilities of a political change in Russia, the Russian exiles' desire to return to a free country only increased.

Even as late as 1930, on the tenth anniversary of the founding of the Russian École Normale in Paris, the Russian exiles inaugurated a military academy for their sons. Not only did Tsarist princes, clergy from the Russian Orthodox Church, Tsarist generals, and other Russian nobility attend the function, but also French army officers, and Sir Henri Deterding, who was the guest speaker. At this time, the threat from Germany was not yet embedded in the minds of the French, who still viewed the communist revolution as the biggest and most dangerous threat to the peace of Europe and its democracies. It was thus only normal that Deterding would tell those assembled for that inauguration: 'The hour of emancipation of your great fatherland is at hand. The liberation of Russia will take place much sooner than we all think. It may even he a matter of a few months!'

Of course, this statement may have been augmented by a few too many glasses of champagne, as it was excessively optimistic and magnified beyond all recognition to reason. But it had the intended effect, which was to prompt an immediate and rousing applause from the Russians, with the French officers no less enthusiastic. The months passed however, and the 'impending' liberation seemed to come and pass without the desired results. Many who had been present at the inauguration of the Russian exile's military academy had been foolish enough to believe that cocktail-hour rubbish. Worse still, they had passed on these false hopes to others in the exile communities of Europe. They now realised bitterly that once again they had been fed false hopes and dashed dreams. To them, it now seemed that the politicians of the western communities were only good at making speeches, but came up far short of actually pushing for a military intervention against the 'Godless Bolsheviks'.

It now seemed as though these Tsarist exiles were destined to live out the rest of their lives without hope of returning to their homeland. This realisation first turned to frustrated cynicism, but eventually changed to anger and bitterness towards those European countries who professed to despise the Reds but seemed too weak willed to do anything about it. Of course, in Germany, where the Nazi Party had come to power in 1933, things were a lot different. Reports from Russian émigrés there stated that even before the Nazis had assumed control of the country, they had fought the Communists on the street in an uncompromising manner. When Germany finally invaded the Soviet Union on 22 June 1941 the majority of the exiles quickly stepped forward to offer their help. Author George Fischer states that their eagerness to deal the hated Bolsheviks a death blow was too much of a temptation for most of these Russian exiles:

> Many of them succumbed under the pressure of their burning anti-Stalinism, to the opportunity of perhaps at last realising their dreams of overthrowing and replacing the Soviet regime. And after so many years of barren exile, it seemed a distinct possibility in 1941–1942.[29]

There were two distinct groups of volunteers, which came from this Russian émigré sector. Some émigrés were Fascists and others who were Russian nationalists. There was a big difference between these two groups. It was the anti-Communist nationalists who were in the majority and who were better organised and taken more seriously:[30]

> NTS was one of the non-Nazi émigré organisations in Germany. Since its foundation in Belgrade in 1930, it was distinguished for its Mussolini-like philosophy of 'solidarism' and intense Russian nationalism, and became – unlike most old émigré organisations exceptionally skilled organisationally and propaganda wise.[31]

At first, many of these Russian volunteers were rejected due to the arrogance of a German Army that had yet to taste defeat. Some were denied service in Russia simply because of their advanced age. Although the real reason was that Hitler did not wish any of them to play any part in the defeat of the USSR, but an exception was made to some of the younger generation that had grown up outside of their parents' homeland. Those living in Germany especially found it easy to join the *Wehrmacht* because they had become German citizens. Those few were used as interpreters at headquarters, or in the numerous propaganda companies that followed the German advance. They were true idealists and their readiness to act on their convictions was what set them apart from the rest. One was quoted as saying:

> I do absolutely nothing against my conscience . . . This war is not terrible for us, Russian patriots, but only joyous; for the Bolshevik yoke over our motherland will he ended . . . I consider myself a warrior of Christ.[32]

A few émigré volunteers even managed to get themselves posted to the *Brandenburg* commandos or even to a front-line German combat division, as was the case with Count Grigori von Lambsdorff, who ended up as an interpreter in the *6. Panzer-Division*. He and another exile, Sergei von der Pahlen, became what were termed *'Sonderführer'* (Special Officer). They served in this combat division for a time until their 'talents' would lead them to serve in purely anti-Communist,

Russian formations.[33] With the exception of these few cases, however, the numerous and repeated requests by these Russian exiles to fight alongside the German Army in Russia were, for the most part, ignored or rudely brushed aside. The request by the leaders of these numerous émigré communities throughout Europe to form an anti-Stalinist Russian government in exile – one which the Russian people and soldiers could rally around in the Soviet Union – was rejected outright. Although it disappointed them greatly, the Russian exiles nonetheless kept up their support for what was now being referred to as the European 'crusade' against communism.

The farther that the German Army penetrated into Russia, the closer they came to seeing their country liberated from the Stalinist yoke. At least at that early stage in the war (1941) this is how these exiles perceived things to be. Little did they realise that Hitler and his henchmen had other plans for the Soviet Union. In Belgrade, the large ex-Tsarist émigré population had witnessed the German invasion of Yugoslavia in April 1941 with mixed feelings. These Russian exiles had many things in common with their Serbian Slavic cousins. For one thing they came from the same religious upbringing. This string tied them to the Serbians vis-à-vis their Orthodox Christian religion. But the subsequent Axis invasion of the Soviet Union in June 1941 tipped the scales in the minds of virtually every Russian émigré in Favour of the German aggressor. Again, as before, their blind hatred of one evil led them to side with another amoral political movement. Undeterred by Germany's arrogance, the Russian émigré community in Yugoslavia in the autumn of 1941 went ahead and declared that an anti-communist Russian exile force had been raised on 12 September 1941, and was ready to fight in Russia. The Russian exiles christened it the '*Otdel'niy Russkiy Korpus*' (*Russiches Schutzkorps*).

An Aging Army Rejoins the Fight

The first signs that the German invasion of the Soviet Union was not going on as planned occurred on 5 December 1941. German forces in front of Moscow – strung out, understrength, frozen by the coldest Russian winter in decades, and attacked by dozens of newly-arrived Siberian divisions – reeled back in shock by the sheer force and weight of the first Soviet winter counter-offensive of the war. Keeping the Germans off balance, the Red Army was able to push back the Nazi invaders in numerous places. German losses now began to mount with even greater speed and abundance than had yet been experienced during the brief summer and autumn campaign season. One of the results of this Soviet counter-offensive was to sober many Germans up as to how difficult it was going to be to defeat the Soviet Union. It was still imperceptible to all but the most 'enlightened' German officers, that Russia could only be defeated with the support and active assistance of the Russian people themselves.

Joseph Goebbels, Hitler's Propaganda Minister, had once commented to Hitler that the Japanese made it a point of establishing puppet governments, albeit strongly leashed to the local Imperial Japanese Army garrison, in order to give the appearance that these conquered countries were allied to Japan and were therefore not vanquished nations. He suggested to Hitler that perhaps this was the correct policy to follow in the East. Hitler's bigoted reply was strongly opposing, and his disapproval of the so-called *untermenschen* (sub-humans) would never waver, even in the face of military defeat. The Soviet winter counter offensive had far-reaching repercussions even behind the German front lines. Men on leave, in the reserves, and the few previously demobilised divisions of the German Army were now once again called forward in order to try and replenish the huge losses being sustained in Russia. All along the German dominated areas of Europe, requests for replacements came forward.

In effect, the German rear-area commands all across Europe, those garrisoning the conquered lands, were ordered to supply men for the Eastern Front and were stripped to the bare minimum. Only in France, where the Germans still faced an undefeated England across the Channel, did they keep a sizable infantry force to watch the British.[34] It is an established fact that from the very beginning of the occupation of Yugoslavia, the Germans had inadequately garrisoned this country. Their answer to this dilemma was to form various locally raised native formations that would help them to control the Yugoslav countryside and her people. Eventually, one such unit turned out to be the *Russiches Schutzkorps*. The Germans re-designated it as the '*Russiches Schutzkorps*', or *Russiches Schutzkorps* on 2 October 1941.

The initial strength of this Russian exile force was a regiment, formed in Belgrade, which contained some 2,000 men. Later in January 1942 this number was raised to some 3,000 men when a second regiment was raised. Each regiment now had around 1,500 men apiece. In the spring of 1942, a more humbled German military began to seek out more of these Russian exiles – the very same ones which they had so arrogantly turned down in the summer of 1941, in order to expand the *Russiches Schutzkorps*. Although the formation was never to exceed several thousand men, it eventually achieved a combat strength of 11,197 men in September 1944 and throughout its history, exactly 17,090 men passed through its ranks.[35] It now seemed that those old Tsarists were needed after all. Though many Russian exiles had been offended by the apparent indifference and arrogance of the Germans, they nevertheless forgave their apparent narrowmindedness and believed that the Germans had learned their lesson.

After all, it had been the Germans who had done more for the Tsarist cause than any other country. An old Arab proverb states that 'the enemy of my enemy is my friend'. Of course, these exiles forgot or ignored the fact that it was the Germans who had slipped Lenin into Russia in 1917, and so the Russian Revolution can be partly blamed on Germany's attempt to get Imperial Russia out of the Great War, but I digress. Of such are strange partnerships made. It was in this way that in the spring of 1942 when these exiles, many of them already in their forties, fifties and sixties, were once again given the chance to fight against communism. Throughout its history, the *Russiches Schutzkorps* would be composed principally of men from this older age group. Only about 10 per cent of the total force would be made up of younger and more physically fit men. This fact explains why the initial mission given to this Russian force by the Germans was that of factory guards, since the task did not require very strenuous physical exertion – something that middle-aged men, and men in their late fifties and early sixties were not capable of.

The Russiches Schutzkorps *is Formed*

Hitler's invasion of the Soviet Union had, as stated before, brought great joy to the Tsarist émigré community all across Europe. On their own initiative and without German consent, the Russian exiles in Yugoslavia had announced the formation of the '*Otdel'niy Russkiy Korpus*' on 12 September 1941. The proclamation from the NTS Propaganda Department stated that Tsarist Brigadier-General M. F. Skorodumov had been placed at the head of the formation. The declaration also stated that the implied goal of the formation was the destruction of the communist system in the Soviet Union and the ouster of Joseph Stalin and the Communist Party from Russian politics. The manifesto also went on to state that the unit was ready to be employed in the Soviet Union to aid in that country's liberation. It was hoped that this statement would send a clear message to the German command that they had nothing to fear from this Russian exile military unit and everything to gain.

The results were not exactly what the Russian exiles anticipated, however. On 15 September 1941, or just three days after the official announcement of the establishment of the unit, the Germans arrested General Skorodumov because the exile group had failed to get prior German approval. They had avoided this of course, because they feared a negative response. They were hoping that by making such a public statement and showing how the formation would help benefit the German war effort, they could avoid the wrath of German arrogance and stupidity. They were wrong. Yet, the German commander in Serbia was keenly aware that his occupation force suffered from a shortage of manpower and units. Most of his forces were second-echelon or rear-area troops that were at best only capable of very limited offensive capabilities. He was not about to turn down the assistance of these exiles, especially given the fact that guerrilla activity was increasing and the war behind the lines in Yugoslavia was expanding.

One source state that about 250 ethnic Germans from Serbia were added to the Corps.[36] The *Russiches Schutzkorps* eventually became such an integral part of the German command that on 1 December 1942 it was incorporated into the *Wehrmacht* and its men now took an oath of allegiance to Adolf Hitler.[37] The unit would be subordinate to the German Military Commander in Serbia for tactical employment, but for other matters it was directly responsible to the OKW. The bulk of the forces under the German Military Commander in Serbia laid in the small number of two-regiment infantry divisions. These units were later re-designated as *Jäger*, or 'light' divisions while assigned to occupation duty in Yugoslavia. These units would be dispersed to various parts of the country (Serbia, Croatia, Bosnia and Herzegovina, etc.) as the need arose. The following were the permanent garrison forces in Serbia as of January 1942:[11]

342. Infanterie-Division
704. Infanterie-Division (later redesignated *104. Jäger-Division*)[38]
714. Infanterie-Division (later redesignated *114. Jäger-Division*)
717. Infanterie-Division (later redesignated *117. Jäger-Division*)
718. Infanterie-Division (later redesignated *118. Jäger-Division*)
Landesschützenbataillon 562 (the *Landesschützen* were regional defence battalions)
Landesschützenbataillon 590
Landesschützenbataillon 592
Serbisches-Freiwilligen-Korps (1,560 Serbian Fascists)
Russisches Schutzkorps (at this time, 3,000 émigrés split into two regiments)
Serbische Staatsgarde und Grenzschutz (12,000 'Nedic' men)

The above forces were slightly augmented in March 1942 when the *Landesschützenbataillon 287* was added to the roster of troops in Serbia and stationed in Belgrade. On 2 October 1941 with the consent and approval of the German command, the Russian émigré unit was finally given the official title of *Russisches Schutzkorps*. It was then that Major-General Boris Alexandrovich Shteyfon (Steifon) was assigned as commanding general of the Russian exile force.[39] One source says that Brigadier-General M. F. Skorodumov was allowed to form the corps if he agreed in advance to step down as its titular head – all simply because he failed to get advance authorisation from the German command.[40] Soon after the *Russisches Schützenregiment 2* was organised, the 3rd was formed as well. In March 1942 the *Russisches Schützenregiment 4* came into existence. By this time, the size of the Corps had risen to around 6,000 men. The organisation of the *Russiches Schutzkorps* looked like this at the start of January 1942:

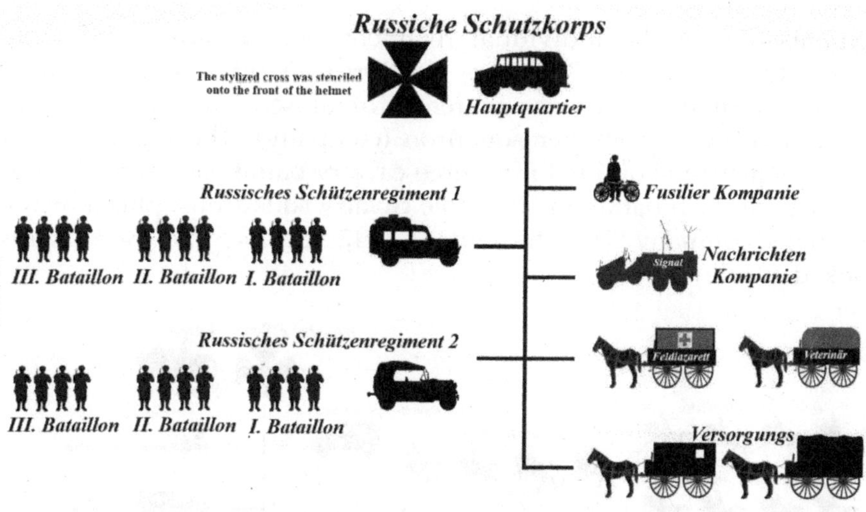

Figure 23. The **Russiches Schutzkorps**, January 1942.

The *Russiches Schutzkorps* grew rapidly in 1942 and by the end of the year it had five regiments: *Russisches Kavallerieregiment 1, Russisches Schützenregiment 2, Russisches Schützenregiment 3, Russisches Schützenregiment 4* and *Russisches Schützenregiment 5*. By December 1942 the Corps had a table of organisation strength of some 8,000+ men. The main units were stationed in the following localities:

Table 17. The *Russiches Schutzkorps*, December 1942

Unit	Location
Hauptquartier (Headquarters)	Belgrade
Russisches Kavallerieregiment 1	Loznica and Kupranj
Russisches Schützenregiment 2	Kraljevo, Zapadne, Morave River Valley
Russisches Schützenregiment 3	Pozarevac, Negotin, Petrovac, Bor and Majdanpek
Russisches Schützenregiment 4	Belgrade
Russisches Schützenregiment 5	Ibra River Valley, and Visegrad up to Banja Koviljaca
Russisches Ersatz und Ausbildungs Bataillon	Belgrade

Organisation of the individual regiments was basically the same and only varied with *Russisches Kavallerieregiment 1,* since it was a cavalry formation and was therefore organised into squadrons of about 150 men apiece per squadron (company). The regiment had twelve squadrons divided into three cavalry battalions. According to one source, each battalion had three cavalry squadrons, plus a heavy weapons company.[41] By the end of 1942 the *Russiches Schutzkorps* looked as follows:

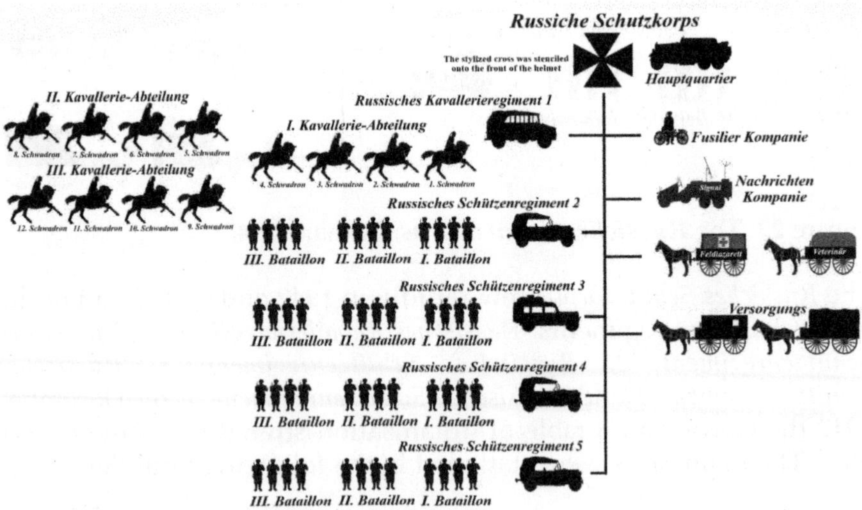

Figure 24. The ***Russiches Schutzkorps,*** December 1942.

Early Operations

The use of the Corps in late 1941 and throughout 1942 was mainly defensive and static in nature. When the Germans launched an anti-partisan operation in mid-January 1942, the *Russiches Schutzkorps* was relegated to garrison duties in the Belgrade-Gradista-Pozarevac-Obrenovac area. In the spring of 1942, the German Military Commander in Serbia wished to employ a combat unit which would soon be going to the Russian Front in an anti-partisan drive.[42] This operation was to concentrate on the approximately 4,000 Partisans in the Sarajevo-Visegrad area.[43] This operation was to be the first instance when units of the Independent State of Croatia would participate.[44] This small Axis force was to be augmented by Italian troops. Unfortunately for the Axis, the Croatian Armed Forces were in a very poor state of readiness. At the end of 1941 the NDH (Croatian Armed Forces) comprised only forty-six weak rifle battalions divided into six divisions and three corps.[45]

Additionally, there were fifteen *Ustashe* (Croatian Fascist Party) combat battalions and the *'Poglavnik'* (Croatian Bodyguard) Regiment, which was a full strength and fully motorised unit. In addition, a special *Ustashe* formation, the *Crna legija* (Black Legion) (two battalions initially) under Major Jure Frantecic had been created in February 1942.[46] There also existed one mountain battery and four specialised battalions comprising railway security, engineer, anti-tank, and signals units. Under German command and alongside German units, all Croatian forces tended to fight well, but their morale suffered when left to their own devices: 'Among individual Croatian units, fresh signs of disintegration appeared, and the Croats complained of the unfavourable influence of the Italians on their own troops'.[47]

Added to these forces were the *Volksdeutsche* (ethnic-German) units that were raised by the Germans and basically attached to the German Order Police organisation. This was initially a six-company battalion based in Esseg (Osijek) with the title: *'Prinz Eugen'*, the same title of the soon-to-be formed (in 1942) *7. SS Freiwilligen-Gebirgs-Division 'Prinz Eugen'*. The official name of this ethnic-German Croatian organisation was the *Einsatzstaffel der Deutschen Mannschaften in Kroatien* (Action Staff of German Troops in Croatia). They wore a uniform similar to the SS but with some slight variations. Between March and August 1942 other ethnic-German Croatian battalions would be raised and were subsequently titled *'Ludwig von Baden'*, *'General Laudon'*, and *'Emanuel von Bayern'*.[48]

One anti-partisan drive followed another during the spring and summer of 1942, but none achieved any significant success in quelling either the communist partisan movement under Joseph Broz Tito, or the Serbian Royalist *Chetnik* guerrilla movement under Colonel Draza Mihailovich. During the latter half of 1942 the *Russiches Schutzkorps* continued its security duties in central and western Serbia. It operated relatively well and began to establish a reputation as a dependable 'German' force. Persistent pleas by its officers to the OKW for permission to employ the *Russiches Schutzkorps* in the Soviet Union continued to be denied. The somewhat justified reason given was that the majority of the men in the Corps were not physically fit to serve in the strenuous and tough conditions of the Russian Front. The request kept being firmly, but ever more politely turned down. There may have been a grain of truth in the answer, which the Germans kept repeating to the frustrated and elderly anti-Communist Tsarist warriors. The absolute truth was that Hitler's plans for a conquered Russia did not include the supplanting of the current, Stalinist regime with one that would be either Royalist, democratic, or even Fascist. The Soviet Union was to become a non-entity, ripe for German colonisation, just as he had written in *Mein Kampf*.[49]

The continued refusal of the OKW to allow the old Tsarists the chance to fight against their hated enemy would slowly but surely sap at the fighting will of the Corps. Especially after many a legionnaire began to question their fight against a people (the Serbs) whom they had many things in common with. The persecution of the Serbian Orthodox Church by the Croatian *Ustashe* and the arming of Bosnian Muslims by the Germans against the revenge killings by Serbian *Chetnik* guerrilla raids also helped to lower the morale of the *Russiches Schutzkorps*. Why, most wondered, were they fighting the Serbian *Chetniks*, when the *Chetniks* themselves were fighting the communists – the very same enemy of the Tsarist exiles? Slowly, an unofficial truce began to develop between members of the *Russiches Schutzkorps* and the royalist Serbian guerrillas under Draza Mihailovich.

1943: The Turning Point

The first three months of 1943 found the Corps increasingly engaged in bitter firefights with small to medium-sized *Chetnik* and Tito communist, partisan bands. Those guerrilla forces had been responsible for 985 incidents of sabotage, ambushes, train derailments, and political murders in the first 90 days of 1943 alone. At this time, aside from the *Russiches Schutzkorps*, the only sizable Axis force in Serbia included the *104. Jäger-Division*, the Serbian Volunteer Corps, the Serbian State and Frontier Guard, and the Bulgarian occupation corps with their 22nd, 24th and 27th Infantry Division. The Serbian Volunteer Corps had proved to be a tough and reliable anti-communist fighting force. On the other hand, the effectiveness and reliability of the roughly 15,000 soldiers of the Serbian State and Frontier Guard was coming more and more into question, especially beginning in early 1943 and onwards.

The summer of 1943 was no different than the first three months of the year. On 25 May 1943 the *Russiches Schutzkorps* battalion guarding the mines at Negotin was attacked when partisan units stormed the local police station and freed some guerrillas. In this small attack, three exiles were killed. The partisans escaped with their freed companions. A day later, in Loznica, eleven suspected *Chetniks* were apprehended by men of the *Russiches Schutzkorps,* whose intelligence officer indicated that an additional 500 Mihailovich guerrillas were still in the area of Valjevo and Cacak. On 28 May 1943 a search and destroy mission by the *Russiches Schutzkorps* around Arangjelovac and Topola, about 54km south of Belgrade, netted a paltry four communist guerrillas killed and one wounded.

This small operation had been organised and planned by the Serbian State Guard in conjunction with units of the *Russiches Schutzkorps*. The major change in policy in 1943 for the Corps was that no longer was this aging force relegated to defensive operations such as guard and escort duties. The employment of the *Russiches Schutzkorps* beginning in 1943 took on a more active role. This was done with the tacit approval of the *Militärbefehlshaber in Serbien* (German Military Commander in Serbia) and may be indicative of several things. First, it indicates that perhaps the need of the Axis occupation forces was increasing so greatly that the Germans even had to fall back on what was definitely considered secondary and low-grade formations for their active anti-partisan operations.

Secondly, it might have been an attempt by either the combined Russian and German command staff or even the German Military Commander in Serbia, or perhaps even the OKW to try and raise the morale of the men in the Corps by using them in more combat-sensitive roles. It may also have been a combination of both reasons. On 2 July 1943 a combined German and Bulgarian sweep south-west of the Serbian town of Aleksinac, about 30km east of Krusevac, netted a meagre thirty-seven *Chetnik* guerrillas. South of Cacak, which lies about 50km south-west of Kragujevac, eleven suspected Titoists (communist guerrillas) were apprehended. That same day west of Cacak, in the area of Uzice, strong *Chetnik* units were identified, while the *Russiches Schutzkorps* was able to drive away a small communist partisan band that had been operating near Ljubovigja, about 18km north-east of Uzice.[50]

On 18 July 1943 the Germans and Bulgarians were still reportedly fighting *Chetnik* units south of Krusevac, citing a great number of enemies as being wounded.[51] While this operation continued, the *Russiches Schutzkorps* formed a 'hunter' command and began operations, first sweeping south-east of Loznica, which was situated around 50km east of Tuzla, disrupting the assembly area of a partisan unit which was about to launch a raid. It took the *Russiches Schutzkorps* exactly three weeks to expel this [tITO] partisan force from their positions. On 10 August 1943 *Chetnik* forces had mixed results against units of the *Russiches Schutzkorps*. Near Cacak, just north-west of Uzice, numerous *Chetniks* were captured, including one high ranking *Chetnik* officer who questioned why anti-communist Russian exiles were fighting the 'Mihailovich Royalist Army'.

At this time, a *Chetnik* listening post was also located and put out of action. This small *Russiches Schutzkorps* success was soon offset. *Chetnik* units operating in and around the town of Krupanj, about 40km west-north-west of Valjevo, were able to free and then mobilise and arm a large number of Serbian farmers who were being held captive by a small detachment of men from the *Russiches Schutzkorps*. Apparently, the Russians were surprised by the *Chetnik* force and 'forced to surrender'. The Serbians spared them all, but took their arms, munitions, and equipment. It is possible that this 'surrender' could have been staged. The communist partisans and royalist *Chetniks* had not failed to attempt to demoralise the men of the *Russiches Schutzkorps* whenever possible. The *Chetnik* guerrillas in particular, because of their anti-communist stance, pro-royalist affiliation and Eastern Orthodox religion, were particularly successful in persuading many Russian volunteers that their fight was not against the Serbian people and therefore, against the *Chetnik* forces.

In spite of numerous German explanations to these Russian exiles, that they were fighting Stalin and communism, although indirectly, by their continued suppression of the 'native' uprising in Serbia, many a Russian volunteer began to have second thoughts about the struggle in which they were now giving their lives. Because the Russians and Serbians had so much in common, slowly but surely this schism began to have a demoralising effect on the capability of the *Russiches Schutzkorps*. This conflict became so great that most of the units in the *Russiches Schutzkorps* began to prefer fighting the Tito partisans. To the exiles, it seemed senseless to engage the Serbian (royalist) guerrilla forces in battle, since they were working just as hard as they were to destroy the communists. Numerous instances now occurred where *Chetnik* and *Russiches Schutzkorps* units would deliberately avoid one another.

Soon, a '*entente tacite*' (tacit understanding) was reached between the *Chetniks* and the *Russiches Schutzkorps*. Only if faced with an aggressive *Chetnik* force, would the line companies and battalions of the *Russiches Schutzkorps* offer battle; and then usually it was undertaken only in self-defence. One more thing must be said about the fighting quality of the *Russiches Schutzkorps* against the communist partisan guerrillas. The truth of the matter is that with the exception of the younger, more physically fit and mobile men in the *Russisches Kavallerieregiment 1*, the rest of the Corps performed poorly when it came to anti-guerrilla operations. The men were just too elderly and out of shape to execute commands on the same level as younger and more physically fit troops. Losses now began to pile up.

On 10 September 1943 the strength of the *Russiches Schutzkorps* had shrunk to a mere 4,769 men. This figure also included the small German cadre staff. Morale had sunk to an all-time low in that month. On 27 September 1943 the unthinkable occurred: seventeen men of the elite *Russisches Kavallerieregiment 1* deserted. An investigation into the incident by the German staff yielded the reason for the desertions. The men had apparently gone over to the *Chetnik* forces because they no longer believed in the German punitive practices in Serbia – in particular, *Unternehmen Maiskolben* (Operation Corncob), the forced internment of the male Serbian population in the countryside in order to deny the partisans and *Chetniks* of a potential recruiting base – had a great detrimental effect on the men of the *Russiches Schutzkorps*.

This order to intern the Serbian farmers was extremely demoralising to the men of the Corps, who saw it as extremely similar in practice and harshness to the way in which the communists in Russian had achieved their goals. The decision to launch and try to implement *Unternehmen Maiskolben* thus had its consequences. However, it seems that when pressed, the Russian exiles could still be counted on. This was the case when on 10 October 1943, in the town of Grube Lissa, with its Antimony mine, *Chetnik* forces attacked and were repulsed by the town's garrison of Russian exile troops. Because of the heightened demands on the *Russiches Schutzkorps,* which caused increasing losses in men killed or wounded, the headquarters staff undertook another recruiting campaign like the one which they had carried out in 1942. During this drive, Russian exiles living in Romania had been targeted. According to the German Army High Command, Adolf Hitler had approved this renewed recruiting campaign in 1943. Once again, the effort was concentrated on exiles and other Russians living in Romania and Bulgaria. A recruiting team was even sent to occupied Odessa, in the Ukraine:

> The efforts of another group of old émigrés, the so-called Schutzkorps (Guard Corps) had some tangible results. The Schutzkorps was a military organisation, consisting of three, later five regiments of old émigré residents living in Yugoslavia; In 1941 it volunteered to help the Germans liberate Russia from Bolshevism. On the whole they were a rather reactionary lot, intrigue-ridden, composed mostly of men in their fifties and sixties. The Germans initially sanctioned the use of the Corps for guard service; later made an anti-partisan combat unit, it was repeatedly thrown into action against Serbian guerrillas. In 1943 it became a regular formation of the Wehrmacht and allowed to extend its recruitment to other countries, including Romania. As a by-product of this permission, in December 1943 the Schutzkorps opened a recruitment bureau in Odessa; the former Café Libman, a popular and centrally located spot, was assigned to the bureau and the Old Russian [tsarist] tricolour flag was displayed in its windows.
>
> The flag and the way the office appeared aroused considerable interest in town. This was, after all, the first endeavour of this sort, and the only one in Soviet territory. But curiosity almost at once turned to hostility. The office lasted only a few months and in that short time had several chairmen, who were relieved one after another. One of its 'Chiefs of Staff' was Senior Lieutenant Zalevsky, a typical old-guard professional military man with monocle and stick, who 'dealt with volunteers as tsarist officers had with their valets'. Odessa officials helped get Zalevsky recalled.
>
> The Schutzkorps recruiters seemed to be offering a third solution, a way of avoiding both the Bolsheviks, who were just then advancing at a menacing pace, and the Germans. Informants agree that those who enlisted did so only because they had completely failed in Odessa – there were relatively few of these or because they feared the returning Soviets. Since the Corps took only volunteers with no next of kin, men with families and belongings could not use the Schutzkorps as a way of getting to Yugoslavia. Still, a few did join though apparently none of them of genuine conviction. Their experience with the Schutzkorps proved abominable; the old White officers looked on the 'Soviet scum' with disdain and scorn.[52]

Things did not go as well as the recruiters had hoped, for on 15 January 1944 a report was passed down from the headquarters of the *Russiches Schutzkorps* to all of the depleted line companies. It said that many of the expected new recruits, which had arrived in Belgrade, had been arrested and turned over German military authorities due to accusations of communist activity. A few of the volunteers fled from Serbia back to Odessa. Vladimir Petrov, a refugee who passed through Odessa on his way westward, describes in his memoirs his encounter at the Recruiting Post for Russian Volunteers with an official who, a year earlier, had been chief of police under the Germans in the North Caucasus region:

> Petrov – 'Is the recruiting successful here?'
>
> Official – 'Well, not too much so ten or fifteen men a week; Life is good in Odessa, so that there aren't many people who want to go and fight. The ones who volunteer are usually those who for some reason have to get out of Odessa quickly. For instance, criminal elements, thieves, sometimes bandits, or simply homeless refugees'.
>
> Petrov – 'Do you think they'll thank you for that type of volunteer?'
>
> Official – He waived his hand. 'I don't give a damn. I'm not looking for any medals for this work. My job is to take them to Belgrade. Usually about half of them desert on the way, but that's outside of my responsibility'.[53]

For all classes in Odessa the Recruiting Office seemed a confirmation of the stereotypes about how reactionary and moribund the émigré population was. It was not that they were 'Whites' of the Russian Civil War that made the *Russiches Schutzkorps* seem undesirable – the only resident political organisation of any consequence was composed of the veterans of the campaigns of 1918–21. This was the *Obshchestvo Byvshik Voinskikh Chinov* (OBCh, Veterans' Society), which had been raised through the efforts of Nikolai Lukich Pustovoitov, an elderly professional soldier who had served as a colonel in the Tsarist army. He had spent his entire Soviet period in Odessa, mostly in hiding:

> Pustovoitov was not the ignorant, pompous, narrow-minded martinet kind of professional soldier; he apparently befriended a number of individuals in 'Transnistrian society'. He persuaded the Romanians to authorise his organisation as a mutual-aid society where anyone who had belonged to any of the earlier [presumably tsarist and 'White'] armies could join. According to the only informant really familiar with its work though perhaps too favourable to it because of his own close association with it and with Pustovoitov – the society also engaged in other activities, such us establishing an orphanage and financing the St. Magdalena church in Odessa.[54]

Although the monarchist spirit of the OBCh was initially rather pronounced, it soon cooled as news of Vlasov's Smolensk Manifesto reached Odessa. Now the *Russiches Schutzkorps*, whose members and recruiters represented the 'old order', were met with opposition from those who wanted to follow Vlasov and his view of a non-communist, non-monarchist Russia:

> Finally, when the Schutzkorps opened offices in Odessa, some pro-Vlasovites, generally the anti-monarchist, nationalist Russian intelligentsia, including some of the older men got the OBCh to apply to the primaria [the administration of the ROA] for permission to recruit replacements for the ROA.[55]

From all of this we can gather that most of the recruits gained in Odessa were, for the most part, the bottom of the recruiting barrel. We cannot also omit the possibility that Soviet intelligence might have tried to infiltrate the *Russiches Schutzkorps* by trying to get some of their agents recruited. Stalin's intelligence network in the Balkans was especially effective, given the size of the communist parties in those countries before the start of the Second World War. In fact, German soldiers and civilians stationed in Bulgaria were particularly singled out for assassination by a very active communist underground. The situation became so bad that the authorities had to post a travel advisory warning for all German nationals, civilian or soldier alike, not to travel individually or in small groups, especially in the Bulgarian countryside.[56]

The Russiches Schutzkorps Engages the Red Army

During the summer of 1944 the *Russiches Schutzkorps* continued to experience difficulty in acquiring replacements to replenish its losses in the field. In the summer, it was pitted against crack units of Tito's partisan army. In April and May 1944, the Corps fought against elements of the Partisan 12th Corps at Loznica and Krupanj. The *Russiches Schutzkorps* also fought the 2nd and 5th Partisan Division at Usca and in the area of the Ibro River by Valjevo in June and July. In August they were engaged against the Partisan Operational Group of Divisions. In September 1944 the *Russiches Schutzkorps* again fought the Partisan 12th Corps in western Serbia. Even before the Corps had completed its withdrawal from Serbia, events outside of Yugoslavia would now set in motion changes that would decisively alter the military balance in that country and the fate of the *Russiches*

Schutzkorps as a result. On 23 August 1944 Marshal Ion Antonescu, Romania's ruler, was killed. King Michael, that country's monarch then surrendered Romania unconditionally to the Soviet Army. Three days later, on 26 August 1944, while troops of the 3rd Ukrainian Front advanced along the Prut River towards Galati, Bulgaria began surrender negotiations as well. Technically not at war with the Soviet Union, the

Bulgarians nevertheless were worried about a Soviet invasion. Events would prove them right. On 27 August units of the 2nd Ukrainian Front advanced through the Focsani-Galati gap and captured the city of Galati the third largest city in Romania. It was on this same day that Romania's new pro-Soviet government declared war on Germany. On 9 September 1944 a pro-Soviet government was installed in Bulgaria. It was a mere formality, since the day before (8 September) the Bulgarians had declared war on Germany as well. In less than a week, the Germans were facing a Bulgarian army of six divisions that was now sweeping into eastern Serbia to aid the Tito partisans. In one of the very last offensive operations of its history, the *Russiches Schutzkorps* was ordered back into Serbia. It was to assist the *7. SS Freiwilligen Gebirgs-Division 'Prince Eugen', 1. Brandenburg-Regiment der Division 'Brandenburg'*, and the *SS-Polizeiregiment 5* to try and trap some partisan units in the area of Valjevo. These partisan formations from the 12th Partisan Corps were trying to reach the Bulgarians coming from the east.

By 25 September the bulk of the *Russiches Schutzkorps* was located in western Serbia. A day later, *'Kampfgruppe Fischer'*, which comprised the *2. Brandenburg-Regiment* (minus its *I. Bataillon*) plus a battalion of the *1. Gebirgs-Division* found themselves fighting Soviet units 5km north of Negotin. The battalion of *2. Brandenburg-Regiment,* together with the *I. Kavallerie-Abteilung, Russisches Kavallerieregiment 1* of the *Russiches Schutzkorps,* defended the heights east of D. Milanovac against attacking Soviet units. Soviet attacks against the combined German and Tsarist Russian force continued into the 27th. As the days wore on however, more and more pressure was placed on the Axis defenders until slowly they were pushed from their positions. By the time this battle had ended, the *Russiches Schutzkorps* had not only engaged units of the Soviet 57th Army but had fought the Partisan 14th Corps as well. For the Corps, the chance to fight the Soviet communists had finally arrived. Its weakness in anti-tank weapons didn't help them in this struggle, since the Soviets were amply armed with modern tanks and mechanised vehicles.

The few tanks that the Corps Headquarters Staff possessed were some obsolete French R35 tanks captured by the Germans and donated to the Corps. Yet, in spite of the chaos going on around it, the *Russiches Schutzkorps* managed to increase its numbers to well over 11,000 men by September 1944. Was this due to the 'opportunity' which the advancing Red Army now afforded these old Tsarist-era émigré volunteers, to fight the communists head on? It is known that many a Russian Guard Volunteer who had 'retired' from the Corps due to wounds inflicted or advancing age, voluntarily rejoined the unit shortly before it was committed against the Red Army. In fact, the breakdown of men in the *Russiches Schutzkorps* in September 1944 was 362 officers, 1,295 non-commissioned officers, and 9,540 enlisted men, for a grand total of 11,197 combatants. The largest single group of Russian exiles, about 5,000 volunteers, had come from Romania.[57]

Of course, these figures soon dwindled one month later, after encountering elements of the Red Army in eastern Serbia. For some unknown reason, on 14 October 1944, the *Russiches Schutzkorps* was renamed by the Germans as the '*Russisches Schutzkorps Serbien*' which roughly translates as the *Russky Korpus v Serbii*, or '*Russiches Schutzkorps* in Serbia'. Nevertheless, the men of this Russian émigré force continued to refer to the formation as the *Russiches Schutzkorps*. On 14 October 1944 the combined Soviet and Yugoslav communist armies began their assault on Belgrade. Five days later they entered the ruined capital. Although the Red Army and (Yugoslav) Tito forces had lost a lot of men in recapturing the city, the German command had lost about 15,000 men in the defence of the Yugoslav capital.

Among the dead were a few hundred men from the *Russiches Schutzkorps*. The remnants of the *Russiches Schutzkorps* withdrew to the Bosnia River Valley, in the area of Brcko and Slavonski Brod in October 1944. It would remain in this area until April 1945. During their withdrawal, the *Russiches Schutzkorps* had made peace pacts with local *Chetnik* forces, who were just as alarmed as the émigré Russians were at the rapid advance of the communists. In fact, during its withdrawal, several *Chetnik* units assisted the Corps against the Tito partisans. With the exception of the *Russisches Kavallerieregiment 1*, the Corps was split up amongst the numerous German battle groups and divisions which were also retreating from Serbia into Bosnia. One such battlegroup was '*Kampfgruppe Rehe*', led by a German major of the same name.

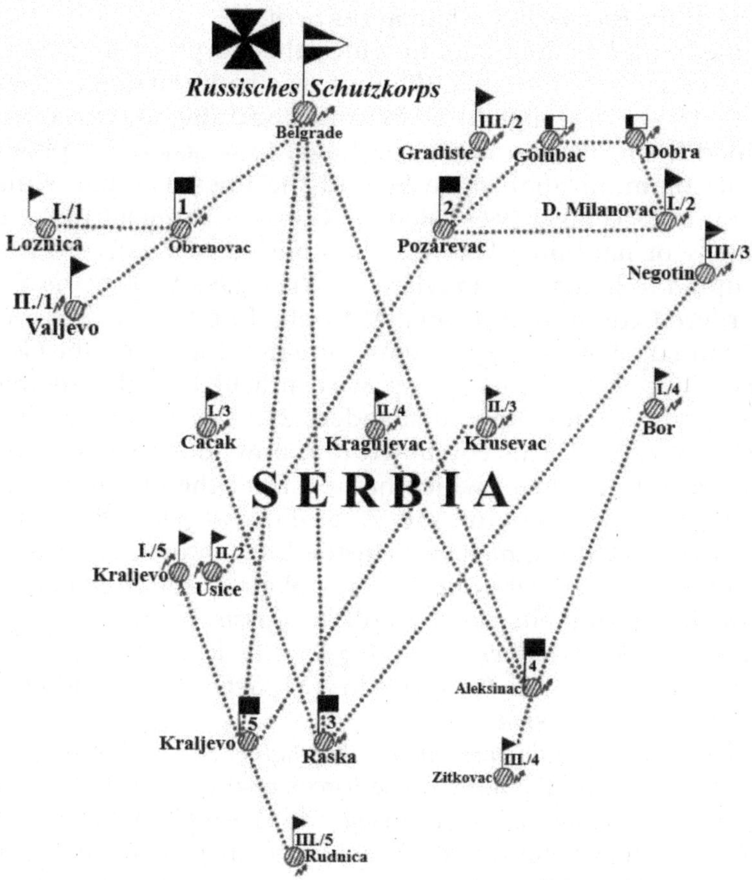

Figure 25. Communications network for the ***Russische Schutzkorps Serbien***, November 1944.

It was composed of one battalion from the *Russisches Schutzkorps Serbien*, one battery from the Nish Artillery School, and a German Naval '*alarm*' unit. It saw action in September 1944 by Orsova Donau, south-west of Turnu Severin, along the Brza-Palauka Road. Another was '*Kampfgruppe Scheurlen*' which contained a battalion of the *Russisches Schutzkorps Serbiens* that had been stationed in Novi Pazar since early October 1944. In addition, this battle group also had two additional battalions of the *Russiches Schutzkorps*, plus the Reserve Battalion, *Luftwaffe-Regiment 'Böhmer'*, two Serbian *Hilfspolizei* (auxiliary police) battalions (also from Novi Pazar), a German 20mm *Flak* battery, a German army 88mm *Flak* battery, plus a score of other scratch formations.[58]

The End of the Russisches Schutzkorps Serbien

After the battle for Belgrade, in which the Corps participated, and the battles in eastern Serbia, the unit was badly mauled. It was so weak that it was no longer used in front-line duties and the Germans relegated the formation to the less hazardous task of keeping their lines of communication open behind the lines. German situation maps for 24 December 1944 listed the Corps as being located around the towns of Jajce and Travnik. This period of relative calm was interrupted in January 1945 when the *Russisches Schutzkorps Serbien* was ordered committed to several fronts. In effect, it was split up. On 13 January 1945 some elements were fighting under the German *XXXIV. Armeekorps*. This group was attached to the regimental battle group of the now disbanded *21. Waffen-Gebirgs-Division der-SS 'Skanderbeg'*. This combined unit now took over the defence of the Brcko bridgehead which had up until then been held by an SS mountain regiment of the *7. SS-Freiwilligen-Gebirgs-Division 'Prinz Eugen'*. That regiment was needed for an intended operation north of Sava – an operation that was planned for 16 January 1945. Meanwhile in Montenegro, the bulk of *Russisches Schützenregiment 4* and *Russisches Schützenregiment 5* of the *Russisches Schutzkorps Serbien* were attached to the German *XXI. Gebirgskorps* and attached to the *104. Jäger-Division*.

At this time the *Arabisches Infanterie-Bataillon 845* was also operating under this German division. These forces beat off communist attacks in the area of Grahovici, near Visegrad. These German forces even launched a small counter-attack, which managed to gain impetus when the *Leichte Artillerie-Abteilung 631*, made up of Eastern troops and armed with Russian 76.2mm M1943 artillery pieces, arrived to lend their support. This Russian artillery battalion was soon attached to the *Russisches Schutzkorps Serbien* in the last weeks of 1944. Numerous guerrilla attacks in the area between Zepce and Maglaj were beaten off by units of the Corps in early January 1945. On 19 January 1945, after defending against numerous counter-attacks, the Corps was ordered to regroup once again. It was to form a new defence line in the area extending from Pavlevac, some 28km south-west of Virovitica to the heights west of Brzaja, some 18km west of Virovitica. A day after being assigned to these new defensive positions, the Russian exile force there had to fight off strong communist partisan units that had advanced behind the positions of the exiles on the north slope of Bila Gora and west and south of Pitomaca. The adjacent units next to the *Russiches Schutzkorps* were *Kampfgruppe 'Moskov'* and the *1. Kosaken-Kavalleriedivision* operating close to the Cossacks, was even considered as a potential cadre for raising another unit of Cossacks, but nothing came of this.

The attempt to regroup the entire remaining elements of the *Russisches Schutzkorps Serbien* proved impossible, although it did manage to organise itself into three separate parts. By far the largest number was the remnants containing *Russisches Schützenregiment 4* and *Russisches Schützenregiment 5* under *XXI. Gebirgskorps*. Another group was fighting alongside the *7. SS-Freiwilligen-Gebirgs-Division 'Prinz Eugen'*, under *XXXIV. Armeekorps*. The third group was the *Russisches Schutzkorps Serbien* units assigned to the *1. Kosaken-Kavalleriedivision* under *LXIX. Armeekorps*. It should be noted here that part of the Corps was used by the Germans to protect the Sarajevo – Bosanski Brod communication line at this time.[59] After January 1945 the German Armed Forces High Command War Diary makes no further mention of the Corps. What is known is that the *Russiches Schutzkorps* continued to fight on in three separate and distinct battle groups right on through February, March and April 1945. In the autumn of 1944 General Vlasov had made an attempt to assimilate numerous anti-communist Russian forces into his own command. Vlasov wanted to absorb the *Russisches Schutzkorps Serbien* into his Russian Army of Liberation (ROA), but nothing ever came of this, primarily because of bitter infighting between the Russian nationalists and those in charge of the various ethnic groups:

> Vlasov rejected such recognition of independence and referred the Ukrainians to the relevant provisions of the manifesto. He declared, however, that once the first ROA divisions were organised, and were joined together with the Cossack Corps, the Steifon Corps [i.e. the *Russiches Schutzkorps*], the Second Ukrainian Division, and Maltsev's air force group, a total of about 100,000 men – he would seriously consider a frontal breakthrough to initiate the revolutionary struggle jointly with the UPA, whose strength was estimated at 50,000 troops.[60]

In late March 1945 an attempt was made once again to merge the *Russisches Schutzkorps Serbien* – this time with the *XV. Kosaken-Kavalleriekorps* which had been absorbed into the *Waffen-SS* in December 1944. But by that time in the war, the Russian exiles were in no mood to join any other unit or organisation. The writing was clearly on the wall, so most of the men in the Corps just wanted to reach the relative safety of the Austrian border where they hoped they could seek asylum. There they expected to surrender to British forces, which they believed understood their situation. On 30 April 1945 General Boris Shteifon died. Command of the Corps was then entrusted to the leader of the *Russisches Kavallerieregiment 1,* Colonel Anatoliy I. Rogozhin, who had been a lieutenant in Tsar Nicholas's 2nd Personal Bodyguard Regiment. Sometime in late April 1945 the remnants of the *Russiches Schutzkorps* surrendered to advancing British troops. The *XV. Kosaken-Kavalleriekorps* – and in fact many Eastern troops hoping to avoid the Red Army – also did as well. But for the anti-communist Russian forces their surrender to the Western powers would prove only a temporary reprieve. At Yalta, Stalin had already squeezed an agreement from Churchill and Roosevelt that all Soviet citizens captured by the Western powers be turned over to the Red Army. Their fate had been sealed months ago. Between 1941 and 12 March 1945 the *Russiches Schutzkorps* had lost 11,506 men killed, while 1,084 men were on leave or sick and 4,500 crossed the Austrian frontier. The following total number of men were killed or wounded in each regiment:[61]

Table 18. *Russiches Schutzkorps* Losses, 1941–1945[62]

Russisches Kavallerieregiment 1	1,823
Russisches Schützenregiment 2	2,432
Russisches Schützenregiment 3	2,229
Russisches Schützenregiment 4	1,960
Russisches Schützenregiment 5	2,041
Ersatz und Ausbildungs Bataillon und Korps-Hauptquartier	1,021
Grand Total:	11,506

Now began a series of forced repatriations from the British camps – all going in one direction: east. This began in earnest as early as May 1945, and continued on as late as February and March 1946. The fate that awaited these anti-communist fighters and their families can well be imagined. Many books have now been written describing the horrors. Many Cossacks or Russians committed suicide rather than go back to the Stalinist hell which they had escaped. The British were indeed most receptive and understanding about the reasons which prompted these Eastern volunteers to take up arms against the Soviet government. Many British officers and ordinary soldiers felt pity for the fate of these troops, but orders were orders, so the British went about carrying out the repatriation orders as dutifully as was in their nature and character. There were three categories which outlined the policy of forced repatriation of Soviet citizens as it had been ratified by the committee representing the three military departments of the United States (Army, Navy and State Department):

1. Soviet citizens captured in German uniform.
2. Former members of the Soviet Armed Forces (because it was thought they might be deserters).
3. People who, though not captured in German uniform, had voluntarily rendered aid and comfort to the enemy.

This last category was the most sinister of the three, since it virtually condemned the families of the volunteers – the old men and women, the children and the wives of the volunteers as well. Numerous cases of family suicides were recorded. The first inkling of a possible loophole in the agreement on forced repatriation occurred on the morning of 29 May 1945 as the men of the British 6th Armoured Division were forcibly handing to the Soviets Cossack soldiers from the *1. Kosaken-Kavalleriedivision*. The men of the 6th Armoured Division had already shown considerable distaste for the whole affair, but had nevertheless proceeded to follow their orders.

While the trucks transporting the prisoners to the Soviet lines were en route, a staff officer at division headquarters reviewed the full agreement. He noted in the fine print that only individuals who were citizens of the Soviet Union *after* 1 September 1939 were to be repatriated. This information was quickly communicated to the British officer in charge of the truck column by radio and the transport was stopped momentarily. In the entire column, they could only find fifty men who were exempt from the forced repatriation order. Although the English were disappointed that only fifty men were spared, it nevertheless was fifty souls that they had saved. Word quickly spread to the internee Russians, numbering in the hundreds of thousands in Allied captivity. Those who could prove this exemption were saved.

Fortunately for the men of the Corps, almost all of them were saved from the clutches of the vengeful Stalinist communist government by qualifying to slip through this apparent loophole. When they were released from captivity, many of these men sought to live out the rest of their lives outside of shattered Europe. Many chose to immigrate to Canada, South America, Australia, and the United States, while some decided to remain in France, Germany, or Austria. Their hopes at seeing a renewal of the Romanov monarchy in Russia was now shattered. Those who had simply wished to rid Russia of communism had to wait 46 years before that dream was finally realised. In 1963, N. N. Protopopoff, a son of one of these exiles, who had served in *Russisches Kavallerieregiment 1*, wrote a book on the history of the *Russisches Schutzkorps Serbien*.

It was privately published in the same printing press that had continued to put out their veterans' magazine, *Nashi Vesti*. The book, written in the Cyrillic alphabet, was basically published for the families of those veterans who had descendants and had remained in contact. This meant that their story remained unknown for the majority of people. This is the reason why to this day their story remains obscure and relatively unknown. But to know their story is to understand part of the causes why Russians sided with one evil (Nazi Germany) in order to destroy another (Stalinist Russia). If for no other reason than this, history should not forget them.

The Pro-German Serbian Volunteer Corps and Greek Security Battalions

Two of the most significant collaborationist formations in the German-occupied Balkans were the *Srpski dobrovoljački korpus* (SDK, Serbian Volunteer Corps), led by Dimitrije Ljotić, and the Greek *Tagmata Asphaleias* (Security Battalions), both of which were organised under German oversight and dedicated primarily to anti-communist operations. A smaller but related example was the *Poulos Polizei-Verband*, a notorious collaborationist militia in Greece commanded by Georgios Poulos. These units shared the common feature of being presented domestically as nationalist defenders against communism, yet in practice they operated as auxiliaries of German security forces, subordinated to the SS and *Wehrmacht*, and implicated in brutal repression against Resistance movements and civilians. The SDK was established in September 1941, initially recruited from fascist supporters of Ljotić's Zbor movement. It began as a militia-sized formation but quickly grew into an organised paramilitary formation. Although its leadership claimed that the SDK existed to defend Serbian national interests, the reality was that it functioned as an instrument of German occupation policy. The Corps was heavily involved in anti-partisan warfare against the communist-led Yugoslav Partisans as well as against rival *Chetnik* factions. Its operations often included punitive expeditions, reprisals, and the persecution of civilians suspected of aiding the resistance. Over time the SDK expanded in size: on 15 February 1942 it numbered 3,685 men, rising to about 4,000 in January 1943, 5,500 by November 1943, and nearly 9,900 in August 1944.

By March 1945, as the Axis position in the Balkans was collapsing, the Corps reached a peak strength of roughly 10,500 men. The retreat of German forces from Serbia in the autumn of 1944 drew much of the SDK with them. Many members accompanied the *Wehrmacht* into Slovenia and Austria, where the unit continued to serve under German command until the war's end, with some members later surrendering to the Allies and others falling into Partisan hands. The Greek Security Battalions emerged somewhat later, being formally organised in 1943 at a time when German occupation authorities faced growing pressure from the communist-led *Ellinikós Laïkós Apeleftherotikós Stratós* (ELAS), the military wing of the National Liberation Front (EAM). These battalions drew their personnel largely from anti-communist, monarchist, and conservative sectors of Greek society, men who feared that communist partisans would dominate Greece after liberation. The Security Battalions were armed, trained, and equipped by the Germans, and their missions paralleled those of the SDK in Yugoslavia: to suppress Resistance activities, secure territory, and relieve German forces for front-line service elsewhere. In June 1944, the collaborationist units in Greece numbered approximately 16,625 officers and men, with estimates of their peak strength rising to about 22,000 later that year. Their geographical focus included Attica, central Greece, and the Peloponnese, where they carried out anti-guerrilla sweeps, village burnings, and executions of suspected ELAS sympathisers. Like the SDK, they quickly earned a reputation for cruelty against civilians.

The collapse of German power in the Balkans in the autumn of 1944 sealed the fate of both the SDK and the Greek Security Battalions. In Serbia, most of the SDK withdrew north with the *Wehrmacht* and continued fighting until the final surrender in Austria in May 1945. In Greece, many members of the Security Battalions attempted to avoid retribution by presenting themselves as patriots fighting only against communists, while others were captured by the resistance and summarily executed. Yet, in the polarised political climate of post-war Greece, some survivors were incorporated into the state security apparatus during the Greek Civil War (1946–9), where their anti-communist credentials became an asset rather than a liability. Both the *Serbisches-Freiwilligen-Korps* and the Greek Security Battalions highlight the complex and often divisive legacy of wartime collaboration in the Balkans. While they presented themselves as nationalist and anti-communist defenders, their reliance on German sponsorship and their participation in repression undermined these claims. At their core, they exemplified how local political factions exploited the German occupation to pursue ideological goals, contributing not only to wartime atrocities but also to the violent political polarisation that marked Yugoslavia and Greece in the immediate post-war years.

Chapter 10

TAPPING THE BALKANS, PART 2: 1943–1944

The Muslim Militia and Legion of the Sanjak, 1943–1945

Among the Axis-occupied countries during the Second World War, Yugoslavia produced numerous irregular formations, often organised along ethnic lines as militias, legions, or auxiliary units. The Muslim Militia of the Sanjak, a mountainous region in eastern Montenegro with a long-standing Muslim population, was one such obscure unit. Historically threatened by their Serbian Orthodox neighbours, the Sanjak Muslims had long maintained village self-defence associations. Following the Axis invasion of Yugoslavia in April 1941, these associations strengthened in response to growing *Chetnik* and communist partisan threats. By the end of 1941, they had evolved into a village guard or militia, equipped with discarded Yugoslav weapons and Italian rifles.

The militia first saw combat in February 1942, assisting *Chetniks* and Italian forces against Tito's partisans near Nova Varos. Despite initial setbacks, the militia remained a key local defensive force. Between January and February 1943, *Chetnik* forces launched massacres against the Sanjak Muslims, killing many civilians and confronting militia members, who managed to inflict limited casualties in return. After recovering from these losses, the militia largely avoided participation in major Axis operations, such as *Unternehmen Schwarz* in May–June 1943, though the German authorities recognised their potential as a local defence force. Following Italy's capitulation in September 1943, the German *118. Jäger-Division* handed over Pljevlja to the militia, maintaining its strength at roughly 5,000 men.

Around this time, SS officer Karl von Krempler took command, establishing the *Höhere SS-und Polizeiführer Sandschak* headquarters and reorganising the unit as *Muselmanengruppe von Krempler*, eventually redesignated as *Polizei-Selbstschutz-Regiment 'Sandschak'*. Under Krempler, the militia underwent formalisation and training, though discipline, equipment, and uniforms remained inadequate. Many members retained their peasant lifestyle, disappearing for days to tend crops. Hafiz Suleyman Pacariz, a respected religious leader, commanded the unit on the ground. From January 1944, the militia supported German and *Chetnik* offensives against the partisans, including efforts to secure central Montenegro roads. Strength and troop reports varied, with numbers ranging from 800 to 5,000 men depending on whether Krempler's forces or those earmarked for a Muslim legion were counted. By March, the militia was formally subordinated to 2. *Panzerarmee* and *Höhere SS-und Polizeiführer Serbien.*

Between April and July 1944, Krempler's forces participated in major anti-partisan operations – *Unternehmen Kammerjäger, Daufgänger* and *Ruebezahl* – facing Tito's divisions in central Montenegro and eastern Sanjak. These operations involved German, Bulgarian, *Chetnik*, Albanian, and Sanjak Muslim units. While the militia occasionally delayed partisan movements, it never achieved decisive results. By mid-1944, the unit was formally redesignated *Polizei-Selbstschutz-Regiment der-SS 'Sandschak'*, although some evidence suggests it never exceeded a single operational battalion. Troop strength was estimated at around 4,000 men, with most remaining militia unincorporated into the formal regiment.

By September 1944, Krempler's regiment was deployed along key routes in western Serbia but became overextended during the German withdrawal from Greece and the Balkans. Partisan offensives in October forced the Sanjak Muslims to retreat to Sarajevo, where most older militiamen deserted or went into hiding. The remaining younger members, including Pacariz, joined *Ustaše* forces under General Vjekoslav Maks Luburic, maintaining the regiment's identity. In March 1945, the Sanjak militia was committed to the front near Ivan Sedlo south-west of Sarajevo. Despite heavy fighting, the German-Croatian defenders could not hold Sarajevo, which fell on 6 April 1945. Survivors joined the Obrana Brigade, later reorganised as the 30th Assault Regiment of the Croatian 18th Assault Division. With the final Axis collapse, most members were either killed, captured, or forced into flight, and the *Polizei-Selbstschutz-Regiment der-SS 'Sandschak'* was formally disbanded in Graz, Austria, in 1945. Commanders:

- *SS-Standartenführer der Reserve* Karl von Krempler: September 1943 – 21 June 1944
- *SS-Oberführer* Richard Kaaserer: 21 June 1944 – 28 November 1944

Before German oversight, the Sanjak Muslims served under Italy's MVAC (Anti-Communist Volunteer Militia). As of February 1943, 780 men served in this Italian-sponsored legion. Ironically, the same *Chetnik* forces that massacred Muslims during January–February 1943 operated under MVAC authority, highlighting the complex and brutal local conflict dynamics. Although the Sanjak Muslims' contribution to the Nazi war effort was militarily negligible, their presence was useful to German authorities as a propaganda tool, a local defensive force, and a counterweight against partisans and rival militias. Nevertheless, the unit remained poorly equipped, under-trained, and heavily dependent on local leadership and German oversight.

Note: For a full history of the *Polizei-Selbstschutz-Regiment der-SS 'Sandschak'*, please refer to *'Hitler's Muslim Allies: German Army and Waffen-SS Islamic Volunteers, 1941-1945'* by Frontline Books (an imprint of Pen & Sword), 2025.

Greek Volunteer Formations in the *Wehrmacht*

Ioannis Rallis (also spelled 'Ralles') was the first eminent Greek political figure to collaborate openly on both a military and political level with the German occupation forces which had ruled Greece alongside the hated Italians since the fall of Greece in 1940. The Germans hoped that Rallis would secure the support of elements of Greece's pre-war political elite, restore order to the country, and establish an anti-Communist front against the *Ethniko Apeleftherotiko Metopo* (EAM) and its military arm, the *Ethnikos Laikos Apeleftherotikos Stratos* (ELAS). EAM was the main movement of the Greek Resistance and had been initially formed by an alliance of the Communist Party of Greece, the Socialist Party of Greece, the Greek Popular Republic and the Agricultural Party of Greece. ELAS was its military arm. Since anti-communism served as a common ground between the Liberal Party and the People's Party, the idea of a united front seemed plausible.

Rallis changed the ministry council and was instrumental in creating the so-called 'Security Battalions' – the collaborationist paramilitary groups equipped by the *Wehrmacht* and dedicated to the persecution of Resistance groups (mainly ELAS). Being more experienced in politics than his predecessors, he was more respected by the Germans and proved more effective against the Resistance movements. All three administrators during the occupation (Georgios Tsolakoglou, Konstantinos Logothetopoulos and Ioannis Rallis) presided over what was in effect a puppet government (1941–4) completely subordinate to the Nazi occupation authorities. Thus, they all failed to prevent the

Nazis from imposing heavy 'reconstruction' fees on Greece, eventually paid by the confiscation of all kinds of crops and precipitating a terrible famine that, according to the Red Cross, cost the lives of about 250,000 people (mainly in the urban areas of the country). They also did not react to the annexation of the northern territories of Thrace and Eastern Macedonia to the Axis partner Bulgaria.

Greece: September 1943 and Italy's Surrender

The collapse of Italy in September 1943 brought the Germans into the forefront in Greece (and elsewhere). Up until the beginning of 1943, the Germans had been content to control Salonika, Crete, and other lesser islands, and to allow the Italians to run the rest of the country as they saw fit. This all began to change in the spring of 1943 when Ioannis Rallis became Prime Minister of Greece, replacing General Georgios Tsolakoglou who had become 'untrustworthy' in the eyes of the Axis. With Rallis' permission, and no approval from the Italians, German troops were moved into the Peloponnese. It wasn't so much the growing guerrilla movement that alarmed the Germans, as it was the success of the Allies in defeating Erwin Rommel's *Afrika Korps* and expelling the Germans and Italians from the African continent altogether. Now Greece went from being a backwater forward supply base to the next possible invasion area for the Allies. Not that the guerrilla movement was not sending alarm signals of the greatest magnitude to German command circles, quite the contrary. An incident which occurred in the Peloponnesian peninsula in the autumn of 1943 clearly shows the danger and increase in partisan activity in Greece, as this following quote describes, which occurred near the Peloponnese village of Kalavryta:

> Toward the end of 1943 Greek guerrillas, striking from mountain hideouts captured eighty German soldiers. They took the captives into the mountains and pushed them over a precipice. Only three of the eighty survived. Nazi retribution was swift and terrible. It was mistakenly directed against the townspeople rather than against the guerrillas.[1]

The Germans, who had for the most part watched anxiously as the ever-worsening Axis military situation increased in direct proportion and relation to the growth of the Greek partisan movement, now were faced with the prospects of governing more Greek territories with one less ally (the Italians). Having been on the sidelines since 1941, they were now thrust into the spotlight in Greece by becoming the *de facto* primary occupying power. They inherited from the Italians an economic 'basket case', and a country on the verge of political and military anarchy. The power vacuum which had been left by the Greek collapse in April 1941, coupled with the famine winter of 1941–2 and two years of Italian mismanagement, had created the conditions which existed in 1943 when the Germans had to take control.

The economic stability of the Greek nation had not much improved since that starvation crisis of 1941–2. Additionally, the Greek populace had to suffer arbitrary Italian policies as much as they had to deal with making a day-to-day living. Resentment of the 'unworthy' Italians, who had invaded Greece in 1940 only to be repulsed by the small Greek Army, only grew. The Italians only succeeded after Germany intervened. It was therefore understandable that Greek contempt and anger for the Italians simmered just beneath the surface. As time wore on, the various Greek guerrilla movements, supported initially by the British, and then also by the Soviet Union (who only backed the communist ELAS units), began to grow and become more emboldened and sophisticated. As diverse as the various political-military guerrilla movements were, they began to take a toll on the enemy.

This then, was the military and political dilemma which Germany had inherited from the Italians in Greece in the autumn of 1943. By this time, Germany was fighting a war of attrition on several fronts. Greece was on a possible Allied 'hit list' for late 1943 to early 1944. The Germans could ill afford to spare troops for Greece, but they did their best to try and reinforce the small German garrison. However, these reinforcements were not sufficient to properly occupy the vast new Greek territories, with hundreds of miles of coastline which they now had to protect from a possible Allied invasion, let alone control the areas deep inside the country. The use of indigenous militia units had already become standard practice in other parts of Nazi-occupied Europe, the Baltic States and the Soviet Union. Up until then, Greece had only supplied a small police and *Gendarmerie* (rural police) force, which was considered unreliable at best. But in the autumn of 1943, with Germany needing more military support, Greece was not to become the exception to the above-mentioned rule.

In fact, the Germans found a 'fertile field' when attempting to recruit anti-communist units into their Army, Order Police and SS forces. The security battalion units set up under the Rallis government, whether they formed part of the five *Evzone* regiments or the regular security battalions, proved to be quite effective against the communist ELAS guerrillas. The vastly differing political ideals of the various Greek guerrilla movements only made the German recruiting efforts easier. Whether they acknowledge it or not, ELAS played a major role in pushing many Greeks into the arms of the Germans.

The British attempted to contain this internecine conflict, but they were unable to eliminate it entirely. The Germans, seeing what was happening, took full advantage of these political differences – expanding the chasm that already existed between the royalists, conservative republicans, socialist, and communists – just as they had already done in other parts of Axis occupied Europe and the USSR. The German watch word in Greece during the last occupation years of 1943–4 was 'divide and conquer'. In this they excelled, thereby laying the groundwork for the creation of Greek collaborationist forces, a subject that has thus far received little, if any, scholarly attention. This subject is historically important, since it details the active participation of perhaps around 50,000 Greeks in the German volunteer movement. This figure has been denied by most Greeks up until the present.

Background: Greek Forces during the Occupation

Before the war the armed forces of the Greek state comprised the Royal Greek Army and Navy, and the State Security Forces (*Somata Kratikcs Asphaleias*). These were the Royal *Gendarmerie* (*Basilikē Chorophylake*), the City Police (*Astynomia Poleon*), the Fire Department (*Pyrosbestike Hyperesia*) and the Rural Guard (*Agrophylake*).[1] Of these the *Gendarmerie* was paramilitary in character, able to police effectively the countryside and intent on the persecution of Communists and other elements disaffected with the regime of Ioannis Metaxas (1936–41). The City Police had forces only in the cities of Athens, Piraeus, Patras and Corfu (Kerkyra), the rest of the country being under the supervision of the *Gendarmerie*. Likewise, the Fire Department and the Rural Guard were of very limited military value and practically unarmed.

The *Gendarmerie*, during the brief Greek-Italian and Greek-German war (28 October 1940 to 30 May 1941), acted as additional Military Police and provided prisoner escorts, as well as a *Gendarmerie* School Battalion that fought during the German airborne assault on Crete. Moreover, the gendarmes helped with the creation of a Militia ('*Politophylake*') whose literal translation was 'Citizen Guard' from older men that had not been conscripted, who were used as guards for military installations of the interior during the war.

The *Gendarmerie* was controlled by the Ministry of the Interior through a *Gendarmerie* Headquarters (*Archegeion Chorophylakes*) based in Athens. The country was divided into several Higher *Gendarmerie* Commands, which in turn were divided into lower *Gendarmerie* headquarters. Under these were *Gendarmerie* sub-commands which controlled the *Gendarmerie* Stations that dotted the provinces.[2] Apart from these, there existed a *Gendarmerie* regiment in Athens. This controlled up to ten companies of gendarmes, without intermediate battalion HQs, as well as a Motorised (Motorcycle) Detachment. Over and above the *Gendarmerie,* composed of seconded gendarmes and policemen and similarly subordinated to the Ministry of the Interior, was the Special Security Branch (*Dieuthynsis Eidikes Asphaleias*) that specialised in the prosecution of communists and other suspects, acting as a secret (and sometimes brutal) service of the State.

Creation of the Greek Security Battalions

On 6 April 1943 the more pro-German Ioannis Rallis was appointed by the Germans to become Prime Minister of Greece, thus replacing Prime Minister Logothetopoulos. With this new appointment, a new phase in German-Greek relations began. Rallis immediately reshuffled his Cabinet and, at the instigation of the SS, began planning the formation of his own security force, soon to emerge as the Security Battalions.[3] The Germans had seen the slow but steady rise in Greek guerrilla activity all across the country, so it was essential that they now tried to take all necessary steps to eliminate, or at least control this growing partisan menace.

With Rallis' permission, the Germans entered the Peloponnese in 1943. This had been done without even consulting the Italians, who had sizable forces there. Up until 1943 the Germans had been content to govern Crete, some smaller islands, and most of Macedonia with its important port of Salonika. But the worsening military situation in North Africa and the growing guerrilla menace in Greece forced them to begin taking measures which would ensure the security of their control in that country. A new Greek security force would be formed that would help assist them in this effort. Initially, one battalion of 1,000 anti-terrorist police was organised, as well as recruiting thousands of villagers and townspeople into local self-defence militias to help fight off guerrilla 'food raids'.[4] The first unit formed was organised on 7 April 1943 in Athens by the Rallis government. Rallis initially ordered the creation of four security battalions. The initial battalion was formed easy enough, but volunteers for the next three proved hard to acquire, given that before the Italian surrender of September 1943, which deprived Germany of a much-needed ally, the Germans were still unsure about arming an all-Greek security force, and the fact that few Greeks were willing to initially volunteer for service.

Only after the Italian surrender in September 1943 did the Germans begin to accelerate the growth of the security battalions, partly due to the initial success of the first security units, and partly out of necessity in acquiring men to replace the Italian garrison units. By the end of 1943 the first three to four *Evzone* battalions had been formed and were actively hunting out the ELAS guerrillas. The *Evzones* were historically elite Greek mountain infantry units, analogous to Scottish Highlanders. They were distinguished by their picturesque white jackets, wide skirts and Albanian-type slippers with turned-up tufted toes. Their typical battle cry was '*Aera! Aera!*'[5]

By December 1943 the first four *Evzone* battalions had been organised. The table of organisation for the *Evzone* mountain battalion called for three rifle companies and a separate machine-gun company. Total effectives in each battalion were to be 22 officers and 539 NCOs and men. Initially, two battalions were stationed in Athens and two in Salonika. By the end of 1943, the *Evzone* battalions were actively participating in searching out and destroying the Greek ELAS communist guerrillas. The Greek *Gendarmerie* force was still thought of as a vital part of the anti-guerrilla forces. A German roster for 15 December 1943 showed that the Greek *Gendarmerie* force, which was supposed to have a complement of 14,923 men, was greatly undermanned, having a deficiency of 4,040 officers, NCOs, and men.[6] In fact, the dated document detailed the numbers of officers and men as to 'paper' strength and 'actual' numbers as follows:

Table 19. Greek Gendarmerie Strength, 15 December 1943

Authorised Strength	**Officers, NCOs, and Men**	**Actual Strength**
1,169	Officers	1,223
13,754	NCOs & Men	9,660[7]
14,923	Grand Total	10,883

The recruitment of men into the *Evzone* battalions also had an effect on the loss of personnel in the *Gendarmerie* force, as testified by the following account:

> In January 1944 Rallis stepped up the pressure on army officers, threatening to penalise any serving officer who refused to 'volunteer' by stopping his pay and food cards. On 22 May the government published a three-page list of such men and announced that they had been placed on the retired list and had forfeited all pension rights. For the first time, regular army NCOs were posted to battalion units. Men were deliberately dismissed from the gendarmerie without rations to force them into the Battalions. Under duress, large numbers of gendarmes and army officers complied; others escaped to the Middle East, or took to the hills.[8]

While the security battalions were in the process of being expanded, the Germans made use of those Italians who still supported a Fascist-Nazi victory by organising them with some additional Greek volunteers into what were to be principally Italian-manned police battalions. The units were raised and (initially at least), operated in the following localities:[9]

- Field Post No. 44 566 – *1. (italienisches) Polizei-Freiwilligen-Bataillon* (1st Police Volunteer Battalion), stationed in Athens
- Field Post No. 47 316 – *2. (italienisches) Polizei-Freiwilligen-Bataillon* (1st Police Volunteer Battalion), stationed in Volos
- Field Post No. 45 542 – *3. (italienisches) Polizei-Freiwilligen-Bataillon* (3rd Police Volunteer Battalion), stationed in Verria

Although the above three police volunteer battalions were supposed to have been composed of both Italians and Greeks, a captured German document dated 12 April 1944, clearly shows that only Germans and Italians comprised the 1st Police Volunteer Battalion in Athens. The German commander is listed as being *Major der Polizei* Mahner, and the numbers of volunteers were as follows:

Table 20. 1st (Italian) Volunteer Police Battalion, 12 April 1944

	Officers	Civilian Officials	NCOs	Men	Total
Germans:	8	3	69	9	89
Italians:	10	0	77	498	585
Total:	18	3	146	507	674
Grand Total:					**674**

Nowhere in this German document does it show that any Greeks were attached to this volunteer battalion. Whether this was also true in the other two volunteer police battalions is as yet unknown. By the time of the German withdrawal from Greece, the above-named 1st and 3rd Battalions were merged into a unit title *Polizei Regiment Nagel*. This unit was led by *Oberstleutnant der Schutzpolizei* (Lieutenant-Colonel of the Police) Gottlieb Nagel, who was Commander of the Order Police 'Athens'. Nagel's staff was small- just two officers, one civilian inspector, and three NCOs, but he had at his disposal an entire *Gendarmerie* platoon: *Gendarmerie Zug No. 40 (mot.)*, under the command of *Leutnant der Schutzpolizei* Westphal. This motorised platoon contained one officer (Westphal), five NCOs, and thirty-four men.[10] With the aid of the German *Befehlshäber der Ordnungspolizei Griechenland* (Supreme Commander of the Order Police in Greece), Rallis was able to eventually increase the number of *Evzone* units from an initial batch of four battalions, into three *Evzone* regiments of three battalions apiece. A German roster for these *Evzone* battalions lists them almost exclusively in southern and central Greece as of 15 August 1944:[11]

Table 21. Pro-German *Evzone* Regiments, 15 August 1944

Unit:	Location:	Operational Control:
1. *Evzonen-Regiment*	Athens	*LXVIII. Armeekorps*
1st Battalion / *Evzone* Regiment 1	Athens	*LXVIII. Armeekorps*
2nd Battalion / *Evzone* Regiment 1	Athens	*LXVIII. Armeekorps*
3rd Battalion / *Evzone* Regiment 1	Athens	*LXVIII. Armeekorps*
2. *Evzonen-Regiment*	Tripolis	*LXVIII. Armeekorps*
1st Battalion / *Evzone* Regiment 2	Tripolis	*LXVIII. Armeekorps*
2nd Battalion / *Evzone* Regiment 2	Tripolis	*LXVIII. Armeekorps*
3rd Battalion / *Evzone* Regiment 2	Tripolis	*LXVIII. Armeekorps*
3. *Evzonen-Regiment*	Yannina	*XXII. Gebirgskorps*
1st Battalion / *Evzone* Regiment 3	Yannina	*XXII. Gebirgskorps*
2nd Battalion / *Evzone* Regiment 3	Yannina	*XXII. Gebirgskorps*
3rd Battalion / *Evzone* Regiment 3	Yannina	*XXII. Gebirgskorps*

Apparently, the very first *Evzone* units to enter the Peloponnese had arrived in the beginning of 1944, as witnessed by this account:

> On 20 January [1944], a detachment arrived in Patras [in the Peloponnese], where it paraded through the streets, apparently to some popular acclaim, before being billeted in the town's school. To drum up local volunteers, officers told their men to visit the 'tavernas' [taverns] and impress the public with their pay, rations and good living conditions.[12]

In addition to these three *Evzone* regiments, the Greek government also formed nine security battalions in Macedonia:[13]

- *I. Griechisches Freiwilligen-Bataillon* – In Verria, then Katerini in September 1944.
- *II. Griechisches Freiwilligen-Bataillon* – In Verria.
- *III. Griechisches Freiwilligen-Bataillon* – In Cervia & Kozani, then only Kozani in September 1944.

IV. *Griechisches Freiwilligen-Bataillon* – In Yiannitsa.
V. *Griechisches Freiwilligen-Bataillon* – In Bordia & Kozani, then Ptolomais in September 1944.
VI. *Griechisches Freiwilligen-Bataillon* – In Bordia & Kozam.
VII. *Griechisches Freiwilligen-Bataillon* – In Sachos & Langada, then Kilkis in September 1944.
VIII. *Griechisches Freiwilligen-Bataillon* – In Sachos & Langada.
IX. *Griechisches Freiwilligen-Bataillon* – In Krija-Wrissi (this unit was formed in September 1944).Volunteer Battalion V – In Bordia & Kozani, then Ptolomais in September 1944.

The Bulgarians also formed three additional Greek volunteer battalions in Macedonia. By 15 August 1944 they had formed the 1st and 3rd Battalions. For some reason, the 2nd Battalion was still in the process of being organised and trained. The 1st Battalion was stationed in Kastoria, while the 3rd Battalion was located in Edessa. The 2nd Battalion was being organised in Florina. These three battalions were more commonly referred to by the names of the towns where they were stationed. These three volunteer battalions contained a large number of members of the old Inner Macedonian Revolutionary Organisation, which sought Macedonian independence. In addition to these three Bulgarian-raised volunteer battalions, plus the nine security battalions formed by the Greek government with German Order Police assistance, the Bulgarians maintained friendly relations with the *Tsaous Andon* militia group, headed by Andronios Fosteridis. Although this band had a British liaison officer (Major Miller), it nevertheless had a non-aggression treaty with the Bulgarian forces in 1944.[14] Its 5,000 men controlled an area north of the Drama district where they operated. They were staunchly anti-communist. This fact is shown by an incident that occurred on 1 January 1944 when an ELAS force, at Major Miller's instigation, was invited to celebrate the New Year with units of the *Tsaous Andon* militia.

No one knows if the incident was premeditated or not, but what is known is that the ELAS group was murderously attacked with guns and axes and cut to pieces. Afterwards, the *Tsaous Andon* militia assisted the Bulgarian military in sweeps and anti-guerrilla drives against the 6th ELAS Division. There were a total 250 Bulgarians in the *Tsaous Andon* militia. One of his lieutenants was Commander Theodoros Mikropoulos, who led the 2nd 'Double' Company of the 26th Nationalist Regiment, stationed in the town of Bairam Tepe. In addition to these 5,000 militiamen, the Bulgarians had organised a small detachment of 300 Muslim Bulgarian volunteers who were sent to operate in western Macedonia in the Kastoria-Florina district. They were called *Comitadjis*. In March 1944 two volunteer battalions were formed on the island of Euboea, named 'Wichos', and 'Euboea', while in July 1944 *Freiwilligen-Bataillon 'Salonika' (bulgarisch)* was formed. In August a volunteer 'half battalion' was organised in Larissa under the auspices of the *4. SS-Polizei-Panzergrenadier-Division 'Polizei'*, while in Karditsa, another volunteer battalion was formed with the aid of the German SD.

This battalion had a political movement backing it, whose initials were EASAD. In September 1944 the German Order Police officially accepted into its ranks the *Poulos Polizei Verband*, even though it had been in existence since the autumn of 1943. Volunteer Battalion 'Salonika' was another unit that, although officially recognised by the German Order Police in July 1944 it had been in action against the *Andartes* (Greek guerrillas) since the previous summer. In fact, on 6 July 1943 the unit was performing security duty in the road between Servia and Elason, about 36km south-west of Servia.[15] In the Peloponnese, total Greek anti-partisan forces eventually amounted to some 8,000–9,000 men. Initially only one locally raised volunteer battalion had been formed. This was the *Polizei-Freiwilligen-Bataillon 'Leonidas'* based in Sparta. It had been equipped with German weapons and uniforms, and even included a German liaison officer.

This unit had been formed in December 1943 by a local wealthy landowner by the name of Leonidas Vrettakos. Vrettakos had lost his brother to the communist ELAS guerrillas, so he had a personal vendetta against the *Andartes*. Being a well to do farmer also meant that he had no desire to see a communist victory. His unit became a serious and continuous threat to the local guerrillas. Its men were drawn from the villages and towns in the surrounding countryside and were intimately familiar with the region and its people. This made them very dangerous. Additional forces in the Peloponnese included an *Evzone* battalion sent to Patras in January 1944. Eventually the entire *2. Evzonen-Regiment* with two additional *Evzone* battalions, not counting the one at Patras, arrived in the Peloponnese. One *Evzone* battalion was stationed at Tripolis, while the third was located at Corinth. To this force, five extra security and *Gendarmerie* battalions rounded up the entire Greek government military in the Peloponnese.

The ELAS guerrilla movement had been growing steadily, especially since the summer and fall of 1943. In fact, by 28 July 1943 the number of combat personnel which ELAS could field was around 16,000 men and women.[16] This force continued to grow in the winter of 1943 and spring of 1944. While this had been going on, ELAS had been steadily eliminating any other potential guerrilla movement. This was in anticipation of the eventual Axis withdrawal from Greece, when the group with the strongest military backing would decide the political future of the country It was for this reason that in April 1944 ELAS attacked and destroyed EKKA, the last non-ELAS resistance movement in central Greece, killing its commander, Colonel Dimitrios Psarros. In anger and frustration, the remnants of EKKA, still wearing their short British battle jackets and ankle boots and carrying Sten guns, simply walked into Patras and volunteered for service in the security battalions.[17] Fighting was bitter all across the countryside. The emotions and politically opposite viewpoints all came to a clash.

On 30 December 1943, in the region of the *LXXXVII. Armeekorps* near Athens, a unit of the volunteer battalions had a shootout with the communists.[18] The battalionists captured 107 guerrillas. A day later by Razzia, near Athens an additional 117 communists were captured. This group included 17 ELAS officers. The spring of 1944 brought no respite between the government and ELAS forces. On 22 February 1944 the *1. Evzonen-Regiment*, which was operating south of Chalkis, was surprised by a large ELAS unit. In the ensuing battle, numerous security men were killed and wounded. Thirty-five *Evzones* were reported missing and presumed captured.[19] Six days later, in the *XXII. Gebirgskorps* area by Agrinion, an *Evzone* assault force surprised an ELAS unit and captured forty communists.[20] On 8 March 1944, a combined German police and *Evzone* force operating in the area of *LXXXVII. Armeekorps* captured 132 communists and killed 21 near Piraeus.[21] That same day, in the Katerini district, a Greek security battalion was attacked and suffered eighty casualties before the *Andartes* could be driven off.[22]

The Fight against the Greek Guerrillas

In the Peloponnese, the ELAS guerrillas had their 3rd Partisan Division, with perhaps 4,500 men split into five guerrilla regiments. From the very beginning, the war there was just as bitter as in the rest of the Greek countryside. In early June 1944 the Germans had decided to organise an anti-guerrilla operation between Tripolis and Sparta that would be aimed at clearing out approximately two entire ELAS regiments in that region of Megalopolis. Beginning on 6 June it employed the use of the *II.* and *III. Bataillon* of *18. SS-Polizei-Gebirgsjäger-Regiment* plus the *SS-Polizei-Gebirgsartillerie-Abteilung*.[23] Additional forces included the *'Leonidas'* Battalion, the *3. Griechisches Gendarmerie-Bataillon* based in Kalamta, and one battalion (the 3rd) of the *2. Evzonen-Regiment* based in Tripolis. Colonel Dertilis, who was initially in charge of the security battalions, had sent Colonel Papadongonas to the Peloponnese to run the security battalions there. By the time of this Axis anti-guerrilla drive in the Peloponnese, Colonel Basileios Dertilis had been replaced by Colonel Ioannis Plytzanopoulos in April or May 1944.

Colonel Plytzanopoulos placed Colonel Dionysios Papadongonas in charge of Greek forces during the operation. Greek Major Manitakis, who commanded the *3. Griechisches Gendarmerie-Bataillon* at Kalamata, would provide supporting infantry for the *SS-Polizei-Gebirgsartillerie-Abteilung*, once it moved south from its staging area in Megalopolis. A battle group of the *117. Jäger-Division*, moving down from Korje, would also support the assault of the bulk of the *18. SS-Polizei-Gebirgsjäger-Regiment*, and the 3rd Battalion of the *2. Evzonen-Regiment*. Colonel Papadongonas was a very diligent and hard-working officer. He had personally placed a strong emphasis on raising volunteers for the security battalions in the Peloponnese.

His units were put under the command of the Ministry of the Interior and regarded as part of the *Gendarmerie*. By the end of the occupation, the total number of Rallis troops in the Peloponnese would amount to some 8,000 men. The German commander of this operation, code-named *'Natter'* ('Asp'), was *Major der Schutzpolizei* Poys, the commander of the *II. Bataillon* of *SS-Polizei-Gebirgsjäger-Regiment 18*. He met Colonel Papadongonas for a meeting as to how best to employ their forces. During this meeting the German major was quite impressed by the German-speaking Greek colonel:

> I found Colonel Papadongonas to be a loyal government career officer with nationalist-royalist leanings. He was stately and impressive, with Greek manners, and very soldierly, and in his roots he seemed kindly.[24]

It appears then, that relations between the German officers and Greek officers of the Ioannis Rallis government were good. This appears to have been the common thread tying the Rallis government forces to the Germans and was based on a hatred of communism. The operation officially ended on 20 June 1944, whereupon the various German units were redeployed elsewhere. The next operation, *Unternehmen Adler.* (Eagle) began on 25 June and lasted until 5 July. During this second operation, the Germans employed the following units:

- *SS-Polizei-Gebirgsjäger-Regiment 18*
- Parts of the *117. Jäger Division*
- *Aufklärungs-Abteilung 116*
- *Aufklärungs-Abteilung 83*
- *Luftwaffen-Jäger-Regiment 22* – belonging to *11. Felddivision (L)*[25]
- Several Greek volunteer battalions[26]

On 5 July the *SS-Polizei-Gebirgsartillerie-Abteilung* withdrew to Sparta, where it then moved on to Tripolis. On the 6 July it crossed the Corinth and on to Athens.[27] The *II. Bataillon / 18. SS-Polizei-Gebirgsjäger-Regiment* was sent to Lamia, while the *III. Bataillon* went on to Amfissa. Colonel Papadongonas continued to feature prominently in events in the Peloponnese. When the last *Wehrmacht* troops left that area in September, 1944 the Greek security battalions there did not withdraw with them. They were set upon by ELAS, and it was through Colonel Papadongonas's efforts that they continued to resist bitterly. This resistance was not always strong.

For example, when the German *117. Jager-Division* abandoned Agrinio and Amfilochia (south-central Greece) from 8–12 September, the 1,000 or so battalionists at Agrinio simply surrendered. From 5–20 September the security battalionists holding Pyrgos, in Ellis held their own before being overwhelmed by elements of the 3rd ELAS Division. On 19 September at Navpaktos, on the north-west coast of the Gulf of Corinth, 650 battalionists surrendered to elements of the 13th ELAS Partisan Division. Major Kapetsonis, an ex-EKKA officer, led this battalion. After EKKA's defeat by ELAS forces, he had crossed over the gulf to Patras in the Peloponnese, where he joined the Greek security garrison there.[28]

Another noteworthy operation, begun on 18 July 1944 about 30km north of Athens, employed the *I. Bataillon* of *18. SS-Polizei-Gebirgsjäger-Regiment*. This battalion was under the command of the *1. Kompanie* commander, *Hauptmann der Polizei* Bothner, supported by a battalion from the *1. Evzonen-Regiment*. This battle group roamed this region north of Athens, hoping to make contact with and destroy elements of the 2nd ELAS Division. There were other anti-guerrilla operations launched jointly. The first two were conducted in 1943 and were launched in the area of operations of the *XXII. Gebirgskorps*. The first one was code-named *'Augustus'*, and was launched in August 1943 in an area south-west of Yannina (in Epirus). In this operation the primary German unit was the *1. Gebirgs-Division*. Greek forces were negligible, and only included some translators and guides. The last major operation for 1943 was a four-step anti-partisan drive whose parts were codenamed *'Panther'*, *'Tiger'*, *'Puma'*, and *'Hubertus'*. These operations ran from October-November 1943 and centred south-east of Yannina, in the southern Pindus Mountain region between Thessaly and Epirus.

Operation Panther was completed on 26 October 1943 and was judged a complete success. Begun in earnest when a column of about 4,000 German infantrymen, supported by eight tanks and by artillery, moved to try and reopen the Kalambaka-Yannina road. They advanced from Trikkala towards Kalambaka. This force was drawn from the *4. SS-Polizei-Panzergrenadier-Division 'Polizei'*, which was in Greece for rest and reorganisation. A second column of troops from the *1. Gebirgs-Division* advanced from Yannina itself towards Driskos, Baltouma Bridge and Gotista. A third colunm comprising the *2. Brandenburger-Regiment,* advanced from Konitsa towards Zagoria.[29] During this eight-day battle, the 4th Regiment of the 1st ELAS Partisan Division was smashed and Kalambaka was taken on the evening of 18 October 1943. The next big anti-guerrilla drive was titled 'Summer Thunderstorm'.

It lasted from 7–11 April 1944 in the Boeotia region, where around 3,000 Axis troops tried to clear the Helicon Mountain area of ELAS troops. In this operation, the Germans used the *III. Bataillon* of *SS-Polizei-Panzergrenadier-Regiment 7* from the *4. SS-Polizei-Panzergrenadier-Division 'Polizei';*[30] *Festungs-Bataillon 1010;* elements of the *11. Felddivision (L),* and the *Deutsche-Arabische Infanterie-Batallion 845.*[31] In addition, the Greek *1. Evzonen-Regiment* from Athens supplied a battalion for the operation, while the *1. (italienisches) Polizei-Freiwilligen-Bataillon* (German and Italian troops) also took part. In this battle, the ELAS guerrillas were defeated, but Axis losses were 250 including 45 battalionists.[32]

Next was a large anti-guerrilla sweep in the northern Peloponnese area involving parts of the *117. Jäger Division* and parts of the *41. Festungs-Division,* plus the Rallis forces stationed in Patras, Aegio, Argos, and Tripolis. This operation lasted from 18–27 April and involved around 3,000 German troops and 1,000 battalionists. *Unternehmen Maigewitter* (Operation May Thunderstorm) was launched on 4 May 1944 in the region south of Edessa, Macedonia. Greek forces involved in this attack included elements of the *III. Griechisches Hilfs-Bataillon (bulgarisch)* (from Edessa), and the *I. Griechisches Hilfs-Bataillon (bulgarisch)* from Kastoria. German forces amounted to around 600 men from *4. SS-Polizei-Division 'Polizei'* in the form of *Kampfgruppe Lange*. For their part, the Andartes were not just sitting back taking all of these offensives lying down.

For example, on the night of 1–2 June, a force of some five battalions from the 5th ELAS Partisan Brigade (13th Partisan Division), totalling 1,700 men, attacked the *7., 9., 10.,* and *11. Kompanie* of *SS-Polizei-Panzergrenadier-Regiment 7* of *4. 4. SS-Polizei-Division 'Polizei'* which were stationed in Amfissa.[33] The town also had a locally raised volunteer battalion for defence. Altogether, the German defenders could count on around 1,500 men. ELAS later claimed 150 enemy dead to their 75 killed and wounded. June also brought a fresh assault against the 3rd ELAS Partisan Division in the southern Peloponnese *(Unternehmen*

Viper) which has already been discussed. In July *Unternehmen Steinadler* was launched in the northern Pindus Mountains against elements of the 8th and 9th ELAS Partisan Divisions. The operation began on 3 July and lasted until 17 July. German forces included some 12,000–15,000 men, which even included some German-raised Albanian *Balisti*.[34]

Elements of the *4. 4. SS-Polizei-Division 'Polizei' Sicherungs-Regiment 639*, and the *104. Jäger-Division*. Greek and Italian troops were substantial, and included the following formations: The 3rd, 5th, & 6th Volunteer Battalions from Kozani; the *3. (italienisches) Polizei-Freiwilligen-Bataillon* from Verria (Italians); The *I. Griechisches Hilfs-Bataillon (bulgarisch)* from Kastoria; the *II. Griechisches Hilfs-Bataillon (bulgarisch)* from Florina; and parts of the *3. Evzonen-Regiment* from Yannina. Accounts from ELAS sources admit to the ferocity of this offensive, admitting that on account of this Axis attack, their forces became separated and cut off. The last major anti-guerrilla operation to be launched in Greece was code-named *'Kreuzotter'* ('Adder'). It began on 5 August and lasted till 25 August. The operation concentrated on the Karpenisi area and also included the region south of Karpenisi and west of Amfissa. This region was held by the German *104. Jäger-Division*. *Polizei-Freiwilligen-Bataillon 'Agrinio'* took part in this operation, advancing with *104. Jager-Division* troops from the Agrinio-Makrynia area towards Thermo and Aetopetra, entering Berikos on 7 August 1944.[35]

Another force from Agrinio advanced towards Ayios Viasis on 6 August 1944. It then turned northwards and took Chouni and Sidera. On 10 August troops of the *104. Jäger-Division* linked up with elements of *SS-Polizei-Gebirgsjäger-Regiment 18*, which were advancing from Amfissa, alongside a Greek volunteer battalion from that town.[36] On 11 August 1944 Viniani was captured by the combined German and pro-Axis Greece force. ELAS sources state that Karouta was defended by 5th Partisan Brigade, which managed to inflict 150 casualties on the 553-man battle group of the *III. Bataillon/SS-Polizei-Gebirgsjäger-Regiment 18* and Greek *'Amfissa'* Security Battalion. By 7 August, a second police battalion advanced towards Karouta but the town wasn't captured by German and Greek forces until 26 August 1944.

On 15 August, in support of this last offensive, *4. SS-Polizei-Division 'Polizei'* units attacked from the Helicon district. The months of August and September 1944 would prove that the Germans were losing all control of the countryside. The problem not only lay in the ever-growing guerrilla menace, but in the advance of the Red Army during the summer of 1944, and the collapse of the southern German army group. Compounding these German military reversals

An excellent photograph of pro-German Norwegian *Ordenspoliti* members. (*Norges Hjemmefrontmuseum*)

Vidkun Quisling inspects members of the Norwegian SS Legion. (*Norges Hjemmefrontmuseum*)

A poor-quality image, but nevertheless an extremely rare photograph of an ethnic-German Serb serving in one of several *Hilfspolizei* battalions which operated in Serbia as part of the German occupation. (*Photo courtesy of Jovan Kovačević*)

Members of the pro-German Greek *Polizei-Bataillon Poulos*. Notice the arm patch on the man holding up a rifle (centre of picture). It appears to be an arm patch of the Greek flag. *(Museum of Modern History (Ljubljana))*

On the left, a pro-German village militiaman. Note the homemade arm patch, which bears a stylised swastika, what appears to be the Greek flag, and the Roman numeral 'V'. On the right, a pro-German Greek *battalionist* officer, wearing a mixture of Greek and German attire and insignia. (*Bundesarchiv*)

SS-Gruppenführer and *Generalleutnant der Polizei* Walter Schimana, seen here inspecting a Greek collaborationist *Evzone* battalion. (*Bundesarchiv*)

A member of the Albanian Gendarmerie and two members of the *21. Waffen-Grenadier-Division der SS 'Skanderbeg'* guard an Albanian farmer, some time in 1944. (*Bundesarchiv*)

Members of the pro-German Serbian Volunteer Corps marching, 1943. The corps, a fascist formation, was led by the virulently anti-Semitic Dimitrije Ljotić. (*Photo courtesy of Jovan Kovačević*)

The commander of the 4th Battalion of the Serbian Volunteer Corps, Miloš Vojnović Lautner. This officer's father was Serbian, while his mother was German. As such, he was an ethnic-German Serb. (*Photo courtesy of Jovan Kovačević*).

Ethnic German members of the *22. SS-Freiwilligen-Kavallerie-Division 'Maria Theresia'* seen here slicing large chunks of bacon. Toward the end of the war, food shortages were common throughout many Axis-held territories. This photograph suggests that men who joined the *'Maria Theresia'* SS Division were relatively well supplied with food. The largest number of men to enlist in the *Waffen-SS* simply out of the need to avoid starvation, occurred in the Netherlands during the so-called 'Hunger Winter' of 1944–5. (*Bundesarchiv*)

Three ethnic-German Romanians serving in the *Waffen-SS*. (*Photo courtesy of Alexey Morozov*)

Spanish volunteers who helped to create the *250. Infanterie-Division* of the *Wehrmacht*. This division fought in the region of Army Group North and was respected by the Russians for its toughness in battle. (*Museo de la División Azul*)

Men of the Spanish *250. Infanterie-Division* of the *Wehrmacht*. After the division was recalled by the Spanish government, a Spanish Legion of two battalions was formed from volunteers who wished to continue fighting. In the late summer of 1944, this regiment-sized unit was disbanded. The volunteers were again asked if they wished to remain on the Eastern Front; this time, only two companies opted to continue. These were absorbed into the *Waffen-SS* as the *Spanish Freiwilligen-Kompanien der SS 101* and *102*. Fifty men from one of these companies later took part in the defence of Berlin in April 1945. (*Museo de la División Azul*)

Flemish volunteers of the *Waffen-SS*, circa 1944. They served in the *23. SS-Freiwilligen-Panzergrenadier-Division 'Nederland'*. (*Kazerne Dossin: Gedenk-, Museum- en Documentatiecentrum*)

A decorated member of the Flemish *Waffen-SS.* He wears the infantry assault badge, the close combat clasp, as well as the Iron Cross. (*Kazerne Dossin: Gedenk-, Museum- en Documentatiecentrum*)

A recruiting poster for the Estonian SS Legion. (*Bundesarchiv*)

Members of the Estonian *Ost-Bataillon 658.* These men would later serve in the *20. Waffen-Grenadier-Division der SS (estnische Nr. 1).* Notice the young boy in the group – no doubt the company or battalion 'mascot'. (*Bundesarchiv*)

Heinz Reinfarth and other SS officers speaking with members of the *Kaminski Brigade* in Warsaw, August 1944. (*Bundesarchiv*)

Bronislav Kaminski, conferring with German *Ordnungspolizei* officers. (*Bundesarchiv*)

Not Germans, but Russian volunteers of the *Kaminski Brigade*. (*Photo courtesy of Alexey Morozov*)

Members of an Armenian battalion of the *Wehrmacht*. They are seen here somewhere in France in 1944. (*Nevington War Museum*)

Armenian volunteers, circa 1943. The full colour Armenian shield is being worn by at least two men. (*Bundesarchiv*)

Georgian volunteers in the *Wehrmacht*, circa 1943. (*Bundesarchiv*)

A high-ranking German officer inspects a Georgian machine-gun crew, some time in 1944. Notice that they are located along a coast. The machine gun appears to be a First World War Maxim machine gun. (*Bundesarchiv*)

An officer in a Georgian unit looks through 'rabbit ear' observation binoculars. (*Bundesarchiv*)

Aserbaidschanisches Bataillon I./111 (the I/111th Azerbaijani Battalion) in Warsaw, August 1944. (*Muzeum Powstania Warszawskiego* [*Warsaw Uprising Museum*]).

Volunteers from the North Caucasus region. Note the '*Bergkaukasien*' arm patch on the right sleeve of the officer on the left. (*Bundesarchiv*)

A very rare photograph of British members of the *Waffen-SS* 'British Free Corps'. South Africans and one or two Irishmen were also found in this unit. These turncoats numbered no more than two dozen and referred to themselves as the 'Legion of St. George'. They wore a very unique cuff band. It was the only *Waffen-SS* cuff band written completely in English. The background was the typical Black cloth but the words 'British Free Corps' were woven in silver or white thread. (*Imperial War Museum*)

Recruiting poster for the British Free Corps. (*Bundesarchiv*)

Swedish volunteers of the *Waffen-SS*, shown here in the region of Narva, 1944. (*Bundesarchiv*)

Finnish members of the *Waffen-SS*, 1943. (*Sotamuseo [Finnish Military Museum]*)

Leon Degrelle, the Belgian Rexist Party leader, seen here as he appeared in 1989, when he was 83 years old. Degrelle was born on 15 June 1906 in Bouillon, in the Belgian province of Luxembourg (southern Belgium). He died in exile on 31 March 1994 in Malaga, Spain. This photograph was purchased from a private collector.

was the collapse of the Antonescu government in Romania, and her subsequent declaration of war against Germany. Shortly after Romania switched sides, Bulgaria did as well. This only added urgency to the situation, since the entire *Heersgruppe* 'E' in Greece was now threatened with being cut off.

As a result, the decision to evacuate Greece was reached in August 1944 and German forces began the withdrawal from the Peloponnese in late August. Actually, *Unternehmen Otterüberquerung* (Operation Otter Crossing) was launched not so much to destroy further guerrilla forces, as it was launched to allow the safe withdrawal of German forces from the Peloponnese by way of the Gulf of Corinth and Patras. The vast majority of the Rallis security battalions were left behind to fend for themselves. The 3rd ELAS Partisan Division and its five regiments had been harassing the Greek and German forces since the summer. One notable mention was the attack on a government train on 23 July at Routsi, near Megalopolis. In this attack, the train was blown up.

It had been carrying around 350 men of the local *Griechisches Hilfs-Bataillon 'Megalopolis'*. Later, ELAS claimed that 310 out the 350 battalionists had been killed.[37] Typically however, these guerrilla attacks were relatively small hit-and-run affairs, at least until the German withdrawal began in late August-September. On 10 August for example, in the southern Peloponnese, an ELAS force wiped out two platoons of German troops, killing seventy-five soldiers. Among the dead were seven battalionists. The withdrawal from the Peloponnese was very noticeable. ELAS attempts to try and prevent or hinder it now began. On 29 August, another ELAS force from the 3rd Peloponnesian Partisan Division attacked German and Greek *Evzone* troops at Skoupa, near Carinthia. They reported eighty enemy dead. The ELAS guerrillas weren't sitting still on the mainland either. One of their biggest successes occurred between 8–12 September, when the Germans finally withdrew from Agrinio and Amfilochia. At Agrinio the remaining security battalion was forced to surrender with their arms. ELAS sources stated that around 1,000 battalionists surrendered there. Not all of Rallis' troops gave up that easily and many desperate, last-ditch battles were fought.

One such action took place from 5–20 September at Pyrgos, in Elis. Kalamta was also very hotly contested, and all attempts to arrange surrender were met with battalionist rifle fire. In these engagements, about another 1,000 battalionists were either killed or captured. Sparta, south-east of Tripolis, and Areopolis were abandoned by the Greek security units, who withdrew to Gythio. On 19 September Argos was taken by 3rd Peloponnesian Partisan Division forces. Inside Tripolis, the commander of the Greek security forces, Colonel Papadongonas, was formally asked to surrender but the amnesty promised ran out on 16 September 1944. Thereupon fighting for Tripolis resumed without an end in sight. The Greek security forces in Tripolis clung on for dear life, for it had been rumoured that many battalionists that surrendered had been killed by ELAS troops. Papadongonas was finally saved when British forces landed at Patras on 4 October 1944. That same week he surrendered to the British. Security battalionists at Pyrgos weren't so lucky however, as it was reported that after a two-day battle, the men who surrendered to the Andartes there were shot. Those were the lucky ones. Seeking revenge for earlier abuses, some Greek collaborators paid dearly as the following excerpt shows:

> On Sunday, 17 September the former governor of Messina and other officials were brought back under ELAS guard from Meligala to Kalamata. As soon as they were marched into the main square, frenzied onlookers broke loose of the ELAS civil police and in ten minutes beat some of the prisoners to death, and strung the others up from lamp-posts. An American radio operator had a good view of the crowd: All of [them] wanted to get in some kind of a blow. Canes, clubs, knives, shoes, rocks, and everything anyone could strike a blow with were used on the group. This was their first chance at vengeance and they took it.[38]

Fighting began to wane after the surrender of Tripolis. On 7 October Corinth was captured by ELAS. In this battle the 3rd Peloponnesian Partisan Division captured 235 of Rallis' *Evzone*s and sent them directly to a concentration camp on Spetse. In the same week that Tripolis surrendered, the security battalions holed up in Gythio (Sythion) actually launched an attack on 3rd Peloponnesian Partisan Division forces now holding Sparta. Their attempt was to actually try and reach British forces in order to surrender to them, but they were defeated on 10 October at Mistra when they were surrounded and forced to surrender.[39] On 12 October 1944 Athens was abandoned by the Germans. A day later, on the 13th, British paratroopers landed in the Greek capital, and three days after that, the New Greek government followed.[40] Another source states that the New Greek government did not enter the capital until the 18 October, but that aside from battles still being fought in the Peloponnese between ELAS forces and security battalionists, order reigned in the rest of the country.[41]

In fact, the Germans were still in the process of withdrawing their forces, and still occupied most of Macedonia and parts of northern Epirus and Pindus. On 23 October, after a brief truce in which ELAS promised to spare them, battalionists surrendered at Monemvasia, in the Peloponnese. A day later, the *Gendarmerie* of Edessa (in Macedonia) surrendered as well, but the town was not entered until 26 October. On that same day, 10th ELAS Partisan Division forces also took Yiannitsa and Skydra. Three days later, they captured Verria, overrunning the local security forces there. This was the last major battle between the *Andartes* and the battalionists. For all intents and purposes, the guerrilla war as it dealt with the Germans and the collaborationist Rallis government was over, but before the year was over, EAM-ELAS was pitted against the newly installed Greek government. In fact, many men of the new government of George Papandreou were former battalionists. A point in fact was Colonel Spiliotopoulos Panagiotis, appointed as the new military commander of the Athens area.[42] The political hatreds and aspirations which all interested parties felt for one another were just too great to cease once the Axis withdrew from Greece. In fact, one British officer commented that by the time the British arrived in Greece in 1942, 'the cards had already been dealt for a serious post-war disturbance'.[43] Now former battalionists would fight for the Papandreou government against EAM-ELAS. A bitter civil war still lay ahead of the starved and war-ravaged Greek nation.

Chapter 11

1943–1944: BLOODBATH IN THE EAST AND THE RUSSIAN ARMY OF LIBERATION

Untermenschen in German Uniform

Beginning with the Nazi invasion of the USSR, a number of German generals supported the organisation of Eastern volunteer formations, but for a long time without success. In the autumn of 1941, Field Marshal Fedor von Bock had sent to Hitler's headquarters a detailed project for the organisation of a Liberation Army of some 200,000 Russian volunteers, and for the formation of a local government in the province of Smolensk. It was returned in November 1941 with the notation that 'such thoughts cannot be discussed with the *Führer*', and that 'politics are not the prerogatives of Army Group Commanders'. Of course, Field Marshal Wilhelm Keitel, who wrote this notation, did not show the project to Hitler.[1] Since the summer of 1941, volunteers made up of Eastern peoples had been employed as sentries, drivers, store-keepers, workers in depots, etc. The experiment had surpassed all expectations. In the spring of 1942, there were already at least 200,000 of them in the rear of the German armies, and by the end of the same year their number was allegedly near 1,000,000.[2]

As stated in a previous chapter, the next step taken by many German commanders in the East (behind Hitler's back) was the organisation of voluntary military troops, called '*Osttruppen*', clad in German uniforms and designed to guard lines of communication, fight Soviet partisans in the rear of the German armies, and sometimes even hold less important sectors of the front. These troops seldom exceeded the strength of a battalion. In the middle of 1942, there were already six such battalions in the rear of Army Group Centre alone. One of the first Russian volunteer formations was RONA – Russian National Army of Liberation – which was organised in the winter of 1941–2 under the command of a Soviet captain called Bronislav Kaminski, who was promoted by the Germans to Major-General. His army – which in fact never exceeded the strength of a division – at first fought against Soviet partisans, and later on the front. In the summer of 1944, after considerable losses, RONA was withdrawn to East Prussia, where Himmler took it over from the *Wehrmacht* and reorganised it into an SS brigade.

After 1943, the morale of the *Kaminski Brigade* dropped, as its men and its leader saw that they had bet on the wrong horse. After they were transferred from the Bryansk region of central Russia, where they had been operating very successfully against Russian partisans, they began to sink into what can best be described as pure existentialism with a freebooter attitude. By 1944 Kaminski's brigade had earned the worst possible reputation among all who had anything to do with it, not excluding Russians from other formations. A particularly gruesome reputation was gained by this brigade during the quelling of the Warsaw Rising in 1944. Only the infamous *SS-Sturmbrigade Dirlewanger,* composed of criminal volunteers from German prisons and concentration camps, could match the deeds of Kaminski's Brigade.[3] After the Warsaw rising, Kaminski was shot by order of his protector Himmler, and the remnants of his brigade were sent to the Vlasov Army which was then being formed. A story was made up that said Polish partisans had ambushed Kaminski's command car. This was done so the already unruly mob of men would not rebel.

As stated earlier in Chapter 8, about the same time that RONA was established, the SD raised its own force of Russians in Belorussia (White Russia). There, Vladimir Vladimirovich Gil, a Red Army officer, was given command of the *Druzhina-SS-Verband,* and near Smolensk, at the end of 1941, the *Abwehr* raised the Russian National People's Army (RNNA). This Russian SS formation was disbanded in 1943 after it defected. The second, known as the *Graukopf Brigade* and backed by the *Abwehr,* met with the same end in 1943, when several desertions forced the Germans to break up the brigade and employ the battalions piecemeal. Besides these formations, a number of volunteer battalions, companies and squadrons were formed. At first, they had unofficial status, but later they were fully recognised. The majority of them, composed of volunteers of Russian nationality, were later incorporated into the Russian Army of Liberation – ROA – which was not an army in the organisational meaning of the word, but a name given to all Russian voluntary formations which recognised General Vlasov as their leader.

The Eastern Legions

In a better condition were the Eastern Legions, the *Ostlegionen*, which, according to Alfred Rosenberg's conception, contained only non-Russian volunteers. Hitler limited them to nationalities living far from the frontiers of the 'Great Reich'. On 30 December 1941 a top-secret memorandum ordered that the Supreme Command was to create, first the Turkestani Legion from volunteers of the following nationalities: Turkomans, Uzbeks, Kazakhs, Kirghiz, Karakalpaks and Tadjiks. Second, the Caucasian-Mohammedan Legion, from Azerbaijanis, Daghestans, Ingushes, Lezghins and Chechens. Third, the Georgian Legion; And fourth, the Armenian Legion.[4] The German employment of so-called *Osttruppen* represents one of the more complex facets of the Eastern Front.

These units were formed from prisoners of war, local volunteers, and conscripts drawn from the non-Russian nationalities of the Soviet Union, including Ukrainians, Georgians, Armenians, Azeris, Turkestanis, Tatars, and others. Their emergence stemmed from both practical military needs and political calculations: as German manpower losses mounted after 1941, the *Wehrmacht* increasingly turned to auxiliary forces to sustain its war effort. Although Nazi racial ideology officially discouraged cooperation with 'inferior' Slavic and Asiatic peoples, expediency often outweighed dogma on the front line. Initially, many *Osttruppen* served in the form of *Hilfswillige* (or 'Hiwis'), auxiliaries attached to German combat units for support tasks such as logistics, construction, and transport. By 1942, however, the German Army had begun to integrate them more systematically into armed formations. *Ost-Bataillone*, composed of several hundred men each, were created and often attached to divisions operating in the Soviet Union.

Their reliability was questioned by many German commanders, who feared desertion or defection, particularly when units were stationed near their ethnic homelands. As a result, *Ost-Bataillone* were frequently redeployed to the Western Front, the Balkans and Italy, where the likelihood of defection was thought to be lower. By 1944, several hundred such battalions were scattered across occupied Europe. The use of *Osttruppen* highlighted the tension between German military pragmatism and the ideological rigidity of the Nazi regime. On the one hand, these auxiliaries provided much-needed manpower, filling gaps in overstretched German formations. On the other, they were never fully trusted and were rarely afforded the status or equipment of regular German soldiers. Their presence in Normandy in June 1944 – where entire *Ost-Bataillone* were captured by the Allies – underscored both the extent of German dependence on these troops and their precarious position within the *Wehrmacht* hierarchy.

Ultimately, the *Osttruppen* illustrate how the German war effort on the Eastern Front was shaped not only by ideology but also by the exigencies of total war. In contrast to the unofficial formations, the Eastern Legions had national committees from the start. It must be explained that a 'legion' was not a tactical formation, but a training centre where national units, mostly battalions, were organised and trained. It seems that the largest formation was the *162. (Turkestanische) Infanterie-Division,* composed of Germans, Turkomans, and Azerbaijanis which, according to its commander, performed like a good German infantry division.[5] According to the testimony of Caucasian leaders, the number of volunteers from the Caucasus who fought on the German side was 102,300.[6] For a more detailed description of these Caucasian volunteers as they stood in October 1944, please refer to Appendix V in this book.

German commanders had great sympathy for the Cossacks, although these did not conceal their political ambition to build their own state, Kazakia. Their bravery, their generally-known hatred of the Soviets, and the services rendered from the very beginning particularly in fighting Soviet partisans, brought quick results. As early as the middle of 1942, a Cossack cavalry formation existed in Mohylev, under the command of a former Soviet major, Kononov, who had crossed over to the Germans at the first opportunity with the greater part of his regiment, and began service on the side of the Germans by guarding the line of communications against Soviet partisans.[7] When in the summer of 1942 the front in the south was moving fast toward the Caucasus and the Volga, the German armies entered territories inhabited by the Cossacks. Composed of many tribes, these had during the civil war in Russia in 1917–20 formed six federated republics: the Cossacks of the Don, of the Kuban, of Terek, of Orenburg, of the Ural, and of Astrakhan. The republics had been liquidated by the Bolsheviks with extreme cruelty. The Cossacks, therefore, greeted the Germans as liberators. The entire population of towns, villages and settlements went out to meet the German troops with flowers and gifts of all kinds, singing their national anthems. Cossack formations of the Red Army were coming over to the Germans in a body, new formations were springing up, apparently from nowhere, in traditional uniforms and armed with swords, pistols, daggers and rifles that had been buried for years.

One of the old and well-known *atamans* (Cossack leaders), Kulakov, who since 1919 had been believed dead, came out of hiding and, accompanied by hundreds of Cossacks in resplendent dress and on magnificent horses, made a triumphant drive into Poltava. Thousands of Cossacks in POW camps offered their services in the fight against the Soviets. Even the remnants of the Kalmuk tribe, estimated at some 60,000–80,000 people, formed and equipped sixteen cavalry squadrons which cleared the steppes of the remaining Soviet units, showing no mercy. *General der Kavallerie* Ernst August Köstring, who knew Russia well and in August 1942 was appointed 'Governor of the Caucasus', thought he was dreaming or watching a great historical film.[8] Such was the Cossacks' revenge for years of terror at the hands of the NKVD – the Soviet State Secret Police.

The recruiting of Cossacks for the fight against the Soviets was patronized by the Cossack National Movement of Liberation, whose aim was the rebuilding of an independent Cossack state. Aside from vague promises of some type of independence, like all the others who threw their lot with the Third Reich, no solid declaration or decree was offered to them. In spite of that, more Cossacks continued to volunteer. In the summer of 1943, the *1. Kosaken-Kavalleriedivision* (1st Cossack Cavalry Division) was formed under the command of *Generalleutnant* Helmuth von Pannwitz. It had six cavalry regiments. Shortly afterwards the division was expanded into the *XV. Kosaken-Kavalleriekorps,* which eventually numbered some 50,000 men. Further, two Cossack brigades and twelve Cossack reserve regiments were formed, and a number of smaller units were attached to German formations. In all, Cossack troops on the German side numbered about 250,000 men.[9]

It should be explained here that the granting of the SS status to the Cossack Corps was Himmler's device, quite often applied, for barring the *Wehrmacht*'s influence in political concerns of the foreign formations. This occurred in February 1945. However, the men of the *XV. Kosaken-Kavalleriekorps* continued to wear a combination of German Army and Cossack attire. The Germans used the Cossacks to fight Soviet partisans, to cover the rear of their armies, and sometimes for action on the front. Later on, some Cossack formations were moved to France and Yugoslavia. The Cossack command objected, on the grounds that the Cossacks should fight only against the Soviets, but in vain. Meanwhile, a small group of German officers and civil servants, in spite of many failures and difficulties, continued their effort to create a Russian Liberation Army out of the hundreds of thousands of Russian volunteers who wanted to fight against the Soviets. Their hopes were revived when at last a Russian 'de Gaulle' was found: the Soviet General Andrey Andreyvich Vlasov, former commander of the 37th and 20th Soviet Armies, and later Deputy Commander of the front on the river Volkhov.[10]

General Vlasov and the Russian Army of Liberation

General Vlasov was the son of a Russian peasant from the Nizhni, Novgorod district who, although far from rich, had been classed by the Bolsheviks as a 'kulak' and treated accordingly. The young Vlasov finished school with the financial aid of his brother, and began to study first theology and later at the Agricultural College of the University at Nizhni Novgorod. In the spring of 1919, he was called up into the Red Army. After a few weeks in a regiment, Vlasov was posted to an officer's school and finished a four-month course, gaining a commission. As a Second Lieutenant he was sent to the front to fight against the 'Whites'.

He did not join the Communist Party until 1930, but from then on, his rise was swift, since he obviously had great ability. In 1938, already a major-general, Vlasov acted as Soviet Military Advisor to Chiang Kai-Shek in China. In December 1939, he returned to Russia and was given command of a division. During the war with Germany, he commanded in turn a tank corps and an army, taking part in the battle of Kiev and in the defence of Moscow. In March 1942 he became Deputy Commander of the Volkhov Front. In mid-June 1942, the Soviet forces operating on the Volkhov River were surrounded in the woods and marshes, without food and supplies, and by the end of the month surrendered to the Germans. Vlasov became a prisoner of war.

The Propaganda IV Section of the *Wehrmacht*, WPrIV, realising that Vlasov was one of the outstanding officers of the Red Army, took immediate interest in him. He was transferred to a special, comfortable camp for important prisoners, where he was subjected to subtle propaganda which played on his aversion to the Soviet system. Soon the German supporters of collaboration with the anti-Soviet movement were convinced that their prisoner was the man they were looking for. His personal charm, his effective manner of speaking, his manners and abilities, and particularly his gift of inspiring confidence as well as his last important position in the Red Army, clearly predestined him to stand at the head of the Liberation Movement and Army, which in spite of Hitler's strict orders was coming into being. In September 1942, still in the POW camp, General Vlasov wrote a leaflet calling on the officers of the Red Army and the Russian intelligentsia to overthrow the Soviet regime of Stalin whom he accused of being guilty of all the disasters which had befallen Russia. However, the leaflet also contained some Nazi propaganda, included without Vlasov's knowledge.[11]

This leaflet was dropped by the *Luftwaffe* in thousands of copies. The German protectors of General Vlasov attached great hopes to it.

They expected that the results of this appeal would finally force Hitler to agree to the formation of the Russian Army of Liberation, and the results were indeed great. Day after day, the German Supreme Command received reports from all army groups that thousands of deserters from the Red Army who were coming over to the Germans, were asking for General Vlasov, and wanted to fight against the Soviets. But these reports infuriated Hitler; on his orders, Field Marshal Keitel forbade everybody, not excluding the General Staff, to present any kind of memorandum or report on the subject of General Vlasov and Russian formations.[12] This failure did not discourage the German supporters of the anti-Soviet movement. They decided to take what constituted a very unusual step under Hitler's regime. Without official authorisation they brought into being in December, 1942 the Russian National Committee, with General Vlasov as chairman.

This was no easy achievement, in view of the strong opposition of the non-Russian nationalities. It was decided that the seat of the Committee would be Smolensk, from where the already prepared 'Smolensk Manifesto' was to be broadcast. In its thirteen points, the Manifesto declared and promised the following: (1) abolition of compulsory labour, (2) abolition of collective farms, and land grants to the peasants, (3) reintroduction of private commerce and handicrafts, (4) termination of terror, (5) personal freedom, (6) freedom of faith, conscience, speech, press, and assembly, (7) free choice of work, (8) guarantee of free development for all nationalities, (9) release of all political prisoners, (10) rebuilding of towns, villages and factories at the expense of the state, and (11) a guarantee of minimum subsistence for all invalids and their next of kin. Moreover, the Manifesto stated that Nazi Germany, led by Adolf Hitler, pursues the aim of creating a New Order in Europe without Bolsheviks or 'capitalists'. This, of course, was an addition put into the Manifesto by the Germans. The Manifesto ended with an appeal to the soldiers and officers of the Red Army to join the Liberation Army which was fighting on the German side. Thus, the promoters of the German-Russian collaboration wanted to present the German authorities with an accomplished fact.[13]

The venture largely misfired. None of the papers controlled by the Germans even mentioned the creation of the Committee and the Manifesto; broadcasting the Manifesto was forbidden; Smolensk was rejected as the residence of the Committee. Soviet citizens in the occupied territories got to know about the Committee and its Manifesto from leaflets which were intended for the other side of the front and were dropped on the German side only 'by mistake'. However, in January 1943 the leaflet campaign had yielded such good results that the Command of Army Groups Centre and North invited General Vlasov, on their own initiative, to go on a tour of their areas and deliver speeches to prisoners of war, Soviet volunteers and the local population.

In March 1943, Vlasov, who had gained personal freedom, visited Smolensk, Mohylev, Bobruisk, Borisov, Orsha, and other places; Everywhere his speeches brought him thousands of supporters. Later, after a short rest, he toured the areas of Army Group North. In March also, his letter appeared in a newspaper; In it, he gave his reasons for taking up the fight against Bolshevism. In the second half of April the storm broke. Field Marshal Keitel demanded to know who had allowed General Vlasov to issue a political proclamation; he also threatened grave consequences if it proved true that Vlasov was appearing in public, and was being called 'the future leader of the Russians'. A few days later, Keitel issued a new order in which he stated: Vlasov is only a prisoner of war, his 'shameless' speeches infuriated the *Führer* who forbade mentioning the name Vlasov in his presence.

The latter should immediately be sent back to the POW camp, and should be kept under special surveillance; if, in future, Vlasov appeared anywhere in public he would be arrested and handed over to the Gestapo.[14] Yet the friends of General Vlasov succeeded in gaining permission for his further stay in Berlin – under 'surveillance', which in fact was rather fictitious. In the meantime, the leaflet campaign was in full swing. Soon all Army Groups and some of the armies reported that the publication of a political declaration and a change of attitude toward the anti-Soviet volunteers were a necessity; Otherwise, the occupation of the Eastern territories would prove an impossible task. Attempts were made also to find a way to Hitler's reason through Rosenberg; But the difficulty was that Rosenberg regarded the creation of the Russian National Committee as contrary to his own conceptions.

After a few months, Rosenberg's opposition relaxed, as General Vlasov abandoned his previous stand of the 'one and undivided Russia', consented to the principle of self-determination of the non-Russian peoples, and agreed that Russia, in a peace settlement, would renounce her claims to the Ukraine and the Caucasus.[15] Before Rosenberg's planned intervention, Hitler once more repeated his view on this question. On 8 June, at a conference with his military advisors and chiefs of services, he declared that the Liberation Army was a dangerous folly. He did not need such an army and would never consent to its organisation. The setting up of any states in the occupied territories was out of the question. There were, unfortunately, too many supporters of such ridiculous schemes in Rosenberg's circle and in the Army too. Instead of forming volunteer troops from them, the Russians would be sent to Germany to work in coal mines, replacing Germans. Vlasov was needed for propaganda work at the front – any activity of his in the rear was inadmissible.

Losses in German formations could be replaced by volunteers from the east only on a very small, never a large scale. Yet, by 1944 one in five men wearing the uniform of the *Feldheer* (Field Army) was an Eastern volunteer.[16] After that conference, Field Marshal Keitel wrote Rosenberg a very sharp letter in which he informed him of Hitler's decision and asked him to forget the planned intervention.[17] Thus Hitler, for the time being, reduced the Russian National Committee, and the Liberation Army which in fact existed only in name, to a mere centre of propaganda, controlled by Germans and working mainly by means of newspapers and pamphlets edited in Russian. However, the result of this propaganda was that, in spite of Hitler's intervention, the Committee and the Liberation Army became a symbol of the Russian nation's fight against the Soviet yoke. The lot of Soviet prisoners in German captivity improved. During 1943 the number of volunteers in the Eastern formations increased allegedly to some 800,000.[18] In September of that year, a new blow fell upon these formations.[19] According to exaggerated comments in German reports, Soviet troops broke through German lines chiefly because of the 'treacherous' behaviour of the Russian volunteer formations. Hitler flew into a rage; He ordered that all Eastern formations be immediately disbanded, and that 80,000 of them, as first contingent, immediately be sent to France as coal-diggers.

He also demanded that the progress of the disbanding was to be reported to him every 48 hours. The Chief of the General Staff was also furious and at first did not want to hear of any delay in carrying out the order. However, when he was finally convinced that the facts were greatly exaggerated, and that it was impossible to withdraw from the front more than 3,000–5,000 men, he decided to intervene. After three days Hitler modified his order; only formations from the broken sector of the front were disbanded. According to a statement of the General of Eastern Troops, seemingly made at that time, there were then on the entire Russian Front 427,000 ex-Soviet soldiers serving in the Eastern formations, who would have to be replaced by German soldiers in case they were disbanded.[20] This figure did not include over 100,000 '*Hiwis*' who were not recognised as soldiers, or Latvian, Estonian and Ukrainian formations. A few days later, when Hitler seemed appeased, he issued a new order: the Eastern troops were to be withdrawn from the Russian Front and sent to other theatres of operation. Thus, in the autumn of 1943, some 70 to 80 per cent of the Eastern troops were gradually withdrawn from the Russian front and moved to Poland, France, Italy, the Balkans, etc. In this way Hitler deprived the Eastern formations of their essential reason for existence – the fight against the Soviets.

The 14. *Waffen-Grenadier-Division der-SS (Ukrainische Nr. 1)*

At the end of April 1943, the formation of a Ukrainian division began. This deviation from Hitler's policy was the result of the deterioration of the general situation on the Eastern Front, and the appearance of Soviet partisans in the south-eastern territories of Poland. The decision to form the Ukrainian division did not meet with the general approval of the Ukrainian population which, discouraged by the German administration, was divided into two camps. The leaders of the underground movement were against the recruitment, but one main consideration turned the scales in its favour: the fear that if the venture was boycotted, Ukrainian youth would be deported to Germany as labourers or enrolled in German auxiliary formations. According to Wolf Dietrich Heike, who served on the staff, the Ukrainian SS division absorbed the following police regiments: *Polizeiregiment 4 (galizisches)*, *Polizeiregiment 5 (galizisches)*, *Polizeiregiment 6 (galizisches)*, *Polizeiregiment 7 (galizisches)* and *Polizeiregiment 8 (galizisches)*.[21]

The Germans, for their part, did not grant special concessions to the Ukrainians. The formation was initially called the *14. Waffen-Grenadier-Division der-SS (Galician Nr. 1)*, which meant that it was under Himmler's control and formally deprived of its national character. However, the Ukrainians received an assurance that the division would be used only on the Soviet front. In June, 1944 the division was engaged, was encircled, and suffered heavy losses fighting its way out. Voluntary enlistment was later replaced by conscription. The initial batch of Ukrainian volunteers for the division turned out to be around 80,000 men; out of which only the most physically fit 13,000 were chosen.[22] In the autumn of 1944, the Germans at last agreed to change the name of the formation to '1st Ukrainian Division', and in March, 1945 it became a part of a future 'Ukrainian Army'.[23] At the end of 1943, a small Ukrainian Legion was organised, which a year later was disbanded by the Germans for refusing to fight the Polish Home Army. The commander of the Legion was shot by the Germans.[24]

The Russian National Committee

The enforced captivity of the Russian National Committee, and of General Vlasov, continued in spite of many efforts on the part of the

German sympathisers of the anti-Soviet movement.[25] An attempt to influence Hitler was made by the *Gauleiter* of Vienna, Baldur von Schirach, who had been won over to the idea of the Russian Liberation Army. Hitler left Schirach's written interpolation without a reply. In the autumn of 1943, the order appeared which directed the Eastern formations from the Russian Front to other theatres of operations; General Vlasov was asked to publish an open letter to the Russian volunteers in which he was to explain that the withdrawal from the Eastern Front was a temporary measure, dictated by the necessity of giving them repose and time for reorganisation. When Vlasov refused his signature, the 'letter' was printed and distributed without his knowledge.

To sum up, by the middle of 1944 the situation of the anti-Soviet movement was as follows: ROA, the Russian Army of Liberation, was not a formation in the sense of a military organisation. Units which bore its name were mostly commanded by German officers, and were dispersed all over Europe; General Vlasov and the Russian National Committee had no influence whatsoever, and were not recognised by the German government; but the soldiers of the ROA saw in them their leaders. In July 1944 a sudden turn occurred. Himmler, always a great enemy of Vlasov and the Russian Liberation Army, finally came to the conclusion that in the critical situation of the Reich it was worthwhile to try a course of policy different from the official one that had so far prevailed. His change of mind was brought about mainly by his closest SS lieutenants.

At that time Himmler was, after Hitler, the most important and powerful person in the Reich. He was Chief of the SS, Hitler's praetorians, Chief of the Police, including the *Gestapo,* Minister of the Interior and, since the attempt on Hitler's life on 20 July, also Commander of the Home Army. He had the full confidence of Hitler, who gave him a free hand in dealing with General Vlasov. The meeting between Vlasov and Himmler was to take place on 21 July 1944. But this date almost coincided with the attempt on Hitler's life; the meeting therefore took place two months later, on 16 September 1944. It resulted in Himmler's consent to the creation of a new committee, called KONR – Committee for the Liberation of the Peoples of Russia – and the KONR Army under Vlasov's command.

The Committee and Army were to embrace all Soviet citizens living under German rule, in order to unite their political and military activities in the fight against Bolshevism. General Vlasov confirmed his declaration in the Smolensk Manifesto, that in the new Russia: 'every people will obtain national freedom, including the right of self-determination. The realisation of this right to national independence and freedom is possible, however, only after destroying Stalin and his clique'.[26] Himmler agreed to this interpretation and promised to help with the formation of the KONR Army. To start with, five divisions were to be organised (of which only two were formed) from among prisoners and workers brought to Germany from the occupied territories in the east; their number reached almost five million. As the majority of the Eastern troops (ROA) was engaged on various fronts, their transfer to the KONR Army was to take place gradually. Thus, the new Committee and its army owed their creation to Himmler who, by taking them under his wing, removed them from the sphere of influence of the *Wehrmacht* and Rosenberg, both of whom he hated.

The creation of the Committee for the Liberation of the Peoples of Russia and the consent to the organisation of its Army, met with strong opposition in many influential German circles; chiefly because the Committee and Army were led by a Russian, Vlasov, and were to embrace nationals of all the peoples of Russia. Not only Rosenberg opposed this but also many high officials and officers. Vlasov's strongest opposition, however, came from the representatives of the non-Russian nations, whose aim was to cut off all bonds with Russia and create their own independent states. In their eyes the KONR was mainly a Russian enterprise and controlled by Russians whom they did not trust. The declaration of 'equality of all peoples of Russia and their real right for national development, self-determination, and state independence' was regarded as merely a concession to circumstances which in the future, as so often in the past, would be forgotten.[27] This time, the non-Russian representatives expressed the experience of hundreds of years of relations between their peoples and Russia. Thus, although Himmler – who wanted only one all-Russian committee rather than several national committees – exercised pressure and made various threats, the following nationals refused to join KONR: Ukrainians, White Ruthenians (Belarusians), Georgians and Cossacks. The Kalmuks, who were labelled as 'Cossacks', decided to join KONR. General Vlasov however, prompted by his closest friends, came to an understanding with certain Ukrainians, White Ruthenians, Cossacks and Georgians who pretended to be 'representatives' of their nations. Thus, for example, the Russian General Balabin joined KONR as 'representative' of the Cossacks although his only grounds for 'representation' was that he had served some time ago in the Cossack troops.

General Vlasov by the way had no illusions; He realised fully his defeat. When one of the Germans congratulated him on the 'satisfactory' solution of the non-Russian representatives, he replied sadly: 'Those?'

'The others are only the shadows of their peoples, but those are the shadows of the shadows'.[28] The majority of the White Russian émigrés declared themselves opposed to KONR and General Vlasov, characterising his programme as 'Bolshevist' because it emphasised preserving the gains of the 1917 Revolution. However, those factions of the old émigrés who realised that a return to the state of affairs before 1917 was impossible backed Vlasov. Yet KONR remained to the end under the influence of the Russians who were Soviet citizens; It was the expression of their protest against the tyranny of Stalin. On 14 November 1944 the Committee for the Liberation of the Peoples of Russia held its inaugural meeting in Prague. Here the Prague Manifesto was proclaimed. In it the aims of the KONR were described:

> a) The overthrow of Stalin's tyranny, the liberation of the peoples of Russia from the Bolshevik system, and the restitution of those rights to the peoples of Russia which they fought for and won in the people's revolution of 1917; b) Discontinuation of the war and an honourable peace with Germany; c) Creation of a new free people's political system without Bolsheviks and exploiters.[29]

The political programme was almost identical with that of the Smolensk Manifesto of December 1942; but it stressed in its very first point the right of the peoples of Russia to self-determination and full national independence. It stated further that it 'decisively rejects all reactionary projects connected with a limitation of the peoples' rights', and that it welcomed Germany's help under conditions which would not impair the honour and independence of Russia. The declaration ended with an appeal to officers and soldiers of the Red Army to stop the war of aggression and turn their arms against the Bolshevik usurpers, and to 'brothers and sisters in the motherland', to continue in the fight against Stalin's tyranny and the war of aggression.

After its first meeting, the Committee for the Liberation of the Peoples of Russia met a few more times in Prague, but it had no opportunity to develop its activity. The end of the Third Reich was approaching with great speed. Besides, German control was constantly hampering the Committee's work, and all decisions and instructions had to be 'coordinated' with the appropriate German commissar. Nevertheless, the publication of the Prague Manifesto made a deep impression on the Russians. First of all, it brought forth a great number of voluntary applications for service in the Liberation Army, a number surpassing all expectations in one single day, 20 November 1944, about 60,000 applications were received. Particularly large was the number of volunteers from among prisoners of war and Soviet refugees who had left their native land voluntarily with the retreating German armies, preferring a wandering life in strange and perhaps unfriendly lands to a return under the NKVD yoke. What is still more puzzling, the desertion from the Red Army to the Germans increased after the publication of the Manifesto, although no one any longer doubted the defeat of Germany. Whatever can be said today about this hope and belief, it remains a fact that it was widespread, particularly in the Red Army.

The KONR Army, called persistently though wrongly 'ROA', Russian Army of Liberation – no such army ever existed as a united military force – had begun to form in November 1944, six months before the end of the war. Its birth was accompanied by shortages of arms and equipment, and by the chaos of the disintegrating Reich. Its short-lived protector, Himmler, realising that the venture was belated, abandoned it to the *Wehrmacht*. The German armies were delaying the transfer of their Eastern troops to General Vlasov's command; many of these formations were by then destroyed or had suffered heavy losses on the Western Front.[30] The leaders of the German economy were protesting against the recruiting of Eastern workers to the Liberation Army. As a result, the five divisions to be organised were cut by the Germans to two – then eventually two and a half divisions, plus a small 'Air Force' consisting of one air squadron. The KONR Army would have never been formed, even as a small force, in such a short time but for the great influx of enlistments, the enthusiasm of the volunteers, and the existence of a skeleton staff which General Vlasov had managed to form during the two years of inactivity.[31]

In spite of all difficulties, General Vlasov formed the Army Headquarters, two infantry divisions, one reserve brigade, an engineer battalion, and a few officers' units, with a total strength of some 50,000 men.[32] On 28 January 1945 he officially took command of the army. Shortly afterwards, the German insignia was removed and replaced by the army's own insignia. The 1st KONR Division, under the command of General Sergei Kuzmich Bunyachenko, was given the title of *600. Infanterie-Division*. Its organisation began in November 1944 in Münsingen (*Truppenübungsplatz Münsingen*), in *Wehrkreis V*. Operational readiness was reached in mid-February 1945. Because of the *Wehrmacht*'s reluctance to part with their Eastern formations, mentioned before, the nucleus of the division consisted of the remnants of the *30. Waffen-Grenadier-Division der SS (Russisches Nr. 2)*, which was greatly reduced during the fighting in France, and the remnants of the Kaminski SS division: *29. Waffen-Grenadier-Division der-SS 'Rona' (Russisches Nr. 1),* which had in fact turned from an effective anti-partisan force from 1941–3, to simply a band of outlaws and freebooters by 1944. When this rabble arrived at the camp where the division was being formed, gangs of armed and unarmed men in all kinds of uniforms, accompanied by women in fancy dresses and bejewelled from head to foot, stepped out of the carriages; officers were distinguished from men only by the number of watches on their wrists – from three to five; order and discipline did not exist. At the sight, General Bunyachenko exclaimed in anger: 'So this is what you're giving me – bandits, robbers, thieves. You'll let me have what you can no longer use!'

The End

In mid-April 1945 the first Russian Liberation Army division, *600. Infanterie-Division,* was near the Oder Front. In late April the *600. Infanterie-Division* took it upon itself to move. It headed south towards Cottbus, then in the direction of the Czech border. The Prague Uprising began on the morning of 5 May 1945 with largely symbolic acts of defiance. Czech civilians tore down German flags, replacing them with national banners, while tram conductors refused *Reichsmarks* and declined to announce stops in German, as mandated. Yet these gestures of resistance quickly escalated: isolated German soldiers and small groups of two to four were attacked – and sometimes killed – on the streets. The German response was swift and brutal, employing rifles and machine guns, turning Prague and its environs into a tense and heavily militarised space. Though American and British bombers were ordered to avoid targeting Czech territory in the same manner as German cities, Prague and its surrounding areas experienced several significant air raids in the war's closing months. These strikes aimed to disrupt German production and transportation networks. Anticipating the relative immunity of Prague to Allied bombardment, the German military had established numerous warehouses, ammunition depots, and other installations within the city and its periphery, including training bases and an SS officer academy.

Seizing the opportunity, Prague's youth stormed these lightly defended facilities and armed themselves. They captured five armoured vehicles – including Hetzer tank destroyers, at least one French AMR-35 tank, and a number of half-tracks – but the most significant gain was the acquisition of hundreds of Panzerfaust anti-tank weapons.[33] Meanwhile, the Czech resistance reached out to Major-General Sergei Kuzmich Bunyachenko of the Russian Liberation Army (ROA), requesting military support. Bunyachenko, aware that the Nazi regime was on the verge of collapse, faced a stark dilemma. He feared the consequences that awaited ROA volunteers at the hands of Stalin's forces, who would show no leniency to those who had served in the Russian Liberation Army. Calculating that aiding the Czechs might provoke Western intervention on their behalf, Bunyachenko saw an opportunity to secure asylum in the West.[34] Two ROA divisions were positioned near Prague: the *600. Infanterie-Division*, which had departed the Oder front without authorisation in late April, and the *650. Infanterie-Division*, stationed west of the city. Both would be deployed to assist in the expulsion of German forces.[35]

The defection and betrayal of the ROA represented a profound blow to German strategic planning. Both divisions had been meticulously trained and exceptionally well-equipped with rifles, mortars, artillery, anti-tank weapons and engineer equipment, rendering them overstrength by 1945 standards. Yet, aside from a brief anti-tank engagement along the Oder, these troops never fired upon the Red Army – a fact that led post-war historian Jürgen Thorwald to describe the Russian Liberation Army as 'an illusion'. On 6 May, elements of the *600. Infanterie-Division* entered Prague around midday, engaging German forces and disarming thousands by 7 May. However, as Czech leaders came to terms with the reality that Western liberation forces would not arrive and that the Red Army would occupy the city, they recognised that continued collaboration with the ROA could jeopardise future Czech-Soviet relations.

The Czech National Council informed Bunyachenko that his forces were no longer welcome. That same day, the ROA withdrew, moving westward in a failed attempt to surrender to Western Allied forces – echoing the broader German effort to avoid Soviet capture. With the ROA's departure, German forces regained the initiative. By 8 May, only a single district of Prague remained under Czech insurgent control, signalling both the courage of the city's defenders and the brutal limits imposed by the strategic and political realities of the closing days of the war. As for the men of the Russian Army of Liberation, a bleak future awaited them in a Siberian gulag. At least, those who were sent there were considered the 'lucky' ones. For the leadership of the ROA, only torture and execution awaited them in Russia.

Chapter 12

CONCLUSIONS

The history of foreign volunteers in German service during the Second World War defies simple characterisation. On the one hand, many of the units created by the Third Reich out of foreign manpower proved militarily negligible, and in some cases even counterproductive. Hastily assembled formations of dubious loyalty and inadequate training rarely matched the expectations of their German sponsors. In the most extreme instances, such as with certain Eastern battalions or ad hoc auxiliary contingents, desertion, mutiny, and poor combat performance rendered these units of little operational value. From a strictly military perspective, their creation often absorbed more effort, resources, and suspicion than they were ever likely to repay.

Yet even these ineffective formations served a broader function in the Nazi war effort. The mere existence of legions, brigades, and 'national' battalions composed of non-Germans provided the regime with potent propaganda imagery. Thousands of photographs and reels of film documented these foreign volunteers parading under swastikas, swearing oaths to Adolf Hitler, or marching to the front alongside German soldiers. Such images circulated widely in the controlled media of the Reich and were further disseminated in occupied Europe and beyond. They allowed Joseph Goebbels and his propagandists to make the apocryphal claim that Nazi Germany was not fighting alone but rather leading a worldwide coalition against Bolshevism. This claim bore little resemblance to the reality of the war, but it offered psychological sustenance both to Germans who longed for reassurance and to collaborators abroad who sought affirmation of their choices.

Nevertheless, it would be a mistake to dismiss the entire phenomenon as merely symbolic. Some foreign formations played a role far more substantial than propaganda. By 1943–4, as the German army on the Eastern Front haemorrhaged manpower, auxiliaries and so-called *Osttruppen* filled increasingly crucial gaps. As previously stated, by the beginning of 1944, fully one out of every five soldiers in the *Ostheer* was a foreign volunteer from the Soviet Union. This is a staggering proportion, one that underscores both the acute manpower crisis facing the *Wehrmacht* and the extent to which Germany relied on coercion, opportunism, and local grievances to sustain its war effort. While these auxiliaries were often relegated to second-line duties such as guarding railways or conducting anti-partisan sweeps, their numbers nonetheless freed German troops for front-line service and prolonged the Reich's ability to wage total war.

In other theatres as well, the contribution of certain foreign contingents was undeniable. In the Balkans, foreign volunteers formed part of the counterinsurgency apparatus that sought to suppress partisan resistance in Yugoslavia and Greece. In Western Europe, collaborationist formations – though smaller in number – provided tangible support in anti-partisan operations and coastal defence. The *Waffen-SS* in particular succeeded in raising divisions from a range of occupied and neutral countries, some of which fought with determination in the final battles of 1944 and 1945. While their combat effectiveness varied widely, several such units achieved a degree of cohesion and battlefield reputation sufficient to mark them as more than symbolic.

The diversity of motives among foreign volunteers complicates any effort to draw simple conclusions. Some were driven by anti-communism, whether genuine ideological conviction or bitter memory of Stalinist policies. Others sought escape from poverty, persecution or captivity, with enlistment offering a chance of survival. Opportunism, coercion, local rivalries, and a desire to secure advantage within occupied societies all played their part. The result was a mosaic of experiences that cannot be reduced to propaganda stooges on the one hand or fanatical collaborators on the other. This complexity is precisely what makes the study of these units so revealing: it exposes the cracks in both the Nazi vision of a racially ordered Europe and the post-war narratives that sought either to glorify or to condemn without distinction.

From the perspective of the Third Reich, the reliance on foreign manpower was both a strength and a weakness. It enabled the German war effort to continue beyond the point where the Reich's own demographic resources should have forced a reckoning. At the same time, it revealed the limits of German control and the contradictions of Nazi ideology. The regime that proclaimed itself the guardian of racial purity was forced, out of desperation, to arm and equip men whom it considered inferior or untrustworthy. This dissonance was papered over by propaganda, but in practice it highlighted the pragmatic compromises that total war demanded. In the long term, the legacy of foreign volunteers in German service has been contested and politically charged. In the immediate post-war years, some sought to frame their participation as a form of pan-European resistance to communism, an argument that resonated during the early Cold War but which downplayed the reality of collaboration with the Nazi state. Conversely, other accounts imposed sweeping condemnations that ignored the diversity of circumstances under which men joined these units. For decades, the subject remained marginalised, overshadowed by both the enormity of Nazi crimes and the national myths constructed in occupied countries after 1945. Only more recently have scholars sought to approach the subject with the nuance it demands, situating foreign volunteers within the broader contexts of occupation, ideology, and survival.

Ultimately, the story of foreigners in German uniform is one of paradox. It reveals how the Nazi regime simultaneously relied upon and distrusted its collaborators, how individuals navigated impossible choices in the shadow of dictatorship and war, and how propaganda could transform marginal contingents into symbols of global struggle. Some of these formations were militarily insignificant, existing more on film reels than on battlefields. Others became integral to the German war effort, particularly on the Eastern Front, where sheer numbers made them indispensable. Taken together, they remind us that the Second World War was not only a conflict between states but also a crucible of coercion, ideology, and opportunism in which millions were compelled to make decisions with profound consequences. As such, the history of these foreign volunteers resists simple moralisation. They were neither the heroic 'European crusaders' of post-war myth nor the faceless traitors of blanket condemnation. They were men caught in the violent currents of the twentieth century's defining conflict, whose choices and fates illuminate both the ambitions of the Nazi regime and the desperate realities of those who served it. Their story, though fraught with distortion and controversy, is essential to understanding the complexity of the Second World War itself. The presence of foreigners in German uniform, particularly those whom Nazi racial ideology did not consider Aryan, exemplified one of the many contradictions inherent in the Third Reich.

Appendix I

A CHRONOLOGICAL LISTING OF VOLUNTEER FORMATIONS IN THE EAST, 1941–1945

1941

August 1941

Eingreifgruppe Tietjen. Formed on 24 August 1941, from the *9. Kompanie* of *Infanterie Regiment 18, 6. Infanterie-Division, VI. Armeekorps, 9. Armee, Heeresgruppe Mitte*. The company was led by *Hauptmann* Georg Tietjen. This anti-partisan force began recruiting Russian volunteers.

October 1941

Abwehr Unternehmen Tiger B. Formed on 18 October 1941, from German personnel from *Regiment z.b.V. 800 'Brandenburg'*. The group was also made up of Russian POWs who had volunteered for service. This unit had been raised by the *Abwehr*.

November 1941

Stabsoffizier der Osttruppen 582. Formed this month under *Korück 582* behind the lines of *9 Armee, Heeresgruppe Mitte*. This staff was organised to control the large influx of Russian volunteers which were beginning to enter German service.

Eingreifgruppe Tietjen. By 1 November 1941, this force comprised 300 Russian volunteers divided into six 'companies' of 50 Russians each.[1] Each of these companies had perhaps 20–25 Germans attached. These German soldiers belonged to the *9. Kompanie* of *Infanterie Regiment*

18. The German company had been split up in order to provide cadre personnel for the Russian companies.

Kriegsgefangenen-Arbeits-Pionier-Bataillon 3. Formed on 12 January 1942, from Russian POWs who volunteered for construction work in the German Army. The POWs came from camps in *Wehrkreis XII* (Military District No. 12) in Germany. The battalion was sent to Oslo, Norway but by the spring of 1942 it had been shifted to south-western Norway.

1942

March 1942

Eingreifgruppe Tietjen. Continued to serve under *Korück 582* of *9 Armee, Heeresgruppe Mitte*. An artillery battery, *Ost-Artillerie-Batterie 582*, of four Soviet-made 76.2mm guns, was added on 1 March 1942.

April 1942

Reiter-Abteilung 207. Formed on 11 April 1942, with two cavalry squadrons. It was attached to the German *207. Sicherungs-Division* behind the lines of *Heeresgruppe Nord*.

Bau-Bataillon 246. This construction battalion was formed from Russian POWs for work in the German Army. Its German cadre staff came from *Reichsarbeitsdienst-Bataillon 246*. This labour battalion had been virtually destroyed while fighting during the cold Russian winter of 1941–2. The battalion was reformed in the region of *4. Panzerarmee, Heeresgruppe B*, in southern Russia with Russian volunteers.

Ost-Kampf-Bataillon Dnieper. Formed on 29 April 1942, from *Sonderstab Hohlfeld* (Special Staff Hohlfeld).

Ost-Bataillon 617. Formed on 28 April 1942, under *Korück 532* of *2. Panzerarmee, Heeresgruppe Mitte*.

Kriegsgefangenen-Arbeits-Bataillon 1. Formed in Arnsberg from Russian POWs that were housed in *Stalag 20* near Thorn (Torun), Poland. The unit was organised by *Reserve-Baubataillon Nr. 6*, and also contained a good portion of Polish POWs. It was created officially on 8 April 1942.

Sonderstab Hohlfeld. This headquarters unit was raised on 29 April 1942, in the region of *Heeresgruppe Mitte* from a German cadre staff to control Russian volunteers. It helped to organise *Ost-Kampf-Bataillon Dnieper* (a former unit of the *Graukopf Brigade*) and other *Ost* battalions for employment in Belarus and the region of central Russia where *Heeresgruppe Mitte* was operating.

Sonderstab Knoth. Same as *Sonderstab Hohlfeld*, except it was stationed in Belarus.

June 1942

Russische-Sicherungs-Abteilung 188. Formed from the *31–34 Hundertschaft* (31st through 34th Centuries, or companies). These were a series of company-sized Russian volunteer formations that had been organised beginning in the autumn of 1941 in the area of *Heeresgruppe Nord* under *18. Armee.*

Russische-Sicherungs-Abteilung 189. Like *Russische-Sicherungs-Abteilung 188* above, this unit was raised by grouping together the *35–38 Hundertschaft* operating in the region of *18. Armee.*

Ost-Kampf-Bataillon Berezina. Formed on 15 June 1942, in Bobruisk, Belarus.

Kriegsgefangenen-Arbeits-Bataillon 1. Sent to northern Norway on 13 June 1942. It became an army troop of *20. Gebirgsarmee.*

Russische-Sicherungs-Abteilung 410. Formed under *X. Armeekorps, 16. Armee, Heeresgruppe Nord.*

Russische-Sicherungs-Abteilung 510. Formed under *X. Armeekorps, 16. Armee, Heeresgruppe Nord.*

Partisanenjäger-Abteilung AOK 16. Formed from six Russian volunteer companies acting in an anti-partisan role. Also contained one artillery battery made up of captured Russian guns. It was employed against the guerrillas behind *16. Armee* lines.

Finnische-Sicherungs-Abteilung 187. Formed from Finnish volunteers using the *27 Hundertschaft* as the core of this battalion. It was employed in the area of *18. Armee, Heeresgruppe Nord.* This unit would eventually be transformed into a purely Russian battalion.

July 1942

Ost-Kampf-Bataillon Duna. Formed in Bobruisk on 14 July 1942, for employment in the region of Belarus and *Heeresgruppe Mitte.* It was a former battalion of the *Graukopf Brigade.*

Ost-Kampf-Bataillon Pripjet. Formed in Bobruisk on 14 July 1942, for use in Belarus and in the area of *Heeresgruppe Mitte.* It was a former battalion of the *Graukopf Brigade.*

Ost-Kampf-Bataillon Wolga. Formed this month in Bobruisk from *Sonderstab Knoth.* It was a former battalion of the *Graukopf Brigade.*

Weißruthenisches Schutzmannschafts-Wachbataillon 46. This was a '*Wach*' (Guard) battalion that was formed in Minsk, Belarus where it remained and operated for most of its history.

Weißruthenisches Schutzmannschafts-Wachbataillon 47. Raised and stationed in Minsk. It was employed in Belarus.

Weißruthenischess Schutzmannschafts-Frontbatallion 48. Raised and stationed in Minsk. It was employed in Belarus.

Ost-Artillerie-Abteilung Schrader. Formed from three volunteer Russian artillery batteries, using captured 76.2mm Russian artillery pieces. It was led by *Hauptmann* Ernst Schrader.

September 1942

Reiter-Abteilung 207. Initially it contained only two squadrons of volunteer Russian cavalry. A third squadron (3. *Kavallerie Schwadron*) was added to this battalion on 7 September 1942.

I. Freiwilligen-Bataillon / Korück 582. Formed from *Eingreifgruppe Tietjen,* which had been expanded from an original six companies into three Russian volunteer battalions. It was still employed in the region of *9. Armee, Heeresgruppe Mitte.*

II. Freiwilligen-Bataillon / Korück 582. Formed from *Eingreifgruppe Tietjen,* which had been expanded from an original six companies into three Russian volunteer battalions. It was still employed in the region of *9. Armee, Heeresgruppe Mitte.*

III. Freiwilligen-Bataillon / Korück 582. Formed from *Eingreifgruppe Tietjen,* which had been expanded from an original six companies into three Russian volunteer battalions. It was still employed in the region of *9. Armee, Heeresgruppe Mitte.*

Reserve-Ost-Kompanie 582. Raised to supply recruits for the above three battalions under *Korück 582.*

Ost-Batterie 582. An artillery battery (Russian guns) formed to provide support for the three Russian volunteer infantry battalions listed above.

Panzer-Zug 582. This was a Russian armoured train that had fallen into German hands. It was at the disposal of *Korück 582.*

Ost-Bataillon 601 Beresina. Attached to *203. Sicherungs Division.* It was a former battalion of the *Graukopf Brigade.* Headquarters Staff and *2. Kompanie* based in the town of Ljuban, about 90km south-east of Bobruisk. A mutiny arose in the ranks of *2. Kompanie* in this battalion on 18 September 1942. After it was all over, three German members of *Geheime Feldpolizei-Gruppe 707* were dead, along with two Russian *Ordnungsdienst* members and three other men who were wounded. Sixty-seven Russian mutineers with three light machine guns and two mortars defected to the partisans. The rebellion occurred basically for three reasons: (1) the Russian volunteers witnessed the abysmal treatment that the Germans meted out on the Russian civilian population, (2) the fact that the Germans refused to establish Russian formations higher than battalion-sized units, and (3) the realisation that Nazi Germany had no interest in establishing an independent Russian government after the war.

Ost-Bataillon 603 Duna. Ordered formed 30 September 1942. Simply a redesignation of *Ost Kampf-Bataillon Duna,* a former battalion of the *Graukopf Brigade.*

Ost-Bataillon 604 Pripjet. Ordered formed 30 September 1942. Simply a redesignation of *Ost Kampf-Bataillon Pripjet,* a former battalion of the *Graukopf Brigade.*

Ost-Bataillon 605 Wolga. Ordered formed 30 September 1942. Simply a redesignation of *Ost Kampf-Bataillon Wolga,* a former battalion of the *Graukopf Brigade.*

Weißruthenisches Schutzmannschafts-Wachbataillon 49. Raised and stationed in Minsk, Belarus this month.

Kriegsgefangen-Bau und Arbeits-Abteilung 180. Formed on 15 September in *Wehrkreis I* (Military District I) in East Prussia from Russian POWs who volunteered for work. The battalion was sent to Oslo, Norway.

Kriegsgefangen-Bau und Arbeits-Abteilung 183. Formed this month in *Wehrkreis I* from Russian POWs who volunteered for service. This battalion was also sent to Norway but was stationed in Drontheim.

1943

January 1943

Ost-Reiter-Abteilung 580.

Genesenden-Bataillon Russland (Forming Cadre Battalion 'Russia'). This unit was established in the *Generalgouvernment* (i.e., Poland) on 18 January 1943 from Russian POWs.

Ost-Bataillon 412. Formed this month by simply re-designating the *Selbstschutz Bataillon des Generalkommando XII. Armeekorps.* It contained four Russian volunteer rifle companies.

Ost-Bataillon 446. This battalion was disbanded and its two companies were transferred to *Ost-Bataillon 82* of *2. Panzer-Division.*

Ost-Bataillon 82. Formed on 1 January 1943, from *Bandenjäger Kompanie Zimmeck,* and the *1.* and *2. Kompanie* of *Ost-Bataillon 446.*

Ost-Bataillon 339. Formed by *339. Infanterie-Division,* which was currently fighting under the *XLVII. Panzerkorps, 2. Panzerarmee, Heeresgruppe Mitte.* Like *Ost-Bataillon 446,* it initially contained only two volunteer Russian rifle companies. The unit began operations south of Kirov, which lies east of Roslav and north of Bryansk.

Ost-Wachbataillon 555. Formed on 15 January 1943, in the region of *Wehrkreis XVII* (Military District No. 17) in northern Austria. The battalion was established using former Russian POWs and served in the capacity of factory guards.

Ost-Bataillon 447. Expanded from a mere one battalion into two battalions this month, and redesignated as follows: *I. Bataillon 447, II.*

Bataillon 447. These two battalions continued to operate under *XLVII. Panzerkorps, 2. Panzerarmee, Heeresgruppe Mitte.*

Ost-Bataillon 556. Formed on 15 January 1943, in *Wehrkreis VIII* (Silesia). The battalion had three rifle companies but no headquarters staff.

Kommandeur der Osttruppen z.b.V. 709. Formed on 28 January 1943, from the *Stabsoffizier der Osttruppen 582*. Still controlled the following units: *Ost Bataillon-628, Ost-Bataillon 629, Ost-Bataillon 630, Ost-Ersatz-Kompanie 582, Ost-Artillerie-Batterie 582*, and *Panzer-Zug 582*.

Kommandeur der Osttruppen z.b.V. 701. Formed on 19 January 1943, from the German liaison command attached to *Ost-Ersatz-Regiment Mitte* located in Bobruisk, Belarus.

Ost-Bataillon 134. Formed using four rifle companies of Russian volunteers. Began forming in January but was deemed ready in March 1943. The battalion served under the *134. Infanterie-Division* of *2. Panzerarmee, Heeresgruppe Mitte.* Two additional platoons of Russian volunteers were also in this German division's engineer battalion. This particular German division had about 2,300 *Hiwis* by April 1943, and an additional 5,600 Russian POWs as acting as labourers. These Russian volunteers thus amounted to almost 8,000 men in the division.

Ost-Bataillon 427. Ordered formed in January 1943 under the German *XXVII. Armeekorps, Heeresgruppe Mitte.* The unit was in action by May 1943.

Ost-Bataillon 667. Formed on 14 January 1943 by simply re-designating the *I. Bataillon der Freijäger-Regiment 16*. It was still operating under *16. Armee, Heeresgruppe Nord.*

Ost-Bataillon 668. Formed in 14 January 1943 by simply re-designating the *II. Bataillon der Freijäger-Regiment 16*. It was still operating under *16. Armee, Heeresgruppe Nord.*

Ost-Bataillon 669. Formed 14 January 1943 in the *16. Armee* area of North Russia, with a staff company and *1.-6. Kompanien.* The battalion originated as *Partisanenjäger-Abteilung der 16. Armee.* It was referred to by this name from March to October 1942. From October 1942 to January 1943, it was known as *III. Bataillon der Freijäger-Regiment 16 (16. Armee).* It was redesignated for a third time as *Ost-Bataillon 669* from 14 January 1943 to 6 July 1944, when it was finally renamed as *Russische Bataillon 669.*

Ost-Bataillon 633. Formed in the region of *Heeresgruppe Mitte* around mid-January 1943.

Ost-Bataillon 634. Formed in the region of *Heeresgruppe Mitte* around mid-January 1943.

Ost-Bataillon 635. Formed in the region of *Heeresgruppe Mitte* around mid-January 1943.

Ost-Bataillon 636. Formed in the region of *Heeresgruppe Mitte* around mid-January 1943.

Ost-Bataillon 637. Formed in the region of *Heeresgruppe Mitte* around mid-January 1943. It was attached to *3. Panzerarmee*.

Ost-Bataillon 642. Formed on 15 January 1943 under *4. Armee, Heeresgruppe Mitte*. It was formed from Russian volunteers and the *5. (Ost)-Kompanie der Wachbataillon 582*, and *Ost-Stab-Kompanie 642 der Bataillon Hopfgartern*.

February 1943[2]

Ost-Bataillon 448. Disbanded this month. Its two companies were handed over *en masse* to *Ost-Bataillon 339*. It was still employed under *339. Infanterie-Division*.

Ost-Bataillon 339. Increased in size from two companies to four by the addition of the two companies of the disbanded *Ost-Bataillon 448* which had been serving under the headquarters of *XLVIII. Panzerkorps*.

Kommandeur der Osttruppen 703. Formed on 1 February 1943, under *3. Panzerarmee, Heeresgruppe Mitte*. This headquarters staff was used to control Eastern battalions.

Kommandeur der Osttruppen 704. Formed this month under *4. Armee, Heeresgruppe Mitte*. This headquarters staff was used to control Eastern battalions.

Kommandeur der Osttruppen 720. Formed this month in the region of *Heeresgruppe Süd*. This headquarters staff was used to control Eastern battalions.

Kommandeur der Osttruppen 721. Formed this month in the region of *Heeresgruppe Süd*. This headquarters staff was used to control Eastern battalions.

Ost-Wachbataillon 555. Sent to southern Russia for use as an army troop unit.

Ost-Bataillon 556. Sent to southern Russia for use as an army troop unit.

March 1943

Ost-Reiter-Abteilung 207. A 4th (reinforced) Cavalry Squadron was added to this cavalry battalion on 15 March 1943.

Ost-Bau-Bataillon 559. Formed on 15 March 1943. It was supposed to be organised into an infantry battalion, but was redesignated a '*bau*' (construction) unit on 26 March 1943. It was also on that day that this battalion was renamed as *Ost-Bau-Bataillon des Befehlshaber Heeresgebiet Süd* ('Eastern Construction Battalion of the Commander of Rear Areas South'). The unit had been partially formed from parts of the German *Bau Bataillon 246*. It contained four companies.

Ost-Bataillon 134. Deemed fully formed this month and attached to *134. Infanterie-Division*.

Ost-Bau-Bataillon 643. Formed on 23 March 1943 under *Korück 559* of *4. Armee, Heeresgruppe Mitte.*

Weißruthenisches Schutzmannschafts-Wachbataillon 46. Still located in Minsk under the *Kommandeur der Schutzpolizei Minsk.*

Ost-Bataillon 604. Stationed in Gomel and attached to *221. Sicherungs-Division.*

Ost-Kavallerie-Schwadron 221. Also stationed in Gomel. It had been raised in December 1942 as *Reiter-Hundertschaft 221*.

April 1943

I. Ostvölk-Genesenden-Bataillon. Formed on 30 April 1943 in the *Generalgouvernment* (i.e., occupied Poland). This was simply a redesignation of *Genesenden-Bataillon Russland.*

Kommandeur der Osttruppen z.b.V. 711. Formed under *18. Armee, Heeresgruppe Nord*. Like all the other *Osttruppen* command staffs, this headquarters' staff was used to control Eastern battalions.

Regimentsstab Findeisen z.b.V. Formed on 9 April 1943 by simply re-designating the *Kommandeur der Osttruppen 710* in the area of *16. Armee, Heeresgruppe Nord.*

Kommandeur der Osttruppen z.b.V. 702. Formed on 19 April under *2. Panzerarmee, Heeresgruppe Mitte*. It had been raised with the help of *Ost-Stab z.b.V. 532* (Eastern Staff for Special Employment 532), under *Korück 532* of *2. Panzerarmee*. This was simply a redesignation of *Ost-Regimentsstab z.b.V*. As all the other HQs staffs like them, this staff was used to control Eastern battalions.

Ost-Bataillon Hansen. Formed on 25 April under *3. Panzerarmee, Heeresgruppe Mitte.*

Weißruthenisches Schutzmannschafts-Wachbataillon 46. Located in Novogrudok, Belarus under the *Kommandeur der Ordnungspolizei Weissrussland.*

Weißruthenisches Schutzmannschafts-Wachbataillon 47. Located in Minsk, Belarus under the immediate control of the *Kommandeur der Schutzpolizei Minsk.*

Weißruthenisches Schutzmannschafts-Wachbataillon 49. Located in Minsk, Belarus under the immediate control of the *Kommandeur der Schutzpolizei Minsk.*

Weißruthenischess Schutzmannschafts-Artillerie-Abteilung 56. Located in Minsk, Belarus under the immediate control of the *Kommandeur der Schutzpolizei Minsk*. Initially contained two batteries of captured Russian artillery, but later a third battery was added: *1.-3. Artillerie Batterie*. This battalion, along with other Belarusian battalions, was used to help create *Polizei-Brigade Siegling* (so-named after Hans Siegling, its commander) in the summer of 1944. *Polizei-Brigade Siegling* in turn, served as the core of *30. Waffen-Grenadier-Division der-SS (russische Nr. 2).*

Ost-Pionier-Bataillon 454. This battalion was raised this month by expanding on the earlier, single eastern engineer company: *Ost-Pionier-Kompanie 454* of the *454. Sicherungs-Division,* which was operating in the rear areas of *Heeresgruppe Süd.*

May 1943

I. / Ost-Bataillon 447. Sent to *Heeresgruppe Süd* under *XLVII. Panzerkorps.* Notice that because the German higher command prohibited volunteer formations being larger than battalion size, the staff of *XLVII. Panzerkorps* did as most other German commands did to get around that order. Two battalions were created (*I.* and *II.*) named *Ost-Bataillon 447.*

II. / Ost Bataillon 447. Sent to *Heeresgruppe Süd* under *XLVII. Panzerkorps.*

Ost-Bataillon 604 Pripjet. Committed to front-line fighting this month.

Ost-Bataillon 308. Formed in the region of *Heeresgruppe Mitte* under *Arko 308* (*Artillerie-Kommandeur 308,* or 'Artillery Commander No. 308'). Interestingly enough, the field post numbers were not assigned until March 1944. It contained only two rifle companies which were used as infantry protection for the artillery observers and batteries.

Ost-Bataillon 427. This unit was finally committed to front-line fighting after almost five months of training and undertaking anti-guerrilla operations behind the lines of *XXVII. Armeekorps, 9. Armee, Heeresgruppe Mitte.*

Ost-Bataillon 268. Formed from three rifle companies of Russian volunteers for service in the *268. Infanterie-Division,* which was then serving under the *4. Armee, Heeresgruppe Mitte.*

Kommandeur der Osttruppen z.b.V. 741. Formed on 20 May 1943, for employment in controlling Eastern units under *Heeresgruppe 'A'.* This month it was employed in the Kuban bridgehead of *Heeresgruppe Süd.*

June 1943

Ost-Bataillon 82. Still operating under *2. Panzer-Division, 3. Panzerarmee, Heeresgruppe Mitte.* This two-company battalion received a much-needed influx of troops when a third company (*3. Kompanie*) and a 'headquarters' company were organised and added this month.

Ost-Nachschub-Bataillon 574. Formed using three supply companies. It was organised by the German *Heer-Kommandeur Ventspils* in Courland, Latvia. It was later expanded to six companies. It was probably formed from Latvian volunteers, although it is possible Russians could have also served.

Ost-Bataillon 600. Formed from four rifle companies under *Heeresgruppe Mitte*.

Ost-Bataillon 601 Beresina. Returned to Bobruisk, Belarus which was its home base and began *Pionier* (engineer) training this month. It would be redesignated as an engineer bridging unit in November 1943 when it was transferred to France. One reason why this battalion was no longer to be a rifle unit was that it was not considered fully reliable by the German command.

Ost-Bataillon 619. Renamed this month as a cadre forming battalion for other Russian units.

Ost-Bataillon 646. Formed this month using three rifle companies of Russian volunteers in the region of *Heeresgruppe Mitte*. It apparently never attained full operational strength. It was disbanded in February 1944.

Ost-Bataillon Weicker. Formed under the staff of the *Kommandeur der Osttruppen 711* (Commander of Eastern Troops 711).

II. Ostvölk-Genesenden-Bataillon. Formed in the *Generalgouvernment* (occupied Poland) on 1 June 1943.

Weißruthenisches Schutzmannschafts-Wachbataillon 47. Still located in Minsk.

4.–7. Ost-Sicherungs-Kompanie der Sicherungs-Bataillon 456. These four Russian security companies were formed and officially added to the German *Sicherungs-Bataillon 456* this month. The *1.-3. Kompanien* contained German personnel. This battalion was operating behind the lines of *2. Armee, Heeresgruppe Mitte*. Later in the summer, two additional Russian companies (numbered *8.* and *9.*) were added.

July 1943[3]

Regimentsstab z.b.V. 709. Formed on 9 July 1943 from *Kommandeur der Osttruppen z.b.V. 709* in the region of *9. Armee, Heeresgruppe Mitte*. As all of the other HQs staffs like them, this staff was used to control Eastern battalions.

Ost-Ersatz-Regiment Mitte. This was simply a redesignation of *Kommandeur der Osttruppen 701*. It contained three Eastern volunteer recruit training battalions numbered *I. II.* and *III.*

August 1943

Ost-Bataillon 412. This month this *Ost* battalion was redesignated as the *III. Bataillon der Grenadier-Regiment 578* of *305. Infanterie-Division*. The unit was located in northern Italy.

Bau-Pionier-Bataillon 246. This was merely a redesignation of *Bau-Bataillon 246*. The new title became effective on 19 August 1943.

Regimentsstab z.b.V. Klobe. Formed on 12 August 1943 by redesignating *Regimentsstab z.b.V. Findeisen*. As all of the other HQs staffs like them, this staff was used to control Eastern battalions.

Regimentsstab z.b.V. 709. This Eastern regimental staff headquarters was officially disbanded on 31 August 1943 after being wiped out.

Kriegsgefangenen-Bau und Arbeits-Bataillon 1. 'Prisoner of War Construction and Work Battalion No. 1'. Attached to *189. Infanterie-Division* in Norway.

Kriegsgefangenen-Arbeits-Abteilung 188. Sent to Bergen and Stavanger in Norway this month after having been stationed in Holland.

September 1943

3. russische Bau-Abteilung. Under the *702. Infanterie-Division, XXXIII. Armeekorps* in Norway.

Kriegsgefangenen-Bau und Arbeits-Abteilung 180. Under *702. Infanterie-Division, XXXIII. Armeekorps*, Norway.

Kommandeur der Osttruppen z.b.V. 712. Ordered formed on 1 September 1943, in the region of *Heeresgruppe Nord*, although it is not known if it was ever fully organised. As all of the other HQs staffs like them, this staff was supposed to control Eastern battalions.

Ost-Bataillon 649. Formed on 12 September 1943 from the *4.-7. Ost Kompanien* of the German *Wachbataillon 581*.

Ost-Bataillon 648. Formed on 12 September 1943 in the region of *2. Armee, Heeresgruppe Mitte* from the *8.* and *9. Ost Kompanien* of *Sicherungs-Bataillon 456*, and the *8.* and *9. Ost Kompanien* of *Wachbataillon 581*.

Ost-Bataillon 680. Formed on 12 September 1943 from the *4.-7. Ost Kompanien* of *Sicherungs Bataillon 456*.

Ost-Bataillon 647. Formed on 12 September 1943 partly from *Wachbataillon 581* under *2. Armee, Heeresgruppe Mitte*.

Ost-Regimentsstab z.b.V. 753. Formed on 12 September 1943 by simply re-designating *Regimentsstab z.b.V. Klobe*. As all of the other HQs staffs like them, this staff was used to control Eastern battalions.

Weißruthenisches Schutzmannschafts-Wachbataillon 45. Formed this month in Baranovichi, Belarus. This original numerical designation ('45') had been assigned previously to an Estonian *Schuma* battalion.

Ost-Regimentsstab z.b.V. 752. Formed in September in the area of *2. Armee, Heeresgruppe Mitte*. As all of the other HQs staffs like them, this staff was used to control Eastern battalions.

October 1943

Kommandeur der Osttruppen z. b.V. 702. Sent to *19. Armee* in southern France on 2 October 1943.

Ost-Bataillon 648. Attached to *Korück 580* on 20 October 1943.

Ost-Bataillon 649. Attached to *Korück 580* on 20 October 1943.

Ost-Bataillon 654. Sent from *Heeresgruppe Nord* to *19. Armee*, in southern France and stationed initially in Châlons-sur-Marne.

Kommandeur der Osttruppen 721. Sent to *7. Armee* in France this month. As all of the other HQs staffs like them, this staff was used to control Eastern battalions.

Ost-Bataillon 627. Sent to the St. Malo in the area of Brittany, France and placed under *7. Armee* this month.

Ost-Bataillon 674. Formed by simply renaming *Ost-Bataillon Weicker* on 21 October 1943.

Ost-Bataillon 661. Sent to southern France towards the end of the month.

Ost-Regimentsstab z.b.V. 751. Formed this month in the region of *9. Armee, Heeresgruppe Mitte*. As all of the other HQs staffs like them, this staff was used to control Eastern battalions.

Kommandeur der Osttruppen z.b.V. 703. Sent to France this month. As all of the other HQs staffs like them, this staff was used to control Eastern battalions.

Ost-Bataillon 615. Sent to the town of Chatillon under the German Administrative Military Commander in France.

Ost-Reiter-Abteilung 281. Sent to *Truppenübungsplatz 'Coetquidan'* (Troop Training Ground 'Coetquidan') in France on 20 October 1943. It now was a part of *7. Armee*.

Ost-Reiter-Abteilung 285. Sent to *Truppenübungsplatz 'Coetquidan'* in France in October 1943. It now was a part of *7. Armee*. *Truppenübungsplatz 'Coetquidan'* had existed as early as the First World War, where it served the American Expeditionary Force (AEF) under General John Pershing as an artillery training centre.

Ost-Bataillon 406. Sent to the *326. Infanterie-Division, 19. Armee* in southern France during the first week in October 1943.

Ost-Ausbildungs-Regiment Mitte. This cadre training regiment was sent to *Truppenübungsplatz 'Coetquidan'* in France in the area of *7. Armee* in this month.

Ost-Bataillon 439. On its way to Bayeux, about 25km north-west of Caen in Normandy, France. It began arriving there on 28 October 1943.

Ost-Regimentsstab z.b.V. 750. Located in Blaye and St. Lucie, north of Bordeaux under *1. Armee*. As all of the other HQs staffs like them, this staff was used to control Eastern battalions.

Ost-Bataillon 642. Sent to *7. Armee* area in France on 30 October 1943.

Ost-Bataillon 669. Sent to *7. Armee* area in France on 30 October 1943.

Ost-Bataillon 643. On its way to *7. Armee* in France, arriving on 24 October 1943. It was stationed in Plancoët, a town north-west of Dinan in north-west France.

Ost-Bataillon 663. Sent to *19. Armee* in southern France. It arrived around mid-October. It contained four rifle companies.

Ost-Bataillon 665. Sent to France on 21 October 1943. It was attached to the *338. Infanterie-Division* under *19. Armee* in France. On 29 October 1943 it arrived in the region of Aimarques, about 5km east of Lunel.

Ost-Bataillon 666. Sent to *19. Armee* and attached to *338. Infanterie-Division*. It was stationed in Rivesaltes, north of Perpignan, France.

Ost-Nachschub-Bataillon 651. This supply battalion was transferred to *15. Armee* in France in this month.

Ost-Artillerie-Abteilung Befehlshaber-Heeresgebiet Süd. This unit was formed from Russian volunteers and captured guns. It contained three artillery batteries. It was now employed in the region of *Heeresgruppe Süd* where it had been raised this month.

Ost-Bataillon Hensel. Arrived in southern France on 8 October 1943, and was placed under the *326. Infanterie-Division* of *19. Armee*.

Ost-Bataillon 681. Transferred to *19. Armee* in France on 23 October 1943. It was originally titled *Ost-Bataillon Hansen*.

Ost-Bataillon 633. Sent to France in late October.

Ost-Bataillon 634. Sent to France in late October.

Ost-Bataillon 635. Sent to north-west France in mid-October.

Ost-Bataillon 642. Sent to north-west France and joined *7. Armee*.

Ost-Bataillon 618. Sent to *15. Armee* in France this month.

November 1943

Kommandeur der Osttruppen z.b.V. 700. Sent to *7. Armee* in France. As all of the other HQs staffs like them, this staff was used to control Eastern battalions.

Ost-Bataillon 669. Sent this month to *7. Armee* in north-west France.

Ost-Bataillon 668. Redesignated as *Ost-Bataillon Schittenhel*.

Ost-Bataillon 339. Sent to Italy and redesignated as the *III. Bataillon der Grenadier-Regiment 871* of the *356. Infanterie-Division*.

Ost-Bataillon 600. Sent to France on 16 November 1943. Stationed in Vannes and assigned directly under the 'German Military Commander France'.

Ost-Pionier-Brücken-Bataillon 601. Eastern Engineer Bridging Battalion. This was simply a redesignation of *Ost-Bataillon 601*. This unit had been undergoing engineer training shortly before it was withdrawn from Russia. It was sent to *19. Armee* in southern France on 5 November 1943. It was stationed in Sorques, north-east of Avignon.

Ost-Bataillon 602 Dnjepr. Sent to *7. Armee* in the Brittany region of north-west France. The battalion arrived on 27 November 1943, and was stationed at St. Malo, in Brittany. It would later be destroyed in July 1944 but would not be officially dissolved until 14 October 1944.

Ost-Bataillon 603 Duna. Left Russia for Denmark at the end of this month.

Ost-Bataillon 604 Pripjet. Disbanded this month.

Ost-Bataillon 605 Wolga. Sent this month to the town of Pont d'Ardres, in the Amiens area south-west of Calais, France. It was attached to *15. Armee*.

Ost-Bataillon 406. Sent to France this month and stationed in Le Bourget, about 10km north of Chamberly. Under the direct control of the *Militär Befehlshaber Frankreich* (German Military Commander France).

Ost-Bataillon 412. Sent to *14. Armee* in Italy, and stationed in and around Villa Nevoso, about 30km north-north-west of Fiume, Italy. It was redesignated as *III. Bataillon der Grenadier-Regiment 578* of *305. Infanterie-Division*.

Ost-Ersatz Bataillon. Located in Bologna, Italy. No apparent numerical designation. It was first listed this month. It is possible that it might have been created from excess Russian personnel from other various German units then stationed in that region of Italy.

Ost-Bataillon 669. Sent to France this month. It was under the direct control of the *Militär Befehlshaber Frankreich*.

Ost-Bataillon 618. Arrived in late October in France and attached to *15. Armee*. On 2 November 1943 it was located in Caffiers, south-south-west of Calais. It was then moved to Valenciennes.

Ost-Bataillon 630. Sent to Brittany, France this month. Located in Bayeux under *7. Armee*.

Ost-Bataillon 629. Sent to *7. Armee* in France this month. On 25 November 1943 it was located in Lannion, Brittany.

Ost-Bataillon 633. Sent to France this month. On 10 November 1943 it was located in Landerneau under *7. Armee*.

Ost-Bataillon 634. Sent to France this month. On 10 November 1943 it was located in Quimperlé, Normandy under *7. Armee*.

Ost-Bataillon 635. Sent to France in late October or early November. It was stationed in Landerneau on 8 November 1943.

Ost-Regimentsstab z.b.V. 750. Sent to France on 8 November 1943, and arrived at Bordeaux in the region of *1. Armee* towards the end of the month. As all of the other HQs staffs like them, this staff was used to control Eastern battalions.

Ost-Bataillon 642. On 1 November 1943, it was located in Beauregard, France about 5km north-north-east of Caen.

Ost-Bataillon 649. Arrived on 17 November 1943, and stationed in Cherbourg, in the Brittany area of France. Attached to *7. Armee*.

Ost-Bataillon 654. Attached to the *19. Armee* in southern France on 14 November 1943, but by 17 November it was attached directly to the *Militärbefehlshaber in Frankreich,* and stationed in Chaumont.

Ost-Bataillon 660. On 18 November 1943, it was still on its way to Belgium, where it would be under the direct control of the *Militärbefehlshaber Belgien-Nord Frankreich.*

Ost-Bataillon 669. On 18 November 1943 it was still on its way to Belgium, where it would be under the direct control of *Militärbefehlshaber Belgien-Nord Frankreich.*

Ost-Bataillon 661. Located in Grasse, France under *19. Armee* as of 2 November 1943.

Ost-Bataillon 680. Sent to France and initially stationed in Mézières. On 1 November 1943, it was located in Sissone, about 20km east of Lyon. It was under the *Militärbefehlshaber in Frankreich.*

Ost-Bataillon 662. Sent to Denmark this month.

Ost-Bataillon 620. Sent to northern Italy towards the end of November.

Ost-Bataillon 617. Sent to Italy this month. It became an independent unit of *LXXV. Armeekorps, Armeeoberkommando Ligurien,* which was then located on the Italian-French border.[4]

Ost-Bataillon 619. Disbanded this month but not officially removed from the German Field Post rolls until February 1944.

Ost-Bataillon 628. Sent to Bruges, Belgium this month. Attached to the *712. Infanterie-Division.*

Ost-Bataillon 616. Sent to north-eastern Italy this month. It was attached to the *71. Infanterie-Division* which was then operating in the Tarvisio-Gorizia-Trieste-Fiume areas. It would later be officially absorbed into this German division as an integral battalion in one of its regiments.

Ost-Bataillon 636. Sent to north-west France under *7. Armee.* By 19 November 1943 it was located at Vannes.

Ost-Bataillon 268. This battalion was sent to northern Italy after its parent German unit, *268. Infanterie-Division,* was destroyed while operating under *XLI. Panzerkorps, 9. Armee, Heeresgruppe Mitte.*

Weißruthenisches Schutzmannschafts-Wachbataillon 47. Attached to the *SS- und Polizeiführer Weissruthenien* for anti-partisan warfare.

Weißruthenisches Schutzmannschafts-Wachbataillon 48. Attached to the *SS- und Polizeiführer Weissruthenien* for anti-partisan warfare.

Weißruthenisches Schutzmannschafts-Wachbataillon 49. Attached to the *SS- und Polizeiführer Weissruthenien* for anti-partisan warfare.

Weißruthenischess Schutzmannschafts-Artillerie-Abteilung 56. Attached to the *SS- und Polizeiführer Weissruthenien* for anti-partisan warfare.

Weißruthenischess Schutzmannschafts-Frontbatallion 60. Attached to the *SS- und Polizeiführer Weissruthenien* for anti-partisan warfare.

Weißruthenisches Ausbildungs-Schutzmannschaftsbataillon. Stationed in Uretschye, Belarus.

December 1943

Ost-Ausbildungs-Regiment Mitte. Simply a redesignation of *Ost-Ersatz-Regiment Mitte*. Sent to Brittany, France this month and attached to *7. Armee*.

Kommandeur der Osttruppen z.b.V. 711. Disbanded on 8 December 1943. Its personnel were then transferred to *Ost-Ausbildungs-Regiment Mitte*.

Kommandeur der Osttruppen z.b.V. 704. Disbanded this month.

Kommandeur der Osttruppen z.b.V. 720. Disbanded this month in the region of *Heeresgruppe Süd*. It was removed from the Field Post rolls in February 1944.

Ost-Bataillon Schottenheimer. Destroyed on 17 December 1943. Not reformed.

Ost-Reiter-Abteilung 207. Disbanded this month after having incurred severe combat losses in Russia.

Ost-Radfahr-Abteilung 285. Simply a redesignation of *Ost-Reiter-Abteilung 285*. This new designation took effect beginning 4 December 1943. The new title implies that the unit was assigned bicycles instead of horses with which to move around on. It was operating under *XXV. Armeekorps* in western France.

Ost-Bataillon 449. Formed by bringing together four independent company-sized units of Russian volunteers which had been in existence since May 1943.

Ost-Pionier-Brücken-Bataillon 605. A redesignation of *Ost-Bataillon 605 Wolga* (605th Eastern Battalion 'Volga').

Ost-Artillerie-Abteilung 752. Formed on 23 December 1943 from four Russian artillery batteries under the control of the *Befehlshaber Heeresgebiet Süd*. These batteries had been formed using captured Russian 76.2mm and 122mm guns. The battalion was now sent to *7.*

Armee in France. In France it was immediately placed under the control of *Kommandeur der Osttruppen 721.*

Ost-Bataillon 268. On 1 December 1943 the remnants of this unit were on its way to the town of Cremona, Italy. It was to be assigned to the *14. Armee.*

Ost-Bataillon 339. On 1 December 1943 this unit was stationed in Milano, Italy under *14. Armee.*

Ost-Bataillon 412. 1 December 1943 this battalion was situated in the town of San Pietro, about 20km north-north-west of Udine, Italy. Udine was near the Italian Slovene border. This region was north-eastern Italy.

Ost-Bataillon 427. This battalion was disbanded this month in Russia.

Ost-Bataillon 556. Sent to Italy from southern Russia this month.

Ost-Bataillon 600. Located in Vannes, France under *7. Armee.*

Ost-Bataillon 616. This *Ost* battalion was redesignated as the *III. Bataillon der Grenadier-Regiment 194* of *71. Infanterie-Division* this month. The *71. Infanterie-Division* was currently located in and around the city of Fiume (Rijeka), near the Istrian peninsula.

Ost-Bataillon 627. On 1 December 1943 it was located north-west of Plancoët, France under the *346. Infanterie-Division, 7. Armee.*

Ost-Bataillon 628. On 2 December 1943 this unit was stationed in Brue under *15. Armee,* but by 8 December it had been moved to Sluis, about 15km north-east of Bruges.

Ost-Bataillon 663. On 5 December 1943 this battalion was listed under the command of the *338. Infanterie-Division, 19. Armee* in southern France. It was assigned to coastal guard duty and its battalion headquarters was situated in Le Salin de Giraud, near Rhone Muendung, France.

Ost-Bataillon 633. On 21 December 1943 this battalion was located in Ploudalmézeau, north-east of Brest, France.

Ost-Bataillon 642. Located in Beauregard, France about 5km north-west of Caen. It was under the control of *7. Armee.*

Ost-Bataillon 653. Arrived in Greve, Denmark this month from Russia.

Ost-Bataillon 662. Located in Hump, Denmark. It contained four rifle companies.

Ost-Bataillon 666. On 21 December 1943 this unit was listed attached to the *326. Infanterie-Division, 19. Armee* in southern France.

Ost-Bataillon 667. Arrived in Mosbjerg, Denmark this month from Russia.

Ost-Bataillon 681. On 21 December 1943 this Eastern battalion was listed as being attached to *326. Infanterie-Division, 19. Armee* in southern France.

Ost-Bataillon 603 Duna. Arrived in Denmark this month from Russia.

Ost-Artillerie-Abteilung 621. Sent to France and attached to the *15. Armee*. It was assigned coastal guard duty as part of the Atlantic Wall artillery defence.

Ost-Wachbataillon 555. Sent to Italy from southern Russia this month.

1944

January 1944

General der Osttruppen beim OKH (General of Eastern Troops by the Army High Command). Attached to this staff were the *Dienststelle des Inspekteurs für Turkvölkische Verbände*.

Ost-Bataillon 628. Officially became the *I. Bataillon der Grenadier-Regiment 745* of *712. Infanterie-Division*.

Ost-Radfahr-Abteilung 285. On 22 January 1944 this battalion was in France, on its way to Argol, about 17km north-west of Chateaulin. It was attached to *7. Armee*.

Ost-Bataillon 339. On 10 January 1944 this Eastern battalion was listed as the *III. Bataillon der Grenadier-Regiment 871* of *356. Infanterie-Division*.

Ost-Bataillon 556. On 8 January 1944 it was in the process of constructing field fortifications under *LXXVI. Panzerkorps* in Italy. It was absorbed officially as the *III. Bataillon der Grenadier-Regiment 955* of *362. Infanterie-Division*.

Ost-Bataillon 620. On 8 January 1944 it was in the process of constructing field fortifications under *LXXVI. Panzerkorps, 10. Armee* in Italy.

Ost-Bataillon 560. Transported to an area south-west of Cassino on 8 January 1944, in order to perform construction duties. On 31 January thirteen Russian volunteers from this battalion deserted with all of their weapons and equipment. This turned out to be the very first case of desertion of Russian volunteers in Italy.

Ost-Bataillon 600. Located in Antwerp, Holland on 15 January 1944.

Ost-Bataillon 634. Stationed just west of Lorient, France on 13 January 1944. Still under *7. Armee*.

Weißruthenischess Schutzmannschafts-Artillerie-Ersatz-Abteilung 56. This was simply a redesignation of *Weißruthenischess Schutzmannschafts-Artillerie-Abteilung 56*. This battalion now only contained 217 men, and was stationed in Smilovichi, a small town that lies squarely between Minsk and Borisov. The battalion was under the control of the *Kommandeur der Ordnungspolizei in Weissruthenien*.

Ost-Wachbataillon 555. Became the *III. Bataillon der Grenadier-Regiment 755* of *334. Infanterie-Division*.

Weißruthenischess Schutzmannschaft-Wachbataillon 47. This former Belarusian guard battalion was now redesignated as a Ukrainian formation and staffed with Ukrainian personnel.

Weißruthenischess Schutzmannschafts-Frontbatallion 48. Located in Slonim, Belarus under the control of the *Kommandeur der Ordnungspolizei in Weissruthenien*.

Weißruthenisches Schutzmannschafts-Wachbataillon 49. Located in Minsk, White Russia under the control of the *Kommandeur der Ordnungspolizei in Weissruthenien*.

Weißruthenischess Schutzmannschafts-Frontbatallion 60.[5] Located in Snov, which lies just east-north-east of Baranovichi, Belarus under the control of the *Kommandeur der Ordnungspolizei in Weißruthenien*.

February 1944

Kommandeur der Osttruppen z.b.V. im Wehrkreis Generalgouvernment. This staff was organised this month in the *Generalgouvernment*, the Polish territories not incorporated into the *Reich*. The date of formation was 15 February 1944. The staff headquarters was located in Kielce. Its purpose was to control eastern troops in Poland.

I. Ost-Bataillon 447. Disbanded this month in the region of *Heeresgruppe Süd*.

II. Ost-Bataillon 447. Disbanded this month in the region of *Heeresgruppe Süd*.

Ost-Bataillon 449. Disbanded this month.

Ost-Nachschub-Bataillon 651. This unit was raised this month from the remnants of *Ost-Bataillon 551* in the region of *Heeresgruppe Süd*.

Ost-Bataillon 551. Disbanded this month in the region of *Heeresgruppe Süd*.

Ost-Bataillon 561. Formed on 1 February 1944, from four Russian volunteer companies. It was raised under the *9. Armee* in the region of *Heeresgruppe Mitte*. It was sent to France at the end of this month.

Ost-Regimentsstab z.b.V. 752. Formed this month in France from the *Kommandeur der Osttruppen z.b.V. 700*. Like all of the other HQ staffs, it was used to control Eastern battalions.

Kommandeur der Osttruppen z.b.V. 702. Disbanded on 28 February 1944. Its staff helped to form the *Schule der Freiwilligen Verbände* (School for Volunteer Formations).

Schule der Freiwilligen Verbände. The School for Volunteer Formations was established near Lyon, France using personnel from the *Kommandeur der Osttruppen z.b.V. 702*.

Kommandeur der Schule der Freiwilligen Verbände. Formed near Lyon, France from the *Kommandeur der Osttruppen z.b.V. 701*.

Ost-Bataillon 439. On 11 February 1944, this unit was performing coastal watch duty under *716. Infanterie-Division, 7. Armee.*

Ost-Bataillon 560. On 1 February this Eastern battalion was building fortifications in the area of *XIV. Panzerkorps* in Italy.

Weißruthenisches Schutzmannschafts-Wachbataillon 46. Now located in Minsk, Belarus under the control of the *Kommandeur der Schutzpolizei Minsk.*

Weißruthenischess Schutzmannschafts-Frontbatallion 48. This battalion was still located in Slonim, Belarus under the control of the *Kommandeur der Ordnungspolizei Weissrussland.*

Ost-Bataillon 268. Disbanded. Its remaining personnel were incorporated into *Ost-Bataillon 560.*

Ost-Bataillon 560. Formed this month in northern Italy from former POWs. The battalion contained four rifle companies. Some of the Russian volunteers came from the disbanded *268. Ost Bataillon.*

Ost-Bataillon 646. Disbanded this month in the region of *Heeresgruppe Mitte.*

Nachschub-Bataillon 581. This German supply battalion contained two German (*1. und 2. Kompanien*) plus six Eastern volunteer companies (*4.-9. Kompanien*). It was disbanded this month in the region of *Heeresgruppe Mitte.*

I. Ostvölk Genesenden Bataillon. Disbanded on 5 February 1944.

Ostvölk-Sicherungs-Bataillon 553. Formed from the *I. ostvölkisches Genesendenbataillon im Generalgouvernement.* This unit was initially staffed with Ukrainian personnel, but in June 1944 it became a purely Russian formation.

II. Ostvölk Genesenden Bataillon. Disbanded on 5 February 1944.

Kommandeur der Osttruppen z.b.V. 741. Officially dropped from the German Field Post rolls this month.

Weißruthenischess Schutzmannschafts-Frontbatallion 64. Formed this month and stationed in Glebokie, Belarus.

Weißruthenischess Schutzmannschafts-Frontbatallion 65. Formed this month and stationed in Novogrudok, Belarus.

Weißruthenischess Schutzmannschafts-Frontbatallion 66. Formed this month and stationed in Slutsk, Belarus.

March 1944

(kosakische) Ost-Reiter-Abteilung 72. Formed this month in the region of *Heeresgruppe Mitte.* Composed of Cossack volunteers.

(kosakische) Ost-Reiter-Abteilung 73/. Formed this month in the region of *Heeresgruppe Mitte.* Composed of Cossack volunteers.

Ost-Regimentsstab z.b.V. 751. Sent from *9. Armee, Heeresgruppe Mitte* to *7. Armee* in France in March. This staff continued to help organise *Ost Bataillon 561* near Cherbourg, France.

Ost-Bataillon 561. This Eastern battalion continued forming under *Kommandeur der Osttruppen z.b.V. 751*, near Cherbourg, France. On 19 March 1944 the battalion was in Nacqueville, just west of Cherbourg. It was attached to the *709. Infanterie-Division*.

Ost-Bataillon 441. On 19 March 1944 it was located in and around Bayeux, France under the *352. Infanterie-Division, 7. Armee*.

Ost-Bataillon 630. Located in Sissone, France.

Weißruthenischess Schutzmannschafts Wachbataillon 49. Stationed in Minsk, Belarus.

Ost-Bataillon 308. Although this unit had been organised and made combat ready in May 1943 it had not received a Field Post number until this month. The unit contained only two companies.

Weißruthenischess Schutzmannschafts Frontbatallion 69. Begins forming this month in Belarus.

Weißruthenischess Schutzmannschafts Frontbatallion 66. Sent to the region of *Heeresgruppe Mitte* and committed to front-line combat.

Freiwilligen-Ost-Stamm-Regiment 4. Formed in February 1944 but officially raised in March. The regiment was to supply Russian and Ukrainian volunteers for the Eastern battalions. Contained the following battalions: *Freiwilligen-Ost-Ersatz-Stamm-Bataillon, Freiwilligen-Ost-Ausbildungs-Bataillon, Freiwilligen-Ost-Genesenden-Bataillon, Ost-Batterie 203*, and *Ost-Reiter-Schwadron 221*. Until 12 June 1944, this regiment served as the replacement unit for all Ukrainian and Russian volunteers. After 12 June 1944, it only supplied recruits for the Ukrainian formations.

April 1944

Ost-Ausbildungs-Regiment Mitte. Disbanded this month. Its three battalions were dispersed as follows: *I. Bataillon* became an independent battalion attached to *265. Infanterie-Division* and stationed in La Baule, France. The *II. Bataillon* became the *IV. Bataillon der Grenadier-Regiment 898* of *266. Infanterie-Division*.

Divisionsstab z.b.V. 136. Formed on 25 April 1944 as a special administrative staff that was supposed to help control non-German, Eastern infantry battalions. This special divisional staff was formed from the staff of *Kommandeur der Osttruppen 721*. The divisional commander was *Generalmajor* Count Christoph zu Stolberg.

Kommandeur der Osttruppen z.b.V. 721. Disbanded this month. Its staff and its personnel were used to form *Divisionsstab z.b.V. 136*.

Ost-Bataillon 663. On 19 April 1944, it officially became the *I. Bataillon der Festungs-Grenadier-Regiment 759* of *338. Infanterie-Division*.

Ost-Bataillon 662. This month it became the *III. Bataillon der Grenadier-Regiment 712* of *416. Infanterie-Division.*

Ost-Bataillon 661. This month it officially became the *IV. Bataillon der Reserve-Grenadier-Regiment 239* of *148. Reserve-Division* under *19. Armee.*

Ost-Bataillon 603. On 30 April 1944 it officially became the *I. Bataillon der Grenadier-Regiment 714* of *416. Infanterie-Division* in Denmark.

Ost-Bataillon 653. On 30 April 1944 it officially became the *II. Bataillon der Grenadier-Regiment 714* of the *416. Infanterie-Division* in Denmark.

Ost-Bataillon 667. On 30 April 1944 it officially became the *III. Bataillon der Grenadier-Regiment 714* of the *416. Infanterie-Division* in Denmark.

Grenadier-Regiment 714 (Ost). It was raised on 30 April 1944 in Denmark. It was created by combining three Eastern battalions: *Ost-Bataillon 603, Ost-Bataillon 653, and Ost-Bataillon 667*. This Eastern regiment was attached to the *416. Infanterie-Division*.

Ost-Bataillon 654. This month it was redesignated as the *III. Bataillon der Grenadier-Regiment 895* of *265. Infanterie-Division.*

Grenadier-Regiment z.b.V. 752. Simply a redesignation of *Ost-Regimentsstab z.b.V. 752*. It controlled the following units: *Ost-Artillerie-Abteilung 752* and *Ost-Pionier-Kompanie 752*.

Ost-Bataillon 643. Contained three rifle companies. It was sent to the Channel Island of Jersey, under the *319. Infanterie-Division*.

Ost-Radfahr-Abteilung 285. On 8 April 1944, it was stationed in Lorient, France under the *7. Armee.*

Ost-Bataillon 412. This Eastern battalion had already become the *III. Bataillon der Grenadier-Regiment 578* when it was transferred to Italy in November 1943. On the night of 19 April 1944 thirteen members of this Russian battalion deserted when American forces dropped thousands of leaflets over the defensive positions of the battalion. The leaflets were printed in Russian and urged these volunteers to surrender.

Ost-Bataillon 68. On 27 April 1944 it was located in the Sissone area on its way to Charleville, France.

Ost-Bataillon 681. In this month it officially became the *IV. Bataillon der Grenadier-Regiment 934* of *244. Infanterie-Division*.

Ost-Bataillon 618. This battalion was apparently a fully motorised *Ost* battalion because it was so listed by the *Heer*. As such, it was part of that army's corps troops.

Ost-Pionier-Bataillon 666. This month it officially became the *IV. Bataillon der Grenadier-Regiment 932* of the *244. Infanterie-Division*.

Ost-Bataillon 665. This month it became the *III. Bataillon der Festungs-Grenadier-Regiment 757* of *338. Infanterie-Division*.

Ost-Bataillon 642. On 12 April 1944 it was renamed as the *IV. Bataillon der Grenadier-Regiment 736* of the *716. Infanterie-Division*.

Ost-Bataillon 439. On 13 April 1944 it was redesignated *IV. Bataillon der Grenadier-Regiment 726* of *716. Infanterie-Division*.

Ost-Bataillon 662. On 30 April 1944 it was redesignated as *III. Bataillon der Grenadier-Regiment 712* of the *416. Infanterie-Division* in Denmark.

Ost-Bataillon 630. It was redesignated this month as the *I. Bataillon der Festungs-Grenadier-Regiment 857* of *346. Infanterie-Division*.

Ost-Bataillon 628. It was redesignated this month as *II. Bataillon der Festungs-Grenadier-Regiment 857* of the *346. Infanterie-Division*.

Ost-Bataillon 629. It was redesignated this month as *IV. Bataillon der Grenadier-Regiment 899* of *266. Infanterie-Division*. It was stationed in the area of St-Malo, France.

Ost-Bataillon 633. On 19 April 1944 it was redesignated as the *IV. Bataillon der Grenadier-Regiment 852* of the *343. Infanterie-Division*.

Ost-Bataillon 634. It was redesignated this month as *III. Bataillon der Festungs-Grenadier-Regiment 895* of *266. Infanterie-Division*.

Ost-Bataillon 649. On 19 April 1944 this unit was redesignated as the *IV. Bataillon der Grenadier-Regiment 729* of *709. Infanterie-Division*.

Weißruthenisches Schutzmannschafts-Wachbataillon 47. On 19 April 1944 this Belarusian battalion was directly under the control of the *SS- und Polizeiführer Weissruthenien* and assigned to anti-partisan warfare.

Weißruthenisches Schutzmannschafts-Wachbataillon 48. On 19 April 1944 this Belarusian battalion was directly under the control of the *SS- und Polizeiführer Weissruthenien* and assigned to anti-partisan warfare.

Weißruthenisches Schutzmannschafts-Wachbataillon 49. On 19 April 1944 this Belarusian battalion was directly under the control of the *SS- und Polizeiführer Weissruthenien* and assigned to anti-partisan warfare.

Weißruthenischess Schutzmannschafts-Frontbatallion 60. On 19 April 1944 this Belarusian battalion was directly under the control of the *SS- und Polizeiführer Weissruthenien* and assigned to anti-partisan warfare.

May 1944

Divisionsstab z.b.V. 136. Began operations against the French *maquisards* (partisans) in the region of Brittany, France.

Ost-Bataillon 82. Disbanded this month in the region of *Heeresgruppe Mitte*.

Kommandeur der Freiwilligen Verbände bei Oberbefehlshaber West- Formed on 18 May 1944, from *Kommandeur der Osttruppen z.b.V. 703*. Used as a liaison between *OB West* and *Ost* troops.

Ost-Batailllon 642. In this month this Eastern battalion became the divisional reserve of *716. Infanterie-Division*. It was also sent closer to the French coastline, adding some much-needed infantry to the coastal defence of the division.

III. (Ost) Bataillon der Grenadier-Regiment 955 of *362. Infanterie-Division*. This was the old *Ost-Bataillon 556* which had been absorbed into this division. The Battalion, along with the rest of *Grenadier-Regiment 955*, fought bitterly in the ruins of Cisterna, Italy. Cisterna was a major rail and road centre east-north-east of Anzio and Nettuno. By 25 May 1944 the town had been captured by the U.S. 3rd Infantry Division.

Ost-Bataillon 615. Transferred this month to Montbard in north-east France.

Ost-Bataillon 669. Transferred this month from the *7. Armee* in France to the northern France-Belgium border area. It was now placed under the control of the *Militärbefehlshaber Belgien-Nord Frankreich*.

Weißruthenisches Heimwehr-Pionierbataillon 1. This unit was formed in Belarus this month using three volunteer companies.

Weißruthenischess Schutzmannschafts-Frontbatallion 64. Simply a redesignation of *Weißruthenischess Schutzmannschafts-Wach Bataillon 64*.

Table 22. Location of the Volunteer Cadre Division in 1944

City	Formation	Nationalities
Lyon	Div. HQ Staff	Various ethnic groups
Lyon	*Schule der Freiwilligen Verbände*	Various ethnic groups
Castres	*Freiwilligen Stamm Regiment 1*	Turkestani, Georgian and North Caucasian
Mende	*Freiwilligen Stamm Regiment 2*	Azerbaijani, Volga Tartar, Armenian
Mende	*Freiwilligen Stamm Regiment 2*	After April 1944: only Russian and Ukrainian volunteers. After June 1944: only Russians
Macon	*Freiwilligen Stamm Regiment 3*	Supplied replacements of Turkestani troops for the German 162. (*Turk.*) *Infanterie-Division*. After June 1944 supplied only Ukrainian volunteers
Namur	*Freiwilligen Stamm Regiment 4*	Supplied Russians and Ukrainians. After June 1944 only Russian volunteers
Langres	*Freiwilligen Stamm Regiment 5*	Supplied replacements for Cossack units

June 1944

Divisionsstab z.b.V. 136. Under the *LXXIV Armeekorps* of *7. Armee*. It was withdrawn from France before the Allies could cut off its escape route and sent to Antwerp, Holland. It was placed at the disposal of *15. Armee* commander.

Russische-Sicherungs-Bataillon 553. This was simply a redesignation of *Ostvölk-Sicherungs-Abteilung 553*.

Russische-Bataillon 556. Formed from the remnants of the Russian-manned *III. Bataillon der Grenadier-Regiment 955*. It now became an independent formation of *10. Armee* in Italy.

Ost-Bataillon 581. Towards the end of the month, it became a part of *'Festung Cherbourg'*, in Brittany.

III Bataillon der Festungs-Grenadier-Regiment 895 of *265. Infanterie-Division*. This was the ex-*Ost-Bataillon 634*. In this month it is drawn into the Normandy fighting and pushed back into the Brittany area in late June.

Ost-Bataillon 636. Caught up in the fighting in Normandy, France under the *LXXXIV. Armeekorps* and destroyed. Not officially removed from the German rolls until 14 October 1944. According to one French source, this Eastern battalion was made up of only two rifle companies.

Ost-Bataillon 681. Located near Gruissan (Aude). It had good discipline and each company was holding a front of about 2km. The uniforms of these volunteers were said to be in excellent condition, which showed unit pride.[6]

IV. Bataillon der Grenadier-Regiment 726 of *716. Infanterie-Division*. This was the ex-*Ost-Bataillon 439*. This month it was caught up in the Normandy fighting.

IV. Bataillon der Grenadier-Regiment 736 of *716. Infanterie-Division*. This was the ex-*Ost-Bataillon 642*. This month it was caught up in the Normandy fighting.

Ost-Reiter-Abteilung Befehlshaber des Heeresgebiets Süd. Disbanded this month in the region of *Heeresgruppe Süd*.

Ost-Pionier-Bataillon 318. Formed on 27 June 1944 by expanding *Ost-Kompanie 59* which was serving under *213. Sicherungs-Division, 4. Panzerarmee, Heeresgruppe Süd*.

Russisches Freiwilligen-Stamm-Regiment 4. Simply a redesignation of *Freiwilligen-Ost-Stamm Regiment 4*.

Kriegsgefangen-Arbeits-Abteilung 188. Disbanded this month.

July 1944

Russische-Bataillon 669. Formed from *Ost-Bataillon 669*. It was transferred on 6 July 1944 from Belgium to Heuberg, Germany in *Wehrkreis V*.

Ost-Bataillon 635. This unit was attached to the remnants of the *353. Infanterie-Division* which now only numbered about four battalions in strength.

Ost-Bataillon Huber. This unit was also said to have joined the battle group of *353. Infanterie-Division*.

The following initial Belarusian battalions were allocated to the forming *Polizei-Brigade Siegling* in eastern Poland:

Weißruthenischess Schutzmannschafts-Frontbatallion 60
Weißruthenischess Schutzmannschafts-Frontbatallion 61
Weißruthenischess Schutzmannschafts-Frontbatallion 62
Weißruthenischess Schutzmannschafts-Frontbatallion 63
Weißruthenischess Schutzmannschafts-Frontbatallion 64
Weißruthenischess Schutzmannschafts-Frontbatallion 65
Weißruthenischess Schutzmannschafts-Artillerie-Abteilung 56

Russisches-Bataillon 617. Simply a renaming of *Ost Bataillon 617*.

Russische-Pionier-Brücken-Bataillon 605. Simply a redesignation of *Ost-Pionier-Brücken-Bataillon 605* on 13 July 1944.

IV. Bataillon der Grenadier-Regiment 899 of 266. *Infanterie-Division*. This was the ex-*Ost-Bataillon 629*. It was destroyed during the fighting for St-Malo in the Brittany region of France. It was officially disbanded alongside the rest of *266. Infanterie-Division* in September 1944.

III. Bataillon der Festungs-Grenadier-Regiment 895 of *265. Infanterie-Division*. This was the ex-*Ost-Bataillon 634*. It was pushed back into Lorient, alongside remnants of *265. Infanterie-Division*. It was still under *XXV Armeekorps* control. This embattled German garrison was named a *'festung'* (fortress). by Hitler. The German garrison actually survived the war trapped in the port city of Lorient, France.

Ost-Bataillon 636. This unit was pushed back into *Festung Lorient*. The garrison in this port town and three others, St. Nazaire, Quiberon Bay, and Dunkirk, survived the war surrounded by Allied troops.

III. Bataillon der Grenadier-Regiment 1059 of *92. Infanterie-Division*. This was the ex-*Ost-Bataillon 560*. In this month it was once again redesignated, this time as *III. Bataillon der Grenadier-Regiment 147* of *65. Infanterie-Division* of *LXXV. Armeekorps* of the *Ligurien Armee* command. The Ligurian Army command controlled the Italian-French border region and the coastline up until the *14. Armee* area of operations.

Ost-Artillerie-Abteilung Befehlshaber-Heeresgebiet Süd. Disbanded this month in the region of *Heeresgebiet Süd*.

IV. Bataillon der Grenadier-Regiment 932 of *244. Infanterie-Division*. This was the ex-*Ost-Pionier-Bataillon 666*. When the *244. Infanterie-Division* was destroyed in and around the southern French port city of Marseille, this Eastern battalion was detached and renamed as *Russisches Ost-Bataillon 666*.

Weißruthenischess Heimwehr-Pionier-Bataillon 2. Raised this month and formed behind the lines of *Heeresgruppe Mitte* in western Belarus.

The following other, similar battalions began forming but did not complete their training this month:

Weißruthenischess Heimwehr-Pionier-Bataillon 3.
Weißruthenischess Heimwehr-Pionier-Bataillon 4.
Weißruthenischess Heimwehr-Pionier-Bataillon 5
Weißruthenischess Heimwehr-Pionier-Bataillon 6.
Weißruthenischess Heimwehr-Pionier-Bataillon 7.
Weißruthenischess Heimwehr-Pionier-Bataillon 8.
Weißruthenischess Heimwehr-Pionier-Bataillon 9.
Weißruthenischess Heimwehr-Pionier-Bataillon 10.
Weißruthenischess Heimwehr-Pionier-Bataillon 11.

Ost-Bataillon 639. This Eastern battalion was composed of Russians and Poles and was located between the Taute River and the Graignes Port des Planques Canal, west of Goucherie between 7–9 July. Elements of the *38. SS-Panzergrenadier-Regiment* of *17. SS-Panzergrenadier-Division 'Götz von Berlichingen'* were interspersed with this Eastern unit for added 'stiffening' to the front lines of this *Ost* battalion.

Ost-Artillerie-Abteilung 752. Attached to the *265. Infanterie-Division* in *Festung Lorient.*

Ost-Regimentsstab z.b.V. 755. Disbanded this month.

August 1944

Ost-Artillerie-Bataillon 621. Destroyed near Dieppe, France this month.

Ost-Artillerie-Abteilung 752. Destroyed defending *Festung Lorient* under the control of the remnants of *265. Infanterie-Division.* It was officially disbanded in October 1944.

Ost-Bataillon 618. Destroyed in the fighting for Normandy.

Ost-Bataillon 675. Also referred to as *Russische-Sicherungs-Abteilung 675.* Created this month using three companies of volunteers. It was formed from Russian stragglers who were rounded up withdrawing from France. They were grouped in Belgium and assigned to *15. Armee.*

Ost-Bataillon 681. This battalion's title had been officially changed to *IV. Bataillon der Grenadier-Regiment 934* of the *244. Infanterie-Division,* but after the destruction of *244. Infanterie-Division* near Marseille, it was once again redesignated as *Ost-Bataillon 681* and assigned as a *19. Armee* troop.

Ost-Bataillon 427. Reformed again in East Prussia.

I. Bataillon der-Grenadier-Regiment 857 of *346. Infanterie-Division.* This was the ex-*Ost-Bataillon 630.* This unit was destroyed in the fighting withdrawal from Normandy.

II. Bataillon der Grenadier-Regiment 736 of *716. Infanterie-Division*. This was the ex-*Ost-Bataillon 642*. This Eastern battalion withdrew to the Alsace region and was attached to the German *19. Armee.*

III. Bataillon der Grenadier-Regiment 726 of *716. Infanterie-Division*. This was the ex-*Ost-Bataillon 439*. Withdrew to the Alsace region and was attached to *19. Armee.*

IV. Bataillon der Grenadier-Regiment 932 of *242. Infanterie-Division*. This was the ex-*Ost-Pionier-Bataillon 666*. After *242. Infanterie-Division* was destroyed in and around Marseille this month, the battalion was detached and redesignated as *Russisches Ost-Bataillon 666.*

Russisches Ost-Bataillon 666. Formed this month. It was simply a redesignation of *IV. Bataillon der Grenadier-Regiment 932* of *242. Infanterie-Division.*

Ost-Pionier-Bataillon 454. Disbanded on 5 August 1944.

Russisches Bataillon 669. Transferred to the Vlasov Army and sent to *Truppenübungsplatz 'Münsingen'.*

Ost-Bataillon 620. Attached to *94. Infanterie-Division* in Udine, north-eastern Italy.

Ost-Bataillon 627. Remnants attached to *15. Armee* as it withdrew from France.

Kommandeur der Schulen der Freiwilligen Verbände. School is withdrawn from Lyon, France in late August 1944.

Weißruthenischess Schutzmannschafts-Frontbatallion 64. Attached to *Waffen-Grenadier-Regiment der SS 76 (russisches Nr. 5)* of the forming *30. Waffen-Grenadier-Division der-SS* (*russische Nr. 2*).

Weißruthenisches Heimwehr-Pionier-Bataillon 3. Disbanded early this month.

Weißruthenisches Heimwehr-Pionier-Bataillon 4. Disbanded early this month.

Weißruthenisches Heimwehr-Pionier-Bataillon 5. Disbanded early this month.

Weißruthenisches Heimwehr-Pionier-Bataillon 6. Disbanded early this month.

Weißruthenisches Heimwehr-Pionier-Bataillon 8. Disbanded early this month.

Weißruthenisches Heimwehr-Pionier-Bataillon 9. Disbanded early this month.

Weißruthenisches Heimwehr-Pionier-Bataillon 7. Deemed ready this month.

Weißruthenisches Heimwehr-Pionier-Bataillon 11. Deemed ready this month.

I. Bataillon der Festungs-Grenadier-Regiment 759 of *338. Infanterie-Division*. This was the ex-*Ost-Bataillon 663*. This month *Grenadier-Regiment 759* was destroyed at Ronetal and as a result, this Eastern battalion now became an independent unit and was once again redesignated as *Ost-Bataillon 663*.

September 1944

Ost-Bataillon 615. Located about 60km south of Dijon under *Kampfgruppe Brodowski.*[7] Used as a screening force for the German outpost line around Givry Chatillon. The battle group under *LXIV. Armeekorps*. It was composed of the following German and Russian units:

- *Ost-Bataillon 615*
- *IV. Bataillon / Sicherungs-Brigade 200*
- *Schwer Batterie (128mm Flak 40) / Flak-Bataillon 157*
- *Provisorisch maschinengewehrzug* (provisional machine-gun platoon)

Freiwilligen-Stamm-Regiment 2. On 17 September 1944, about 100 men from this regiment was located just west of Belfort, France.

Ost-Bataillon 654. Located in the Belfort, France area under *19. Armee.*

Ost-Bataillon 662. When *416. Infanterie-Division* was transferred from Denmark to the Rhine River region of Germany, this Russian battalion, which had been acting as *III. Bataillon der Grenadier-Regiment 712* of *416. Infanterie-Division*, was detached and remained in Denmark. Its title reverted back to *Ost-Bataillon 662*.

Ost-Bataillon 666. Attached this month to the *IV. Luftwaffen-Feldkorps* which was then operating in the Alsace region.

(russisches) Aufklärungs-Verband „Porsche" (Reiter) This unit was an Eastern formation formed during this month using four Russian volunteer cavalry squadrons.

Kommandeur der Osttruppen z.b.V. im Wehrkreis Generalgouvernement. This unit was disbanded on 30 September 1944, in Petrikau.

Weißruthenisches Heimwehr-Pionier-Bataillon 1. Disbanded this month.

Weißruthenisches Heimwehr-Pionier-Bataillon 2. Disbanded this month.

Weißruthenisches Heimwehr-Pionier-Bataillon 7. Disbanded this month.

Weißruthenisches Heimwehr-Pionier-Bataillon 11. Withdrew into East Prussia along with the rest of *Heeresgruppe Mitte*.

Weißruthenischess Schutzmannschafts-Frontbatallion 65. Disbanded this month.

October 1944

Divisionsstab z.b.V. 136. Disbanded in Holland on 30 October 1944. The staff now supplied two battalions of troops with stomach ailments of four companies apiece.

Weiss. Schuma Frontbatallion 64. Disbanded officially this month. Its remaining men were absorbed into the *Waffen-Grenadier-Regiment der-SS 76 (russische Nr. 5)* of the forming *30. Waffen-Grenadier-Division der-SS (russische Nr. 2)*.

Ost-Bataillon 602 Dnjeper. Destroyed while fighting on 14 October 1944.

Ost-Bataillon 654. Assigned to *Waffen-Grenadier-Regiment der-SS Nr. 77 (russische Nr. 5)* on 21 October 1944 of the forming *30. Waffen-Grenadier-Division der-SS (russische Nr. 2)*.

Ost-Artillerie-Abteilung 621. Disbanded on 28 October 1944. Its remnants are then sent to join the Vlasov Army at *Truppenübungsplatz Münsingen*.

Ost-Artillerie-Bataillon 752. Destroyed in August 1944 but officially disbanded on 28 October 1944. Its remnants were now sent to join the Vlasov Army.

I. Bataillon / Festungs-Grenadier-Regiment 759 of *338. Infanterie-Division*. This was the ex-*Ost-Bataillon 663*. The battalion was caught on the west bank of the Rhone River by the advancing Allied forces and forced to surrender. Remnants of the battalion were sent to the Vlasov Army at *Truppenübungsplatz Münsingen* in November 1944.

Ost-Bataillon 665. This battalion had been designated as the *III. Bataillon der Festungs-Grenadier-Regiment 757* of *338. Infanterie-Division*, but this month it was detached from the regiment and employed by *19. Armee* as an independent army unit.

IV. Bataillon der Grenadier-Regiment 726 of *716. Infanterie-Division*. This was the ex-*Ost-Bataillon 439*. This Eastern battalion was detached from *716. Infanterie-Division* and became an independent battalion. In November 1944 its members were sent to *Truppenübungsplatz Münsingen* to join the Vlasov Army.

IV. Bataillon der Grenadier-Regiment 736 of *716. Infanterie-Division*. This was the ex-*Ost-Bataillon 642*. After *716. Infanterie-Division* was virtually destroyed this month; it too was detached and redesignated as *Russische Bataillon 642*. It was later sent to *Truppenübungsplatz Münsingen* in November 1944.

I. Bataillon der Festungs-Grenadier-Regiment 759 of *338. Infanterie-Division*. This was the ex-*Ost-Bataillon 663*. It was detached and its remnants sent to join the forming Vlasov Army at *Truppenübungsplatz Münsingen*.

Ost-Bataillon 635. Destroyed in Normandy months ago but officially disbanded on 14 October 1944. Its surviving personnel were sent to other Eastern battalions.

Ost Regimentsstab z.b.V. 753. Located in Courland, Latvia.

November 1944

Russische Bataillon 642. Sent to join the Vlasov Army at *Truppenübungsplatz Münsingen*.

Ost-Bataillon 681. Sent to *Truppenübungsplatz Münsingen* to join the Vlasov Army.

Ost-Bataillon 665. Withdrawn from *19. Armee* and sent to *Truppenübungsplatz Münsingen*.

Russische Bataillon 556. Sent from Bologna to Verona this month. Acting as a guard unit.

General der Freiwilligen-Verbände beim Chef GenStdH. Formed on 25 November 1944, from the following two staffs: *Dienststelle des Inspekteurs für Turkvölkische Verbände und General der Osttruppen beim OKH, Kommandeur der Schulen der Freiwilligen Verbände*. Sent to *Truppenübungsplatz Münsingen* to help raise the Vlasov Army divisions.

December 1944

Nachschub-Bataillon 574. Simply a redesignation of *Ost-Nachschub-Bataillon 574*.

Ost-Bataillon 628. Also known as *I. Bataillon der Grenadier-Regiment 745* of *712. Infanterie-Division*. This battalion arrived at *Truppenübungsplatz Münsingen* on 13 December 1944 and joined the Vlasov Army.

Ost-Bataillon 630. Also known as *I. Bataillon der Grenadier-Regiment 857* of *346. Infanterie-Division*. This unit arrived at Münsingen this month to join the Vlasov Army.

Ost-Bataillon 663. Sent to *Truppenübungsplatz Münsingen* to join the Vlasov Army.

Ost-Bataillon 618. Although destroyed in August 1944 it was officially crossed off the German rolls this month. Remnants of this battalion joined the Vlasov Army at *Truppenübungsplatz* Münsingen.

Ost-Bataillon 605. Sent to *Truppenübungsplatz Münsingen* and disbanded. Its men incorporated into the forming Vlasov Army.

(kosakische) Reiter-Abteilung 580. Simply a redesignation of the Cossack-manned *Ost-Reiter-Abteilung 580*. Although it now contained Russian volunteers, it nevertheless still had a good percentage of Cossack volunteers. Still attached to *2. Armee,* and now operating in the Deutsche-Eylau area of East Prussia.

Russische Aufklärungs-Abteilung 684. Formed using four squadrons of Russian cavalrymen. This was simply a redesignation of *Aufklärungs-Verbände Porsche*. It was located in Aalborg, Denmark as an army troop.

Russische Sicherungs-Bataillon 553. Sent to *Truppenübungsplatz Münsingen* to join the Vlasov Army.

Ost-Bataillon 7. Formed this month using five Russian rifle companies which had been previously operating independently of one another. It was employed under the *7. Infanterie-Division* which was currently in East Prussia.

Russische Bataillon 600. Simply a redesignation of *Ost-Bataillon 600*.

Ost-Artillerie-Abteilung 56. When *30. Waffen-Grenadier-Division der-SS (russische Nr. 2)* was finally disbanded in December 1944, this unit was sent to *Truppenübungsplatz Münsingen* to join the Vlasov Army.

Ost-Bataillon 654. When *30. Waffen-Grenadier-Division der-SS (russische Nr. 2)* was finally disbanded in December 1944, and sent to *Truppenübungsplatz Münsingen* to join the Vlasov Army.

Bataillon Murajew. When *30. Waffen-Grenadier-Division der-SS (russische Nr. 2)* was finally disbanded in December 1944, and sent to *Truppenübungsplatz Münsingen* to join the Vlasov Army.

Weißruthenischess Schutzmannschafts-Front-Bataillon 60. When *30. Waffen-Grenadier-Division der-SS (russische Nr. 2)* was finally disbanded in December 1944, and sent to *Truppenübungsplatz Münsingen* to join the Vlasov Army.

Weißruthenischess Schutzmannschafts-Frontbatallion 64. When *30. Waffen-Grenadier-Division der-SS (russische Nr. 2)* was finally disbanded in December 1944, and sent to *Truppenübungsplatz Münsingen* to join the Vlasov Army.

Weißruthenischess Schutzmannschafts-Frontbatallion 65. When *30. Waffen-Grenadier-Division der-SS (russische Nr. 2)* was finally disbanded in December 1944, and sent to *Truppenübungsplatz Münsingen* to join the Vlasov Army.

1945

January 1945

Bau-Pionier-Bataillon 851. First appeared in 1945 but almost immediately sent to join the Vlasov Army at *Truppenübungsplatz Münsingen*.

Ost-Bataillon 666. Sent to *Truppenübungsplatz Münsingen* to join the Vlasov Army.

Ost-Pionier-Brücken-Bataillon 601. As of 29 January 1945, this battalion was still under *LXIV Armeekorps* of *19. Armee*.

III. Bataillon der Grenadier-Regiment 194 of *71. Infanterie-Division*. This was the ex-*Ost-Bataillon 616*. This Russian battalion was detached from its German division which was sent to Hungary this month and was redesignated as *Russische Bataillon 616*. The unit was eventually transferred to Italy and became an independent unit of *14. Armee*. Later it was attached to *10. Armee*.

III. Bataillon der Grenadier-Regiment 755 of *344. Infanterie-Division*. This was the ex-*Ost-Wachbataillon 555*. This battalion was now detached from the *334. Infanterie-Division* and became an independent unit of *14. Armee*. It was now redesignated as *Russische Bataillon 555*.

Russische Bataillon 555. See *III. Bataillon Grenadier-Regiment 755 / 344. Infanterie-Division*.

III. Bataillon der Grenadier-Regiment 147 of *65. Infanterie-Division*. This was the ex-*Ost-Bataillon 560*. This month it was detached from this German division and made an independent battalion. It was also redesignated as *Russische Bataillon 560*.

Russische Bataillon 560. This battalion became *III. Bataillon der Grenadier-Regiment 147 / 65. Infanterie-Division*.

Ost-Pionier-Brücken-Bataillon 601. Attached to *Panzer-Brigade 106*, according to an order of battle dated 29 January 1945.

Russische Pionier-Bataillon 905. First identified in January 1945 serving as an independent unit of *5. Panzerarmee* in the Eifel area of the Ruhr region.

Bau-Pionier-Bataillon (K) 1. Simply a redesignation of the *Kriegsgefangenen-Arbeits-Bataillon (Pionier) 1*. It was still attached to the *20. Gebirgsarmee* in northern Norway.

Ost-Bataillon 627. Still attached as an independent unit of *15. Armee*.

Russische Bataillon 600. Sent to *Truppenübungsplatz Heuberg*.

Russisches Freiwilligen-Stamm-Regiment 4. Located in the Eifel area and attached to the *272. Volksgrenadier Division*.

Ost-Freiwilligen-Genesenden-Stamm-Bataillon. This battalion was stationed in Altneuhaus, Oberpfalz in central Bavaria.

February 1945

III. Bataillon/Grenadier-Regiment 871/356. Infanterie-Division. This was the ex-*Ost-Bataillon 339*. When this German division was transferred from Italy to Hungary this month, this Russian battalion was detached and re-designated as *Russische Bataillon 339*. It was then used as an army troop for *10. Armee*.

Ost-Bataillon 666. Sent to *Truppenübungsplatz Münsingen*, where it was disbanded and its men incorporated into the forming Vlasov Army.[8]

Russische Bataillon 308. Disbanded this month. Its men were sent to *Truppenübungsplatz Münsingen* to join the Vlasov Army.

Ost-Bataillon 675. Disbanded this month at *Truppenübungsplatz Heuberg*. Its men were then transported to *Truppenübungsplatz Münsingen*, where they were incorporated into the forming Vlasov Army. Specifically, this battalion joined *600. Infanterie-Division (russische Nr. 1)*.

600. Infanterie-Division (russische Nr. 1), 650. Infanterie-Division (russische Nr. 2), and two ROA brigades: *Russische Grenadier-Brigade 599* and *Panzerjäger-Brigade R (russisch). Grenadier-Regiment 578 / 305. Infanterie-Division* These two divisions and brigades were created from many Eastern battalions. Those definitively identified include: *Ost-Bataillonen 308, 427, 600, 603, 605, 618, 621, 628, 630, 653, 654, 662, 663, 666, 667, 674, 675, 681; Ost-Artillerie-Bataillonen 582, 752;* and *Ost-Pionier-Bataillone 601, 851.*[9]

March 1945

III. Bataillon der Grenadier-Regiment 578 of *305. Infanterie-Division*. This was the ex-*Ost-Bataillon 412*. This Eastern battalion became an independent unit of *10. Armee* in this month and was detached from *305. Infanterie-Division*. In addition, it was redesignated as *Russische Bataillon 412*.

Russische Bataillon 412. See *III. Bataillon der Grenadier-Regiment 578 / 305. Infanterie-Division.*

Ost-Pionier-Brücken-Bataillon 601. Sent to *Truppenübungsplatz Münsingen* this month and disbanded. Its men were used to help form the Vlasov Army.

Grenadier-Regiment 1604 (russische). This regiment was formed by simply redesignating of *Grenadier-Regiment 714 (Ost) / 416. Infanterie-Division* which was located in Denmark at this time. It contained *Ost-Bataillon 603, 653, and 667* as the *I., II.*, and *III. Bataillone* in the regiment. *Russische Bataillon 620*. Formed by simply redesignating as *II. Bataillon der Grenadier-Regiment 274* of *94. Infanterie-Division*. This was the ex-*Ost-Bataillon 620*. This month it was detached from *94. Infanterie-Division* and made an independent unit in the *14. Armee* in Italy.

Russische Reiter-Abteilung 580. Still under 2. *Armee*, but now located in West Prussia.

April 1945

Russische Grenadier-Brigade 599. Formed near Aalborg, Denmark on 16 April 1945 but later transferred to Viborg. Although this brigade was attached to *Division z.b.V. 614*, it formed part of the Vlasov Army and contained the following regiments: *Grenadier-Regiment 1604 (russisch), Grenadier-Regiment 1605 (russisch),* and *Grenadier-Regiment 1607 (kaukasisch).*

Grenadier-Regiment 1604. was sent to *3. Panzerarmee, Heeresgruppe Vistula,* on the Oder River this month. It was located in Prenzlau.

Grenadier-Regiment 1605 (*russische*). Formed this month from *Ost-Bataillon 662* and *Ost-Bataillon 674*. It was located in Viborg, Denmark.

Grenadier-Regiment 1607 (kaukasisch). Formed this month. Even though this regiment was formed from the *Georgisches Infanterie-Bataillon 799* and the *Nordkaukasischen Infanterie-Bataillon 836,* they were nevertheless officially a part to the Vlasov Army. The regiment was stationed in Viborg, Denmark.

On 5 May 1945, General Sergei Bunyachenko, a leading ROA officer in Vlasov's staff, asked Vlasov for permission to send the ROA to fight alongside Czech patriots in Prague. Bunyachenko argued that with the Red Army advance ever closer, the only hope that the men of the ROA had to avoid any retribution was to fight against the Germans and hope that the Western Allies would give them asylum in the West. This last-minute attempt by these Russian collaborator forces to distance themselves from the Germans would prove to be fruitless. They had bet on the wrong horse and would now suffer the consequences.

The War in the East lasted from 22 June 1941 until 8 May 1945. During that time, the Germans exacted a terrible toll on the population of Eastern Europe.[10] However, German losses also proved to be significant, especially given that Germany in 1939 contained only about 80 million people, as compared to the USSR, which possessed 190 million citizens. On average, and on a 'quiet day', Hitler's *Ostheer* was losing 3,000–5,000 men on the Eastern Front. Final losses for the Germans during the campaign in the East were as follows: 1,105,987 killed, 1,018,059 missing or taken prisoner, plus 3,498,411 wounded, for a grand total of 5,622,411 casualties on the Russian Front from 22 June 1941 to 8 May 1945.[11]

Appendix II

LITHUANIAN VOLUNTEER FORMATIONS, 1941–1945

At the beginning of the German occupation, the Provisional Government of Lithuania urged members of the Lithuanian police to return to their former positions. An initial batch of about 3,000 police officers of the former Independent State of Lithuania returned to work. This amounted to about 40 per cent of the pre-Russian and pre-German occupation numbers. The public police of Lithuania divided into the following three parts:

1. The city police precincts.
2. The regional and district police precincts,
3. The self-defence battalions (with accompanying auxiliary police stations).

Police officers had the right to wear their former Lithuanian Police uniforms, though they were obliged to wear armbands on their left sleeve by the Germans with the words 'In the service of the German Police' or 'In the service of the German Security Police'. On 22 August 1941, there were 1,849 full-time positions assigned for the police in 22 regions throughout Lithuania. On 1 August 1941, the regional police had 750 horses, 1,000 bicycles, 40 motorcycles, 10 passenger cars, and 10 trucks for signals and communications duties. In August 1943 there were 4,043 Lithuanian policemen employed in the system of the public police of Lithuania. The activity of the Lithuanian police brought positive results for the German occupation since they helped to maintain order.

Germany therefore was able to use the Lithuanian police to achieve their goals, among which included fighting the partisans and assisting the Nazis in the Jewish Holocaust. On 25 July 1941, the General

Commissioner for Lithuania, Theodor Adrian von Renteln, assumed control of the country. What reward was given to the Lithuanians for helping to expel the Russians? Instead of allowing a Lithuanian government to assume control, the Germans banned it and jailed its leaders. In its place, they installed a seven-member Lithuanian *Generalrat* (Directorate or General Council), headed by General Petras Kubiliûnas.[1] They did, however, use a small number of these Lithuanian partisan volunteers, organising them into self-defence units of 500–600 men apiece and placing them under German *SS* and police control. This occurred within a week of their occupation of Kaunas. The Germans had succeeded in forming the core of the so-called *Litauisches Bataillone der nationalen Arbeit* (*Tautinio darbo apsaugos batalionas,* TDA), also known by the German term *'Hilfspolizei'*.[2] The majority of the TDA-men were later organised into the auxiliary police battalions known as the *Schutzmannschaft* (Self-Defence). This was the beginning of the Lithuanian self-defence battalions. In short order, five Lithuanian battalions were created in the summer and autumn of 1941:

Table 23. Initial Lithuanian Police Battalions Created in 1941

Battalion No.	Station Post in 1941	Officers	Men
1	Vilnius	10	334
2	Vilnius[3]	18	450
3	Minsk, Belarus	24	607
4	Vilnius	8	253
5	Vilnius[4]	22	288

Beginning in early 1942, von Renteln attempted to mobilise the Lithuanian male population with the explicit assistance of the Lithuanian General Council. This would have made it appear that the Lithuanian people themselves were mobilising to aid in the German war effort. Yet one more example of how poorly the Lithuanians were treated by the Germans is the issue of forced labour. In 1943, while only 10,000 Latvians and 3,000 Estonians had been drafted for work in German factories, an estimated 40,000 Lithuanians had been forced to do so, many beginning in May 1942 when thousands had been sent to District Hesse to work in armaments factories there. By mid-1942, there were nineteen Lithuanian self-defence battalions being employed in the USSR and Lithuania.[5]

According to the Lithuanian General Council, in mid-1942 there were 16,000 Lithuanians in the self-defence battalions: 6,000 in the *Hilfspolizei* (auxiliary police) and 10,000 in the various other self-defence battalions.[6] In 1944, all Lithuanian self-defence units were redesignated as police battalions. A good number of the Lithuanian battalion members were drawn into the apparatus of destruction as prison guards, performing escort duty for those driven to mass execution sites, and, finally, as shooters themselves. The more extreme wing of these volunteers were the so-called Voldemarists, who were followers of Augustinas Voldemaras, the former charismatic prime minister and opponent of Smetona. They were thoroughly racist and neo-Nazi in their thinking, so they had no trouble fitting into the newly-formed Lithuanian Nationalist Party (*Lietuvių nacionalistų partija*). Its emblem was the swastika. The Lithuanian police battalions which were most implicated with the *Shoah* were the *Schutzmannschaft-Bataillon 2 (litauisches)*, and later *Schutzmannschaft-Bataillon 12 (litauisches)* which was commanded by Antanas Impulevičius.

Table 24. Lithuanian Police Battalions in German Service

No.	Date	Comments
1[7]	Jul. '41	Created on 31 July 1941, as the *Litauisches Schutzmannschaft-Bataillon 1 Vilnius*. Renamed *Litauisches Polizei-Frontbatallion 1* in July 1942. It was disbanded in October 1944, with the remnants of the battalion going to the *21. Luftwaffen-Feld-Division.*
2	Jul. '41	Created on 31 July 1941, from the *Litauisches Schutzmannschaft-Bataillon 2 Vilnius*. Renamed *Litauisches Polizei-Front-Bataillon 2* in March 1942. Sent to Lublin, Poland in July 1942 and used to guard prisoners of war and SS death camps. Broken up officially in April 1943.
2	Mar. '43	An entirely new *Litauisches Schutzmannschaft-Bataillon 2* was raised in March 1943 in Kaunas. On 31 July 1944 it became part of *Litauisches Polizeiregiment 1,* which the Germans referred to as *Litauisches Regiment Siauliai.* The regiment was employed under *5. Panzer-Division* from 28 August – 7 September 1944.[8] *Litauisches Schutzmannschaft-Bataillon 2* was removed from combat and reformed as a police unit in Danzig in October 1944: *Litauisches Polizei-Front-Bataillon 2*. It took part in the defence of Danzig from 15–30 March 1945.

No.	Date	Comments
3	Jul. '41	Initially created as a construction battalion on 31 July 1941 but renamed *Litauisches Polizei-Front-Bataillon 3* in March 1942. Sent to Minsk, Belarus in July 1942 where it remained for most of 1942 and 1943. It spent most of its existence fighting the partisans in the surrounding countryside. It was disbanded in Danzig in September 1944 with the remnants going to the *Litauisches Freiwilligen-Polizeiregiment 2*.
4	Aug. '41	*Litauisches Schutzmannschaft-Bataillon* 4. Formed as a self-defence battalion in Vilnius on 15 August 1941. Renamed *Litauisches Polizei-Front-Bataillon 4* in March 1942. Sent to Ukraine in July 1942 and served there into 1943. It was initially used to guard *Durchgangslager 4* (Prisoner of War Transit Camp No. 4) in Stalino. In March 1943 it was rebuilt in Kaunas (Kovno), Lithuania. Two references state that it was disbanded in November 1943,[9] while another says it was split up a year later, in November 1944.[10]
5	Sep. '41	Formed in Kaunas as the *Kaunas Schutzmannschaft-Bataillon 5* in September 1941. Renamed *Litauisches Polizei-Front-Bataillon 5* in November 1941. In July 1942 it was transferred to *Korück 584* behind the lines of *16. Armee.* From 1 January 1943, until 22 March of that same year the battalion was used to guard the principal prisoner of war transit camp behind the lines of *Heeresgruppe Nord.* It later returned to anti-partisan warfare under *Korück 584.* On 29 July 1943 the battalion was still listed under the command of *Korück 584.*[11] On 21 September 1944 the battalion was disbanded after heavy losses and poor morale. The battalion retained two companies which were used as construction units building fortifications under *Sonderstab Oberst Köhl.* This staff controlled a number of construction units of *Heeresgruppe Kurland.* The two remaining companies were now redesignated as *Litauisches Bau-Bataillon 5* of *Sonderstab Köhl.* It remained as part of *Division z.b.V. 300* from 6–22 November 1944. It remained under the control of *Sonderstab Oberst Köhl* until 31 December 1944. Between 3 January and 14 March 1945 it was employed guarding Russian prisoners of war in Courland, Latvia. It surrendered there to Russian forces on 9 May 1945.

No.	Date	Comments
6	Jul. '42	Formed in Vilnius as *Litauisches Polizei-Front-Bataillon 6* in July 1942 and used to guard stationary posts. In September 1942 it was transferred to the *Kommandeur der Ordnungspolizei in Litauen* (Commander of the Order Police in Lithuania). This headquarters was located in Kaunas. Part of the battalion was used to help form *Litauisches Polizei-Front-Bataillon 256* when *Litauisches Polizei-Wachbataillon 6* was disbanded in November 1944.
7	Sep. '41	Originally this unit was *Litauisches Schutzmannschaft-Bataillon 4* in Kaunas, Lithuania. It was redesignated as *Litauisches Polizei-Front-Bataillon 7* in March 1942 and sent to Ukraine. In July 1942 it was located in Vinnitsa, on the Bug River guarding Russian POWs. Vinnitsa lies south-south-west of Zhitomir. By March 1943 the battalion was back in Kaunas (Kovno), but that same month it was used to once again guard Russian prisoners of war. This time they were assigned to guard prisoners behind the lines of *Heeresgruppe Nord.* In June 1943 the battalion returned to Kaunas.
8	Oct. '41	Originally this unit was *Litauisches Schutzmannschaft-Bataillon 6* in Kaunas, Lithuania. It was renamed as *Litauisches Polizei-Front-Bataillon 8* in March 1942. It was sent to Vilnius that same month before being transferred to Ukraine. In July 1942 it guarded Russian POWs behind the lines of *Heeresgruppe Süd* in the area around the city of Uman. In November 1943 it was disbanded.
9	Sep. '41	Formed in September 1941 as the *Kaunas Schutzmannschaft Hauptquartier Stab H.* Expanded through recruitment and renamed in July 1942 as the *Litauisches Polizei-Wachbataillon 9*. The battalion was used to guard fixed installations. One source states that the battalion was used to form *Litauisches Freiwilligen-Polizeiregiment 1* in Danzig in October 1944, while another source states that it was used to form the *Litauisches Freiwilligen-Polizeiregiment 3.*

No.	Date	Comments
10	Jul. '42	*Litauisches Polizei-Wachbataillon 10* was created in Panevezys in July 1942. It was employed guarding stationary (fixed) installations. In September 1942 the battalion was released from its guard duties in and around Panevezys and was sent to Kaunas (Kovno). Part of the battalion was disbanded in February 1943. The remaining companies were employed under the command of *1. Luftwaffen-Feld-Division* from 6 April to 30 July 1943.
10	Jun. '43	While the remnants of the original *Litauisches Polizei-Wachbataillon 10* were fighting alongside *1. Luftwaffen-Feld-Division,* a totally new *Litauisches Schutzmannschaft-Bataillon 10* was created in Kaunas and pronounced combat ready in June 1943. The remnants of the old battalion were withdrawn from the front lines and absorbed into the new battalion sometime in July 1943. From that month the new *Litauisches Schutzmannschaft-Bataillon 10* was deployed behind the lines of *16. Armee* was initially employed guarding Russian prisoners.
11	Sept. '41	Formed as *Litauisches Schutzmannschaft-Bataillon 3* from Kaunas on 13 August 1941. Renamed in March 1942 *Litauisches Polizei-Wachbataillon 11* while stationed in Vilnius. Sent to Ukraine in July 1942, where it was stationed in Korosten. It apparently remained as a guard there for about five months. In December 1942 the battalion was moved to the area north of Polotsk and attached to *Kampfgruppe von Gottberg* from 26–31 December 1943. It was withdrawn from front-line action on 1 January 1944 due to heavy losses and performed guard duty from 1–9 January 1944. In the meantime, it was also reformed. From 10–11 January 1944 it was temporarily committed once again and attached to the *32. Infanterie-Division* of *16. Armee.* It was returned to Korosten towards the end of January 1944. It remained there performing guard duty until the front lines reached it in late October 1943. While serving as a part of *454. Sicherungs-Division,* it suffered heavy losses once again during the defence of Korosten (north-west of Kiev) in late November 1943.[12] As a result, it had to be disbanded.

No.	Date	Comments
12	Aug. '41	Formed as the *Litauisches Schutzmannschaft-Bataillon 2* from Kaunas on 7 August 1941. Reformed as *Litauisches Polizei-Front-Bataillon 12* in Kaunas in July 1942 and sent that same month to Minsk, Belarus. There it remained until June 1944 when it took part in the general withdrawal from Belorussia.
13	Aug. '41	Formed as the *Litauisches Schutzmannschaft-Bataillon 1* from Kaunas on 7 August 1941. Reformed in July 1942 as *Litauisches Polizei-Front-Bataillon 13*. That same month it was sent to *Korück 584* of *16. Armee*. From 1 January 22 February 1943 the battalion performed guard duty. It then returned to fighting the partisans under *Korück 584*. On 29 July 1943 the battalion was still operating under the command of Korück 584 of *16. Armee*. In January and February 1944, the battalion followed the general withdrawal of *Heeresgruppe Nord* back into the Baltic States with the Red Army following close behind. In June 1944 the Soviet summer offensive brought the Red Army once again to the Lithuanian border, which they crossed on 5 July 1944. On 13 July the Red Army entered Vilnius. One account says that *Litauisches Polizei-Front-Bataillon 13* remained in Vilnius, acting as the rearguard of the withdrawing German Army. Instead of withdrawing into East Prussia, the battalion was pushed northwards into Courland, Latvia. The defence of Vilnius and the withdrawal took a heavy toll on the battalion and in September 1944 it was reformed as a construction battalion. It was then renamed as the *Litauisches Bau-Bataillon 13*. On 22 October 1944, it was attached to *Feld-Division 12 (L)* of *16. Armee* in the Courland Pocket. From 6–24 November 1944 it served under the command of the *126. Infanterie-Division*. From 29 November to 31 December 1944, the battalion was attached to the *32. Infanterie-Division*. While under the control of this German division, it was temporarily assigned to *Gruppe Oberstleutnant Thomaschki* from 14–31 December 1944. On 8 January 1945 it was placed under the direct control of the X. *Armeekorps*. From 13–28 January 1945 it was attached to the *132. Infanterie-Division*. From 19–24 March 1945 the battalion was part of the rear-area security by Pavilosta under *Sonderstab Oberst Köhl*. From 28–30 March 1945 it was attached to *Gruppe von Gise*, a battlegroup under the command of X. *Armeekorps*.

No.	Date	Comments
14	Jul. '42	Formed in Siauliai in July 1942 as *Litauisches Polizei-Wach Bataillon 14*. It performed guard duty in fixed and stationary emplacements and localities. In September 1942 it was transferred to the *Kommandeur der Ordnungspolizei* (KdO) in Lithuania, whose headquarters was located in Kaunas. It appears that the battalion served until the end of the war.
15	Nov. '41	Formed in November 1941 as *Vilnius Eisenbahn-Sicherheits-Bataillon* (Vilnius Railway Security Battalion). Renamed as *Litauisches Polizei-Front-Bataillon 15* in July 1942. That same month it was transferred to Baranovichi, in Belarus where it performed guard duty and anti-partisan operations. From 12 September to 31 December 1942, when the battalion was transferred to the rear of *Heeresgruppe Nord* and placed under *Korück 584* of *16. Armee.* Between 1 January 22 February 1943 the battalion performed POW guard duty behind the lines of *Heeresgruppe Nord.* In July 1943 it returned to Belarus where it returned to fighting the partisans in that region. In September 1944 it became a part of *Litauisches Freiwilligen-Polizei-Regiment 2.*
251	Jul. '42	Formed in Kaunas. Garrisoning Kaunas, Lithuania.
252	Jul. '42	Formed in Kaunas. Garrisoning Kaunas, Lithuania.
253	Jun. '43	Formed in Prienai, Lithuania. In April 1944 this battalion was located in Kaunas, Lithuania. On 13 July 1944 it became a part of *Litauisches Freiwilligen-Polizeiregiment 1.*
254	Sep. '42	Formed in Vilnius, Lithuania. In April 1943 it was stationed in Sharkovshchina under the KdO of Belarus. In January 1944, it was still stationed in Sharkovshchina. In September 1944 it became a part of *Litauisches Freiwilligen-Polizeiregiment 2.*
255	Sep. '42	Formed in Kaunas, Lithuania. In March 1944 it had 277 men and was attached to *Kampfgruppe von Curt von Gottberg*. In April 1944 it was stationed in Slutsk, Belarus.
256	Nov. '44	Formed in Kaunas, Lithuania.
257	Apr. '44	In April 1944 this battalion was located in Vilnius, Lithuania. On 13 July 1944 it became a part of *Litauisches Freiwilligen-Polizeiregiment 1.*

No.	Date	Comments
263	May '44	Formed in May 1944 but disbanded in August 1944.
264	May, '44	Formed in May 1944 but disbanded in August 1944.
265	May, '44	Formed in May 1944 but disbanded in August 1944.
301	Mar. '44	Created in March 1944 in Mariampole as part of *Sonder-Regiment Kaunas.*
302	Mar. '44	Created in March 1944 in Vilnius as part of the *Sonder-Regiment Vilnius.* Transferred into the *Luftwaffe* in May 1944 as airfield guards.
303	Mar. '44	Created in March 1944 in Trakai as part of *Sonder-Regiment Mariampole.* Transferred into the *Luftwaffe* in May 1944 as airfield guards.
304	Mar. '44	Created in March 1944 in Vilnius as part of *Sonder-Regiment Vilnius.* Transferred into the *Luftwaffe* in May 1944 as airfield guards.
305	Mar. '44	Created in March 1944 in Kalvarija as part of *Sonder-Regiment Kalvarija.* Transferred into the *Luftwaffe* in May 1944 as airfield guards.
306	Mar. '44	Created in March 1944 in Vilnius as part of *Sonder-Regiment Vilnius.* Transferred into the *Luftwaffe* in May 1944 as airfield guards.
307	Mar. '44	Created in March 1944 in Marijampolė as part of *Sonder-Regiment Marijampolė.* Transferred into the *Luftwaffe* in May 1944 as airfield guards.
308	Mar. '44	Created in March 1944 in Ukmerge as part of as part of *Sonder-Regiment Kaunas.* Transferred into the *Luftwaffe* in May 1944 as airfield guards.
309	Mar. '44	Created in March 1944 in Kalvarija as part of *Sonder-Regiment Kalvarija.* Transferred into the *Luftwaffe* in May 1944 as airfield guards.
310	Mar. '44	Created in March 1944 in Seredzius as part of *Sonder-Regiment Kaunas.* Transferred into the *Luftwaffe* in May 1944 as airfield guards.
311	Mar. '44	Created in March 1944 in Mariampole as part of *Sonder-Regiment Mariampole.* Transferred into the *Luftwaffe* in May 1944 as airfield guards.
312	Mar. '44	Created in March 1944 in Kalvarija as part of *Sonder-Regiment Kalvarija.* Transferred into the *Luftwaffe* in May 1944 as airfield guards.

Appendix III

LATVIAN VOLUNTEER FORMATIONS, 1941–1945

The Latvian contribution to the German war effort in the Second World War amounted to 104,000 men. Latvians served in the *Luftwaffe, Kriegsmarine* and *Heer*. By far most of the men who served fought in army battalions. In the case of Latvia, the Germans were able to raise two Latvian SS divisions: *15. Waffen-Grenadier-Division der-SS (Lettische Nr. 1)* and *19. Waffen-Grenadier-Division der-SS (Lettische Nr. 2)*. Latvians also served, albeit in lesser numbers, in the German Order Police, as well as the SS Security Service. What follows is a listing of the principal Latvian formations, with a brief history of each unit.

Latvian *Schutzmannschaft* (Self-Defence) Battalions

Lettische Front-Bataillon 16 Zemgale

This battalion was formed in Riga on 4 September 1941. It was led by Colonel Gustavs Mangulis between 4 September and 11 December 1941. From 12 December 1941 until 30 January 1943 the battalion was led by Lieutenant-Colonel Rudolfs Kocins. The unit was incorporated into the Latvian SS Legion as the *I. Bataillon / Waffen-Grenadier-Regiment der-SS* 32 *(Lettische No. 3)*. Between October and December 1941, the battalion fought at Dno, then Staraya Russa carrying out railway security duty and anti-guerrilla operations. Between December 1941 and January 1943, it was assigned to rear-area security behind *16. Armee* lines. However, the battalion was sent into front-line action when it was brought into Cholm on 16 January 1942. There it was surrounded with German forces and survived the siege in the spring of 1942. One source states that this security duty was performed from 12 September to 2 December 1942. The battalion eventually returned to Latvia, where it was disbanded at Ilukste on 30 January 1943.

Lettische Polizeibataillon 16 E

This battalion was formed in Riga and Bolderāja on 21 March 1942. The unit was led by Lieutenant-Colonel Osvalds Meija from 21 March until 14 August 1942. On 18 May 1942, the battalion was redesignated as *Lettische Polizeibataillon 266 E*. The unit was then stationed at Balderaja between March 1942 and November 1944. From 14 August 1942 until 9 February 1943 the commander of the battalion was Major Alfons Skrauja. Major Nikolajs Tiltins led the unit between 9 February 1943 and November 1944. In November 1944 the battalion was transferred to Germany where it was eventually absorbed into the *15. Waffen-Grenadier-Division der-SS (Lettische Nr. 1)*.

Lettische Front-Bataillon 17 Vidzeme

This battalion was formed in Riga on 21 December 1941. Major Alfons Skrauja led this battalion between 21 December 1941 and 21 July 1942. From 21 July 1942 until May 1943, the battalion was led by Captain J. Nikans. The unit was in the area of Lepel, Belarus performing rear-area security duty from December 1941 until May 1942. However, one source states that the battalion was transferred to Ukraine in late March 1942. That same source says that from May 1942 to May 1943, the unit was stationed in Dnepropetrovsk, Ukraine. It performed the same duties there as it did in Belarus. While in Dnepropetrovsk, the unit was also responsible for providing guards for *Durchgangslager IV* (Prisoner of War Transit Camp No. IV) that was stationed in the area. The *4. Kompanie* of the battalion apparently remained in Riga while the rest of the battalion was in Ukraine. The unit was finally disbanded in the autumn of 1943.

Lettische Polizeibataillon 17 E Rēzekne

This battalion was formed on 18 March 1942 in Kraslava.[1] It was initially led by Lieutenant-Colonel Raimonds Bebris. On 18 May 1942 the formation was redesignated the *Lettische Schutzmannschaft-Bataillon 267*. The last commander of this unit was Captain N. Plavenieks. Between March and November 1942, the battalion was said to have been stationed in Kraslava, Latvia. In November 1942 it was sent to the Velikiye Luki region to carry out anti-partisan operations. It remained there until July 1944 when it was pushed back, along with the rest of the German Army, into the Courland Pocket in Latvia. It remained in Courland until the end of the war. One unconfirmed report says that the battalion commanders were Major Alfons Skrauja (21 December 1941 to 21 July 1942), and Captain J. Nikans (22 July 1942 to May 1943).

In addition, that in May 1943 the battalion was disbanded and absorbed into the Lettisches Polizeibataillon 25. The company commanders were: 1st Company: Captain Jānis Purmalis, 2nd Company: Captain Augusts Sūna, 3rd Company: 1st Lieutenant Arnolds Vilks.

Lettische Front-Bataillon 18 Kurzeme

This battalion was assigned Field Post No. 39350. This unit was formed on 4 September 1941 in Riga. The first battalion commander was Captain Karlis Bems, who led the unit until 16 December 1941. Colonel Karlis Lobe took command of the unit from 16–30 December 1941. Thereafter Colonel Arvids Kurse assumed control. Kurse was a former Latvian Army general who had accepted the rank of colonel under the Germans. He led the battalion until 21 February 1942 when Major Fridrichs Rubenis assumed command. Between September 1941 and May 1942, the unit was stationed in Riga, Latvia. It next moved to the Minsk region in May 1942, where it carried out rear-area security duties until May 1943 when it was returned to Riga. In July 1942 the unit was stationed briefly in Stolpce under the Commander of the Protection Police Minsk. From Stolpce the unit planned, launched, and took part in several anti-guerrilla operations. In June 1943 it was officially dissolved and its men were transferred into the *Waffen-SS*. Major Fridrichs Rubenis led the battalion until 1 June 1943 when the formation was incorporated into the Latvian SS Legion as the *III. Bataillon / Waffen-Grenadier-Regiment der-SS 33 (Lettische Nr. 4)*.

Lettische Polizeibataillon 18 E Ērgļi

This battalion was formed on 18 March 1942 in Liepāja (Libau) in Latvia. Colonel Janis Rucelis led this unit until 1943 when Major Aleksandrs Tomass assumed command of the battalion. Tomass held this post until 3 February 1944 when the unit was officially disbanded. The battalion was redesignated as the *Lettische Schutzmannschaft-Bataillon 268* on 18 May 1942. Between March and July 1942, the unit was stationed in Liepāja, but in July 1942 it was transferred to the Dnepropetrovsk region, in Ukraine, where it carried guard duties and also took part in anti-partisan operations.

Lettische Front-Bataillon 19 Latgale

This battalion was raised on 16 December 1941 in Riga. The first commander was Captain K. Porietis, who led the unit until 14 January 1942. Major Gustavs Praudins next led the unit until 7 August 1942 when a German officer, *Hauptmann der Schutzpolizei* Heufeldt assumed command. Heufeldt led the battalion until 30 January 1943 when it was disbanded and its men incorporated into the Latvian SS Legion as the *II. Bataillon / Waffen-Grenadier-Regiment der-SS 32 (Lettische Nr. 3).* From December 1941 until May 1942 the unit remained in Latvia. In May 1942 it was sent to Krasnoye Selo and remained there performing guard duties and occasionally taking part in front-line service until January 1943.

Lettische Polizeibataillon 19 E

Field Post No. 15205 was assigned to this unit. This battalion was raised on 18 March 1942 from Latvian customs and border guard personnel. On 18 May 1942 it was redesignated as *Lettisches Polizei-Wachbataillon 269*. It operated in the Baltic coast region for most of its existence. In July 1942 it became a part of *Kampfgruppe Jeckeln*. It operated between 7 January and 20 February 1943 under the *2. SS Infanterie-Brigade (motorisiert)* of *18. Armee.*[2] It then performed frontier guard duty in Latvia until the summer of 1943, when it was disbanded and its men were incorporated into the forming *II. Bataillon / Waffen-Grenadier-Regiment der-SS 42 (Lettische Nr. 4).*

Lettische Wachbataillon 20 Riga

This unit was raised in Riga on 4 September 1941. The initial commander was Captain K. Porietis, who led the battalion until 4 December 1941. At that time, Captain Karlis Bems assumed control of the unit and led it until 14 January 1942 when Captain K. Porietis resumed command of the unit. Porietis led the formation again from 11 March until late 1942, when Major Oskars Tiltins assumed command. Tiltins led the battalion until October 1942, when Lieutenant-Colonel Peteris Uzans assumed control. From 1941 until 1944 the formation was stationed in Riga. While in Riga it protected the city's port, as well as numerous warehouses, plus the bridges over the Daugava River. The battalion was absorbed into the *Lettische Freiwilligen-Polizeiregiment 1 Riga* as the *IV Bataillon* on 11 August 1943. On 10 October 1944, the battalion was evacuated to Liepāja. On 25 October, the unit was transported to Danzig along with the Inspector General of the Latvian-SS Legion, *SS-Gruppenführer und Generalleutnant der Waffen-SS* Rūdolfs Bangerskis, and his staff. A day later the police regiment was renamed *Waffen-Grenadier-Regiment der-SS 'Riga'*. In December 1944 the *IV Bataillon,* along with the rest of the regiment, was disbanded and its men were transferred *en masse* to the *15. Waffen-Grenadier-Division der-SS (Lettische Nr. 1).* At this time, this Latvian SS division was stationed in Lyck, West Prussia.

Battalion commanders:

Captain Kārlis Porietis (4 September–4 December 1941)
Captain K. Bēms (4 December 1941–14 January 1942)
Captain Kārlis Porietis (14 January 1942–11 March 1942)
Captain Oskars Tiltiņš (11 March–October 1942)
Lieutenant-Colonel Pēteris Užāns (October 1942–September 1944)
Captain O. Šeturiņš (September–19 November 1944)

Lettische Polizeibataillon 20 E Abrene
The battalion was assigned Field Post No. 47162. This unit was formed on 9 May 1942 in Abrene, Latvia. The formation was later redesignated as the *Lettische Polizei-Frontbataillon 270* on 18 May 1942. Captain P. Saulite led the unit from 9 May 1942 until 18 February 1943. Between May 1942 and February 1943, it trained continuously as an engineer unit. It was listed as part of the *281. Sicherungs-Division (Heeresgruppe Nord)* between 12 September 1942 and 22 February 1943. On that day two companies of the battalion were said to be operating under *II Armeekorps.* The *Lettische Polizei-Frontbataillon 270* served under the control of the *Befehlshaber der Ordnungspolizei Ukraine und Russland-Süd* beginning in September 1942. It was redesignated as the *Lettische Ost-Pionier-Bataillon 672* in March 1943. Its various construction companies were employed in repairing the Sebezh to Opochka road and bridges.

Lettische Polizei-Front-Bataillon 21 Liepāja
The battalion was assigned Field Post No. 45849. This unit was formed on 25 February 1942 in Lipeja (Libau). According to German records, the formation was not raised until April 1942. Between 25 February and 20 August 1942, the commander of the battalion was Lieutenant-Colonel Teodors Rutulis. It apparently came under the control of the Commander of the Order Police Riga in April 1942. In July 1942 it was listed as part of *Kampfgruppe Jeckeln* and served in the region of Krasnoye Selo until January 1943. In the summer of 1943, the battalion was absorbed into the Latvian SS Legion. From 1–20 July 1943 the unit fought under the *2. SS-Infanterie-Brigade (motorisiert)* of the *18. Armee* on an emergency basis. Police Captain Jakob assumed command of the battalion from 20 August until 30 January 1944.

Lettische Polizei-Front-Bataillon 22 Daugava
Field Post No. 19620 and later, 09939. This battalion was formed on 25 February 1942 in Riga and Bolderāja. The first commander was Lieutenant-Colonel Gerbers, who led the unit from its inception until

October 1942, when Captain H. Vanags assumed command. The battalion was sent to Warsaw, Poland in July 1942 where it performed guard duty until October of that same year. In October it was sent to Stalino, in Ukraine. Captain Vanags led the unit until 7 February 1943. In March and again in June 1943 the battalion was sent to Maevsk and Zaporozhe (Zaporizhzhia) in south-eastern Ukraine. The city lies along the banks of the Dnipro River. The battalion then moved on to Zhitomir. It operated as a police battalion and carried out anti-partisan duty there.

Between August and December 1943, the battalion was performing security tasks around Luck (Lutsk). Between December 1943 and February 1944, it returned to Latvia. On 7 February 1944 the formation was absorbed into *Lettische Polizeiregiment* 2. This regiment was a mixed bag of older men, some without much combat experience, and some only partially armed. Command of the regiment was given to Lieutenant-Colonel of the SS Nikolajs Rusmanis. The unit was ordered withdrawn to Germany in late 1944 but by the time the regiment arrived at the embarkation point, nearly 40 per cent of the regiment had deserted. The remnants were eventually merged with *15. Waffen-Grenadier-Division der-SS (Lettische Nr. 1)* in West Prussia.

Lettische Polizei-Front-Bataillon 23 Gauja

The battalion was assigned Field Post No. 15576, then later Field Post No. 56833. This Latvian formation was formed on 25 February 1942 in Riga and Bolderāja. Captain Kristaps Brigaders led the battalion from the unit's inception until the end of the war. In March 1942 the unit was sent to Ukraine. In July 1942 and July 1943, it was stationed in Dnepropetrovsk. In June 1943 the unit had returned to Riga, where it was reformed and re-organised as a police battalion. In July 1942 it was assigned to guard *Durchgangslager 4,* and again in July 1943. One source states that the battalion was stationed in Kerch in eastern Crimea in late 1943.

Between 26 January and 5 February 1944, the battalion was part of an emergency front-line combat formation under-SS Battlegroup Prützmann. Prützmann's emergency combat group was under control of the *XIII. Armeekorps* of *4. Panzerarmee.* It would incur heavy losses between March and July 1944, making a fighting withdrawal through Kremianetz, Podkamien, Brody, and other western Ukrainian towns. The battalion was returned to the Baltic States and next served under the German *215. Infanterie Division, I. Armeekorps, 16. Armee* from 1 August through 15 September 1944. It continued to fight under *215. Infanterie Division,* but as part of *XLIII. Armeekorps, 16. Armee.* The unit was apparently withdrawn from the Courland Pocket in Latvia in the autumn of 1944. German reports place the formation in Danzig in October 1944, where it was apparently reformed as a police battalion and assigned a new Field Post number (Nr. 56833). However, one Latvian source claims that the battalion spent the rest of the war in the region of Bauska, Courland, in Latvia.

Lettische Polizei-Front-Bataillon 24 Talsi

This battalion was assigned Field Post Nr. 48276, and later Field Post Nr. 40019. The unit was formed on 1 March 1942 in Lipaja (Libau). In April 1942 the Germans listed the battalion as a formation available to the *Kommandeur der Ordnungspolizei* (KdO, Commander of the Order Police) in Riga. Between 1 March 1942 and 9 February 1943 Colonel Alfreds Veveris led the battalion. Between May and July 1942, the unit was stationed in Minsk, Belarus. In July 1942, however, the battalion was transferred to Stankov where, under German orders, it took part in numerous anti-guerrilla operations. In October 1942 the battalion was sent to the Leningrad front, where it served under the *2. SS Infanterie Brigade (motorisiert).* Major Alfons Skrauja led the battalion from 9 February until 18 April 1943. By March 1943 the unit was once again under the KdO Riga, but in April the battalion was no longer in the Latvian capital. On 18 April 1943 it was fighting on the Leningrad front. It was there that the unit was disbanded and its personnel used to form the Latvian Legion's *I. Bataillon / Waffen-Grenadier-Regiment der-SS 33 (Lettische Nr. 4).*

Lettische Polizeibataillon 25

This battalion was assigned Field Post No. 41246. This unit was formed on 6 March 1942 in Liepāja. The unit was initially under the command of Captain R. Aluts, who led the battalion from 6 March until June 1942. In June Lieutenant-Colonel Karlis Plikausis assumed control of the unit and led the battalion until 7 February 1944. It was then that the unit was disbanded and its men absorbed into the *Lettische Polizeiregiment 2 Liepāja.* In July 1942 the unit was sent to Ukraine, where it operated in the region of Korosten, and Ovruch, near Zhitomir. The battalion was assigned to help collect and guard the grain harvest in that region. The unit was withdrawn from Russia and returned to Latvia in the beginning of 1944.

Lettische Polizei-Front-Bataillon 26 Tukums

This battalion was assigned Field Post No. 42181. It was formed on 6 March 1942 in Tuckums. In April 1942 the battalion came under the control of the KdO Riga. The first commander, Lieutenant-Colonel Gredzens, led the unit from 6 March until 31 August 1942. The battalion was sent to Begoml in Belarus in July 1942 where it came under the control of the Commander of the Order Police Minsk. One report states that the battalion was stationed in and around the Belarusian capital. It was there that the unit was employed in numerous anti-guerrilla drives.

Colonel Alfreds Veveris assumed control of the battalion on 1 September 1942, and led the formation until 9 February 1943. Lieutenant-Colonel Karlis Aperats assumed command of the unit from 9 February until 23 April 1943. The battalion was attached to the *1. Luftwaffen-Feld-Division* under the *18. Armee* from 7 January until 27 March 1943. It operated in the Novgorod region as a front-line unit beginning in December 1942.[3] The battalion then served in the *2. SS Infanterie-Brigade (motorisiert)*, which was then operating under *18. Armee* (1 April to 6 May 1943). In June the unit was disbanded and its men were incorporated into the Latvian SS Legion as the *II. Bataillon / Waffen-Grenadier-Regiment der-SS 33 (Lettische Nr. 4)*.[4]

Lettische Polizei-Front-Bataillon 27 Burtnieki

This battalion was formed in Riga and Mangalsala (Magnisholm) on 14 March 1942. The first commander was Captain Karlis Rems, who led the unit until 20 July 1942. The battalion was transferred to Ukraine in March 1942 and placed in the front line in the region of Grishino. In July 1942 the unit was sent to Krivoi-Rog, where it performed guard duty for *Durchgangslager 4*. Shortly thereafter the formation was returned to the front line, but in January 1943 it was once again sent to Krivoi-Rog. Between February and March 1943, the unit was assigned to the Bela Gora region. There it was attached to the *19. Panzer-Division* of Battlegroup Lieutenant-General Gustav Schmidt which was then operating under *1.Panzerarmee*.

The unit remained under the *19. Panzer-Division* from 13 February until 5 March 1943. Colonel Karlis Ziverts assumed control of the battalion from July 1942 and led it until April 1943. This was probably the most trying period for the men in the *Lettisches Polizei-Frontbataillon 27*. On 23 March the unit was attached to the *3. Panzer-Division* of *1. Panzerarmee*. They remained with the *3. Panzer-Division* until 27 March 1943. In the beginning of April 1943, the battalion was still in the Bela Gora region. It had sustained such heavy losses that it was disbanded. It wasn't until June, however, that the battalion was finally removed from the German Field Post rolls.

Lettische Polizei-Front-Bataillon 28 Bārta

This battalion was formed on 9 March 1942 in Liepāja (Libau) and given Field Post No. 43965. The initial commander was Lieutenant-Colonel Gramatins, who led the unit from 9 March until 6 June 1942. After Gramatins Major Ernests Smits assumed command of the battalion and led the unit from 6 June 1942 until 13 July 1943. In July 1942 the battalion was sent to Krivoi-Rog in Ukraine, where it helped to guard Prisoner of *Durchgangslager 4*. It remained in the Krivoi-Rog region of Ukraine performing guard duty and occasional anti-partisan sweeps until July 1943, when the battalion was recalled to Latvia and disbanded. The men of the battalion were to be absorbed into the Latvian SS Legion.

Lettische Polizei-Front-Bataillon 267 Rēzekne
Lettische Polizeibataillon 268 Ērgļi
Lettische Polizei-Wacht-Bataillon 269
Lettische Polizei-Front-Bataillon 270

Lettisches Schutzmannschaft-Bataillon 266 E

Lettisches Schutzmannschaft-Bataillon 266 E was formed on 21 March 1942 in Riga. It was a redesignation of *Schutzmannschaft-Bataillon 16 E*. The battalion was renamed on 18 May 1942. In October 1944 it was absorbed into the *Lettisches Freiwilligen-Polizeiregiment 1 Riga*. The commanders were as follows: from 21 March 1942 – 14 August 1942: *Oberstleutnant* Osvalds Meija; from 14 August 1942 – 9 February 1943: *Hauptmann* Alfons Skrauja; from 9 February 1943: *Major* Oskars Tiltiņš; From 1943 – 1944: *Hauptmann* Kārlis Kaliņš (temporary); then from 1944 – October 1944: Hauptmann Andrejs Tauriņš. In October 1944 the final commander was: *Oberstleutnant* Kārlis Gerbers.

Lettische Polizei-Front-Bataillon 271 Valmiera

This battalion began forming in Libau in July 1942 but was not ready until 15 January 1943. The battalion was shifted to Belarus in the late summer of 1942 and stationed at Hansevicze, near Minsk. Captain J. Avotins was the initial battalion commander who led the unit until 13 August 1944. The battalion spent all of 1943 in Belorussia performing anti-partisan operations. In March and April 1943, the battalion was posted to Uretschye and Slutsk.[5] While in Belarus, the unit would be under the control of the KdO *Kommandeur der Ordnungspolizei Weissruthenien* (Commander of the Order Police White Ruthenia). In January 1944 the unit listed a strength of only 304 officers, non-commissioned officers, and men. At this time, the battalion was quartered in Dokschyze.[6] Most of 1944 was spent performing the same type of duty.

A German roster of available anti-partisan forces for April 1944 listed *Lettische Polizei-Front-Bataillon 271* as currently performing an anti-guerrilla operation in Belorussia.[7] The month of May 1944 found the unit operating in the region of Minsk. In June the unit took part in the anti-partisan operation, named 'Cottbus', which proved to be the largest German anti-guerrilla drive of the war. The battalion had been stationed at Slutsk when the operation began.[8] Between July and November 1944, the main period in which *Heeresgruppe Mitte* was crushed in Belorussia, and pushed into Poland and Prussia, the battalion was employed on the front line. It operated in the Sigulda and Dobele regions of Latvia. Trapped in the Courland Pocket in Latvia, the battalion was assigned to the *VI. SS-Freiwilligen-Armeekorps*.

The commander of the battalion between 13 August and November 1944 was Lieutenant-Colonel Birzulis. According to survivors of the battalion, it was through the good leadership of Colonel Birzulis that *Lettische Polizei-Front-Bataillon 271* survived the trying summer and autumn months of 1944. On 11 October 1944 *VI. SS Freiwilligen Armeekorps* was located in the region of Dzukste. The battalion was part of a reserve which on 15 October helped to repel a Soviet attack around Nabadzini and Puces. This marked the last independent action of the battalion. Later that month the unit was disbanded and the remnants were absorbed into the *Waffen-Grenadier-Regiment der-SS 43 (Lettische Nr. 5)*. One German source lists *Lettische Polizei-Front-Bataillon 271* as being located in Danzig in October 1944, but this seems highly unlikely.

Lettische Polizei-Front-Bataillon 272 Daugavgrīva

This battalion was formed in Riga and Bolderāja on 1 July 1942. Lieutenant-Colonel Gustavs Mangulis became the commanding officer and held that post until August 1942. In October 1942 one company from the battalion was detached. It became the cadre of a new battalion: *Lettische Polizei-Front-Bataillon 274*. The *Lettische Polizei-Front-Bataillon 272* remained in Warsaw performing guard duty until the end of April 1943, when it was sent on to Dnepropetrovsk in Ukraine. Before it was sent, the battalion took part in the liquidation of the Jewish ghetto in Warsaw. The battalion arrived in Dnepropetrovsk in May 1943. During this time, Lieutenant-Colonel Julijs Taube led the unit. The battalion was disbanded in late 1943 and absorbed into the Latvian SS Legion.

Lettische Polizei-Front-Bataillon 273 Ludza

The battalion was formed in Ludza (Lüdzen), in the Latgale region of eastern Latvia, on 1 July 1942 and remained in existence until 15 July 1943. During this period it was commanded by Lieutenant-Colonel

Birzulis. Initially assigned to guard duties in Ludza and along the Latvian border, the unit consisted of twelve officers, seventeen non-commissioned officers, and 143 NCOs and enlisted men, forming a company-sized formation. In March 1943, the battalion was attached to Operational Staff Schröder, a special formation under the command of SS Brigadier General and Major-General of the Police Walther Schröder, who served as SS and Police Leader Latvia. As part of this battlegroup, the unit participated in anti-partisan operations in the Ludza region, including a punitive action known as *Unternehmen Winterzauber*. These operations formed part of a broader, planned deployment of SS, police, and auxiliary police forces in the area. On 15 July 1943, the battalion was disbanded and fully absorbed into the *Lettisches Polizei-Frontbataillon 276*.

Lettische Polizei-Front-Bataillon 274

This battalion was formed on 1 October 1942 in Warsaw. In November it detached one company to help establish *Lettische Polizei-Front-Bataillon 272*. It was intended that this company would be the core of a new battalion but circumstances prevented this. The 'battalion' was shifted from Warsaw to Bobruisk in Belarus in late October 1942, where it remained until 30 September 1944. In that month it was ordered disbanded. During its existence, the battalion was really a company in size. Nevertheless, it took part in anti-partisan sweeps in Belarus. The commander of the unit during its entire history was Lieutenant Brummers. The formation was stationed in Bobruisk, Belarus between October 1942 and October 1943. It then served in the front lines in the Polotsk region, from October 1943 to March 1944 under *Kampfgruppe Jeckeln*. From March until September 1944 the formation was on guard duty in Riga, Latvia.

Lettische Polizei-Front-Bataillon 275

This 'battalion' was in reality only a reinforced rifle company, like *Lettische Polizei-Front-Bataillon 272*. It performed guard duty in Riga from mid-October until early December 1942. The KdO Riga raised this unit on 16 October 1942. The formation was assigned to Captain Kuginieks, who led the company from inception until 7 December 1942 when it was disbanded. Its men were absorbed into another *Schutzmannschaft* formation. One Latvian source states that this reinforced company was absorbed by the *Lettische Polizei-Front-Bataillon 276*, while a German reference states that it was absorbed into the ranks of *Lettische Polizei-Front-Bataillon 278*. Whichever is the case, the men served in *Kampfgruppe Knecht* (Battlegroup Knecht), an emergency anti-partisan force that was organised in early February 1943 under the command of *Oberst der Schutzpolizei* Karl Knecht.[10]

This combat group was raised in conjunction with *Kampfgruppe Schröder* (two to three battalions) and was to perform operations against the growing partisan menace on the Latvian-Lithuanian-Russian border. Both battlegroups were to operate independently of one another, but were to coordinate drives.[11] German and Latvian language sources regarding the history of *Lettische Polizei-Front-Bataillon 275* concur that the men from this company-sized battalion ended up serving in the *Lettische Polizeiregiment 1 Riga*. Records state that both *Lettische Polizei Frontbatallion 276 and Lettische Polizei Frontbatallion 278* were absorbed into the *Lettische Polizeiregiment 1 Riga* when it was formed in August 1943. Prior to that they both saw service under *Kampfgruppe Knecht.*

Lettische Polizei-Front-Bataillon 276 Kuldīga

This battalion was raised on 7 December 1942 in Kuldiga, Latvia although unconfirmed German records say that the unit was not raised until February 1943. It was common practice for a formation to be raised in one month, and for its Field Post Number not to appear for several months later. This may explain the apparent discrepancy with regard to when the unit was formed. Lieutenant-Colonel Osvalds Meija led the battalion from December 1942 until 15 July 1943. Lieutenant-Colonel Birzulis assumed command of the unit from 15 July until 11 August 1943. The battalion was disbanded on that date and its men were used to create the *IV. Bataillon / Lettische Polizeiregiment 1 Riga*. Between December 1942 and August 1943, the unit had served as guards for rear-area installations in Vilaka, Latvia. The only period in time when the battalion was not on guard duty was in February–March 1943 when it was attached to *Kampfgruppe Knecht*. This entire battlegroup of four *Schutzmannschaft* battalions and three independent support platoons numbered 2,500 men.

Lettische Polizei-Front-Bataillon 277 Sigulda

This unit was also formed in Riga on 7 December 1942. Lieutenant-Colonel Julijs Taube took charge of the unit from December 1942 until 11 August 1943 when the battalion was absorbed into the Latvian SS Legion. This battalion also took part in anti-partisan operations under *Kampfgruppe Knecht* in February 1943 and again in the autumn. The unit was deployed between the towns of Pustina, Asune, and Pizani in that month. In March 1943 the battalion was once again back in Riga. It performed guard duty in the Indra region until absorbed into the Latvian SS Legion in August 1943. One month before, in July 1943 it had taken on the remnants of *Lettische Polizei-Front-Bataillon 282* into its ranks. Apparently *Lettische Polizei-Front-Bataillon 282* had taken heavy losses and was ordered disbanded.

Lettische Polizei-Front-Bataillon 278 (Dobele)

This battalion, which was also raised on 7 December 1942, was led from its inception until 11 August 1943 by Lieutenant-Colonel Gredzens. The battalion had been formed from men recruited in Riga and Bolderāja. The first actions of the unit included security duties in the Ludza region of Latvia. In February 1943 the battalion was part of *Kampfgruppe Knecht*. After the battlegroup was disbanded in late March 1943, the unit went back to guard duty in the Ludza region.[12] In August 1943 the battalion was disbanded and its men were used to form the *II. Bataillon / Lettische Polizeiregiment 1 Riga*. The police regiment was under the command of *Waffen-Standartenführer der-SS* Roberts Osis. The *Lettische Polizeiregiment 1 Riga* eventually found itself in Danzig, East Prussia and soon after, was absorbed into the *15. Waffen-Grenadier-Division der-SS (Lettische Nr. 1).*

Lettische Polizei-Front-Bataillon 279 Cēsis

This battalion was raised on 4 January 1943 in Riga and Bolderāja. Initially command of the battalion fell on Major Oskars Tiltins, but by 15 July 1943 the battalion was under the control of Lieutenant-Colonel Alberts Kleinbergs.[13] The main responsibility of this unit between January and July 1943 was the protection of rear-area facilities in the area of Zilupe, Latvia. In February 1943 the unit formed part of *Kampfgruppe Knecht*. As such, it took part in *Bandenkampf Unternehmen Winterzauber* (Anti-Partisan Operation 'Winter Magic'), which ran from 16 February to 30 March 1943. Latvian records indicate that in mid-July 1943 *Lettische Polizei-Front-Bataillon 279* was disbanded and its men were used to replenish *Lettische Polizei-Front-Bataillon 278.*

Lettische Polizei-Front-Bataillon 280 Bolderāja

The *Lettische Polizei-Front-Bataillon 280* was organised and raised in Riga and Bolderāja on 23 January 1943. Colonel Karlis Lobe was its only commanding officer,[14] holding this post until 9 April 1943 when the battalion was disbanded. This unit took part in *Unternehmen Winterzauber* (Winter Magic) under *Kampfgruppe Schröder*. This was the second combat group raised in February 1943 in the Ostland region that was employed in helping to combat the guerrilla menace on the Latvian-Lithuanian-Russian frontier. The battalion's main region of responsibility was Zilupe, Latvia where it performed numerous anti-partisan sweeps between March and July 1943. This battlegroup was under the command and control of *SS-Brigadeführer und Generalmajor der Polizei* Walther Schröder and his staff.[15] After the war, Karlis Lobe managed to emigrate to Sweden. In 1967 there was an attempt (on 14 June 1967) to hold him partly responsible for the deaths that occurred during *Winterzauber*, but the Swedish government refused to allow him to be extradited.[16]

Lettische Polizei-Front-Bataillon 280 B

The *Lettische Polizei-Front-Bataillon 280 B* was formed by Captain Eduards Hermanis Ozoliņš on 2 August 1943 in Riga, from Vidzeme county police officers and policemen. Most of the officers had served in the Latvian army and therefore had military training and experience. The rest of the men were a combination of older and younger men with no experience whatsoever. When the battalion was formed, it consisted of consisted of 603 officers, NCOs and enlisted men (twenty-five officers, 139 instructors and 439 enlisted). The weapons provided to the battalion by the Germans included French rifles and various machine guns from the First World War. Like *Lettische Polizei-Front-Bataillon 282 A,* the machine-guns provided were from the First World War and were from numerous countries. The battalion was outfitted with the Russian-made Pulyemyot Maksima PM1910 heavy machine-gun, the Austro-Hungarian *Maschinengewehr (Schwarzlose)* M-7, and the German-manufactured MG-08 (*Maschinengewehr 08*). The battalion wore German police uniforms with headgear.

Lettische Polizei-Front-Bataillon 281 Abrene

According to German records, the existence of the *Lettische Polizei-Frontbataillone 281, 282,* and *283* is questionable. This is quite puzzling. The *Lettische Polizei-Front-Bataillone 281* was said to have been raised in Riga and Bolderāja on 23 January 1943. Apparently, the battalion had been created specifically for employment during *Unternehmen Winterzauber*. Its area of activity was in the Zilupe region of Latvia, mainly performing guard duty. The battalion was supposed to have served under *Kampfgruppe Schröder* in March 1943. As far as combat experience was concerned, the officers and most of the NCOs in the battalion had already seen combat, but the majority of the enlisted personnel had not. *SS-Standartenführer* Voldemars Veiss was said to have led the battalion from 23 January until 9 April 1943 when the battalion was finally disbanded. Born in 1897, the 46-year-old Veiss would later reach the rank of *SS Oberführer* and obtain the post of deputy commander of the *19. Waffen-Grenadier-Division der-SS (Lettische Nr. 2)* in 1944.

Lettische Polizei-Front-Bataillon 281 A

The *Lettische Polizei-Front-Bataillon 281 A* was established in Daugavpils on 15 May 1943 by Captain Kārlis Mihelsons. It was created using county police officers and guards. At the end of May the battalion consisted of 488 officers, NCOs and enlisted personnel. The unit had fifteen officers, sixty-eight NCOs and 405 enlisted men. From the second half of May until 2 July 1943 the battalion performed railway security duty in and around Vilnius. By 4 July the unit was back on Latvian soil and stationed in Vilaka. The battalion's designation was changed from *Lettische Polizei-Front-Bataillon 281 A* to *Lettische Polizei-Front-Bataillon 312* on 29 July 1943. However, on 12 August the unit was ordered absorbed into *Lettische Polizeiregiment 1 Riga,* becoming the *III. Bataillon* of the regiment.

Lettische Polizei-Front-Bataillon 282 Venta

The battalion was said to have been raised on 5 March 1943 in Riga and Bolderāja employing 266 men from the Rēzeknes battalion. The battalion had been created for *Unternehmen Winterzauber* although it was established twenty-five days before the end of the operation (30 March 1943). The unit eventually reached a strength of 466 men (eighteen officers, 142 NCOs and 306 enlisted personnel). The commanding officer throughout its brief existence was Captain Janis Zilvers. The company commanders were as follows: *1. Kompanie,* Captain Leonhards Trrēzins, *2. Kompanie,* Captain Jānis Avotiņš, *3. Kompanie,* Captain Kārlis Kronis. As with the previous three or four battalions, this unit was also posted to the region of Zilupe, Latvia where it undertook numerous anti-guerrilla drives, being heavily engaged. On 15 July 1943 the remnant parts were finally absorbed into the *Lettische Polizei-Front-Bataillon 277.*

Lettische Polizei-Front-Bataillon 282 A

The *Lettische Polizei-Front-Bataillon 282 A* was established in Riga under the leadership of Captain A. Jumis on 2 August 1943. The personnel had come from many police officers and policemen from the Kurzeme and Zemgale provinces. Most of the officers were experienced, having served in the Latvian Army before the Soviet occupation in 1940. However, the overwhelming majority of the enlisted men were raw recruits with no experience whatsoever. These recruits were rather young, with some being only 17. The good thing was that the non-commissioned officers had prior military service, which meant they were capable of teaching the raw recruits.

At the time of its formation, the battalion comprised a total of 599 officers, NCOs and men (twenty-four officers, 114 NCOs and 461 enlisted personnel). The armaments assigned to the battalion were not top-of-the-line weapons or equipment. The Germans armed the Latvian volunteers of this battalion with Belgian rifles and various heavy machine guns of the First World War from several empires.

These included the Russian-made Pulyemyot Maksima PM1910 heavy machine-gun, the German-manufactured MG-08 (*Maschinengewehr 08*), the Austro-Hungarian *Maschinengewehr (Schwarzlose)* M-7, and even a few 7.7mm water-cooled Vickers heavy machine guns. The battalion wore German police attire with Romanian headgear. In February 1944, the battalion was stationed in Kurzeme.

Lettische Polizei-Front-Bataillon 311 Valmiera

Official German military records state that the *Lettische Polizei Frontbatallion 311* and *Lettische Polizei Frontbatallion 312* were never really formed. However, Latvian sources state that in fact they were created, although they existed very briefly. Therein is where the confusion lies. The *Lettische Polizei Frontbatallion 311* was organised and raised in Valmeira on 12 May 1943. The unit performed railway security duty guarding the rail line between the Meitene and Valka regions of Latvia. The unit did this work from May until 2 July 1943 when the battalion was officially disbanded. The commander of this battalion was Colonel Eduards Ozolins.

Lettische Polizei-Front-Bataillon 312

Apparently, although German records list this *Schuma* battalion as never having been formed, it in fact did exist before as *Lettische Polizei-Front-Bataillon 281 A.* It was merely renumbered on 29 July 1943. it became the *III. Bataillon / Lettische Polizeiregiment 1 Riga*. The confusion comes from the fact that the Germans did not employ the unit at all when it was raised on 15 May 1943 in the city of Daugavpils. Instead, it began to train and equip there. When the Germans made requests for the unit to be employed as part of the *Lettische Polizeiregiment 1 Riga,* the battalion was simply redesignated the *III. Bataillon* of the regiment. Between 15 May and 11 August 1943, the formation was in training. It was led by Lieutenant-Colonel Karlis Mikelsons.[17]

Lettische Polizei-Front-Bataillon 313

The unit was assigned Field Post No. 39428. German records list this unit as having been raised in November 1943 as a police battalion, but Latvian sources state that the battalion was actually organised on 2 August 1943 in Riga. The first commanding officer was police Major Jumis. Under Major Jumis, the battalion carried out various anti-partisan operations in the Vilnius district (Lithuania) and Molodechno (Belarus) regions between August and October 1943. During that time the *Lettische Polizei-Front-Bataillon 313* and *Lettische Polizei-Front-Bataillon 316* took part many in battles against the partisans in the Vilnius district, while the four battalions of *Lettische Polizeiregiment 1 Riga* fought against Soviet partisans in the Braslava district of Western Belarus. From October 1943 and 30 January 1944, the battalion saw further action against the guerrillas and even some front-line service in the Sebezh and Nevel regions.

At this time *Lettische Polizei-Front-Bataillon 313* was attached to *Kampfgruppe Jeckeln*.[18] By 7 February 1944 command of the unit had been assigned to Captain K. Blitte. This occurred when the battalion became the *III. Bataillon / Lettische Polizeiregiment 2 Liepāja*, whose commander was *SS-Standartenführer* Janis Grosbergs. This second Latvian police regiment saw action against Soviet partisans in the area along the Daugava River beginning in February 1944. Apparently, *Lettische Polizei-Front-Bataillon 31*, which had by now been absorbed into *Lettische Polizeiregiment 2 Liepāja*, came under the control of the *263. Infanterie-Division* of *VIII. Armeekorps, 16. Armee.* The battalion remained under this division from 16 January to 10 February 1944. From 14–19 February the unit fought under the battlegroup of the 83. *Infanterie-Division* of *VIII. Armeekorps, 16. Armee.*

This period of time involved front-line fighting. The battalion was lost in September 1944 when *Lettische Polizeiregiment 2 Liepāja* was destroyed. In this same month a replacement *Lettische Polizeiregiment 2 Liepāja* was ordered formed in order to replace the one that had been destroyed. This new regiment was to be named 'Kurzeme' (Courland). It began to assemble at *SS-Truppenübungsplatz Seelager* (SS Military Training Area Seelager), near Dundaga, on 21 September 1944. The initial formation date of the new regiment was 16 September 1944 in Riga. The new *Lettische Polizeiregiment 2 Liepāja* was a mixed bag of older men with few arms and little training.

Lettische Schutzmannschaft-Bataillon 314

The unit was assigned Field Post No. 27288. This battalion began forming in May 1944. From the beginning there was difficulty in obtaining enough weapons so a decision was made to form this unit into an engineer construction battalion. This was done and by July 1944, when the formation was redesignated. It was attached to Army Group North as an army group support formation. It ended the war trapped in Courland, Latvia. The unit was lost in December 1944 when its personnel were used to replenish Latvian ground combat units.

Lettische Schutzmannschaft-Bataillon 315

The unit was assigned Field Post No. 56540. This battalion was raised in January 1944 and was, from the very beginning, intended to become a construction unit. It served in the region of Army Group North and was trapped in Courland. It was disbanded in April 1945.

Lettische Schutzmannschaft-Bataillon 316

This battalion was formed, according to Latvian records, on 2 August 1943 in Riga and Bolderāja. Between August and October 1943, the battalion was used against the Lithuanian and Russian communist guerrillas in the Vilnius, Lithuania region. In November 1943 the German Field Post Records finally gave the unit a number (No. 36570). Colonel Eduards Ozolins initially led the formation, but by 7 February 1944 Major Arturs Bergs was commanding the battalion. When this unit was incorporated into the *Lettische Polizeiregiment 2 Liepāja,* Major Natins assumed control. From 17–31 December 1943 the battalion formed part of *Kampfgruppe Jeckeln,* then under *VIII. Armeekorps, 16. Armee.* The unit saw front-line service under this combat group in the Nevel and Sebezha areas.

The battalion was once again under the control of *Kampfgruppe Jeckeln* from 5–11 January 1944. Thereafter the battalion served with the *263. Infanterie-Division* between January 16 and 10 February 1944. It then saw employment under the remnant battlegroup of the *83. Infanterie-Division* from 14–19 February 1944. The battalion again saw service with *Kampfgruppe Jeckeln* between 19 July and 8 August 1944. This last employment was the largest that SS General Friedrich Jeckeln had ever organised. There were so many native auxiliary and German units that Jeckeln's ad-hoc divisional headquarters staff was upgraded to corps level. The *Lettische Schutzmannschaft-Bataillon 316* was disbanded in September 1944, when the *Lettische Polizeiregiment 2 Liepāja* was lost.

Lettische Schutzmannschaft-Bataillon 317

The unit was assigned Field Post No. 09505. This unit was formed on 18 October 1943 in Riga and Bolderāja. The first commander who led the unit until 14 February 1944 was Captain Z. Krummins. Between October 1943 and February 1944, the battalion was employed against the guerrillas in the Zilupe and Olaine regions of Latvia. On 14 February 1944 the unit became a part of *Lettisches Polizeiregiment* 3. This regiment was led by *Obersturmbannführer der Waffen-SS* Alberts Kleinbergs. The battalion was employed in the front lines under this police regiment until September 1944 when the unit was disbanded.

Lettische Schutzmannschaft-Bataillon 318

The unit was assigned Field Post No. 11441. This battalion was formed on 25 October 1943 in Riga and Bolderāja. Captain Rudolfs Abeltins led this unit until 14 February 1944. Between October 1943 and February 1944, the battalion was employed in rear-area security duty in the Vecslabada region of Latvia. On 14 February 1944 the formation was incorporated into the *Lettische Polizeiregiment 3*. Like the *Lettische Schutzmannschaft-Bataillon 317*, the *Lettische Schutzmannschaft-Bataillon 318* was employed in the front lines until September 1944, when *Lettische Polizeiregiment 3* was destroyed. From 6–15 July 1944 *Lettische Polizeiregiment 3* was attached to the *290. Infanterie-Division*, which was then under *II. Armeekorps, 16. Armee.*

Lettische Schutzmannschaft-Bataillon 319

Formed on 25 October 1943 in Riga. The Germans placed it in their rolls as a police battalion in March 1944. Major Oskars Tiltins commanded the unit from 25 October 1943 until 8 May 1944. The battalion spent the months of October and mid-November 1943 in Riga. Between November 1943 and March 1944, the unit was performing guard duty in the Sebezha and Indra regions of Latvia. On 16 January 1944 a German order of battle roster listed the *Lettische Schutzmannschaft-Bataillon 319* as a battalion attached directly to *VIII. Armeekorps* command. German records listed the battalion in March 1944 as a police battalion but by December 1944 their designation had changed to that of a 'front' battalion. The months of March and April 1944 were spent on furlough in Olaine, Latvia. Between April and July 1944, the unit was performing rear-area security in the Aluske and Gulbene regions of Latvia.

On 17 September 1944 the battalion was attached to *215. Infanterie-Division* of *XLIII. Armeekorps, 16. Armee.* It served in *Kampfgruppe Kleffel* from 27–29 October 1944, working directly under the control of *16. Armee* headquarters. Between 30 October 30 and 4 November 1944, the battalion was assigned to *Kampfgruppe General von Mellenthin (16. Armee).* The unit was pushed out of Latvia and thus evaded the fate of *Heeresgruppe Nord* which would become trapped in Courland.[19] According to German records, the battalion was stationed in Danzig in October 1944.

Lettische Schutzmannschaft-Bataillon 320

This battalion was formed on 21 December 1943 in Riga, Latvia. Captain Levings led this unit throughout its existence. The battalion performed guard duty in the Jelgava, Kegums, Liepāja, and Salaspils regions of Latvia. The formation was disbanded on 20 September 1944. According to German records, this battalion was never formed.

Lettische Schutzmannschaft-Bataillon 321

The unit was assigned Field Post No. 10865. This battalion was formed on 22 December 1943 at Daugavpils, Latvia. The first commander of the unit was Lieutenant-Colonel Jekabs Zeltins. On 14 February 1944 the battalion became the *III. Battalion* of *Lettische Polizeiregiment 3*. That same day

Captain Fridichsons was made the new battalion commander. Between December 1943 and February 1944, the unit performed rear-area security in the Abrene area. On 14 February 1944 the formation was assigned to *Lettische Polizeiregiment 3.* Between 19 July through 3 August 1944 the battalion was attached to *Kampfgruppe Jeckeln* as the *III. Bataillon* in the regiment.

Lettische Schutzmannschaft-Bataillon 322

This unit was raised on 23 July 1944 in Riga and Bauska. Between 1 August and 15 September 1944, the battalion was attached to *215. Infanterie-Division,* which was then operating under the *I Armeekorps, 16. Armee.* On 17 September 1944 the unit was still under *215. Infanterie-Division,* but was attached to *XLIII. Armeekorps, 16. Armee.* Between 27–29 October 1944 the unit was attached to *Kampfgruppe Kleffel* which formed part of 16th Army. By 30 October *Lettische Schutzmannschaft-Bataillon 322* was placed under *Kampfgruppe von Mellenthin (16. Armee).* The battalion remained with *Kampfgruppe von Mellenthin* until 4 November 1944. In October 1944 the formation was located in Danzig.

In December 1944 the unit was designated as a 'front' battalion. The German field post system assigned a number to this unit late in the war, in February 1945 and renamed it as a police battalion. By 30 March 1945 the battalion was trapped in Courland and serving under the *19. Waffen-Grenadier-Division der-SS (Lettische Nr. 2).* This Latvian SS division was a part of *VI. SS Freiwilligen Armeekorps, 16. Armee.* The commander of this battalion from December 1943 until 8 May 1945 was Captain A. Kikuts. Apparently, the battalion must have been returned to Courland, Latvia from Danzig, West Prussia. It is possible that many of these '300' series numbered Latvian battalions may have been created from the Latvian Depot Brigade.

Lettisches Polizei-Frontbataillon 266 E

The battalion existed from 24 March to 6 November. The Field Post Number assigned was 09654. By 4 April 1944 the HQ staff and the 1st–4th Companies were ready. From 10 March to 26 June 1944, it helped to secure the construction work on the HKL against partisan attacks. From 15–17 March 1944 the battalion took part in an operation against the 1st Kalinin and Drissa Partisan Brigade. This took place just south-west of Kljastinj. From 5–10 April it fought the partisans in *Unternehmen Richard.* The battalion was stricken from the roll of active units on 9 November 1944.

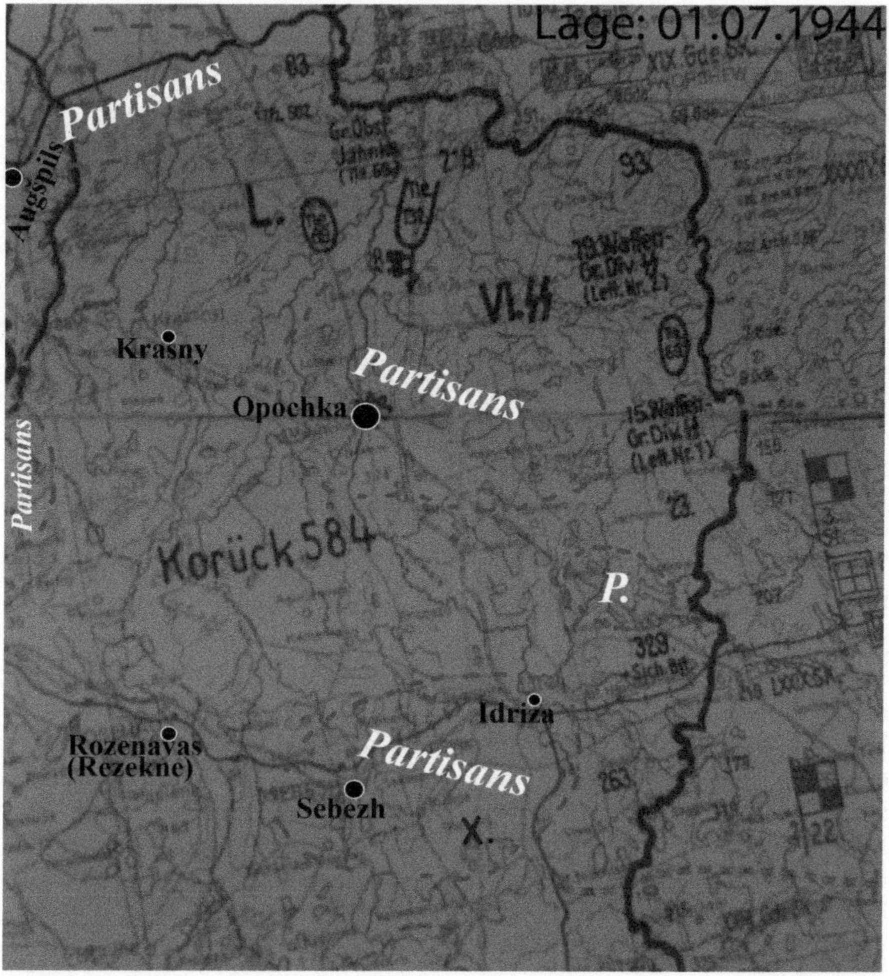

Figure 26. Once *Unternehmen Frühlings**fest*** ended, ***Lettische** Polizeiregiment* **3** was transferred to Sebezh, where it was assigned to *Korück 584*. There was a large partisan force in that region that was threatening the rear of *X Armeekorps*. This map depicts the German and Russian deployment of forces in the region of *16.Armee*.

Latvian Police Regiment Established on 1 August 1943

Lettische Polizeiregiment 1 Riga

The *Lettische Polizeiregiment 1 Riga* was organised near the Latvian-Belarusian border region using four battalions. *Lettische Polizeiregiment 1* was sent to the front lines in February 1944, attaching itself to the *VIII. Armeekorps*. It later withdrew and eventually became involved in heavy fighting around Daugavpils, taking heavy losses. The regiment was organised as follows:

- *I. Bataillon (Lettische Schutzmannschaft-Bataillon 277. Sigulda)* Lieutenant-Colonel Taube
- *II. Bataillon (Lettische Schutzmannschaft-Bataillon 278 Dobele)* Lieutenant-Colonel Kleinberg
- *III. Bataillon (Lettische Schutzmannschaft-Bataillon 281 Abrene, a.k.a. Lettische Polizei-Front-Bataillon 312)* Captain Michaelson
- *IV. Bataillon (Lettische Schutzmannschaft-Bataillon 276 Kuldīga)* Lieutenant-Colonel Birzulis

Latvian Police Units Formed on 7 February 1944

Lettische Polizeiregiment 2 Liepāja

This unit was involved in heavy fighting around Daugavpils, taking heavy losses. Commander: Lieutenant-Colonel Jānis Grosbergs. Towards the end of the month, the German command ordered that the entire regiment (3,000 men) was to proceed to the Latvian-Belarusian frontier region, between Drisa and Polotsk. There the regiment was not only ordered to perform security duties, but the Germans wanted to use the regiment in constructing defence works, such as building bunkers, strongpoints, digging a network of trenches, etc. The regiment was created using the following Latvian battalions:

- *I. Bataillon (Lettische Polizei-Front-Bataillon 22)* Lieutenant-Colonel Kārlis Gerbers
- *II. Bataillon (Lettische Polizeibataillon 25)* Lieutenant Colonel Kārlis Plikausis
- *III. Bataillon (Lettische Polizei-Front-Bataillon 313)* Captain Voldemārs Gravelis
- *IV. Bataillon (Lettische Schutzmannschaft-Bataillon 316)* Captain Ansis Voldemārs Eglītis.

Lettische Polizeiregiment 3 Cēsis

The regiment began its operational history fighting partisan forces. From 6–9 April the regiment engaged a partisan 'battalion' of around 150 men in the Osvejas district. The regiment was able to disperse this partisan force. Two days later the unit left for Vetrino. The regiment travelled by train through Polotsk before reaching its final destination. Once the unit arrived at Vetrino, the regiment was assigned to *Kampfgruppe Jeckeln*. Under this command, it took part in *Unternehmen Frühlingsfest,* fighting south of Vetrino. After the operation was concluded, the regiment was sent to Sebezh, where a large partisan force threatened the rear of *16. Armee* forces fighting in the region.

On 26 June 1944 the Germans were forced to commit the Latvian police regiment to front-line fighting. The unit, which had no anti-tank guns, was thrown in front of advancing Red Army tank forces, with predictable results. The regiment was involved in heavy fighting around Daugavpils, where it took heavy losses. The regiment was officially withdrawn from fighting on 24 July. A month later the unit was officially disbanded. At that time the regiment contained seventeen officers, 149 non-commissioned officers and 528 enlisted men. These were transferred over to *Lettische Polizeiregiment 1 Riga. Lettische Polizeiregiment 3 Cēsis* had been created using the following three Latvian *Schutzmannschaft* battalions:

I. Bataillon (Lettische Schutzmannschaft-Bataillon 317)
II. Bataillon (Lettische Schutzmannschaft-Bataillon 318)
III. Bataillon (Lettische Schutzmannschaft-Bataillon 321)

Police battalions formed on 2 October 1944

Lettische Polizei Bataillon z. b. V. 1 Meiers.

This battalion had been established in June 1944 in order to employ Latvian military disciplinary cases. The battalion was established in Bolderāja. Command of the battalion was given to Captain Jānis Meiers. In peacetime, Meiers had been a lawyer. Meiers had been chosen to lead the unit partly out of the fact that he had legal experience and that would serve him well, given that the battalion was a penal formation. The Ia (adjutant) in the battalion was Captain Arnold Kisis. By 1 July the battalion contained nineteen officers (many who, like the commander, were lawyers), seventy non-commissioned officers and 259 enlisted personnel. The convicts came from Latvian police, border guard, SD and *Schutzmannschaft* units. The crimes committed varied widely. Some were Latvian communists or draft-dodgers from the Salaspils concentration camp.

Others were soldiers accused of theft, Black Market activities, assaulting a superior officer, cowardice, desertion and even murder. In order to easily identify the men as belonging to this penal battalion, its members were forced to wear a red triangle on their field blouse.

The battalion contained three rifle companies. The German Field Post Number assigned to the battalion was 66668. Training was brief, lasting only until the end of July. The battalion's first engagement was in the defence of the Latvian capital of Riga. As a result, the formation took heavy casualties. Krukenberg was so impressed by the fact that the battalion never had a deserter and by the performance of the battalion in the defence of Riga, that he pardoned all of the surviving members of this penal battalion. In August 1944, the remnants of *Lettische Polizei Bataillon z. b. V. 1 Meiers* became a part of *Kampfgruppe Krukenberg* when the battalion was absorbed into *Lettische Grenzschutzregiment 5*. When the battalion was absorbed into this border guard regiment, Captain Arnold Kisis assumed command of the remnants of the battalion.

Lettische Polizei Bataillon z. b. V. 2

Unfortunately, no information has been forthcoming regarding this formation. It supposedly ceased to exist in October 1944, but aside from that, it is not known when the unit was created and who commanded it.

Appendix IV

ESTONIAN VOLUNTEER FORMATIONS, 1941–1945

During the Second World War, Estonia, like many other countries, found itself in a complex and turbulent situation. Here's an overview of Estonian involvement during that time.

One of the notable instances of Estonian involvement was through the Estonian Legion, which was part of the *Waffen-SS,* the combat branch of the SS. The Estonian SS Legion was formed in 1942, primarily composed of Estonian volunteers who were motivated by various factors, including opposition to the Soviet occupation of Estonia, a desire to fight against communism, and promises of Estonian independence by the Germans. It's important to note that not all Estonian Legion members were necessarily ardent supporters of Nazi ideology; many joined for pragmatic reasons related to Estonia's geopolitical situation. *20. Waffen-Grenadier-Division der-SS (estnische Nr. 1)* was the official designation of the Estonian Legion, and it participated in several battles on the Eastern Front alongside German forces.

On the other hand, there were also Estonians who resisted both Nazi and Soviet occupations. Partisans known as the Forest Brothers waged guerrilla warfare against both occupying forces, seeking to restore Estonian independence. These resistance fighters operated mainly in the forests and rural areas of Estonia and continued their struggle well into the post-war period. Additionally, there were Estonians who fought on the side of the Soviet Union as part of the Red Army.

These individuals were often conscripted or forcibly mobilised into Soviet service. Some Estonians also served in Soviet partisan units operating behind German lines. After the war, Estonia fell under Soviet occupation once again, and those who had fought alongside the Germans, including members of the Estonian Legion, faced persecution and repression from Soviet authorities. Many Estonians who had fought with the Germans fled to Western countries or joined the Forest Brothers in continuing resistance against Soviet rule. The involvement of Estonian volunteers during the Second World War is a complex and multifaceted aspect of Estonian history, shaped by geopolitical circumstances, ideologies, and the desire for national independence. It is important to approach this topic with nuance and an understanding of the various factors that influenced individual choices and actions during that turbulent period.

During the Second World War, numerous Estonian battalions were formed to serve alongside German forces, initially within the framework of the *Wehrmacht* and later the *Waffen-SS*. Here are some of the notable pro-German Estonian battalions: *20. Waffen-Grenadier-Division der-SS (estnische Nr. 1)*. From October 1942 to May 1943, the unit was called the Estonian SS Legion. On 5 May 1943 it was renamed as the *3. SS-Freiwilligen-Brigade (estnische)* – 3rd Estonian SS Volunteer Brigade. The unit was declared a division on 24 January 1944. The division was the most significant formation composed of Estonian volunteers who served under the *Waffen-SS*. It was formed in 1942 and saw action on the Eastern Front. The division participated in battles such as the Battle of Narva and the Battle of the Tannenberg Line. The 3rd Estonian SS Volunteer Brigade was formed on 5 May 1943 from Estonian units already serving within the German Army. It was involved in battles against Soviet forces during the later stages of the war, including the battles around the Estonian city of Tartu. Just like the *(estnische) SS-Freiwilligen-Brigade*, which was later numbered *3. SS-Freiwilligen-Brigade (estnische)*, the *4. SS-Freiwilligen-Brigade (estnische)* was also established, but in 1944. The organisation of *3. SS-Freiwilligen-Brigade (estnische)* in July 1943 looked like this:

SS-Freiwilligen-Grenadier-Regiment 1 (estnische)
SS-Freiwilligen-Grenadier-Regiment 2 (estnische)
SS-Panzerjäger-Abteilung (estnische)
SS-Artillerie-Abteilung (estnische)
SS-Flak-Abteilung (estnische)
SS-Nachrichten-Kompanie (estnische)
SS-Feldersatz-Bataillon (estnische)

It participated in operations against Soviet forces in Estonia. The Estonian police battalions were auxiliary police units created by the German occupation authorities in Estonia. While not directly part of the *Waffen-SS*, they collaborated closely with German forces in various operations. Estonian police battalions were involved in anti-partisan actions and security duties in occupied territories. These pro-German Estonian units were part of the broader collaboration between Nazi Germany and various national groups in occupied territories during the Second World War. The motivations for Estonians to join these units were complex and varied, including opposition to Soviet occupation, promises of Estonian independence, and ideological factors. However, it's important to note that not all Estonians supported these collaborations, and many remained neutral or actively resisted both German and Soviet occupations.

Estonian, Latvian and Lithuanian volunteers were recruited into the *Wehrmacht* by the commands of both the *16. Armee* and *18. Armee,* as well as *Heeresgruppe Nord.* In accordance with an agreement concluded between *Reichsführer-SS* Heinrich Himmler and the *Oberkommando des Heeres* (OKH –High Command of the Army), the recruiting of volunteers in the rear of the German army groups in the East was in the confines of the SS and the police system. Until the summer of 1942, units no bigger than a battalion could be formed from these Eastern volunteers. The *Wehrmacht* was the first to start recruiting. From August 1941 to January 1942, six battalion-sized units, named and numbered: *(estnische) Sicherungs-Bataillone 181, 182, 183, 184, 185,* and *186* were created in Estonia from around 4,000 Estonian volunteers. These battalions operated in the rear of the German *18. Armee,* but sometimes also ended up on the front lines, depending on necessity. These Estonian security battalions were reorganised in the autumn of 1942. Given field losses because of combat, including men who had signed on for one year and had not renewed their service contract, plus men who left the security battalions to serve in the Estonian SS Legion, there were only enough men to create three Estonian Eastern battalions: *(estnische) Ost Bataillone 658, 659* and *660.* These battalions fought in the rear of the *18. Armee,* until the beginning of 1944. Thereafter, the remaining men in these three battalions were sent to the forming *20. Waffen-Grenadier-Division der-SS (estnische Nr. 1).*

Beginning in September 1941, the *Höhere SS- und Polizeiführer Estland* command began recruiting Estonian men. To increase the number of volunteers, around 4,000 Estonian POWs – men who had defected from the Russian Army and were being held in prisoner of war camps, were offered the chance to be freed on the condition that they volunteer for service in the *Wehrmacht.* Many of these men initially joined the *Schutzmannschaft* battalions, but later ended up serving in the *Waffen-SS.* Recruits also came from southern and central Estonia. Eventually four so-called 'self-defence' battalions were created: *(estnische) Schutzmannschaft-Bataillone 37, 38, 39,* and *40,* as well as *(estnische) Schutzmannschaft-Reserve-Bataillon 41* and *Schutzmannschaft-Pionier-Bataillon 42*. In 1943 the battalions numbered '37', '38', and '40' were eventually retitled as *(estnische) Polizei Bataillon 37, (estnische) Polizeibataillon 38,* and *(estnische) Polizeibataillon 40.* That same year *Schutzmannschaft-Bataillone 39* was renamed *Schutzmannschaft Polizei-Wacht-Bataillon 39.* For administrative purposes, these battalions were under the German Order Police system. Nevertheless, they served under the control of the German security divisions behind the lines of Army Group North. In 1942 these six Estonian battalions amounted to some 3,000 men. In the spring of 1943 *(estnische) Schutzmannschaft-Polizei-Wacht-Bataillone 39* was disbanded due to heavy losses. The other battalions (minus *(estnische) Schutzmannschaft Pionier Bataillon 42)* were eventually sent to Germany in 1944, where they were used to flesh out the *20. Waffen-Grenadier-Division der-SS (estnische Nr. 1).*

In the autumn of 1941, the Germans recruited additional Estonian volunteers to help create nine more battalions. These were named and numbered as *(estnische) Polizei-Füsilier-Bataillone 29, 30, 31, 32, 33,* and *34.* The 36th Battalion was referred to as *(estnische) Schutzmannschaft-Front-Bataillon 36,* while the 35th Battalion was titled *(estnische) Polizei-Ersatz-Bataillon 35,* and used as the replacement battalion for the other police units. Initially, all of these new battalions were employed in all manner of security and coastal watch duties. The 30th through the 32nd Battalions never completed training, given that there were insufficient men to man them. As a result, these three battalions only had the strength of a reinforced company each. When conditions at the front worsened, *(estnische) Polizei-Füsilier-Bataillone 29, 30, 31, 32,* and *33* were sent into combat in the Leningrad front.

Schutzmannschaft-Front-Bataillon 36, which began active service with 23 officers, 161 non-commissioned officers, and 254 enlisted men, was initially sent to Belarus, where it took part in anti-partisan operations. Next it was sent to eastern Ukraine, where it guarded POW camps in the Stalino and Makeyevka coal mines. The disaster at Stalingrad forced the battalion's employment at the front from 22 November to 31 December 1942. During that time the battalion suffered thirty-nine killed, ninety-seven wounded, and eleven missing. the unit was returned to Estonia in January 1943 and dissolved, with numerous soldiers from the now-defunct battalion enlisting in the Estonian SS Legion. *(estnische) Polizei-Füsilier-Bataillon 29, (estnische) Polizei-Füsilier-Bataillon 33, and Schutzmannschaft-Front-Bataillon 36* were disbanded in 1943. *(estnische) Polizei-Ersatz-Bataillon 35* remained in the Baltic States until September 1944 when it was evacuated to Germany. The *(estnische) Polizei-Füsilier-Bataillon 34* was under the control of the paramilitary construction service, the *Organisation Todt*. It is not known how many men served in these battalions but the figure has to be in the several thousands.

On 28 August 1942, the Estonian *Waffen-SS* Legion was established as a voluntary unit. The formation and training of the new unit took place *SS-Truppenubungslager Debica* (SS Military Training Camp Debica), located near Krakow, Poland. At the beginning of 1943, there was an initial batch of 1,000 Estonian volunteers which would form the core of the new unit. Most of them had been transferred from the Estonian security battalions or the *Schutzmannschaft* battalions. Around 800 men were used to form the first motorised battalion of the *Waffen-SS* which was named 'Narva'. This Estonian *Waffen-SS* battalion was deployed to Ukraine in the spring of 1943. The Estonian self-defence force (*Omakaitse*), a nationalist militia that was created spontaneously in the summer of 1941, was disbanded by the Germans after the Soviets had been driven out of Estonia.

But the Germans soon reestablished it, giving it the status of an auxiliary police force. This paramilitary organisation contained more than 40,000 members, including around 4,000 officers and senior NCOs. In the autumn of 1942, the *Omakaitse* fell under the jurisdiction of the *Wehrmacht*, while full-time volunteers were reorganised into security and defence battalions under the control of the *SS- und Polizeiführer Estland* (*SS-Brigadeführer und Generalmajor der Polizei* Hinrich Möller). Five such battalions were established, and were given the ancillary numbers 29 to 33. They thus became *(estnische) Polizei-Füsilier-Bataillon 29*, *(estnische) Polizei-Füsilier-Bataillon 30*, *(estnische) Polizei-Füsilier-Bataillon 31*, *(estnische) Polizei-Füsilier-Bataillon 32*, and *(estnische) Polizei-Füsilier-Bataillon 33*. In April of 1943 there were more than 2,600 men in these new units. In the spring of 1943, an additional five battalions had been created: *(estnische) Polizei-Füsilier-Bataillon 286*, *(estnische) Polizei-Wacht-Bataillon 287*, *(estnische) Polizei-Füsilier-Bataillon 288*, *(estnische) Polizei-Füsilier-Bataillon 289*, and *(estnische) Polizei-Füsilier-Bataillon 290*.

The *(estnische) Polizei-Füsilier-Bataillon 286* was organised from regular Estonian police officers who were to have served for a period of only four months, but whose term of service was later extended to six months. The *(estnische) Polizei-Wacht-Bataillon 287* consisted mostly of men who from 1942 to 1943 had defected to the German side near Velikije Luki, from the Red Army's Estonian Rifle Corps. This battalion was employed as guards for German prisoner of war camps. The *(estnische) Polizei-Füsilier-Bataillon 288*, and *(estnische) Polizei-Füsilier-Bataillon 289* consisted of men from several reserve battalions. The *(estnische) Polizei-Füsilier-Bataillon 290* was made up of ethnic-Russians who had been living in Estonia. The *(estnische) Polizei-Füsilier-Bataillon 286, (estnische) Polizei-Füsilier-Bataillon 288,* and *(estnische) Polizei-Füsilier-Bataillon 289* were all earmarked for anti-partisan operations in Belarus. These battalions were sent there in the autumn of 1943. At the beginning of 1944, they returned to Estonia and disbanded. The *(estnische) Polizei-Wacht-Bataillon 287* was sent to Germany in September 1944 where it was used to replenish the *20. Waffen-Grenadier-Division der-SS (estnische Nr. 1).*

Given that by the end of 1942 the number of Estonians who were willing to serve in the German armed forces had dwindled to a trickle, the decision was made by the German command to institute a draft. This occurred in February 1943. It targeted Estonian men from the 1919–24 classes. They were, however, given the choice between serving in a combat unit or working in Germany. Those who opted for combat could join either as a *'Hilfswilliger'* (the word literally translates to 'willing to help', but in this context, it means 'volunteer') in the *Wehrmacht* or in the Estonian *Waffen-SS* Legion. Through this draft, some 5,000 men were drafted into the Estonian SS Legion. The Estonian SS Legion was reorganised as follows: *3. (estnische) SS-Freiwilligen-Brigade,* with *45. SS-Freiwilligen-Grenadier-Regiment* and *46. SS-Freiwilligen-Grenadier-Regiment.* In June 1944 the title of the regiments was changed to: *45. Waffen-Grenadier-Regiment der-SS* and *46. Waffen-Grenadier-Regiment der-SS.* Each of these two regiments contained two infantry battalions. The *I. Bataillon* contained *1.-4. Kompanie,* while the *II. Bataillon* contained *5.-8. Kompanie.* Finally, each regiment also had a *13. Kompanie* (infantry guns) and *14. Kompanie* (anti-tank guns). When the brigade was later expanded to division size, these regiments received a third battalion. The *3. (estnische) SS-Freiwilligen-Brigade* completed its organisation with an artillery battalion, an engineer battalion and a flak battalion. In early October 1943, the brigade was sent to Belarus to take part in anti-partisan operations, but given the emergency at the front, it was soon diverted to the front lines around Nevel.

In October 1943, some 3,300 Estonians from the 1925 class were called up and sent to Debica, Poland for induction into the *Waffen-SS.* In January 1944 it was the turn of the 1924 class. In January 1944 the Soviets had broken through along the Leningrad front, thus threatening Estonia directly. As a result, on 30 January 1944 another conscription of Estonian males between the ages of 21 and 40 was implemented (basically the 1904–23 classes). Estonia's prime minister at the time, Jüri Uluots, gave a radio speech to the nation where he supported the call up given the threat that the Red Army was on the verge of entering

Estonian territory. By April 1944, 38,000 men had been inducted based on this latest call-up. In August 1944, around 2,600 Estonian youth born in 1926, were also drafted. On 24 January 1944, the *3. (estnische) SS-Freiwillige-Brigade* was renamed the *20. Waffen-Grenadier-Division der-SS (estnische Nr. 1)*. The newly-designated division took until the summer of 1944 to reach division level (about 15,000 men). The remaining 23,000 men were used to establish six border guard regiments and four police fusilier battalions: *(estnische) Polizei-Füsilier-Bataillone 286, 288, 291,* and *292*. These police fusilier battalions were used initially on coastal guard duty. The following is a complete list of the battalions formed during the war:

(estnische) Polizei-Füsilier-Bataillon 29
(estnische) Polizei-Füsilier-Bataillon 30
(estnische) Polizei-Füsilier-Bataillon 31
(estnische) Polizei-Füsilier-Bataillon 32
(estnische) Polizei-Füsilier-Bataillon 29
(estnische) Polizei-Füsilier-Bataillon 33
(estnische) Polizei-Füsilier-Bataillon 34
(estnische) Polizei-Ersatz-Bataillon 35
(estnische) Schutzmannschaft-Frontbatallion 36
(estnische) Polizei-Bataillon 37 (commander: *Major* Martin-Friedrich Bergman)
(estnische) Polizei-Bataillon 38
(estnische) Schutzmannschaft-Polizei-Wacht-Bataillon 39
(estnische) Polizei-Bataillon 40
(estnische) Selbstschutz-Reserve-Bataillon 41
(estnische) Schutzmannschaft-Pionier-Bataillon 42
(estnische) Polizei-Füsilier-Bataillon 286
(estnische) Polizei-Wacht-Bataillon 287
(estnische) Polizei-Füsilier-Bataillon 288
(estnische) Polizei-Füsilier-Bataillon 289
(estnische) Polizei-Füsilier-Bataillon 290
(estnische) Polizei-Füsilier-Bataillon 291
(estnische) Polizei-Füsilier-Bataillon 292
(estnische) Polizei-Füsilier-Bataillon 293
(estnische) Polizei-Füsilier-Bataillon 521
(estnische) Grenzschutz-Regiment 1 [1]
(estnische) Grenzschutz-Regiment 2
(estnische) Grenzschutz-Regiment 3
(estnische) Grenzschutz-Regiment 4
(estnische) Grenzschutz-Regiment 5
(estnische) Grenzschutz-Regiment 6

Major formations:
(estnische) 3. SS Freiwilligen Brigade
(estnische) 4. SS Freiwilligen Brigade
20. Waffen-Grenadier-Division der-SS (estnische Nr. 1)

Evolution of an Estonian SS formation:
(estnische) SS Legion
(estnische) SS-Freiwilligen-Brigade
3. (estnische) SS-Freiwilligen-Brigade
20. Waffen-Grenadier-Division der-SS (estnische Nr. 1)

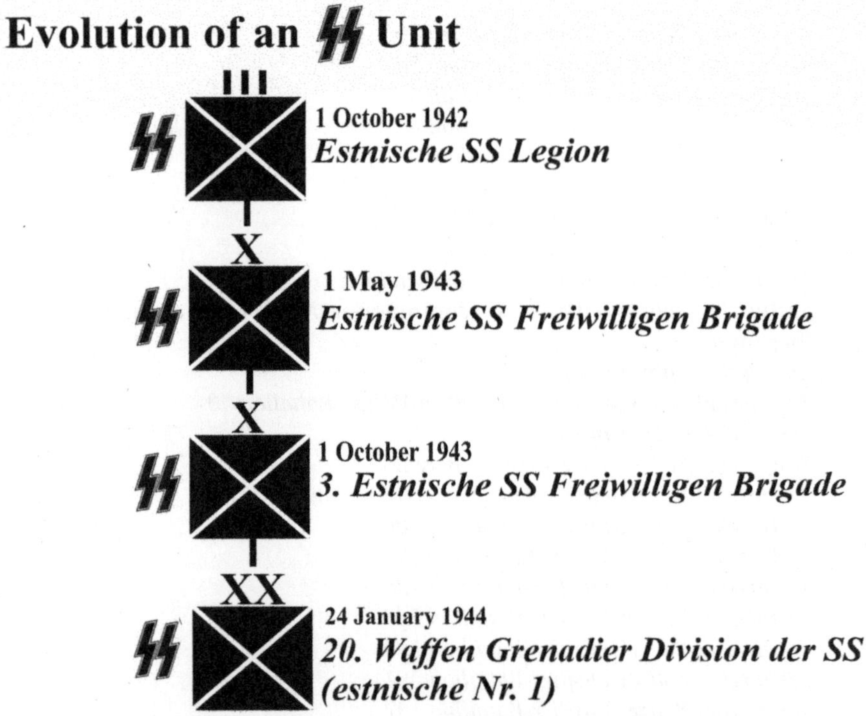

Figure 27. The illustration above depicts the evolution of an Estonian SS regiment to division level.

Appendix V

CAUCASIAN VOLUNTEERS, OCTOBER 1944

Table 25. Caucasian Volunteers, October 1944

In Legion and Field Battalions		
Armenians	11,000	
Azerbaijani	13,600	
Georgian	14,000	
North Caucasian	10,000	
		48,600
Construction and Supply Units		
Armenians	7,000	
Azerbaijani	4,795	
Georgian	6,800	
North Caucasian	3,000	
		21,595
In German Units as *Hiwis*		
	25,000	25,000
In the *Waffen-SS* & *Luftwaffe*		
	7,000	7,000
	Grand Total	**102,195**

NOTES

Introduction

1 Bundesarchiv, N 756/183a, *22. SS-Freiwilligen-Kavalleriedivision 'Maria Theresa' – Fernschreiben, Geheime Kommandosachen, Aktennotiz, Lageplanskizzen.*

Chapter 2: Recruitment of Ethnic Germans in the Newly-Annexed Territories

1 The *Abwehr* was the military intelligence service of the *Wehrmacht* during the Nazi era, operating from 1921 until 1944. Its name literally means 'defence' or 'repulsion', reflecting its original role as a counterintelligence agency.

2 Robert S. Wistrich, *Wer war im Dritten Reich? Ein biographisches Lexikon* (Frankfurt am Main: Fischer Taschenbuch Verlag, 1992), p. 252.

3 Hans Werner Neulen, *An deutscher Seite: Internationale Freiwillige von Wehrmacht und Waffen-SS* (München: Universitas Verlag, 1985), p. 205.

4 Ibid.

5 Franz W. Seidler, *Die Kollaboration 1939-1945* (München: F. A. Herbig, 1995), p. 387.

6 The *68. Infanterie-Division* also contained a sizable number of ethnic Germans from the *Warthegau* region.

7 Rudolf Aschenauer, *Krieg Ohne Grenzen: Der Partisanenkampf gegen Deutschland 1939-1945* (Leoni am Starnberger: Druffel Verlag, 1982), p. 164.

8 Wolfgang Schumann and Ludwig Nestler, eds., *Die faschistische Okkupationspolitik in Polen 1939–1945,* vol. 2 of *Europa unterm Hakenkreuz: Die Okkupationspolitik des deutschen Faschismus 1938–1945* (Berlin [DDR]: Deutscher Verlag der Wissenschaften, 1978), p. 163.

9 The *Selbstschutz* were ethnic-German Poles who supported the German invasion of Poland.

10 Schumann and Nestler, *Die faschistische Okkupationspolitik in Polen 1939–1945,* vol. 2, p. 193.

11 During the first half of the Polish occupation (1939–42), approximately 630,000 people were expelled from the annexed territories.

12 Tadeusz Piotrowski, *Poland's Holocaust: Ethnic Strife, Collaboration with Occupying Forces and Genocide in the Second Republic, 1918-1947* (Jefferson: McFarland and Company Inc., 1998), p. 23.

13 Robert L. Koehl, 'The Deutsche Volksliste in Poland 1939–1945', *Journal of Central European Affairs* 15 (1955), pp. 354–66.

14 Norbert Spannenberger, 'Chapter 3. The Ethnic Policy of the Third Reich Toward the Volksdeutsche in Central and Eastern Europe', in *Territorial Revisionism and the Allies of Germany in the Second World War: Goals, Expectations, Practices*, ed. Marina Cattaruzza, Stefan Dyroff, and Dieter Langewiesche (New York: Berghahn Books, 2015), pp. 56–71,

15 Doris L. Bergen, 'The Nazi Concept of "Volksdeutsche" and the Exacerbation of Anti-Semitism in Eastern Europe, 1939-45', *Journal of Contemporary History* 29, no. 4 (October 1994), pp. 569–82.

16 All numbers are estimates based on German recruitment efforts, military archives, and post-war demographic studies. The figures include both conscripts and volunteers unless stated otherwise.

17 John J. Kulczycki, *Belonging to the Nation* (Cambridge, MA: Harvard University Press, 2016), estimate of 295,000 (low) to 500,000 (high) *Volksdeutsche* serving in the *Wehrmacht / Waffen-SS*.

18 Wilhelm Deist et al., eds, *Germany and the Second World War*, vol. 10 (Oxford: Oxford University Press, 2003), 'Deutsche Volksliste', early-1944 category figures for Warthegau, Danzig-West Prussia, East Upper Silesia,

19 The *606. Infanterie-Division* was formed on 11 April 1945 by simply renaming the *Division z.b.V. 606* under the framework of the *541. Volksgrenadier Division.*

20 Bundesarchiv, Barch. RH 7A / 1119, RH 7 / 2240, *606. Infanterie-Division (z.b.V.).*

21 NARA RG-238 *Arbeitsbesprechung am 23. April 1940, Diensttagebuch des Generalgouverneurs Hans Frank, Bd. 9*, pp. 40–1.

22 Krüger to Gunst, 14 November 1939, W. Gunst SS Officer file (former BDC), RGp-242, A3343 / SSO / 043A / 321, NARA; judgment in proceedings against Friedrich Paulus, May 26, 1977, p. 6, file 4 Ks 1 / 74, State Prosecutor's Office in Frankfurt am Main.

23 *Ortskommandantur I/524* to *Amt I*, Memorandum on the Conversation with Police Commanders at Army Headquarters XXXII on 8 December 1939 and 10 December 1939, file *Ortskommandantur I/524*, sygn. 31, pp. 378–9, WAPL; Globocnik to Chief, District Lublin, 13 February 1940, file *Gouverneur, Distrikt Lublin*, sygn. 891, p. 10, WAPL, and NARA RG-242 A3343 / SSO, 0156B / 242-243, formerly the Berlin Document Center – now under the administration of the *Bundesarchiv*, Berlin. Documents of the

Labor Office, Biała-Podlaska to Labor Department, Lublin, 18 July 1940, file Gouverneur, District Lublin, sygn. 746, pp. 41–3, WAPL.

24 David Littlejohn, *Foreign Legions of the Third Reich, Volume 4 – Poland, The Ukraine, Bulgaria, Romania, Free India, Estonia, Latvia, Lithuania, Finland and Russia* (San Jose: R. James Bender, 1987), p. 19.

25 Steen Bille, *The German Minority in Denmark: Ethnicity and Identity Politics in Northern Schleswig, 1920–1950* (Aarhus: Aarhus University Press, 2005), p. 112.

26 Ronald Tarnstrom, *French Arms* (Lindsborg, KS: Trogen Books, 2001), p. 824.

27 Paul Dostert, 'Die Luxemburger im Reserve-Polizeibataillon 101 und der Judenmord in Polen', *Hémecht: Journal d'histoire luxembourgeoise*, no. 4 (2000), p. 10.

28 Antonio J. Munoz, *Hitler's Green Army: The German Order Police and Their European Auxiliaries, 1933–1945, Volume 1: Western Europe and Scandinavia* (New York: Europa Books, 2000), p. 91.

29 Jean Krier, 'Luxembourg Volksdeutsche and Military Conscription', *Journal of Modern European History* 12, no. 3 (2014), pp. 301–20.

30 Joachim Lund, *Luxembourg and the German Occupation 1940–1945* (New York: Praeger, 1984), pp. 45–78.

31 Later the title of this *Waffen-SS* unit changed to *5. SS-Freiwilligen-Sturmbrigade 'Wallonien'*. The final title change occurred when the brigade was expanded to division level in October 1944 and named *28. SS-Freiwilligen-Grenadier-Division 'Wallonien'*. This is how Luxembourgers ended up serving in the Belgian-Walloon SS division *'Wallonien'*.

Chapter 3: Germanic Volunteers and the Crusade Against Bolshevism

1 David Littlejohn, *Foreign Legions of the Third Reich, Volume 1 – Norway, Denmark, France* (San Jose: Roger James Bender Publishing, 1979), p. 61.

2 Ibid., pp. 50–1.

3 Franz W. Seidler, *Die Kollaboration, 1939–1945: Zeitgeschichtliche Dokumentation in Biographien* (Grabert Verlag, 1995), p. 331.

4 Carlos Caballero Jurado and Paul Hannon, *Resistance Warfare 1940–45*, Osprey Men-at-Arms Series No. 169 (London: Osprey Publishing, 1985), p. 8.

5 Littlejohn, *Foreign Legions of the Third Reich, Volume 1*, p. 60.

6 Bo Lidegaard (ed.), *Dansk Udenrigspolitiks historie*, vol. 4 (Copenhagen: Danmarks Nationalleksikon, 2003), pp. 462–3.

7 Lars Larsen and Jens Pank Bjerregaard, *Danish Volunteers of the Waffen-SS: Freikorps Danmark 1941-43* (Barnsley: Pen & Sword Military, 2018), p. 125.

8 Ibid., p. 137.

9 NARA T-175, Roll 108, 111, 120. *Akten des 11. SS-Pz.Gre.Div. Nordland, 1943-1944.*

10 Claus Bundgård Christensen, Niels Bo Poulsen, and Peter Scharff Smith, *Under Hagekors og Dannebrog: Danskere i Waffen SS 1940–45* (Copenhagen: Aschehoug, 1998), pp. 212–13.

11 NARA T-312 Rolls 1624-1637. *Akten des Armee-Abteilung Narwa, 1944.*

12 Tony Le Tissier, *Race for the Reichstag: The 1945 Battle for Berlin* (London: Routledge, 1999), pp. 181–2.

13 Christensen, Poulsen, and Smith, *Under Hagekors og Dannebrog*, p. 49.

14 In 1864 this province had been taken by a combined German and Austrian force, and forced Denmark to cede that southern Danish region. In 1920 the region had voted to become a part of Denmark by a 4 to1 majority.

15 Samuel W. Mitcham, *The German Defeat in the East, 1944–45* (Westport, CT: Praeger, 2001), pp. 42–3.

16 Rebecca W. Wennberg, *Ideological Incorrectness beyond 'Political Religion': Discourse on Nazi Ideology among Scandinavian National Socialist Intellectuals, 1933–1945* (PhD diss., Royal Holloway, University of London, 2016), pp. 105–06.

Chapter 4: Western European Volunteers and the Crusade Against Bolshevism: France and Spain

1 For a comprehensive history of the German occupation of France, please see *Hitler's War Against the French Resistance*, 1940-1945 (Frontline Books).

2 Krisztián Bene, *La collaboration militaire française dans la Seconde Guerre mondiale* (Éditions Codex, 2010), p. 52.

3 David Littlejohn, *The French Foreign Legion in the Second World War* (London: Macmillan, 1972), pp. 78–80.

4 Owen Anthony Davey, 'The Origins of the Légion des Volontaires Français contre le Bolchevisme', *Journal of Contemporary History* 6, no. 4 (1971), p. 31.

5 Rolf-Dieter Müller, *The French Volunteers of the Waffen-SS*, trans. David Johnston (London: Greenhill Books, 2014), p. 45.

6 Ibid., pp. 46–8.

7 Bene, *La collaboration militaire française dans la Seconde Guerre mondiale*, p. 63.

8 NA T-315/1685, file 36509/11. *Sicherungs Regiment 36 Ia, 26.12.42. Betr.: Unternehmen Ankara. Gefechtsbericht, 19.-24.12.42, 1; ibid, 25.1.43. Betr.: Unternehmen Ankara II. Gefechtsbericht, 17.-21.1.43.*

9 According to Tessin, *Sicherungs Regiment 36* belonged to *286. Sicherungs Division* until it was transferred to *221. Sicherungs Division* in February 1943, or a month after the *Ankara I* operation.

10 Withdrawn from the regiment in May 1944.

11 Existed from September 1943 to March 1944.

12 Becoming the regiment's *I Battalion, II Battalion,* and *III Battalion* respectively.

13 Ben Sheppard. *German Army Security Units in Russia, 1941-1943: A Case Study.* A thesis submitted to the Faculty of Social Science and Commerce of The University of Birmingham for the degree of Doctor of Philosophy, Institute for German Studies Faculty of Social Science and Commerce: The University of Birmingham, June 2000, p. 167.

14 Ibid.

15 J. G. Shields, *Charlemagne's Crusaders: French Collaboration in Arms, 1941-1945* (French Cultural Studies, 2007), pp. 92–5.

16 Littlejohn, *The French Foreign Legion in the Second World War,* pp. 84–5.

17 Müller, *The French Volunteers of the Waffen-SS,* p. 49.

18 Shields, *Charlemagne's Crusaders,* pp. 112–14.

19 Davey, 'The Origins of the Légion des Volontaires Français contre le Bolchevisme', pp. 44–5.

20 Rolf Michaelis, *French Units in the Waffen-SS* (Atglen, PA: Schiffer Publishing, 2025), pp. 7–9

21 The *SS-Junkerschule* (literally 'SS Officer Cadet School') was the *Waffen-SS*'s specialised academy for training future commissioned officers – the SS equivalent of a military officer school like the German Army's *Kriegsschule* or West Point for the United States Army. It was created because Himmler wanted the SS to have its own self-contained system for producing leaders, independent of the regular German Army. While the *Wehrmacht* emphasised conventional military science, the *SS-Junkerschule* combined this with intense ideological indoctrination in National Socialism, racial doctrine, and loyalty to Hitler.

22 Jean Mabire, *La Brigade Frankreich: Le premier combat des SS français* (Paris: Grancher, 2005), pp. 88–93.

23 Michaelis, *French Units in the Waffen-SS,* pp. 42–5.

24 Tony Le Tissier, *SS Charlemagne: The 33rd Waffen-Grenadier Division of the SS* (Barnsley, UK: Pen & Sword Military, 2010), pp. 117–21.

25 In June 1942, Joseph Darnand was petitioning the Germans to allow the SOL to operate in occupied France.

26 Littlejohn, *Foreign Legions of the Third Reich Volume 1,* p. 174.

27 Philippe Burrin, *France Under the Germans: Collaboration and Compromise* (New York: The New Press, 1996), p. 441.

28 Yann Stephan, *A Broken Sword: Policing France During the German Occupation* (Ann Arbor, MI: University of Michigan, Office of International Criminal Justice, 1991), p. 37

29 Burrin, *France Under the Germans*, p. 443.

30 Littlejohn, *Foreign Legions of the Third Reich Volume 1*, p. 176.

31 Ibid, pp. 177–8.

32 Ibid.,p. 277.

33 Ian Ousby, *Occupation: The Ordeal of France 1940-1944* (London: John Murray, 1997), p. 304.

34 Jean-Pierre Sourd, *True Believers: Spanish Volunteers in the Heer and Waffen-SS, 1944–1945* (New York: Europa Books, 2004), p. 50.

35 Stephan, *A Broken Sword*, p. 84.

36 Serge Jacquemard, *La bande Bonny-Lafont* (Paris: Fleuve Noir, 1992), pp. 55–62.

37 Jean-Pierre Sourd Donnat, 'The French "Selbstschutzpolizei", 1943–1944', *Axis Europa Magazine*, no. 15 (Fall 1998): 3.

38 The province had been ceded by France after the Franco-Prussian War of 1870.

39 Jean-Pierre Sourd, *True Believers*, p. 46.

40 Bundesarchiv Freiburg, RH 26-1002, Verband 803: Regiment 3 Brandenburg, Panzergrenadier-Division 'Brandenburg', 1944-1945.

41 With these identity cards the French government could hopefully track down the members of the *Selbstschutzpolizei.*

42 Stephan, *A Broken Sword*, p. 37.

43 Von Gebsattel happened to be the cousin of *Oberst* Baron von Stauffenberg.

44 *SS-Dienstalterliste der Schutzstaffel der NSDAP: SS-Obergruppenführer bis SS-Standartenführer. Stand vom 1. Oktober 1944*, ed. SS-Personalhauptamt (Berlin: Reichsdruckerei, 1944), p. 29.

45 Pierre Philippe Lambert and Gérard Le Marec, *Vichy 1940–1944: Organisations, Mouvements et Unités de l'État Français* (Paris: Jacques Grancher, 1992), p. 210.

46 Christian de La Mazière, *The Captive Dreamer* (New York: Saturday Review Press, 1974), pp. 15–28.

47 Robert Forbes, *For Europe: The French Volunteers of the Waffen-SS* (Bayeux, France: Éditions Heimdal, 2006), pp. 45–8.

48 Jean Mabire, *Division Charlemagne* (Paris: Fayard, 1974), pp. 102–05.

49 Adrian Gilbert, *The Waffen-SS: A Handbook* (London: The History Press, 2019), pp. 241–4.

50 Forbes, *For Europe*, pp. 331–3.

51 Mabire, *Division Charlemagne*, pp. 152–4.

52 Perry Pierik, *From Leningrad to Berlin: Dutch Volunteers in the German Waffen-SS* (Bedford: Aberjona Press, 1998), pp. 198–200.

53 Gilbert, *The Waffen-SS*, p. 243.

54 David M. Glantz, *When Titans Clashed: How the Red Army Stopped Hitler* (Lawrence: University Press of Kansas, 1995), pp. 266–8.

55 Earl F. Ziemke, *Stalingrad to Berlin: The German Defeat in the East* (Washington, D.C.: U.S. Army Center of Military History, 1968), pp. 429–30.

56 Forbes, *For Europe*, pp. 340–2.

57 Glantz, *When Titans Clashed*, pp. 268–9.

58 Mabire, *Division Charlemagne*, pp. 198–202.

59 Gilbert, *The Waffen-SS*, p. 244.

60 Forbes, *For Europe*, p. 342.

61 Ibid., p. 343.

62 Mabire, *Division Charlemagne*, pp. 289–91.

63 Ibid., pp. 302–04.

64 Gilbert, *The Waffen-SS*, p. 245.

65 Forbes, *For Europe*, p. 344.

66 Pierik, *From Leningrad to Berlin*, pp. 200–02.

Chapter 5: Western European Volunteers and the Crusade Against Bolshevism: Belgium, and the Netherlands

1 Bruno De Wever, 'Military Collaboration in Belgium', in *Die Bürokratie der Okkupation: Strukturen der Herrschaft und Verwaltung im besetzten Europa*, ed. Wolfgang Benz, Johannes Houwink ten Cate, and Gerhard Otto (Berlin: Metropol Verlag, 1998), p. 153.

2 Kurt Mehner, *Die Waffen-SS und Polizei 1939–1945* (Norderstedt: Militär-Verlag Klaus D. Patzwall, 1995), p. 318.

3 Kurt Mehner, *Die Geheimen Tagesberichte der Deutschen Wehrmachtführung im Zweiten Weltkrieg 1939–1945*, vol. 6 (Osnabrück: Biblio Verlag, 1984–1990), p. 533.

4 Yvonne de Ridder Files, *Quest for Freedom: A Story of Belgian Resistance in World War II* (Santa Barbara: The Narrative Press, 2000), p. 22.

5 Ibid., p. 135.

6 Massimiliano Afiero and Ramiro Bujeiro, *Belgian Waffen-SS Legions & Brigades, 1941–1944: Wallonie, Wallonien, Flandern & Langemarck* (Oxford: Osprey Publishing, 2021), p. 15.

7 Conrad Schellong would be promoted to *SS-Obersturmbannführer* on 9 November 1944, with his promotion being backdated to 22 September 1944.

8 David Littlejohn, *The Patriotic Traitors: The Story of Collaboration in German-Occupied Europe 1940–1945* (New York: Doubleday & Company, Inc., 1972), p. 173.

9 Before the war, there were various Flemish right-wing parties, but on 11 Maay 1941 the Germans ordered that all pre-war political parties in Flanders were join the VNV.

10 Neulen, *An deutscher Seite*, p. 74.

11 Littlejohn, *The Patriotic Traitors*, p. 160.

12 De Wever, *Military Collaboration in Belgium*, p. 163.

13 Georg Tessin, *Verbände und Truppen der deutschen Wehrmacht und Waffen-SS 1939–1945*, vol. 1 (Osnabrück: Biblio Verlag, 1979–1990), p. 294.

14 Bruno De Wever, *Oostfronters: Vlamingen in het Vlaams Legioen en de Waffen-SS* (Tielt: Lannoo, 1984), p. 167.

15 Littlejohn, *The Patriotic Traitors*, p. 179.

16 Carlos Caballero Jurado and Paul Hannon, *Resistance Warfare 1940–45*, Men-at-Arms Series, no. 169 (London: Osprey Publishing, 1985), p. 18.

17 De Wever, *Oostfronters*, pp. 35–42.

18 Jonathan Trigg, *Hitler's Flemish Lions: The History of the 27th SS-Freiwilligen Grenadier Division Langemarck* (Stroud: Amberley, 2007), pp. 197–206.

19 Robin Lunsdem, *Himmler's Black Order: A History of the SS, 1923-45* (Godalming: Bramley Books, 1999), pp. 75–82.

20 Littlejohn, *The Patriotic Traitors*, pp. 154–5.

21 Gerhard Hirschfeld, *Nazi Rule and Dutch Collaboration: The Netherlands under German Occupation, 1940–1945* (Oxford and New York: Berg, 1988), pp. 34–42; L. de Jong, *Het Koninkrijk der Nederlanden in de Tweede Wereldoorlog*, vol. 3 ('s-Gravenhage: Staatsuitgeverij, 1969–1991), esp. pp. 175–200.

22 Hirschfeld, *Nazi Rule and Dutch Collaboration*, pp. 45–60; L. de Jong, *Het Koninkrijk*, vol. 3, pp. 201–12.

23 Hirschfeld, *Nazi Rule and Dutch Collaboration*, pp. 58–65; L. de Jong, *Het Koninkrijk*, vol. 4, pp. 90–104.

24 L. de Jong, *Het Koninkrijk*, vol. 5, pp. 13–22, 220–7; Hirschfeld, *Nazi Rule and Dutch Collaboration*, pp. 97–116.

25 L. de Jong, *Het Koninkrijk*, vol. 6, pp. 312–39; Hirschfeld, *Nazi Rule and Dutch Collaboration*, pp. 141–66.

26 Hirschfeld, *Nazi Rule and Dutch Collaboration*, pp. 117–23; L. de Jong, *Het Koninkrijk*, vol. 6, pp. 40–53.

27 L. de Jong, *Het Koninkrijk*, vol. 10, pp. 718–22; Philip Rees, *Biographical Dictionary of the Extreme Right Since 1890* (London: Routledge, 1990), s.v. 'Anton Mussert'.

28 Hirschfeld, *Nazi Rule and Dutch Collaboration*, pp. 140–7; N.K.C.A. in 't Veld, *De SS en Nederland: Documenten uit SS-archieven 1935–1945* ('s-Gravenhage: Nijhoff, 1976), pp. 221–8.

29 Hirschfeld, *Nazi Rule and Dutch Collaboration*, vol. 6, pp. 339–46.

30 De Jong, *Het Koninkrijk*, vol. 8, pp. 247–53; H. Amersfoort and P.H. Kamphuis, eds, *May 1940: The Battle for the Netherlands* (London: Brassey's, 1990), pp. 309–12.

31 Hirschfeld, *Nazi Rule and Dutch Collaboration*, pp. 161–6; De Jong, *Het Koninkrijk*, vol. 10a, pp. 92–101.

32 De Jong, *Het Koninkrijk*, vol. 10a, pp. 102–9; in 't Veld, *De SS en Nederland*, pp. 315–20.

33 Hirschfeld, *Nazi Rule and Dutch Collaboration*, pp. 162–4; De Jong, *Het Koninkrijk*, vol. 10b, pp. 405–12.

34 De Jong, *Het Koninkrijk*, vol. 12, pp. 717–26; J.C.H. Blom, 'The Persecution of the Jews in the Netherlands: A Comparative Western European Perspective', *European History Quarterly* 19, no. 3 (1989), pp. 333–51.

Chapter 6: The 'Propaganda Legions' Part 1, 1941–1945

1 Martin Gilbert, *The Second World War: A Complete History* (New York: Henry Holt, 1989), p. 278.

2 The Japanese invasion in 1944 of north-eastern India failed. Soon after the four divisions of anti-British volunteers began to suffer large numbers of desertions. By the end of the war, Bose was on the island of Formosa (today's Taiwan). There, he boarded a Japanese bomber in the afternoon of 18 August 1945. Almost as soon as the plane had taken off, an explosion tore one of the engines from it. People who witnessed the event claim that it sounded like a bomb explosion. Miraculously, Bose survived the crash, but was badly burned. He lingered in a hospital until the evening, where he was treated for broken bones and third-degree burns. He died sometime around 9:30 pm that same day.

3 Rudolf Hartog, *Im Zeichen des Tigers: Die Indische Legion auf deutscher Seite 1941–1945* (Herford: Busse Seewald, 1991), p. 155.

4 Ibid., p. 156.

5 Neulen, *An Deutscher Seite*, p. 357.

6 NARS Microfilm Series T-175, Roll 191, Frame 2729186.

7 Ibid.

8 David Littlejohn, 'The Indian Legion', *The Military Advisor* (San Jose: Bender Publications), vol. 6, no. 3 (Summer 1995), pp. 28–33.

9 With the exception of the *Osttürkischer-Waffenverband der-SS,* which had the individual honour of having a green background cloth for their cuff band and collar tabs.

10 With the exception of the highly motivated *9. Kompanie.*

11 Plans were already in effect during the late summer of 1944 to incorporate the regiment into the *Waffen-SS,* but nothing came of this, basically because at the time the *SS-Hauptamt* was too busy with other, more pressing matters

Chapter 8: 1941–1942: Attrition in the East. Enrolment of Non-Aryans Begins

1 These forces were split up as follows: 3.8 million Germans, 473,000 Romanians, 475,000 Finns, 50,000 Slovakians, and some 45,000–50,000 Hungarians.

2 Antonio Muñoz, *Forgotten Legions: Obscure Formations of the Waffen-SS, 1943-1945* (Boulder: Paladin Press, 1991), p. 301.

3 Antonio Muñoz, *For Croatia & Christ: The Croatian Army in World War II, 1941–1945* (New York: Axis Europa, 1996), p. 12.

4 This figure seems a bit too small since an earlier census, taken in 1944 showed that approximately 69,000 Estonians were then serving in the German Armed Forces: 5,000 in the *Heer,* 20,000 in the *Waffen-SS,* 20,000 in the SS Border Guard Regiments, 9,000 in the *Schutzmannschaft* police battalions, 5,000 in the 'Omakaitse' self-defence forces, and 10,000 in the German *Luftwaffe, Kriegsmarine* and *Organisation Todt* (Nationalised *'Todt'* Construction Work Force).

5 This regiment was initially in the *Osttürkischer Waffenverband der SS* but later transferred to the *Kaukasicher Waffenverband der SS.*

6 This also included about 20,000 men held in German prisoner of war camps.

7 Mainly in the *Kosaken-Kavalleriekorps* of two cavalry divisions and one *'Plastun'* (Cossack infantry) brigade/division, then serving in Yugoslavia. In addition, there were about 17,000 Cossacks, and 20,000 dependents under General Timofey Ivanovich Domanov in northern Italy – titled the Special Armed Cossack Corps. Due to the advanced age of a majority of these combatants, they did not serve under the *Kosaken-Kavalleriekorps* in Yugoslavia. This number also included various, smaller sized Cossack forces elsewhere.

8 According to a wartime memorandum by Caucasian leaders dated 15 July 1944, the total number of Caucasians bearing arms for Hitler's Germany was 102,300.

9 George Fischer, *Soviet Opposition to Stalin* (Cambridge, MA: Harvard University Press, 1952), p. 51.

10 Ihor Kamenetsky, *Hitler's Occupation of Ukraine (1941–1944): A Study of Totalitarian Imperialism* (Milwaukee: Marquette University Press, 1956), p. 61.

11 A more precise number of Latvians serving in the German Armed Forces during July 1944 can be obtained in *Latvian Legion* by Arthur Silgailis. In it, the author listed the numbers of Latvian volunteers in July 1944 as follows: (1) In the *VI. Waffen-Armeekorps der SS (Lettische)*: 31,446 men; (2) In other units of the Legion: 972 men; (3) In the *Schutzmannschaft* front line police battalions: 14,884 men; (4) In the border guard regiments: 12,118 men; (5) In the *Schutzmannschaft Einzeldienst* of the German Order Police: 5,240 men; (6) In the Order Police Auxiliary Group 'C': 22,262 men; (7) In the Latvian Air Force Squadron *'Lettland'*: 628 men; (8) In the *Wehrmacht* as *Hiwis* (*Hilfswilliger*, or volunteers): 12,159 men; (9) In the Organisation 'Todt', Fireman, Factory Guards, and other auxiliary organisations: 10,585 men. Total number as of 1 July 1944 stood at 110,294 Latvian volunteers serving in the German Armed Forces. To this must be added the number of Latvians killed, wounded, or listed as missing in action from 22 June 1941 to 1 July 1944: 3,914 killed, 7,305 wounded and 1,362 missing. So altogether about 122,875 Latvian men had served in one branch of service or another in the German Armed Forces from 22 June 1941 to1 July 1944.

12 A. Redcliffe, *Lessons Learned from the Partisan War in Russia*, MS no. P055C, Office of the Chief of Military History, Department of the Army, Washington, D.C., p. 3.

13 Alexander Pronin, *Guerrilla Warfare in the German Occupied Soviet Territories 1941–1945*, PhD diss., Georgetown University Graduate School, Georgetown, 1965, p. 152.

14 Jürgen Thorwald, *The Illusion: Soviet Soldiers in Hitler*'s *Armies* (New York: Harcourt Brace Jovanovich, 1975), pp. 29–30.

15 Pronin, *Guerrilla Warfare in the German Occupied Soviet Territories 1941–1945*, p. 172.

16 Alex Alexiev, *Soviet Nationalities in German Wartime Strategy, 1941–1945* (Santa Monica: Rand Corporation, 1982), p. 27.

17 Pronin, *Guerrilla Warfare in the German Occupied Soviet Territories 1941–1945*, pp. 171–2.

18 Alexander Dallin, *German Rule in Russia, 1941–1945* (London: Macmillan & Co., Ltd., 1957), p. 537.

19 BA-MA. RH 26-113/13.Divisional Order – (Ia Nr. 693/42 geh.),

20 Veit Scherzer, 'Die Ärmelabzeichen der russischen Freiwilligen im Bereich der 113. Infanterie-Division', *Militaria Magazine*, vol. 18, no. 4 (July-August 1996). P. 102.

21 Thorwald, *The Illusion*, p. 53.

22 Antonio Muñoz, *The Kaminski Brigade: A History, 1941-1945* (New York: Europa Books, 2003), pp. 6–7.

23 Ibid., p. 24.

24 Sean Ryan, 'The Carpatho-Ukraine Contribution: The First Ukrainian Volunteers of the German Army, 1939', *Axis Europa Magazine*, vol. 3, no. 11 (1997), pp. 3–6.

25 Roman Ilnytzkyi, *Deutschland und die Ukraine 1934–1945*, 2 vols., vol. II, pt. II (Munich: Osteuropa-Institut, 1958), p. 139.

26 Fischer, *Soviet Opposition to Stalin*, p. 43.

27 Ibid.

28 Thorwald, *The Illusion*, p. 96.

29 Matthew Cooper, *The Nazi War Against Soviet Partisans, 1941-1944* (New York: Stein and Day Publishers, 1979), p. 121.

30 Thorwald, *The Illusion*, p. 97.

Chapter 9: Tapping the Balkans, Part 1: 1941–1943

1 Muñoz, *Forgotten Legions*, p. 259.

2 Nino Arena, *Soli Contro Tutti: Friuli-Venezia Giulia 1941–1945 (Guerra – Guerriglia – Controguerriglia)* (Rimini: Edizioni Ultima Cruciata, 1993), p. 250.

3 Stefano Di Giusto, *I Reparti Panzer nell'Operationszone Adriatisches Küstenland (OZAK) 1943–1945* (Mariano del Friuli: Edizioni Della Laguna, 2004), p. 75.

4 Werner Regenberg, *Armored Vehicles & Units of the German Order Police 1935–1945* (Atglen: Schiffer Publishing, 2002), p. 92.

5 Muñoz, *Hitler's Green Army*, p. 333.

6 Jože Pirjevec, *Tito: Die Biografie*, trans. Klaus Detlef Olof (Munich: Kunstmann, 2018), p. 174.

7 *Kampfgruppe 2* remained in Skofljica until February 1944 when it was shifted to Velike Lasce.

8 *Kampfgruppe 6* was stationed in this town beginning in January 1944.

9 *Kampfgruppe 7* was stationed in this town beginning in February 1944.

10 On 10 September 1944 a new Home Guard formation was raised from the Slovenian *Domobranci* who had been defending the towns of Velike Lasce, Ribnica and Kocevje (Dolenjska region). The unit was named 'Schmitz' after the German commander who was in charge of these Home Guard troops, *Major der Schutzpolizei* Schmitz.

11 The SS police regiments used may have been *SS-Polizeiregiment 14* and part of *SS-Polizeiregiment 25*, although post-war Slovenian sources state that it was *SS-Polizeiregiment 14* and *SS-Polizeiregiment 17*.

12 NARA, T-501, Roll 261, Frame 000547.

13 Roland Kaltenegger, *Operationszone Adriatisches Küstenland: Der Kampf um Triest, Istrien und Fiume 1944/45* (Graz: Leopold Stocker Verlag, 1993), p. 77.

14 NARA, T-501, Roll 266, Frame 518.

15 Ibid., Frame 539.

16 Matjaz Klepec, *Tüchern ist getränkt mit unserem Blut: Das Schicksal der Heimatwehrmänner (Domobranci)* (Buenos Aires: Editorial Baraga, SRL, 1973), p. 50.

17 Stevan K. Pavlowitch, *Hitler's New Disorder: The Second World War in Yugoslavia* (New York: Columbia University Press, 2008), p. 112.

18 Ibid., p. 114.

19 Klepec, *Tüchern ist getränkt mit unserem Blut*, p. 50.

20 Jozo Tomasevich, *War and Revolution in Yugoslavia, 1941–1945: Occupation and Collaboration* (Stanford: Stanford University Press, 2001), p. 127.

21 George Lepre, *Himmler's Bosnian Division: The Waffen-SS Handschar Division 1943–1945* (Atglen, PA: Schiffer Publishing, 1997), p. 42.

22 Ibid., pp. 43–4.

23 Ibid., p. 45.

24 Ibid., pp. 46–7.

25 Pavlowitch, *Hitler's New Disorder*, p. 118.

26 Tomasevich, *War and Revolution in Yugoslavia*, p. 131.

27 John Cox, *The History of Serbia* (Westport, CT: Greenwood Publishing Group, 2002), p. 90.

28 Otto Kumm, *Vorwärts, 'Prinz Eugen'! Geschichte d. 7. SS-Freiwilligen-Division 'Prinz Eugen'* (Coburg: Munin Verlag, 1978), p. 243.

29 Fischer, *Soviet Opposition to Stalin*, p. 19.

30 Ibid., p. 20.

31 NTS stands for 'The National Alliance of Russian Solidarists'.

32 Nikolai Fevr, *Solntse Voskhodit na Zapade* (Buenos Aires: Novo Slovo, 1950), pp. 20–1.

33 Carlos Caballero Jurado, 'Against Stalin and Stalinism: Count Grigori von Lambsdorff, 1936–1945', *Axis Europa Magazine*, no. 14 (1998), p. 11.

34 Historians have argued that the Germans could have sent more infantry divisions to Russia from France without significantly lowering their defensive capabilities in the West in 1942, but the Dieppe raid in the middle of that year convinced the German High Command that retaining a large force of troops in France and the Low Countries was a safer option.

35 D.P. Vertepov, ed., *Russkii Korpus na Balkanakh vo vremia II Velikoi voiny, 1941–1945 g.g.: Istoricheskii ocherk i sbornik vospominanii soratnikov* [*The Russian Corps in the Balkans during World War II, 1941–1945: An Historical Study and a Collection of Memoirs by Companions-in-Arms*] (New York: Nashi Vesti, 1963), pp. 404–5.

36 J. Lee Ready, *The Forgotten Axis: Germany's Partners and Foreign Volunteers in World War II* (Jefferson, NC: McFarland & Company, 1985), p. 53.

37 NARA, T-501, Roll 253, Frame 78.

38 The *704. Infanterie-Division* was redesignated as the *104. Jager-Division* on 1 April 1943. It was transferred to Greece in late June or early July 1943.

39 David Littlejohn, *Foreign Legions of the Third Reich, Volume III – Albania, Greece, Czechoslovakia, Hungary, and Yugoslavia* (San Jose, CA: R. James Bender Publishing, 1985), p. 259.

40 Samuel J. Newland, *Cossacks in the German Army, 1941-1945* (Portland, OR: Frank Cass & Co. Ltd., 1991), p. 188.

41 George F. Nafziger, *Foreigners in Field Gray: The Russiches Schutzkorps and Italian Soldiers in the Wehrmacht* (Privately published: Pisgah, 1995), p. 58.

42 Paul N. Hehn, *The German Struggle Against Yugoslav Guerrillas in World War II: German Counter-Insurgency in Yugoslavia, 1941–1943* (New York: Columbia University Press, 1978), p. 84.

43 The unit in question was the *342. Infanterie-Division,* which was to remain in Serbia until the end of January 1942 but by March it was in the Rzhev area under *9. Armee, Heeresgruppe Mitte* (Army Group Center).

44 The Russian exiles wanted a return of the Romanov Royal line in Russia as well as being Eastern Orthodox.

45 Hehn, *The German Struggle Against Yugoslav Guerrillas,* p. 74.

46 Muñoz, *For Croatia & Christ,* p. 26.

47 Hehn, *The German Struggle Against Yugoslav Guerrillas,* p. 84.

48 Hugh Page Taylor, 'Action Detachments of the German Troops in Croatia, 1941–1943', *The Military Advisor* 10, no. 3 (1999), p. 24.

49 *Mein Kampf: 'My Struggle'* – Adolf Hitler's political diatribe.

50 Kurt Mehner, *Die Geheimen Tagesberichte der Deutschen Wehrmachtführung im Zweiten Weltkrieg, 1939–1945,* 12 vols., vol. 9 (Osnabrück: Biblio-Verlag, 1988), p. 86.

51 Ibid, pp. 143–4.

52 Alexander Dallin, *Odessa, 1941-1944: A Case Study of Soviet Territory under Foreign Rule,* RM-1875, ASTIA Doc. No. AD 123552 (Rand Corporation: Santa Monica, 1957), pp. 279–80.

53 Vladimir Petrov, *My Retreat from Russia* (New Haven: Yale University Press, 1950), p. 208.

54 Dallin, *Odessa*, p. 282.

55 Ibid., p. 285.

56 Paul Leverkühn, *German Military Intelligence* (London: Ebenezer Baylis & Sons Ltd., 1954), pp. 147–51.

57 Littlejohn, *Foreign Legions of the Third Reich, Volume III*, p. 259.

58 Antonio Muñoz, 'The Serbian State and Frontier Guard, 1941-1945 – Part II', in *Axis Europa Magazine*, Volume I No.2, 1995, p. 7.

59 Jozo Tomasevich, *The Chetniks: War and Revolution in Yugoslavia, 1941-1945* (Stanford University Press: Stanford, 1975), p. 446n.

60 Sven Steenberg, *Vlasov* (Alfred A. Knopf: New York, 1970), p. 164.

61 Vertepov, *Russkii Korpus na Balkanakh vo vremia II Velikoi voiny, 1941–1945 g.g*, p. 404.

62 These figures do not include the total number of men wounded and killed from each regiment

Chapter 10: Tapping the Balkans, Part 2: 1943–1944

1 Robert H. Jackson, *Tyranny on Trial: The Evidence at Nuremberg* (Dallas: Southern Methodist University Press, 1954), p. 199.

2 For example, mainland southern Greece (including Euboea but excluding the Peloponnesus) was under the Higher *Gendarmerie* Command of Mainland Greece (*Anotera Dioikesis Chorophylakes Stereas Hellados*) based in Athens. The prefecture of Euboea was controlled by the *Gendarmerie* Command of Euboea (*Dioikesis Chorophylakes Euboias*) based in Chalcis. This HQ had four subordinate *Gendarmerie* Sub-Commands (*Hypodioikeseis Chorophylakes)* which controlled about twenty-five *Gendarmerie* Stations (*Stathmoi Chorophylakes*) throughout the prefecture. The total number of *Gendarmes* in Euboea was about 400 men.

3 Mark Mazower, *Inside Hitler's Greece: The Experience of Occupation* (Yale University Press: London, 2001), p. 120.

4 J. Lee Ready, *World War Two, Nation by Nation* (London: Arms & Armor Press, 1995), p. 112.

5 Benton, William. *Encyclopedia Britannica* (Chicago, Encyclopedia Britannica, 1963), Volume 8, 930.

6 NARS Microfilm T-78, Roll 450, Frame 6426601.

7 This included 2,460 NCOs and 7,200 enlisted men as listed in NARS Microfilm T-78, Roll 450, Frame 6426601.

8 Mazower, *Inside Hitler's Greece*, p. 325.

9 H. J. Neufeldt, J. Huck and Georg Tessin, *Zur Geschichte der Ordnungspolizei 1936-1945* (Koblenz: Bundesarchiv, 1957), Part II, p. 72.

10 NARS Microfilm T-501, Roll 259, Frames 000535-000542.

11 NARS Microfilm T-78, Roll 410, Frames 6378310-6378312.

12 Mazower, *Inside Hitler's Greece*, p. 325.

13 Neufeldt et al, *Zur Geschichte der Ordnungspolizei 1936-1945*, p. 73.

14 Office of Strategic Services (OSS), Information Report, December 1944–February 1945, GAX-77, "Macedonia, Thrace, Tsaous, PAO, British, Nationalists, Kaltsef, Zervas, Miller," dated April 21, 1945, accessed December 9, 2025, https://www.elia.org.gr/userfiles/pdf_archieve/1945%204-2145%20Macedonia,%20Thrace,%20Tsaous,%20PAO,%20British,%20Nationalists,%20Kaltsef,%20Zervas,%20Miller,%20226-211-WN20331-d%20(GAX-77).pdf

15 Kurt Mehner, *Die Geheimen Tagesberichte der Deutschen Wehrmachtführung im Zweiten Weltkrieg 1939-1945* (Osnabrück: Biblio Verlag, 1988), Volume 7, p. 98.

16 Janusz Piekalkiewicz, *Krieg auf dem Balkan 1940-1945* (München: Südwest Verlag GmbH & Co. KG, 1984), p. 221.

17 Mazower, *Inside Hitler's Greece*, p. 325.

18 Mehner, *Die Geheimen Tagesberichte der Deutschen Wehrmachtführung im Zweiten Weltkrieg 1939-1945*, Volume 9, p, 153.

19 Ibid., Volume 9, p. 362.

20 Ibid., Volume 9, p. 382.

21 Ibid., Volume 10, p. 24.

22 Ready, *World War Two, Nation by Nation*, p. 415.

23 Minus the 3rd Police Mountain Artillery Battery which was employed with the 1st Battalion of the 18th SS Police Mountain Regiment in the Athens area.

24 Hermann Franz, *Gebirgsjäger der Polizei: Polizei-Gebirgsjäger-Regiment 18 und Polizei-Gebirgsjäger-Artillerie-Abteilung, 1942 bis 1945* (Bad Nauheim: Verlags Hans-Henning Podzun, 1963), p. 131.

25 Antonio J. Munoz, *Goring's Grenadiers: The Luftwaffe Field Divisions, 1942–1945* (New York: Europa Books, 2002), p. 147.

26 Rolf Michaelis, *Der Einsatz der Osdnungspolizei 1939-1945: Polizeibataillone – SS-Polizeiregimenter* (Berlin: Michaelis Verlag, 2008), p. 75.

27 These batteries later supported the 2nd and 3rd Battalions at Amfissa and Lamia.

28 Major General Stefanos Sarafis, *ELAS: Greek Resistance Army* (London: Merlin Press, 1948), p. 458.

29 Ibid., p. 435.

30 Friedrich Housemann, *Die Guten Glaubens Waren: Geschichte der SS Polizei Division: 4. SS Polizei Panzer Grenadier Division* (Osnabrück: Munin Verlag GmbH, 1973), Volume 2, p. 332.

31 Antonio Muñoz, *Lions of the Desert: Arab Volunteers in the German Army, 1941-1945* (New York: Europa Books, 1995), p. 35.

32 Serafis, *ELAS*, p. 441.

33 Housemann, *Die Guten Glaubens Waren*, p. 315.

34 For more information on the *Balisti*, please see *Axis Europa Magazine*, July-September 1996 (Whole Number 9).

35 Serafis, *ELAS*, p. 452.

36 Franz, *Gebirgsjäger der Polizei*, p. 147.

37 Serafis, *ELAS*, p. 449.

38 Mazower, *Inside Hitler's Greece*, p. 358.

39 Serafis, *ELAS*, p. 461.

40 Janusz Piekalkiewicz. *Krieg auf dem Balkan 1940-1945*, (München: Südwest Verlag, 1984), p. 281.

41 Brigadier E. C. W. Myers, *Greek Entanglement* (London: Rupert Hart-Davis, 1955), p. 271.

42 Mazower, *Inside Hitler's Greece*, p. 364.

43 Myers, *Greek Entanglement*, p. 284.

Chapter 11: 1943–1944: Bloodbath in the East and the Russian Army of Liberation

1 Jürgen Thorwald, *Wen sie verderben wollen: Bericht des großen Verrats* (Stuttgart: Steingrüben Verlag, 1952), pp. 82–3.

2 Fischer, *Soviet Opposition to Stalin*, p. 45.

3 Heinz Guderian, *Panzer Leader* (London: E. P. Dutton, 1952), p. 356.

4 Fischer, *Soviet Opposition to Stalin*, p. 48.

5 Ibid., pp. 48–9.

6 Ibid., p. 51.

7 Thorwald, *Wen sie verderben wollen*, p. 80.

8 Ibid., pp. 118–19.

9 Ibid., pp. 119–20.

10 Sven Steenberg, *Vlasov* (New York: Alfred A. Knopf, 1970), p. 21.

11 Boris Dvinov, *Vlasovskoye Dvizhenye v Svieti Dokumentov* (New York: privately published, 1950), p. 78.

12 Thorwald, *Wen sie verderben wollen*, pp. 173–4.

13 Fischer, *Soviet Opposition to Stalin*, pp. 58–60.

14 Thorwald, *Wen sie verderben wollen*, p. 220.

15 Fischer, *Soviet Opposition to Stalin*, pp. 62–3.

16 Ibid., p. 63 and see also Appendix II, pp. 176–87.

17 Apparently, this rule was ignored by the divisional commander of the German *134. Infanterie-Division* who, according to author, Alexander Dallin (*German Rule in Russia, 1941-1944*) stated that its personnel consisted of 50 per cent Russian and other Eastern volunteers by late 1942.

18 Fischer, *Soviet Opposition to Stalin*, p. 45.

19 Thorwald, *Wen sie verderben wollen*, pp. 283–5.

20 Fischer, *Soviet Opposition to Stalin*, p. 45.

21 Wolf-Dietrich Heike, *The Ukrainian Division 'Galicia', 1943-45: A Memoir*, trans. Andriy Wynnyckyj, ed. Yury Boshyk, intro. John A. Armstrong (Toronto: Shevchenko Scientific Society, 1988), pp. 57–9.

22 James R. Bender and Hugh Page Taylor, *Uniforms, Organisation, & History of the Waffen-SS*, vol. 4 (San Jose: R. James Bender Publishing, 1986), pp. 25–7.

23 L. Ortynskyj, 'Prawda o Ukraińskiej Dywizji', *Kultura*, no. 11/61 (1952), pp. 109–16.

24 Ibid., p. 85.

25 This initially included most of the staff of *Fremde Heer Ost* (Foreign Armies East) headed by Reinhard Gehlen, but including officers that were 100 per cent committed to realising a Russian Liberation Army, like Captains Wilfried Strik-Strikfeldt, Sven Steenberg, and Egon Peterson (among the more 'active' elements), but later included most of the higher ranking generals on the Russian Front, as well as officers within the SS organisation and within the Nazi political leadership.

26 Fischer, *Soviet Opposition to Stalin*, p. 74.

27 Ibid., 196; see 'Prague Manifesto', Appendix IV.

28 Thorwald, *Wen sie verderben wollen*, p. 424.

29 Fischer, *Soviet Opposition to Stalin*, pp. 196–9.

30 Antonio J. Muñoz, *Hitler's Eastern Legions, Volume II: The Osttruppen* (New York: Europa Books, 1997), pp. 7–15.

31 This was based on the so-called *'Dabendorf'* group who had organised a training school for Russian volunteers by that same name and staffed by Russian officers.

32 Fischer, *Soviet Opposition to Stalin*, p. 97.

33 The *Panzerfaust* was a disposable, single-shot anti-tank weapon that was invented by a German team of engineers at the company Hugo Schneider AG (HASAG) in Leipzig. The weapon was developed under the leadership of Heinrich Langweiler. The *Panzerfaust* was first produced in 1943 and saw its initial use on the Eastern Front. It was designed as a simple, cost-effective weapon that could be operated

by infantry with minimal training, giving German soldiers the ability to destroy armoured vehicles at close range, even heavy tanks. There were several versions of the *Panzerfaust* developed during the war, with incremental improvements in range, penetration power, and ease of use. The first version, the *Panzerfaust 30*, was named for its effective range of 30m. Later versions, like the *Panzerfaust 60* and *Panzerfaust 100*, increased the range and penetration ability of the anti-tank round.

34 What Bunyachenko didn't know, however, was that the Western Allies had already discussed the issue of Russian collaborators with Stalin and had agreed that all Russians taken by their forces were to be handed over to the Red Army. The only exception were those Russians who were not citizens of the USSR prior to 22 June 1941. Because of his high rank, Bunyachenko was sent to Moscow to stand trial. He was found guilty of treason and executed on 1 August 1946.

35 BA/MA R-55 / 616, s. 34.

Appendix I: A Chronological Listing of Volunteer Formations in the East, 1941–1945

1 Fifty men is more akin to a reinforced platoon than a company, but if you add the approximately 25–30 Germans that were attached to each of the 50-man Russian units, then you get a figure of 75–80 men. That number is more like a half-company in size. No doubt, the hope was to gather more volunteers and increase the size of each company to about 125–150 men.

2 In the beginning of this month, the German *6. Armee* surrendered at Stalingrad.

3 Kursk offensive launched at the beginning of this month.

4 BA RH 20-28, 14 AE0.3 lfm, *Armeeoberkommando Ligurien, 1 Jan. – 31 Dez. 1944.*

5 The area and town of Baranovichi have also been part of north-eastern Poland.

6 Coudry, Georges. *Les Camps Sovietiques Les Russes Livres a Stalin en 1945* (Albin Michel: Paris, 1997), p. 131.

7 This battlegroup was led by *Generalleutnant* Friedrich Wilhelm Konrad von Brodowski. The *kampfgruppe* fought in the Vosges Mountains in the autumn of 1944. When captured in late 1944, Brodowski was accused by the French of being behind the order to send security troops to central France in June 1944. That decision eventually led to the Oradour-sur-Glane massacre that same month. Shortly thereafter, the French claimed that he had been shot while trying to escape on 28 October 1944. Most historians agree that the likely scenario was that Brodowski was murdered in retaliation for the massacre.

8 According to one French source, the Allies captured around 74,000 Eastern troops between June and December 1944. By the end of the war, the Allied tally was around 104,000. If these numbers are to be believed, then the Allies must have taken prisoner another 30,000 *Osttruppen* in 1945. In December, the first Vlasov division began forming at *Truppenübungsplatz Münsingen*. In order to fully organise this, the first of two all-Russian divisions of the ROA, numerous *Ost* battalions were disbanded and their men sent to help form these two divisions.

9 *OKH/GenFreiwVerb, Nr.604/44 gKds, Stand 08.10.44,* Bundesarchiv Militärarchiv (Sven Steenberg Collection).

10 Including those parts of the USSR that were referred to as European Russia.

11 Percy Ernst Schramm, *Kriegstagebuch des Oberkommandos der Wehrmacht: 1940–1945,* 8 vols. (Herrsching am Ammersee: Pawlak Verlag, 1982), vol. 8, pp. 1508–11.

Appendix II: Lithuanian Volunteer Formations, 1941–1945

1 Piotrowski, *Poland's Holocaust,* p. 164.

2 Lithuanian Battalions of National Work.

3 Later sent to perform guard duty for a while in Maydanek Concentration Camp in Poland.

4 Performing guard duty in the Vilnius region.

5 Antonio Muñoz. 'Lithuania's Volunteer Police Battalions', in *Europa Magazine,* New York: Europa Books, Issue 14, summer 1998, p. 38.

6 Piotrowski, *Poland's Holocaust,* p. 165.

7 The initial first five battalions were created from the Lithuanian Home Guard, which included a good number of LNP members.

8 Tessin, et al, *Zur Geschichte der Ordnungspolizei 1936-1945,* p. 585.

9 Antonio J. Muñoz, *Hitler's Eastern Legions, Volume 1: The Baltic Schutzmannschaft, 1941–45* (New York: Europa Books, 1998), p. 35.

10 Carlos Caballero-Jurado and Nigel Thomas. *Germany's Eastern Front Allies (2) Baltic Forces* (London: Osprey Men-at-Arms Series, Osprey Publishing, 2002), p. 36.

11 Muñoz, *Hitler's Eastern Legions. Vol. I,* p. 156.

12 Rolf Hinze, *Rückzugskämpfe in der Ukraine 1943-1944* (Dusseldorf: Selbstverlag, Meerbusch, 1991) p. 161.

Appendix III: Latvian Volunteer Formations, 1941–1945

1 One unconfirmed report says that the battalion was established on 21 December 1941.

2 In its capacity as part of SS Battlegroup Jeckeln.

3 Just north of Lake Ilmen in the area of Army Group North.

4 Which later became the 19th Latvian SS Division.

5 NARS Microfilm T-175, Roll 225, Frame 2764109

6 Ibid, Frame 2764393.

7 NARS Microfilm T-175, Roll 174, Frame 2709404.

8 Antonio J. Muñoz, *The Druzhina SS Brigade: A History, 1941–1945* (New York: Europa Books, 1999), p. 42.

9 Schroeder held this position until October 1944.

10 Please see the section of this book covering Battlegroup Knecht.

11 Led by SS Brigadier-General and Major-General of the Police Walther Schröder. The battlegroup contained the 280th Latvian Self-Defence Battalion, and 281st Latvian Self-Defense Battalion.

12 Like all other SS and police battlegroups, SS Police Battlegroup 'Knecht' would be re-formed numerous times.

13 Kleinbergs would eventually become the commander of the 3rd Latvian Volunteer Police Regiment. His rank would reach that of a Lieutenant-Colonel of the SS.

14 Lobe would later win the German Cross in Gold while leading a unit of the Latvian SS.

15 Basically, the staff and personnel of the SS and Police Leader Latvia were used to form the temporary anti-partisan headquarters combat group. *SS-Brigadeführer* Hinrich Möller was the head of the SS and Police Leader Estonia command from 4 August 1941 to 1 April 1944. Then SS Brigadier-General and Major-General of the Police Walther Schröder assumed control from 1 April to 19 October 1944.

16 Ruth Bettina Birn, 'Zaunkönig an Uhrmacher: Große Partisanenaktionen 1942/43 am Beispiel des Unternehmens Winterzauber', *Militärgeschichtliche Zeitschrift* 60, no. 1 (June 2001), p. 101.

17 On 11 August 1943 the battalion officially became the III. Battalion of the Latvian 1st Police Regiment.

18 The specific time periods for their employment under-SS Police Battlegroup Jeckeln was 17–31 December 1943. The battalion once again served under the mixed SS and police battlegroup between 5–11 January 1944.

19 Army Group North was redesignated Army Group Courland.

Appendix IV: Estonian Volunteer Formations, 1941–1945

1 The German police controlled these border guard regiments, but the men wore *Wehrmacht* uniforms and were under tactical command of the *Ostheer*. In May 1944 the regiments were renamed *SS Polizei Grenzschutz Regimenter* (SS police border guard regiments). Regiments No. 2, 4 and 6 were merged under *Division z.b.V. 300* (Division for Special Employment No. 300).

BIBLIOGRAPHY

Primary Sources

Belgian State Archives (CegeSoma), *het Rijksarchief voor de Studie van Oorlog en Samenleving – Die 373. Infanterie-Bataillon (Légion Wallonie), SS Legioen Vlaanderen.*

Bundesarchiv, BArch RH 7A/1119, RH 7/2240, *606. Infanterie-Division (z.b.V.).*

Bundesarchiv, BArch RH 26-68/45-60, *Geschichte der 68. Infanterie-Division.*

Bundesarchiv, BArch N 756/183a, *22. SS-Freiwilligen-Kavalleriedivision 'Maria Theresa' – Fernschreiben, Geheime Kommandosachen, Aktennotiz, Lageplanskizzen.*

Bundesarchiv-Militärarchiv, MA R-55 / 616, s. 34. *Wlassow und die Russische Befreiungsarmee (Russkaya osvoboditel'naya armiya).*

NARA T-74, Rolls 1-20. *Umsiedlungswesen und volksdeutsche Angelegenheiten* (covers resettlement and ethnic German affairs).

NARA T-175, Roll 108, 111, 120. *Akten des 11. SS-Pz.Gre.Div. Nordland, 1943-1944.*

NARA T-175, Roll 191, *Die Indisches Legion.*

NARA T-312 Rolls 1624-1637. *Akten des Armee-Abteilung Narwa, 1944.*

NARA T-314, Rolls 870, 912, 1025 – German Military Personnel Files (*Wehrmacht*).

NARA T-334, Rolls 35, 56, 320, 321 – *Akten des Reichskommissars für die Festigung des deutschen Volkstums* – RKFDV (Records of the Reich Commissioner for the Strengthening of Germandom).

NARA T-501, Rolls 85-86. *Akten des Oberkommandos der Wehrmacht, rückwärtiger Raum und besetzte Gebiete.*

NARA T-501, Roll 90. *Akten über die Militärverwaltung, Besatzungsmaßnahmen und Rekrutierungswesen in eingegliederten Gebieten.*

NARA, T-501, Roll 266. *Operationszone Adriatisches Küstenland: Die Nedić-Männer in Istrien; SNVZ-Truppen in Istrien.*

NARA RG-238 *Arbeitsbesprechung am 23. April 1940, Diensttagebuch des Generalgouverneurs Hans Frank, Bd. 9.*

NARA A3343 (Series RS). RuSHA *(Rasse-und-Siedlungs-Hauptamt). Personelle und Volksdeutsche Aufzeichnungen.*

Trial of the Major War Criminals before the International Military Tribunal. Nuremberg: U.S. Army, 1946. 22 vols.

United States Holocaust Memorial Museum. 'The 1939 German "Minority Census" Database'. USHMM Collections online (microfilm). Accessed 11 August 2025.

In't Veld, N.K.C.A. *De SS en Nederland: Documenten uit SS-archieven 1935-1945.* Individual items reprinted inside it (e.g., German SS orders, correspondence, reports from 1935–1945), 's-Gravenhage: Nijhoff, 1976.

Secondary Sources

Dissertations

Pronin, Alexander, *Guerrilla Warfare in the German Occupied Soviet Territories 1941-1945*, PhD diss., Georgetown University Graduate School, Georgetown, 1965.

Wennberg, Rebecca W., *Ideological Incorrectness beyond 'Political Religion': Discourse on Nazi Ideology among Scandinavian National Socialist Intellectuals, 1933-1945*, PhD diss., Royal Holloway, University of London, 2016.

Articles

Bergen, Doris, 'The Nazi Concept of "*Volksdeutsche*" and the Exacerbation of Anti-Semitism in Eastern Europe, 1939-1945', *Journal of Contemporary History* 29, no. 4 (1994), pp. 569–82.

Birn, Ruth Bettina, 'Zaunkönig an Uhrmacher: Große Partisanenaktionen 1942/43 am Beispiel des Unternehmens Winterzauber', *Militärgeschichtliche Zeitschrift* 60, no. 1 (June 2001), p. 101.

Blom, J.C.H., 'The Persecution of the Jews in the Netherlands: A Comparative Western European Perspective', *European History Quarterly* 19, no. 3 (1989), pp. 333–51.

Davey, Owen Anthony, 'The Origins of the Légion des Volontaires Français contre le Bolchevisme', *Journal of Contemporary History* 6, no. 4 (1971), pp. 29–45.

Dostert, Paul, 'Die Luxemburger im Reserve-Polizeibataillon 101 und der Judenmord in Polen', *Hémecht: Journal d'histoire luxembourgeoise*, no. 4 (2000), pp. 5–22.

Jurado, Carlos Caballero, 'Against Stalin and Stalinism: Count Grigori von Lambsdorff, 1936-1945', *Axis Europa Magazine*, no. 14 (1998), p. 11.

Kamphuis, P.H., ed., *May 1940: The Battle for the Netherlands*, London: Brassey's, 1990.

Koehl, Robert L., 'The Deutsche Volksliste in Poland 1939-1945', *Journal of Central European Affairs* 15 (1955), pp. 354–66.

Krebs, Gerhard, 'Zwangsrekrutierung in Elsass-Lothringen und Luxemburg', *Vierteljahrshefte für Zeitgeschichte* 50 (2002), pp. 289–312.

Krier, Jean, 'Luxembourg *Volksdeutsche* and Military Conscription', *Journal of Modern European History* 12, no. 3 (2014), pp. 301–20.

Littlejohn, David, 'The Indian Legion', *The Military Advisor*, San Jose: Bender Publications, vol. 6, no. 3 (Summer 1995), pp. 28–33.

Muñoz, Antonio. 'The Serbian State and Frontier Guard, 1941–1945 – Part II', *Axis Europa Magazine*, Vol. I, No. 2 (Bayside, 1995), p. 7.

Ortynskyj, L., 'Prawda o Ukraińskiej Dywizji', *Kultura*, no. 11/61 (1952), pp. 109–16.

Ryan, Sean, 'The Carpatho-Ukraine Contribution: The First Ukrainian Volunteers of the German Army, 1939', *Axis Europa Magazine*, vol. 3, no. 11 (1997), pp. 3–6.

Scherzer, Veit, 'Die Ärmelabzeichen der russischen Freiwilligen im Bereich der 113. Infanterie-Division', *Militaria Magazine*, vol. 18, no. 4 (July-August 1996), p. 102.

Sourd Donnat, Jean-Pierre, 'The French "Selbstschutzpolizei", 1943-1944', *Axis Europa Magazine*, no. 15 (Autumn 1998), p. 3.

Taylor, Hugh Page, 'Action Detachments of the German Troops in Croatia, 1941-1943', *The Military Advisor* 10, no. 3 (1999), p. 24.

Books

Afiero, Massimiliano, and Ramiro Bujeiro, *Belgian Waffen-SS Legions & Brigades, 1941–1944: Wallonie, Wallonien, Flandern & Langemarck*, Oxford: Osprey Publishing, 2021.

Alexiev, Alex, *Soviet Nationalities in German Wartime Strategy, 1941–1945*, Santa Monica: Rand Corporation, 1982.

Amersfoort, H., and P.H. Kamphuis, eds, *May 1940: The Battle for the Netherlands*, London: Brassey's, 1990.

Arena, Nino, *Soli Contro Tutti: Friuli-Venezia Giulia 1941-1945 (Guerra – Guerriglia – Controguerriglia)*, Rimini: Edizioni Ultima Cruciata, 1993.

Bender, James R., and Hugh Page Taylor, *Uniforms, Organisation, & History of the Waffen-SS*, Vol. 4, San Jose: R. James Bender Publishing, 1986.

Bene, Krisztián, *La collaboration militaire française dans la Seconde Guerre Mondiale*, Éditions Codex, 2010.

Bernard, Philippe, *La guerre à l'Est: Les Malgré-nous*, Paris: Perrin, 2003.

Bille, Steen, *The German Minority in Denmark: Ethnicity and Identity Politics in Northern Schleswig, 1920-1950*, Aarhus: Aarhus University Press, 2005.

Caballero Jurado, Carlos, and Paul Hannon, *Resistance Warfare 1940-45*. Osprey Men-at-Arms Series No. 169, London: Osprey Publishing, 1985.

Caballero-Jurado, Carlos, *La Espada del Islam: Voluntarios Árabes en el Ejército Alemán 1941-1945*, Alicante: García Hispan, Editor, 1990.

Carnier, Pier Arrigo, *L'armata Cosacca in Italia 1944-1945*, Milan: Gruppo Ugo Mursia Editore, 1990.

Christensen, Claus Bundgård, Niels Bo Poulsen, and Peter Scharff Smith, *Under Hagekors og Dannebrog: Danskere i Waffen SS 1940–45*, Copenhagen: Aschehoug, 1998.

Cooper, Matthew, *The Nazi War Against Soviet Partisans, 1941-1944*, New York: Stein and Day Publishers, 1979.

Cox, John, *The History of Serbia*, Westport, CT: Greenwood Publishing Group, 2002.

Dallin, Alexander, *German Rule in Russia, 1941-1945*, London: Macmillan & Co., Ltd., 1957.

De Jong, L., *Het Koninkrijk der Nederlanden in de Tweede Wereldoorlog*, 14 vols, Gravenhage: Staatsuitgeverij (later Martinus Nijhoff/Staatsuitgeverij), 1969–1991.

De Wever, Bruno, 'Military Collaboration in Belgium', in *Die Bürokratie der Okkupation: Strukturen der Herrschaft und Verwaltung im besetzten Europa*, edited by Wolfgang Benz, Johannes Houwink ten Cate, and Gerhard Otto, Berlin: Metropol Verlag, 1998.

De Wever, Bruno, *Oostfronters: Vlamingen in het Vlaams Legioen en de Waffen-SS*, Tielt: Lannoo, 1984.

Deist, Wilhelm, Bernhard R. Kroener, and Militärgeschichtliches Forschungsamt (Germany), *Germany and the Second World War*, Vol. 10, Oxford: Oxford University Press, 2003.

Di Giusto, Stefano, *I Reparti Panzer nell'Operationszone Adriatisches Küstenland (OZAK) 1943-1945*, Mariano del Friuli: Edizioni Della Laguna, 2004.

Dostert, Paul, *Luxembourg in the Second World War*, Luxembourg: Editions Saint-Paul, 1994.

Dvinov, Boris, *Vlasovskoye Dvizhenye v Svieti Dokumentov*, New York: privately published, 1950.

Fevr, Nikolai, *Solntse Voskhodit na Zapade*, Buenos Aires: Novo Slovo, 1950.

Files, Yvonne de Ridder, *Quest for Freedom: A Story of Belgian Resistance in World War II*, Santa Barbara: The Narrative Press, 2000.

Fischer, George, *Soviet Opposition to Stalin*, Cambridge, MA: Harvard University Press, 1952.

Forbes, Robert, *For Europe: The French Volunteers of the Waffen-SS*, Bayeux, France: Éditions Heimdal, 2006.

Gilbert, Adrian, *The Waffen-SS: A Handbook*, London: The History Press, 2019.

Gilbert, Martin, *The Second World War: A Complete History*, New York: Henry Holt, 1989.

Glantz, David M., *When Titans Clashed: How the Red Army Stopped Hitler*, Lawrence: University Press of Kansas, 1995.

Guderian, Heinz, *Panzer Leader*, London: E. P. Dutton, 1952.

Hartog, Rudolf, *Im Zeichen des Tigers: Die Indische Legion auf deutscher Seite 1941–1945*, Herford: Busse Seewald, 1991.

Hehn, Paul N., *The German Struggle Against Yugoslav Guerrillas in World War II: German Counter-Insurgency in Yugoslavia, 1941–1943*, New York: Columbia University Press, 1978.

Heike, Wolf-Dietrich, *The Ukrainian Division 'Galicia', 1943-45: A Memoir*, translated by Andriy Wynnyckyj, edited by Yury Boshyk, introduction by John A. Armstrong, Toronto: Shevchenko Scientific Society, 1988.

Hirschfeld, Gerhard, *Nazi Rule and Dutch Collaboration: The Netherlands under German Occupation, 1940–1945*, Oxford and New York: Berg, 1988.

Hoffmann, Joachim, *Die Ostlegionen 1941-1943*, Freiburg: Verlag Rombach, 1986.

Ilnytzkyi, Roman *Deutschland und die Ukraine 1934-1945*, 2 vols, Vol. II, pt. II, Munich: Osteuropa-Institut, 1958.

Kaltenegger, Roland, *Operationszone Adriatisches Küstenland: Der Kampf um Triest, Istrien und Fiume 1944/45*, Graz: Leopold Stocker Verlag, 1993.

Kamenetsky, Ihor, *Hitler's Occupation of Ukraine (1941-1944): A Study of Totalitarian Imperialism*, Milwaukee: Marquette University Press, 1956.

Kleitmann, K. G., *Die Waffen-SS: eine Dokumentation*, Osnabrück: Verlag 'Der Freiwillige' GmbH, 1965.

Klepec, Matjaz, *Tüchern ist getränkt mit unserem Blut: Das Schicksal der Heimatwehrmänner (Domobranci)*, Buenos Aires: Editorial Baraga, SRL, 1973.

Kulczycki, John J, *Belonging to the Nation*. Cambridge, MA: Harvard University Press, 2016.

Kumm, Otto, *Vorwärts, 'Prinz Eugen'! Geschichte d. 7. SS-Freiwilligen-Division 'Prinz Eugen'*, Coburg: Munin Verlag, 1978.

La Mazière, Christian de, *The Captive Dreamer*, New York: Saturday Review Press, 1974.

Lambert, Pierre Philippe, and Gérard Le Marec, *Vichy 1940–1944: Organisations, Mouvements et Unités de l'État Français*. Paris: Jacques Grancher, 1992.

Larsen, Lars, and Jens Pank Bjerregaard, *Danish Volunteers of the Waffen-SS: Freikorps Danmark 1941-43*, Barnsley: Pen & Sword Military, 2018.

Le Tissier, Tony, *Race for the Reichstag: The 1945 Battle for Berlin*, London: Routledge, 1999.

Le Tissier, Tony, *SS Charlemagne: The 33rd Waffen-Grenadier Division of the SS*, Barnsley, UK: Pen & Sword Military, 2010.

Lepre, George, *Himmler's Bosnian Division: The Waffen-SS Handschar Division 1943–1945*, Atglen, PA: Schiffer Publishing, 1997.

Leverkühn, Paul, *German Military Intelligence*, London: Ebenezer Baylis & Sons Ltd., 1954.

Lidegaard, Bo, ed., *Dansk Udenrigspolitiks historie*, Vol. 4, Copenhagen: Danmarks Nationalleksikon, 2003.

Littlejohn, David, *The Patriotic Traitors: The Story of Collaboration in German-Occupied Europe 1940–1945*, New York: Doubleday & Company, Inc., 1972.

__________, *The French Foreign Legion in the Second World War*, London: Macmillan, 1972.

__________, *Foreign Legions of the Third Reich, Volume 1 – Norway, Denmark, France,*

San Jose: Roger James Bender Publishing, 1979.

__________, *Foreign Legions of the Third Reich, Volume 3 – Albania, Greece, Czechoslovakia, Hungary, and Yugoslavia,* San Jose: R. James Bender Publishing, 1985.

__________, *Foreign Legions of the Third Reich, Volume 4 – Poland, The Ukraine, Bulgaria, Romania, Free India, Estonia, Latvia, Lithuania, Finland and Russia,* San Jose: Roger James Bender Publishing, 1987.

– – –, *Lessons Learned from the Partisan War in Russia.* MS no. P055C. Office of the Chief of Military History, Department of the Army, Washington, D.C.

Lumsden, Robin, *Himmler's Black Order: A History of the SS, 1923-45,* Godalming: Bramley Books, 1999.

Lund, Joachim, *Luxembourg and the German Occupation 1940-1945,* New York: Praeger, 1984.

Mabire, Jean, *La Brigade Frankreich: Le premier combat des SS français,* Paris: Grancher, 2005.

__________, *Division Charlemagne*, Paris: Fayard, 1974.

Mazower, Mark, *Inside Hitler's Greece: The Experience of Occupation,* London: Yale University Press, 2001.

Mehner, Kurt, *Die Geheimen Tagesberichte der Deutschen Wehrmachtführung im Zweiten Weltkrieg 1939–1945,* 12 vols, Osnabrück: Biblio Verlag, 1984–1990.

__________, *Die Geheimen Tagesberichte der Deutschen Wehrmachtführung im Zweiten Weltkrieg, 1939-1945, 12* vols, Vol. 9, Osnabrück: Biblio-Verlag, 1988.

__________, *Die Waffen-SS- und Polizei 1939-1945,* Norderstedt: Militär-Verlag Klaus D. Patzwall, 1995.

Meyer, Hermann, *Von der Zwangsrekrutierung zur Rehabilitierung: Die Geschichte der 'Malgré-nous'*, Strasbourg: Editions La Nuée Bleue, 1997.

Michaelis, Rolf, *French Units in the Waffen-SS,* Atglen, PA: Schiffer Publishing, 2025.

Mitcham, Samuel W., *The German Defeat in the East, 1944-45,* Westport, CT: Praeger, 2001.

Müller, Rolf-Dieter, *The French Volunteers of the Waffen-SS,* translated by David Johnston, London: Greenhill Books, 2014.

Munoz, Antonio J., *The Kaminski Brigade: A History, 1941-1945,* New York: Europa Books, 2003.

__________, *Goring's Grenadiers: The Luftwaffe Field Divisions, 1942–1945,* New York: Europa Books, 2002.

__________, *Hitler's Green Army: The German Order Police and Their European*

Auxiliaries, 1933-1945, Volume 1: Western Europe and Scandinavia, New York: Europa Books, 2000.

__________________, *The Druzhina SS Brigade: A History, 1941–1945*, New York: Europa Books, 1999.

___________, *Forgotten Legions: Obscure Formations of the Waffen-SS, 1943-1945*, Boulder: Paladin Press, 1991.

___________, *The Last Levy: Waffen-SS Officer Roster, 1 March 1945*, New York: Europa Books, 2001.

_______, *Hitler's Eastern Legions, Volume 1: The Baltic Schutzmannschaft, 1941–45.* New York: Europa Books, 1998.

___________, *Hitler's Eastern Legions, Volume II: The Osttruppen*, New York: Europa Books, 1997.

___________, *For Tsar and Country: A History of the Russiches Schutzkorps, 1941-1945*, New York: Europa Books, 1999.

___________, *Slovenian Axis Forces in World War II, 1941–1945*, New York: Europa Books, 1996.

___________, *Hitler's Eastern Legions, Volume II: The Osttruppen*, New York: Europa Books, 1997.

___________, *For Croatia & Christ: The Croatian Army in World War II, 1941-1945*, New York: Europa Books, 1996.

Myers, Brigadier E. C. W., *Greek Entanglement* (London: Rupert Hart-Davis, 1955).

Neulen, Hans Werner, *An deutscher Seite: Internationale Freiwillige von Wehrmacht und Waffen-SS*, München: Universitas Verlag, 1985.

Newland, Samuel J., *Cossacks in the German Army, 1941–1945*, Portland, OR: Frank Cass & Co. Ltd., 1991.

Pavlowitch, Stevan K., *Hitler's New Disorder: The Second World War in Yugoslavia*, New York: Columbia University Press, 2008.

Petrov, Vladimir, *My Retreat from Russia*, New Haven: Yale University Press, 1950.

Pierik, Perry, *From Leningrad to Berlin: Dutch Volunteers in the German Waffen-SS*, Bedford: Aberjona Press, 1998.

Piotrowski Tadeusz, *Poland's Holocaust: Ethnic Strife, Collaboration with Occupying Forces and Genocide in the Second Republic, 1918-1947*, Jefferson: McFarland and Company Inc., 1998.

Pirjevec, Jože, *Tito: Die Biografie*, translated by Klaus Detlef Olof, Munich: Kunstmann, 2018.

Ready, J. Lee., *The Forgotten Axis: Germany's Partners and Foreign Volunteers in World War II*, Jefferson, NC: McFarland & Company, 1985.

Redcliffe, A., *Lessons Learned from the Partisan War in Russia.* MS no. P055C. Office of the Chief of Military History, Department of the Army, Washington, D.C.

Redžić, Enver, *Bosnia and Herzegovina in the Second World War*, New York: Frank Cass, 2005.

Rees, Philip, *Biographical Dictionary of the Extreme Right Since 1890*, London: Routledge, 1990.

Regenberg, Werner, *Armoured Vehicles & Units of the German Order Police 1935–1945*, Atglen: Schiffer Publishing, 2002.

Rigg, Jonathan Mark, *Hitler's Jewish Soldiers: The Untold Story of Nazi Racial Laws and Men of Jewish Descent in the German Military*, Lawrence: University Press of Kansas, 2002.

Schramm, Percy Ernst, *Kriegstagebuch des Oberkommandos der Wehrmacht: 1940–1945*, 8 Vols, Herrsching am Ammersee: Pawlak Verlag, 1982.

Schumann, Wolfgang, and Ludwig Nestler, eds. *Die faschistische Okkupationspolitik in Polen 1939–1945*. Vol. 2 of *Europa unterm Hakenkreuz: Die Okkupationspolitik des deutschen Faschismus 1938–1945*. Berlin (DDR): Deutscher Verlag der Wissenschaften, 1978.

Seidler, Franz W., *Die Kollaboration, 1939–1945: Zeitgeschichtliche Dokumentation in Biographien*, Grabert Verlag, 1995.

Shields, J. G., *Charlemagne's Crusaders: French Collaboration in Arms, 1941-1945*, French Cultural Studies, 2007.

Silgailis, Arthur, *Latvian Legion*, San Jose, CA: R. James Bender Publishing, 1986.

Spannenberger, Norbert, 'Chapter 3. The Ethnic Policy of the Third Reich Toward the *Volksdeutsche* in Central and Eastern Europe', in *Territorial Revisionism and the Allies of Germany in the Second World War: Goals, Expectations, Practices*, edited by Marina Cattaruzza, Stefan Dyroff, and Dieter Langewiesche, New York: Berghahn Books, 2015, pp. 56–71.

Steenberg, Sven, *Vlasov*, New York: Alfred A. Knopf, 1970.

Stephan, Yann, *A Broken Sword: Policing France During the German Occupation*. Ann Arbor, MI: University of Michigan, Office of International Criminal Justice, 1991.

Tarnstrom, Ronald, *French Arms*, Lindsborg, KS: Trogen Books, 2001.

Tessin, Georg, *Verbände und Truppen der deutschen Wehrmacht und Waffen-SS 1939–1945*, 18 vols, Osnabrück: Biblio Verlag, 1979–1990.

Thorwald, Jürgen, *Wen sie verderben wollen: Bericht des großen Verrats*, Stuttgart: Steingrüben Verlag, 1952.

__________, *The Illusion: Soviet Soldiers in Hitler's Armies*, New York: Harcourt Brace Jovanovich, 1975.

Tomasevich, Jozo, *War and Revolution in Yugoslavia, 1941-1945: Occupation and Collaboration*, Stanford: Stanford University Press, 2001.

Trigg, Jonathan, *Hitler's Flemish Lions: The History of the 27th SS-Freiwilligen Grenadier Division Langemarck*, Stroud: Amberley, 2007.

Vertepov, D. P., ed., *Russkii Korpus na Balkanakh vo vremia II Velikoi voiny, 1941-1945 g.g.: Istoricheskii ocherk i sbornik vospominanii soratnikov* [*The Russian Corps in the Balkans during World War II, 1941–1945: An Historical Study and a Collection of Memoirs by Companions-in-Arms*], New York: Nashi Vesti, 1963.

Yerger, Mark C., *Allgemeine-SS*, Atglen, PA: Schiffer Publishing, 1997.

Zakić, Mirna, 'The Waffen-SS Division 'Prinz Eugen' and Anti-Partisan Warfare in Yugoslavia, 1942–1944', in *Ethnic Germans and National Socialism in Yugoslavia in World War II*, edited by Mirna Zakić, Cambridge: Cambridge University Press, 2017, pp. 209–38.

Ziemke, Earl F., *Stalingrad to Berlin: The German Defeat in the East*, Washington, D.C.: U.S. Army Centre of Military History, 1968.

INDEX OF NAMES

INDEX OF FORMATIONS

Commands

SS Commands & Formations

SS Murder Kommandos

Army Groups, Armies & Corps

Divisions

Brigades & Regiments

Battalions & Companies

Kampfgruppen

West European Units

Luftwaffe Commands & Units

Nazi Militias & Groups

Secret Field Police, Order Police Commands & Units

Other Eastern Foreign & Irregular Units

Schutzmannschaft Battalions

Experimental Eastern Units

Ethnic German, Pro-German Balkan & German-Raised Italian Forces

SLOVENIAN

BOSNIAN MUSLIMS

CROATIAN

RUSSIAN ÉMIGRÉ

GREEK

SERBIAN

ITALIAN

Eastern Troops

Lithuanian Commands & Units

Latvian Commands & Units

Estonian Formations & Units

Cossack Commands & Units

Turkestani Commands and Units

Georgian Commands and Units

North Caucasian Commands and Units

Ukrainian Formations

Company-sized units

Command & Control Units

Engineer & Construction Units and Commands

Finnish Units

White Russian Formations

Convalescent & Replacement Units

Other Units

Russian Formations

'Ost' Battalions (Russian Formations)

Other Russian Formations

Italian RSI Forces

Bulgarian Forces

Croatian Units

Russian Partisan Units

Russian Units

Western Allied Units

Yugoslav Partisans

Greek Partisan Formations & Units

Operational Code Words